Fundamentals of Literacy Instruction and Assessment, Pre-K–6

Fundamentals of Literacy Instruction and Assessment, Pre-K–6

edited by

Martha C. Hougen, Ph.D.
The University of Texas at Austin

and

Susan M. Smartt, Ph.D.
Vanderbilt University
Nashville

Baltimore • London • Sydney

Paul H. Brookes Publishing Co.
Post Office Box 10624
Baltimore, Maryland 21285-0624
USA

www.brookespublishing.com

Typeset by Spearhead Global, Inc., Bear, Delaware.
Manufactured in the United States of America by
Sheridan Books, Chelsea, Michigan.

The individuals described in this book are composites or real people whose situations are masked
and are based on the authors' experiences. In all instances, names and identifying details have been
changed to protect confidentiality.

Library of Congress Cataloging-in-Publication Data

Fundamentals of literacy instruction and assessment, pre-K–6 / edited by Martha C. Hougen and
Susan M. Smartt.
    p.   cm.
  Includes bibliographical references and index.
  ISBN-13: 978-1-59857-205-6—ISBN-10: 1-59857-205-9   1. Language arts (Elementary)
2. Language arts (Early childhood) I. Hougen, Martha Clare.   II. Smartt, Susan M.
  LB1576.F768 2012
  372.6—dc23

                                                 2011049365

British Library Cataloguing in Publication data are available from the British Library.

2021	2020	2019	2018	
10	9	8	7	6

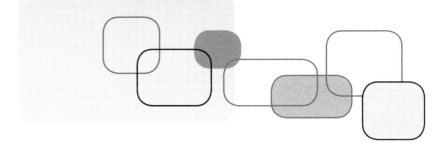

Contents

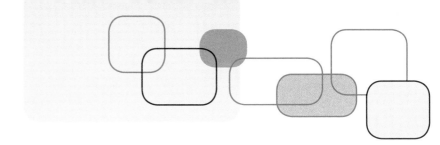

About the Editors

Martha C. Hougen, Ph.D., Principal Investigator, College and Career Readiness Initiative: English/Language Arts Faculty Collaborative, The Meadows Center for Preventing Educational Risk and Vaughn Gross Center, College of Education, The University of Texas at Austin, 1 University Station D4900, Austin, Texas 78712

Dr. Hougen's recent work has focused on improving preservice teacher education by providing university teacher educators with ongoing professional development and collaborative opportunities. Dr. Hougen received her master of education degree in special education from American University and her doctorate in educational administration from The University of Texas at Austin.

Dr. Hougen has worked with struggling readers as a general and special education teacher, public school administrator, and university faculty member. She consults with national organizations, state departments, universities, and school districts across the country regarding teacher education, reading, special education, and the development of higher education faculty collaboratives.

Dr. Hougen's publications focus on improving instruction for students with reading difficulties through the implementation of research-based practices. Awards Dr. Hougen has received recently include the National Educator of the Year, 2007, from the Council for Exceptional Children, Division of Learning Disabilities, and the Outstanding Administrative Leadership in Reading Award from the Texas State Reading Association, 2006.

Susan M. Smartt, Ph.D., Senior Research Associate, National Comprehensive Center for Teacher Quality, Vanderbilt University, Nashville, Tennessee 37240

Dr. Smartt holds a doctorate in school psychology from Tennessee State University and a master's degree in special education and reading from Peabody College of Vanderbilt University. At Vanderbilt, Dr. Smartt engages in research focusing on improving teacher preparation for reading teachers. Dr. Smartt also provides educational consulting services and teacher training to states and local school districts focusing on school reform, reading intervention for low-performing schools, using data to inform practice, developing response to intervention initiatives, and implementing scientifically based literacy programs.

Dr. Smartt owned and directed a reading clinic for 20 years in which she provided comprehensive psychoeducational assessments and tutoring services. She has been a classroom teacher, a reading coach, a reading specialist, a principal, a university faculty member, and a researcher. Her publications include authorship and coauthorship of journal articles, edited volumes, and books on research-based reading intervention and policy initiatives, including *Next STEPS in Literacy Instruction: Connecting Assessments to Effective Interventions* (Paul H. Brookes Publishing Co., 2010), with Deborah R. Glaser, Ed.D. She travels the country extensively, presenting workshops for classroom teachers and administrators.

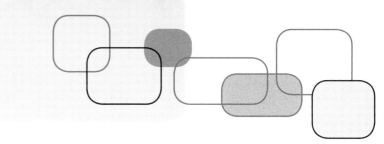

About the Contributors

Stephanie Al Otaiba, Ph.D., Associate Professor, School of Teacher Education, College of Education and Florida Center for Reading Research, Florida State University, 2010 Levy Avenue, Tallahassee, Florida 32310

Dr. Al Otaiba was a special educator before receiving her Ph.D. from Vanderbilt University. She conducts research related to early literacy, learning disabilities, and teacher training. She teaches undergraduate and graduate classes, and serves on the editorial boards of numerous education journals.

Suzanne Carreker, Ph.D., CALT-QI, Deputy Director of Programs, Neuhaus Education Center, 4433 Bissonnet, Bellaire, Texas 77401

Dr. Carreker, a past president of The Houston Branch of The International Dyslexia Association (HBIDA) and a current vice president of the national International Dyslexia Association board, is a frequent speaker at regional and national conferences and has authored a number of multisensory curricula and journal articles. She was the recipient of the 2009 HBIDA Nancy LaFevers Award for her contributions to students with dyslexia and other related learning differences in the Houston community.

Christie L. Cavanaugh, Ph.D., Investigator, FPG Child Development Institute, University of North Carolina at Chapel Hill, CB 8040, Chapel Hill, North Carolina 27599

Dr. Cavanaugh, with more than 30 years in education, has teaching experience in early intervention, early childhood, elementary, and special education in addition to teaching language development, emergent literacy, beginning reading, and intervention at the undergraduate and graduate levels. She has presented, published, and provided professional development nationally. Her primary research interests and areas of expertise are related to language and emergent literacy, beginning reading instruction, and supporting at-risk schools and children through prevention and intervention efforts and implementation of effective, evidence-based practices.

Stephen Ciullo, Ph.D, Researcher, The Meadows Center for Preventing Educational Risk, College of Education SZB 228, The University of Texas at Austin, 1 University Station D4900, Austin, Texas 78712

Dr. Ciullo was a special education teacher in a public school for 6 years. At The University of Texas at Austin, he has worked on several Institute of Education Sciences–funded research projects. Currently he teaches education courses at the University of Texas and works on a reading comprehension project at the Meadows Center for Preventing Educational Risk. Dr. Ciullo's primary research interest is reading comprehension interventions for middle-grade (4th–8th) at-risk readers and students with learning disabilities.

Darcy Dycha, M.Ed., Educational Coordinator, The Children's Learning Institute, University of Texas Health Science Center at Houston, 700 Fannin Street UCT 2400B, Houston, Texas 77030

Ms. Dycha has 18 years of experience in education including work as a regular classroom teacher, graduate school instructor, and statewide coordinator for Texas Reading First. In addition, she has served as an elementary literacy consultant as part of the Alberta Initiative for School Improvement in Canada. She currently works on the development team for Texas Primary Reading Inventory and is a curriculum writer for the Eager Building Vocabulary and Early Reading Strategies project.

Susan M. Ebbers, Doctoral Candidate, University of California, Berkeley, California 94720

Ms. Ebbers is an educational consultant, author, and researcher. After 15 years in public and private education, she began writing research-aligned vocabulary, morphology, and decoding curricula, published by Sopris West. Visit her blog, *Vocabulogic*, created to connect teachers with researchers and to diminish the verbal gap that separates students of high and low levels of linguistic insight.

Jan Hasbrouck, Ph.D., Educational Researcher and Consultant, Gibson Hasbrouck & Associates, 396 Washington Street, Suite 370, Wellesley, Massachusetts 02481

Dr. Jan Hasbrouck is an educational consultant, author, and researcher. Dr. Hasbrouck worked as a reading specialist and coach for 15 years and later became a professor. She is the author and coauthor of several books and her research in reading fluency, academic assessment and interventions, and coaching has been widely published. She and Dr. Vicki Gibson have partnered to form Gibson Hasbrouck & Associates, with the mission to provide high-quality professional development to educators nationally and internationally.

Heather A. Haynes, M.A., Doctoral Candidate, Special Education Department, Beach Center on Disability, University of Kansas, 1200 Sunnyside Avenue, Lawrence, Kansas 66045

Ms. Haynes was an elementary school teacher, reading instructional coach, and reading technical assistance specialist. At the University of Kansas, she is currently a doctoral student fellow in the Response to Intervention Leadership Preparation Program in the department of special education. Ms. Haynes' primary research interests are reading instruction, teacher preparation, and integrating academic and behavioral interventions and supports.

Elfrieda H. Hiebert, Ph.D., Research Associate, University of California, 1156 High Street, Santa Cruz, California 95064

Dr. Hiebert has been on the faculties of the University of Michigan and the University of California, Berkeley, and is currently a research associate at the University of California, Santa Cruz. She has recently initiated a not-for-profit organization, TextProject, aimed at increasing students' reading levels through appropriate texts. She has authored or edited 10 volumes and has published numerous research articles on text features and beginning reading acquisition.

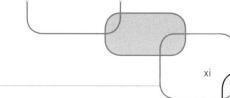

Kristie Hotchkiss, M.S., Project Coordinator for College & Career Readiness Initiative, College of Education, The University of Texas at Austin, 1 University Station, Austin, Texas 78712

Ms. Hotchkiss is a project coordinator for the College & Career Readiness Initiative: English/Language Arts Faculty Collaborative where she facilitates and provides ongoing professional development and collaborative opportunities in adolescent literacy to higher education faculty. She has 32 years of teaching experience with at-risk populations as a reading specialist, has worked at the Vaughn Gross Center on the Texas Adolescent Literacy Academies project, and as an instructional designer for English/language arts for an educational computer software company. Ms. Hotchkiss earned her B.A. from the University of Northern Colorado and her M.S. from Oregon State University in secondary education.

Natalie G. Olinghouse, Ph.D., Assistant Professor, Educational Psychology Research Scientist, Center for Behavioral Education and Research, 249 Glenbrook Road, University of Connecticut, Storrs, Connecticut 06269

Dr. Olinghouse is assistant professor at the University of Connecticut. Her research and teaching interests include writing instruction and assessment, standards-based reform, and reading and writing connections. Dr. Olinghouse also has 12 years of public school teaching experience.

Colleen Klein Reutebuch, Ph.D., Senior Field Trainer/Analyst, The Meadows Center for Preventing Educational Risk, College of Education, The University of Texas at Austin, 1 University Station D4900, Austin, Texas 78712

Dr. Reutebuch's interests include interventions and instructional practices to enhance vocabulary and content area knowledge and to improve reading difficulties. She currently directs grants from the Institute of Education Sciences and conducts research focused on improving reading outcomes for English learners in the middle grades.

Joshua Wilson, M.S., Doctoral Student, Educational Psychology Department, 249 Glenbrook Road, University of Connecticut, Storrs, Connecticut 06269

Mr. Wilson was a special education teacher for 7 years, working in both private and public settings. At the University of Connecticut, he is currently the project manager of an Institute of Education Sciences–funded research project and teaches a class on assessment in special education. Mr. Wilson's primary research interests are writing development and writing assessment.

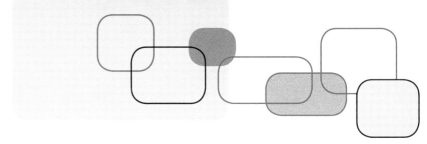

Preface

Since the early 2000s there has been a strong convergence of new evidence about how to teach literacy and how to intervene with students who struggle to learn to read and write. The editors and contributors to this text are passionate about sharing this evidence and the instructional strategies supported by the research. Teachers and administrators, and those who prepare them, must have knowledge of this research and evidence-based practices to address the needs of our diverse student population. Support personnel, such as instructional coaches, school psychologists, speech-language pathologists, and reading specialists, will find the information useful in providing more targeted support for teachers and students. In addition, the information in this text will assist school personnel to implement a response-to-intervention model successfully.

Fundamentals of Literacy Instruction and Assessment, Pre-K–6 is meant to be among the first texts teachers study about literacy. In addition to the information the text contains, teachers are guided in applying the information with students. The information and application with students are essential to those new to the literacy field. The text provides the essential background information and experiences that will enable teachers to comprehend more in-depth texts addressing complex aspects of teaching literacy.

Parents are a child's first teacher and lifelong advocates for their children. This book provides the information parents need to collaborate with school personnel and to advocate for effective evidence-based instruction for their children.

This text refers to the most recent standards addressing literacy, including the Common Core State Standards, the International Reading Association Standards for Reading Professionals, and The International Dyslexia Association Knowledge and Practice Standards for Teachers of Reading. This text is an invaluable resource for those preparing for reading licensure examinations and for teacher educators who understand the value of a text that supports new literacy and practice standards.

Martha C. Hougen and Susan M. Smartt have dedicated their lives to improving the literacy skills of our nation's students. Between them, they have spent years teaching students in classrooms and clinics. They have worked in school districts and at universities training teachers, undergraduate students, and graduate students, to be effective educators. They have conducted research, prepared documents and publications, written articles and books, and presented at international and national conferences. In this text, they have combined their experiences and knowledge with that of the esteemed contributors and other nationally renowned researchers to synthesize the most critical aspects of reading and writing instruction that educators must know.

The text is designed to provide essential foundational knowledge about literacy instruction and assessment practices, supporting educators in the common goal of enabling each student to become a competent and critical lifelong reader and writer.

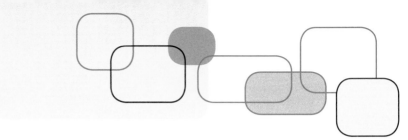

Acknowledgments and Credits

We would like to acknowledge and thank our esteemed contributors. We appreciate them sharing their vast knowledge and experience with us. Their input has been invaluable in creating a text to promote effective literacy instruction.

We thank the innumerable literacy professionals, teachers, researchers, professors, administrators, and colleagues who have contributed to our knowledge of literacy instruction and practice by providing us with the opportunity to work with them, to study their work, and to be mentored by these individuals.

Finally, we want to acknowledge and express our gratitude to the students and teachers whom we have had the privilege to know. It is from them that we have learned the most about how to teach and motivate learners; they have been our guides as we continually strive to become more effective educators.

We would like to credit the following people for their contributions to this book:

Karen S. Chan, who created the graphic design for the following figures:
2.3, 8.1, 8.2, 10.1, 10.2, 10.3, 10.4, 10.5, 10.6, 10.7, 12.2, and 14.2.

Photographer Michael Cerza for the photographs in this book, with the exception of the photograph on page 176, for which we would like to credit Darcy Dycha, and the photograph on page 62, for which we would like to credit Colleen Klein Reutebuch.

Karen S. Chan, Genise Henry, Dorian Henry, and Kamela V. Syed for appearing in the role of teachers in the photographs.

*To the teachers and students who have enriched our lives
by their dedication and motivation to be the best they can be*

1

Becoming an Effective
Literacy Teacher

Introduction

by Martha C. Hougen

Congratulations for choosing to become a teacher, one of the most important, rewarding, and challenging occupations. You are in the unique position of changing the lives of students, either by supporting your students achievement or by contributing to their failure. You, of course, want to help students to succeed, to learn, and to be prepared for college and careers when they leave school. The first years of school are of immense importance: you are the one to teach the basics of literacy to young students and to instill in them a love of reading and of learning. The contributors to this book have a passionate dedication to ensuring that the students in our schools succeed and that their teachers are knowledgeable and effective. We hope to impart the passion, the motivation, and the knowledge to enable you to be that wonderful teacher your students will always remember as contributing to their success.

A teacher's critical responsibility is to teach students to read well. This book will guide your reading instruction. It is not meant to be the one and only book you will use on how to teach reading; it is the first, introductory book. As you will learn, there are huge volumes dedicated to every aspect of reading, and new research is being published every day. This book is meant to be an overview so that when you do tackle the more complicated texts, you will have the background information you need to understand the information presented.

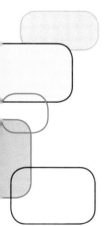

Objectives: After studying this chapter you will be able to do the following:

1. Provide an overview of the text and explain its purpose.
2. Explain your responsibilities as a tutor.
3. Define and discuss what constitutes effective instruction.
4. Define and discuss what constitutes differentiated instruction.
5. Discuss common instructional challenges presented by students at risk for educational failure, including students from economically disadvantaged backgrounds, students who are English language learners, and students who have disabilities.
6. Define scientifically based research and explain why it is important.
7. Share the contents of two relevant web sites that support literacy instruction.
8. Explain your responsibilities as a classroom teacher in a response to intervention (RTI) model.
9. Articulate the big idea questions and explain the rationale for the questions.
10. Describe the role of the Common Core State Standards and other relevant standards.
11. Begin preparations to tutor a student.

PART I: OVERVIEW OF TEXT

This text is organized by the critical components of reading instruction for students in grades Pre-K–6. The chapters follow the typical development of reading skills. Although students learn at different rates, all students master basic reading skills in a similar sequence when first learning to read, from recognizing sounds to decoding words. At the same time, oral language, listening, vocabulary, fluent reading, and comprehension skills are developing in the early reader. Learning to write is another crucial skill students must master to communicate effectively. In addition, writing reinforces the development of reading skills and facilitates learning content. Finally, discussions about recent legislation and policies will be presented, including current initiatives to guide and support student success through the adoption of Common Core State Standards and the implementation of a multitiered system of supports, often referred to as RTI (response to intervention). The last two chapters "put it all together," illustrating how everything you learned in this book, from effective instruction and assessment to national policies and initiatives, can be implemented seamlessly in your classroom.

Chapter 1: Becoming an Effective Literacy Teacher: Introduction

In this chapter, you will learn about some of the challenges you will face as a teacher. You will read an explanation of major initiatives and considerations, to be discussed more thoroughly later in the book. Your responsibilities as a tutor are outlined, and you are provided a template of a recommended lesson plan format.

Chapter 2: The Critical Components of Effective Reading Instruction

Several national reports have recently published converging evidence about what constitutes an effective reading program and how to effectively and efficiently teach students. The critical components of reading instruction and the features of effective instruction are introduced in this chapter and are elaborated upon throughout the text.

Chapter 3: Oral Language and Listening Skill Development in Early Childhood

The years before children enter school are some of the most important to developing the foundation for literacy. You will learn about oral language and listening skill development and how you can promote these skills with your students. If children enter your classroom without these skills, you will be confident about what to do to address these gaps.

Chapter 4: Phonological Awareness: A Critical Foundation for Beginning Reading

One of the most researched prerequisites of learning to read is phonemic awareness. You will learn about this important component, how to teach it, and how to guide students from an awareness of sounds to an understanding of the alphabetic principle (i.e., that sounds can be mapped to letters), and to beginning reading.

Chapter 5: Effective Phonics Instruction

Knowledge about how sounds are represented by letters, why words are spelled the way they are, and how to decode, or read, words is discussed in this chapter. After studying this chapter, rarely will you answer a student's query about why a word is spelled the way it is with, "I don't know. It just is." The knowledge you will learn and will share with your students will decrease some of the frustration about spelling difficult words and determining the meaning of obtuse vocabulary.

Chapter 6: Beginning Handwriting, Spelling, and Composition Instruction

Learning the correct ways to form letters, write phrases and sentences, and spell words are important skills not often explicitly taught in the early grades. This chapter provides a guide to systematically teaching these skills.

Chapter 7: The Common Core State Standards and Text Complexity

At this point, you will know the basics of teaching early reading skills. It is time for your students to practice reading. Now is a crucial time in their reading development. The text you select for your students to read can accelerate their reading progress *or* can frustrate them and slow their reading achievement. This chapter will help you select texts that are not too easy, not too hard, but just right. The expectations of the Common Core State Standards are reviewed, and the use of the Lexile system to determine reading levels of texts is explained.

Chapter 8: Fluency Instruction

You have taught your students to decode words, but they still appear to struggle, reading word by word. It is time to work with them to develop reading fluency, reading with accuracy, expression, and at an appropriate rate or speed. This chapter provides the information you need to teach students to read with fluency and comprehension.

Chapter 9: What Is Important to Know About Words of Written Language

The history of the English language is fascinating. There are more words in the English language than in any other alphabetic language. English has also been open to integrating words from other languages. When you know the clues that words contain, such as their origin, root, and original meaning, you will find English spellings more predictable than not. This chapter will introduce you to the history of the language, unlock clues, and increase your understanding of the English language.

Chapter 10: A Comprehensive, Interactive Approach to Vocabulary Development

Too many students are entering our schools with inadequate vocabulary knowledge. Poor vocabulary is a huge barrier to comprehension. This is apparent when "good" readers enter the upper elementary grades and seem to suddenly struggle with understanding what they are reading. You will learn multiple ways to increase your students' vocabulary knowledge and word consciousness.

Chapter 11: Comprehension, Grades K–3

Often, teachers spend a lot of time asking students questions about what they have read and too little time teaching them how to comprehend text. This chapter provides multiple strategies for teaching young students how to develop comprehension skills.

Chapter 12: Comprehension, Grades 4–6

As the text students read becomes more complicated and dense, different comprehension strategies are required. This chapter discusses research-based strategies you can share with your students.

Chapter 13: Strategic, Meaningful, and Effective Writing Instruction for Elementary Students

Earlier in the book, you learned about beginning writing skills. This chapter discusses more sophisticated writing, writing for different purposes and audiences, and various genres of writing. The ability to express oneself in writing is an important prerequisite skill for success in college and careers.

Chapter 14: Disciplinary Literacy

Recent research has determined and state standards are requiring that students learn to read and write in the disciplines. This chapter provides an overview of what it means to read and write as a historian, a scientist, and a mathematician as well as in English/language arts. Reading and writing in the disciplines becomes increasingly important when students enter secondary school.

Chapter 15: Current Laws, Policies, Initiatives, Common Core State Standards, and Response to Intervention

The past decade has seen significant changes in the laws affecting education. The Elementary and Secondary Education Act (ESEA) of 1965 (PL 89-10, PL 94-142) and the Individuals with Disabilities Education Improvement Act (IDEA) of 2004 are, as this book is published, in the process of being reauthorized.[1] The Common Core State Standards, the Texas College and Career Readiness Standards, and standards developed by professional organizations such as the International Reading Association[2] and The International Dyslexia Association[3] provide guides to instruction. New assessments and certification requirements for teachers are being developed. This chapter explains these developments and how they may affect your instruction.

Chapter 16: Putting It All Together: Becoming an Effective Literacy Teacher

You may feel overwhelmed at this point. This chapter helps you weave everything you have learned into a coherent, seamless instructional plan. You will learn how to organize your instruction as well as how to manage your class for differentiated instruction in varying grouping formats.

Chapter 17: Ten Tips to Becoming an Effective Teacher

This final chapter shares 10 tips to becoming an effective teacher. These tips and the knowledge you have learned by studying this text give you the foundation for becoming a truly great teacher.

Glossary

A glossary is provided at the end of the book. Refer to the glossary often to ensure you understand the terms discussed.

Appendixes

The appendixes provide additional resources for you, including lesson plan formats, activities for tutoring, and more information about certain topics. Be sure to look at Appendix A to learn how to make a sticky board to use with your tutee! The sources for several sets of standards are provided; use the the standards as guides to plan your instruction.

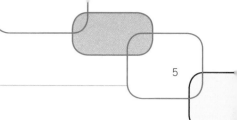

Organization of Chapters

Classroom Scenario

Each chapter begins with a scenario similar to what you may experience as a teacher. The scenarios are designed to help you focus on one aspect of reading, using examples of actual students and teachers. Your instructors may supplement the scenarios with case studies, providing you additional information about students and their achievement data so that you can make informed instructional decisions.

Objectives

The learning objectives are stated in each chapter. The objectives address the most important points you need to master. At least one will address an objective or activity for you to implement with a student you will be tutoring.

Big Idea Guiding Questions

Six big idea questions are addressed in each chapter. These questions are meant to guide your learning, to clarify the most critical aspects of effective reading instruction, and to emphasize research-based best practices. At the end of the text, you will be able to answer the following questions for the critical components of reading and writing:

Big Idea Questions about Reading Instruction

1. What is it (the component)? Why is it important? What does the research say?
2. What should students know and be able to do at specific grade levels, Pre-K–6?
3. How do we assess what students know and how much they are learning?
4. How do we use assessments to plan instruction?
5. How do we teach this component effectively, efficiently, and in a manner appropriate to the age/grade level of our students?
6. How do we develop instructional plans that incorporate standards and evidence-based strategies?[4]

Opportunities for Application Assignments

Suggested opportunities to apply what you have learned are provided at the end of each chapter. The In-Class Assignments are to be completed with your peers during class. The Tutoring Assignments are to be completed with the student being tutored. The Homework Assignments are to be done on your own. The more practice you have applying the concepts and activities presented in this text, the more effective you will be as a teacher.

Suggested Resources, Web Sites, and Readings

There are many resources available online. The most helpful ones are included in this text. Judicious use of these resources will enhance your teaching and save you time. Be sure to explore them.

Notes and References

Detailed references with citations and notes regarding the content presented are provided at the end of each chapter. Refer to the notes for more information about a topic and the supporting research.

Tutoring

During this course, you are expected to work with at least one student who is in kindergarten or grades 1–6. The authors suggest you select a student in grade 1 or 2 for the first half of the semester and a student in grades 4–6 for the second half. This will provide an opportunity to work with a beginning reader, practicing the early literacy instructional strategies presented in this book, and to teach the higher-level comprehension and writing strategies needed by students in upper elementary grades.

The text is designed for you to tutor a student for 1 or 2 hours per week. Your instructor will facilitate placing you with a student, providing the details about securing school and parental permission and explaining the work you are expected to complete with that student. This text will discuss the elements of tutoring, including assessing your student, determining instructional objectives, selecting appropriate materials, using research-based activities and strategies, and evaluating your instruction.

You need to begin assembling your "Tutoring Toolbox." The toolbox consists of materials you should bring to every tutoring session. You will be taught how and when to use each item as you read this text. Your toolbox should include the following:

- Paper, pencils (regular, red, and blue), crayons, note cards
- A wipe-off white board, markers, and eraser
- Sticky notes
- Scissors, glue
- A selection of books to read aloud, appropriate to the grade level of your student
- Progress-monitoring instruments (graphs, selected text)
- A stop watch
- Small chips and a Say-It-Move-It chart (see Appendix B)
- A puppet
- A large, sticky board (see Appendix A)
- The San Diego Quick Assessment: available to download from http://www.homeschooling.gomilpitas.com/articles/060899.htm
- Other materials as determined by your instructor

Lesson Plan Development and Delivery

Effective teachers plan ahead and deliver thoughtful instruction, informed by data, to meet the instructional needs of each student. A lesson plan template is provided to support you in this endeavor (see Appendix D). When you first begin creating lessons, you will spend hours designing just what you want. At first, you will rarely deliver it as you had anticipated. However, you will learn to be an efficient, effective teacher with an appropriate pace and well-timed instruction. If you use this template, or one provided by your instructor, you will make the best use of every minute during your instructional time. Think about this: If you waste just 5 minutes per day organizing materials or arranging groups for 180 school days, you have wasted more than 15 hours of instructional time! If you squander 20 minutes per day, you have deprived your students of 90 hours of instruction; that is about 3 weeks' worth of learning.

Our students do not have time to waste. You should feel a sense of urgency when you are teaching, making the best use of every minute. When you have planned well, you will be an efficient and effective teacher while maintaining a comfortable, positive classroom environment. Each part of the recommended lesson plan will be discussed as you proceed through the book. A blank copy is provided in Appendix D.

Also included in Appendix D is a sample of a completed lesson plan. Extra support, or scaffolding, is provided in the form of a script. You may want to write out what you are going to say for the first few lessons to be sure you know what you want to say and to ensure you explain concepts explicitly.

Expectations and Responsibilities of a Tutor

You will be working with one or more students during the semester. Each student deserves your respect and best effort. In reality, the student will be your teacher! You are expected to come prepared to each tutoring session, to dress and act as a professional educator, and to respect your student. Your responsibilities include respecting the confidential nature of your work. You must not discuss your student with anyone other than the student's teacher and your instructor. Do not include your student's name or photograph on anything you submit in class. If you are allowed to review test data or other personal information about the student, you must keep that information confidential. Student confidentiality is protected by the Family Educational Rights and Privacy Act (FERPA) of 1974 (PL 93-579).[5] It is a federal law that protects the privacy of students' education records. The law applies to all schools that receive funds under an applicable program of the U.S. Department of Education. Stricter confidentiality laws apply to students who qualify for special education services.

Initial Assessment of the Student

Before an instructional plan can be designed for a student, you need to know what the student knows and what he or she needs to learn. Some of this information can be obtained by talking with the student, the teachers, and perhaps the parents. However, you should also obtain more objective data about specific skills.

It is probable that the school in which you are tutoring administers assessments several times a year. You may be able to study those instruments and scores and administer a version of the school's assessment. The school and your instructor will help you determine whether it is appropriate for you to administer the assessment used by the school.

Your instructor may recommend an assessment. If not, there are several available. One assessment, used by many districts across the country, is the Dynamic Indicators of Basic Early Literacy Skills-NEXT (DIBELS), available for students in grades K–6, in Spanish and English.[6] The appropriate assessment can be downloaded at no cost at https://dibels.uoregon.edu/measures/index.php?action=download/.

However, it is essential that you also download the administration and scoring guide and the training videos and that you practice the administration and scoring of the assessments several times (five minimum) before you administer the assessment to a student. Ideally, your instructor will provide training in how best to use this instrument.

Another free assessment that provides a quick check of a student's reading abilities is the San Diego Quick Assessment available for download at http://www.homeschooling.gomilpitas.com/articles/060899.htm.

There are also several inexpensive assessments that will provide a global overview of the student's strengths and needs. One is the Quick Phonics Screener (QPS), which is available at http://www.readnaturally.com/products/qps.htm.[7] The QPS is an untimed, criterion-referenced assessment that measures a student's ability to pronounce the phonetic elements in real and nonsense words, grades K–adult. Teachers administer only those tasks that are appropriate for a student's age, grade, and performance level. Teachers can quickly and accurately diagnose students' strengths and instructional needs. Results can be used to monitor students' progress as their phonics skills develop.

Other screening assessments can be found in the book, *CORE Assessing Reading–Multiple Measures*. This resource also includes several Spanish versions of assessments (e.g., Spanish Phonemic Awareness, Phonics Survey, Spelling, a Verbal Language Scale).[8]

If the student is in the second semester of first grade or older, a reading fluency assessment can be administered in which the student reads on grade-level–connected text for 1 minute. This will be explained in depth in Chapter 8. If the material available in the classroom is used, the assessment is considered a curriculum-based assessment. There are also numerous commercially produced texts appropriate to measure oral reading fluency. Later in this text you will learn how to analyze tests of oral reading fluency.

PART II: OVERVIEW OF INSTRUCTIONAL CONSIDERATIONS AND CURRENT INITIATIVES

Throughout the text, current research and effective instructional practices is explained. This section provides a brief overview of these considerations and initiatives including evidence-based effective instruction, differentiation of instruction, the features of effective instruction, the Common Core State Standards, and ways to provide multitiered systems of support, such as the response to intervention model.

Three Critical Considerations for Effective and Efficient Instruction

This text addresses three practices crucial for effective and efficient instruction: 1) use of effective instructional strategies, validated by evidence-based research; 2) differentiation of instruction for students who may need acceleration and for those who may need instructional interventions due to economic disadvantage, because of a disability, or who are English language learners; and 3) implementation of the features of effective instruction to ensure that all students learn.[9]

1) Use of effective instructional strategies, validated by evidence-based research a practice that selects instructional strategies based upon sound research, is crucial. There are myriad programs, materials, and salespeople who will bombard you, selling the panacea for all educational instructional needs. However, you must select carefully and spend your money and time on materials and strategies that have been rigorously tested by scientific research. This means that the strategies have been studied with many different types of students, in different environments, by several researchers. The strategies are found to be effective with most of the targeted students (no strategy is effective with all students). Rigorous, scientific research is much more than a single study with a small group of students (e.g., the "it worked in my room" results are not sufficient to make important instructional decisions for large numbers of students). Rather, the research must be replicated with many groups of students with similar attributes to those you teach. You can be confident that the strategies presented in this text are based on research, have been used successfully with many students, and have a high likelihood of being effective when used correctly with your students.

2) Differentiation of instruction for students who may need acceleration and for those who may be at risk due to economic disadvantage, because of a disability, or who are English language learners is the second crucial practice. Differentiation addresses the wide range of needs presented by the students, who will have vastly different backgrounds, ways of learning, strengths, and areas in need of intensive support. Some of your students will enter school reading well; others may not know any letters or sounds. Students learn at different rates, and they have a wide variety of background experiences. Throughout this text, ideas will be presented about how to teach differently, or differentiate, for students to meet their individual needs. Differentiation may mean using different materials and activities, teaching smaller groups of students, using assistive technology, or sometimes even changing the learning objectives. Differentiating instruction based upon student needs will ensure that students master the skills taught to them.

Let us explore the specialized needs of students likely to be in your class.

Accelerated students are those who learn quickly and may need to be challenged with more advanced material. These students are referred to as gifted and talented, advanced, or exceptional. However, you will encounter students who have not been identified as gifted, yet need accelerated instruction in certain subjects, and you will have students who are identified as gifted who are not gifted in all areas and may need scaffolded instruction in specific subjects. Therefore, teachers must observe and note the progress of students to know how to adjust instruction to keep the accelerated students engaged and motivated while providing additional support as needed.

At-risk students include those who may find learning in your classroom challenging because they come from economically disadvantaged homes, have disabilities, or are English language learners. Learning how to address their needs and how to include their parents are essential skills for an effective teacher.

Students from economically disadvantaged homes often have different background knowledge and have developed fewer school-ready skills than children from more affluent backgrounds. Often, children from impoverished homes have few, if any, experiences with books or being read to. Their vocabulary knowledge is typically much less than that of middle-class students.[10] Teachers need to make an extra effort to ensure that students develop the listening and oral language skills to be ready to learn to read. One maxim that helps many teachers is "Don't commit assumacide."[11] Do not assume your students know how to hold a book, conduct a conversation with a peer or with adults, or express their ideas in writing. Explicit instruction in acceptable behaviors in school as well as in academic subjects is required.

Classes will include students with disabilities. Federal legislation has been enacted to ensure that all children with disabilities have available to them a free appropriate public education (FAPE) that emphasizes special education and related services designed to meet their unique needs and prepare them for further education, employment, and independent living.[12]

Under the federal law, Individuals with Disabilities Education Improvement Act (IDEA), students may qualify for special education and related services if they are deemed to have one or more of the following disabilities:

- Autism
- Deaf-blindness
- Deafness
- Developmental delay
- Emotional disturbance
- Hearing impairments
- Intellectual disability
- Multiple disabilities
- Orthopedic impairment
- Other health impairment
- Specific learning disability
- Speech or language impairment
- Traumatic brain injury
- Visual impairment, including blindness

It must also be determined that their educational performance is adversely affected due to the disability.[13] The law prescribes criteria for identification and assessment, rights of parents and students, and responsibilities of school personnel.

Approximately 13% of school children have disabilities.[14] These percentages are different in various states because states have different criteria for placing students in special education. The most common disabilities encountered in classes are specific learning disabilities. A specific learning disability is a neurological disorder that may make it difficult for students to acquire academic and social skills. Currently, more than 2.5 million students have been diagnosed with learning disabilities, and they represent 42% of all students with disabilities.[15] Students with reading disabilities comprise approximately 80%–85% of all children diagnosed as having a specific learning disability.[16]

The definition of "specific learning disability" in the IDEA of 2004 is as follows:

> The term "specific learning disability" means a disorder in one or more of the basic psychological processes involved in understanding or in using language, spoken or written, which may manifest itself in imperfect ability to listen, think, speak, read, write, spell, or do mathematical calculations.
>
> The term includes such conditions as perceptual disabilities, brain injury, minimal brain dysfunction, dyslexia, and developmental aphasia.
>
> The term does not include a learning problem that is primarily the result of visual, hearing, or motor disabilities; of mental retardation; of emotional disturbance; or of environmental, cultural, or economic disadvantage.[17]

Identified students must have an individualized education program (IEP) that educators must follow. You should receive a copy of the IEP for all students with disabilities in your class. Be sure to work with the special education teacher to provide appropriate instruction for identified students.

The strategies and teaching practices suggested in this text will support students with specific learning disabilities in reading and writing. It is likely that these students will need more intensive instruction, in smaller groups and for longer periods of time, than other students. You will be able to provide much of the instruction based on what you learn in this text. However, be sure to work with the student's special education teacher to determine how the two of you may collaborate. The special education teacher may be involved in providing small group or inclusion support. You can learn more about the specifics of what and how to teach students with specific learning disabilities by working together.

The most common specific learning disability is dyslexia. Dyslexia is a language-based disability that is typically manifested in students having difficulty with specific language skills, particularly reading. Difficulty spelling, writing, and pronouncing words are also common factors in dyslexia. In some states, students receive special education services and accommodations through Section 504 of the Rehabilitation Act of 1973 (PL 93–112). Whatever the circumstances are in your state, the chances are very strong that you will be teaching students with dyslexia. Because the range of severity in dyslexia varies from mild to severe, students in your class with dyslexia may or may not be officially identified (certified) as specific learning disabled, and, therefore, the students may or may not be receiving special education services. Nevertheless, you will be responsible for your students' instruction and academic success. Typically, students with dyslexia have poor awareness of the sequence of sounds in words, have difficulty with some speech sounds, read slower than their peers, demonstrate poor spelling, exhibit illegible or poor handwriting, have trouble comprehending longer reading assignments, have poor reading stamina, and/or have difficulty memorizing math facts. These difficulties are often "unexpected" because these students often have a large oral vocabulary and in-depth knowledge about certain subjects.

The most accepted definition of dyslexia is the one provided by The International Dyslexia Association (IDA):

> Dyslexia is a specific learning disability that is neurological in origin. It is characterized by difficulties with accurate and/or fluent word recognition and by poor spelling and decoding abilities. These difficulties typically result from a deficit in the phonological component of language that is often unexpected in relation to other cognitive abilities and the provision of effective classroom instruction. Secondary consequences may include problems in reading comprehension and reduced reading experience that can impede the growth of vocabulary and background knowledge.[18]

The International Dyslexia Association (IDA) maintains a web site that provides valuable information for teachers and parents of children with dyslexia: http://www.interdys.org.

Go to the IDA web site and look for the Fact Sheets. They provide information on many of the elements that pertain to students with dyslexia (e.g., spelling, attention deficit hyperactivity disorder (ADHD), causes of dyslexia, teaching programs and practices). In addition, recently The IDA has published standards on teaching students to read and preventing reading difficulties: Knowledge and Practice Standards for Teachers of Reading. The standards are integrated in this text and can be obtained at http://www.interdys.org/standards.htm.[19]

Another common disability is ADHD. Students with ADHD may have difficulties with sustaining attention and may be overly active. They often receive special education services under "other health impaired" and/or "specific learning disability" if appropriate. However, many children with ADHD are protected under a different law: Section 504 of the Rehabilitation Act of 1973. Section 504 requires that individuals with a disability that substantially limits a major life activity be protected with accommodations that enable them to be successful in school and in the workplace. You will likely have students with ADHD in your classes, and the strategies and activities provided in this text will support the educational achievement of these students.

English language learners are students for whom English is not their first language. People living in the United States speak hundreds of different languages. The most common language, other than English, is Spanish. The census of 2010 concludes that Hispanics make up 16.3% of the total population, and 46% live in California and Texas.[20]

A great deal has been learned about how to best support students who are learning English. It is now known, for example, that we do not have to wait until they are proficient in English to begin reading instruction in English.[21] English language learners can be taught to read in English along with their peers. Some districts offer dual language programs where both English speakers and English learners learn English and a second language, usually Spanish. Other districts teach students to read in their home language first, and when they are proficient in their home language, they are taught to read in English. Research is not definitive about which approach is best for English language learners.[22]

Students who are learning English need direct instruction to increase their vocabulary, and it may take several years for them to reach academic levels of vocabulary and comprehension.[23] They must continue to receive intensive vocabulary and comprehension instruction throughout their schooling.

Another important finding is that the teacher does not have to speak the language of the students to be an effective teacher.[24] Using effective instructional strategies, as described in this book, is essential for supporting student achievement. Excellent, effective teaching of the core reading program benefits students who are learning English as well as English speakers as long as the instruction is systematic, explicit, and direct, and ample practice opportunities are provided.[25]

There are four stages of second language acquisition as shown in Figure 1.1, and it is important for teachers to be able to recognize the stage of each student. There are different expectations and methods to teach students at each stage.

A source that provides an excellent overview of the differences between Spanish and English letter sounds and patterns is the *Teaching Reading Sourcebook* by Honig, Diamond, and Gutlohn.[26]

3) Features of effective instruction Effective implementation of the features of effective instruction will ensure that your students learn the content you are teaching.[27] For many years, researchers in education have studied what constitutes good teaching. We know the skills teachers need to master to be effective. Effective teachers manage their classrooms well and make sure that all students are engaged in learning. The five features of effective instruction, listed in Figure 1.2 and explained in detail in the next chapter, are the basis for excellent teaching, no matter what you teach.

You will consider these features as you plan lessons to teach and as you evaluate lessons you taught to determine how to impress your instruction.

Stages of second language development and suggested instructional practices

Stage	Students may:	Suggested instructional practices
• Preproduction	• Communicate in their native language • Remain silent	• Use normal pronunciations & speech • Provide "think-alouds" & modeling • Set clear goals for learning & provide immediate feedback • Actively involve students • Restate students' responses • Use photos & artifacts • Pair students with language buddies • Accept nonverbal responses
• Early production	• Use simple words or phrases • Use telegraphic speech • Understand more English than they can produce	• Allow wait time when you ask a student to respond • Post printed labels and word lists • Post "yes/no" & "either/or" questions • Focus on the meaning of a students' response, not the syntax or pronunciation
• Speech emergence	• Use new vocabulary • Communicate using sentences • Ask simple questions • Understand spoken English with the support of pictures, objects, actions • Understand more English than they can produce	• Continue to build vocabulary by using synonyms, webbing, semantic mapping • Use texts with illustrations that connect to the text & to the students' background • Structure opportunities for students to discuss content with English-speakers
• Intermediate and advanced fluency	• Express thought and feelings more effectively • Ask and respond to higher-level questions ("what if", "how," "why").	• Explain idiomatic and slang expressions • Provide many opportunities for students to write • Help students transfer their knowledge, of reading in their native language, to reading in English

Figure 1.1. Stages of second language development and suggested instructional practices. (*Source:* Vaughn Gross Center at the University of Texas, 2007.)

1. Explicit instruction with modeling
2. Systematic instruction with scaffolding
3. Multiple opportunities for students to respond and practice
4. Ongoing progress monitoring
5. Immediate corrective feedback

Figure 1.2. Features of effective instruction. (*Source*: Vaughn Gross Center for Reading and Language Arts, 2007.)

Working with Parents

Parents of all students and especially of students who are at risk should be included in decisions about their children. Sometimes, it is difficult for parents to come to the school to meet with you: they may work more than one job, have other children to care for, or be uncomfortable because of previous negative experiences with schools. However, it is important that their child's teacher reaches out to them and includes them whenever possible. Share good news about their children as well as your concerns. If personal meetings are difficult to arrange, send home notes and make phone calls sharing the child's positive accomplishments. (Figure 1.3) When you have established a history of sharing positive reports with parents, it is much easier to obtain their support when you have to deal with something that is not so positive.

Respect the parents' talents, whether it is reading in their first language to their child, sharing their work experiences or special skills with the class, or talking about their native culture. Parents are their child's first teacher, and they know more about their child than you do. Enlist them as your partner in educating their child.

You will consider these features as you plan lessons to teach and as you evaluate lessons you taught to determine how to improve your instruction.

Common Core State Standards

In an effort to unify curriculum, increase achievement across the nation, and ensure that all students are college and career ready upon completion of high school, several national organizations collaborated to create standards to guide education.[28] The standards address Mathematics and English Language Arts & Literacy in History/Social Studies, Science, and Technical Subjects, K–12. The (CCSS) were released in June 2010, and states are in the process of adopting the standards. As of May 2011, 44 states had adopted the standards. Texas and Alaska have developed their own standards.[29] Assessments related to the standards are in development.

September 12, 2011

Dear Mr. and Mrs. Novosel,

I am delighted to have Michael in my classroom! Today he completed his reading assignment and shared a story with the class.

I look forward to meeting you at the Open House.

Sincerely,
Ms. Jones

Figure 1.3. Positive note sent to parent.

The mission of the CCSS is the following:

The CCSS provide a consistent, clear understanding of what students are expected to learn, so teachers and parents know what they need to do to help them. The standards are designed to be robust and relevant to the real world, reflecting the knowledge and skills that our young people need for success in college and careers. With American students fully prepared for the future, our communities will be best positioned to compete successfully in the global economy.[30]

The complete CCSS for English/Language Arts are available at http://www.corestandards.org/the-standards/english-language-arts-standards. The Texas College & Career Readiness Standards, adopted in 2008 for the state of Texas, are similar to the CCSS and are available at http://www.thecb.state.tx.us.

Two other sets of standards are referred to throughout the text: the standards developed by the International Reading Association[31] and those developed by The International Dyslexia Association.[32] Upon examination of the standards, you will note agreement as to the most important skills that students must be taught.

Standards in education are intended to clarify the expectations of students and to increase the rigor of instruction. The intent is that all students, no matter what state or zip code they live in, will receive an excellent education, preparing them for further education and/or a career.

Multi-Tiered Systems of Support or Response to Intervention

In 2004, federal legislation reauthorized the Individuals with Disabilities Education Improvement Act enacting federal policies addressing special education. Several significant changes addressed how students with learning disabilities would be assessed, found qualified for services, and provided with instruction. Most importantly for classroom teachers is the requirement that students who are struggling are provided with immediate intervention instruction to address the student's difficulties in the general education classroom. Models designed to provide intervention instruction are commonly referred to as RTI or Multi-Tiered Systems of Support (MTSS). The purpose is to prevent students from failing by addressing their needs immediately with effective, evidence-based instruction. This intervention instruction can take place in any grade and in any location. Intervention instruction must be provided and the student's progress (response to the intervention) documented before the student can be considered for special education services.

Most RTI models include three or four levels of service, called tiers. They include the following (Figure 1.4):

- Tier 1 is the strong core classroom instruction with differentiated instruction as needed (i.e., small group instruction addressing specified skills). It is essential that this instruction, which all students receive, is of the highest quality, is evidence-based, and is highly effective. This text concentrates on core classroom instruction in literacy. If Tier 1 instruction is effective, there is decreased need for the intensive instruction provided in the subsequent tiers.

- Tier 2 is more specialized, intensive instruction with a small group of students who all need to learn the same skill. Usually the general education teacher provides this differentiated instruction in the classroom in small groups of five or six students.

- Tier 3 is an even more intense form of instruction, usually for a longer period of time and in smaller groups. The students who receive Tier 3 instruction need focused, differentiated instruction, smaller groups, more time, and more explicit instruction. Typically, an instructional specialist or a reading specialist provides the intervention instruction. Some districts provide Tier 3 instruction through a special education placement, but other districts include Tier 3 in the general education continuum of services.

- Tier 4 typically refers to instruction provided through special education services, taught by a special education teacher.

Multilevel prevention system

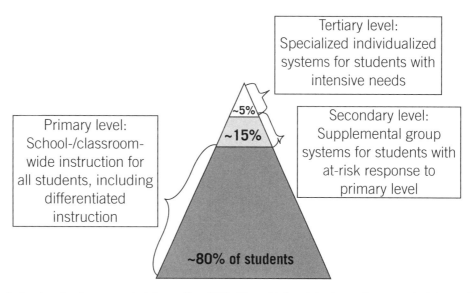

Figure 1.4. Levels of response to intervention (RTI). (From National Center on Response to Intervention [2010]. *What is RTI?* Washington, DC: U.S. Department of Education, Office of Special Education Programs, National Center on Response to Intervention.)

It is important to note that the federal legislation does NOT require a district or state to adopt a RTI model, nor does it dictate how many tiers a district must have, who must provide the instruction, or for how long a student must remain in a tier. At this point, those decisions are left up to the individual local school districts. However, the federal law does require that students receive immediate intervention instruction when it is first noticed that they are not achieving as expected.

Another change in the law was how students are found eligible for special education as having a learning disability. This is a complicated process that is still being discussed and will not be addressed in this text. Suffice it to say that the most important thing for you to remember about the law is that you, as a teacher, must be aware of your students' progress and be sure to provide effective instruction to ensure each student makes adequate progress. (Adequate progress will be defined in later chapters.)

The RTI model is discussed in detail in Chapter 15. More information is available from the National Center on Response to Intervention at http://www.rti4success.org.[33]

CONCLUSION

Whether you are a reading teacher, a general education teacher, a special education teacher, a reading specialist, an interventionist, a math teacher, a science teacher, a history teacher, or an administrator, this book will provide you with the basics of what you need to know to teach students to read well. Study it carefully, complete the suggested exercises, tutor a student, investigate the suggested references and web sites, and you will be able to teach each of your students to read and write.

Again, congratulations on your choice of career, and thank you for what you do to support students to reach high levels of achievement so that they are prepared to be successful in college and careers.

APPLICATION ASSIGNMENTS

In-Class Assignments

1. Review the objectives from Chapter 1. With a partner, take turns paraphrasing each objective, 1–10, and your understanding of the objective. Note those for which you need more information.

2. Explain the following to a partner: expectations of you as a tutor, how you should dress and act in the school, your responsibilities as a tutor, how you should relate to your student, the teachers, and the parents.

3. With a partner, brainstorm a list of your concerns about tutoring a student. Discuss your concerns with the class and elicit suggestions from your colleagues and instructor.

4. With a partner, discuss some activities you can do with your student the first time you tutor.

Tutoring Assignments

1. Obtain a student with whom to work during the semester. Secure parental permission, arrange with the school about a schedule, and complete the requirements of your instructor and university.

2. Assemble your Tutoring Toolbox.

3. Obtain an initial assessment tool. Your instructor will provide additional information and training about the assessments you are to use with your student.

4. Review the Lesson Plan Template and Example in Appendix B. Draft a plan for your first tutoring session. An effective first session might include a read aloud and an informal discussion of the book.

Homework Assignments

1. Download and read *Put Reading First* (http://lincs.ed.gov/). Be prepared to discuss the five components of reading at the next class.

2. Select and study an initial assessment tool appropriate for your student. Practice administering it.

3. Observe an entire reading period, usually 60–120 minutes, in a local school. Note what was directly taught to students and for how long.

4. Describe how the teacher you observed followed or did not follow the lesson plan template provided. Provide specific examples. Be prepared to submit your observations to your instructor.

5. Describe how the teacher you observed differentiated for students in the class, paying particular attention to students with disabilities, students who are English language learners, and students who are accelerated.

ENDNOTES

1. The U.S. Department of Education, The Elementary and Secondary Education Act. Retrieved from http://www2.ed.gov/policy/elsec/leg/esea02/index.html The Individuals with Disabilities Education Improvement Act. Retrieved from http://idea.ed.gov

2. International Reading Association Standards for Reading Professionals, Revised 2010. Retrieved April 15, 2010 from http://www.reading.org/General/CurrentResearch/Standards/ProfessionalStandards 2010.asp

3. The International Dyslexia Association, Knowledge and Practice Standards for Teachers of Reading. Retrieved April 20, 2011, from http://www.interdys.org/Standards.htm

4. Deb Simmons, Texas A&M University, created these questions to guide her students. Dr. Simmons graciously gave us permission to use these questions to help guide your learning.

5. The Family Educational Rights and Privacy Act (FERPA) (20 U.S.C. § 1232g; 34 CFR Part 99). Retrieved April 23, 2011, from http://www.federalregister.gov/articles/2011/04/08/2011-8205/family-educational-rights-and-privacy

6. Dynamic Measurement Group (2010).

7. Hasbrouck (2011).
8. Diamond & Thorsnes 2008.
9. The features of effective instruction are supported by substantial convergent research. The citations for the supporting research are provided in Chapter 2 as each feature is discussed. The particular wording and format used in this text is adapted from The features of effective instruction. (2007).
10. Hart & Risley (1995).
11. Anita Archer, personal communication.
12. U.S. Department of Education. Retrieved April 23, 2011, from http://idea.ed.gov/
13. A useful website that includes the definitions and other information about IDEA and students with disabilities is http://nichcy.org/disability/categories
14. United States Department of Education Institute of Education Sciences. Retrieved April 25, 2011, from http://nces.ed.gov/fastfacts/display.asp?id=64
15. The National Center for Learning Disabilities. Retrieved April 20, 2011, from http://www.ncld.org.
16. Fletcher, et al. (2007); Corteilla (2011), p. 9.
17. IDEA [34 CFR 300.8(c)(10)]. Retrieved April 23, 2011, from http://idea.ed.gov/
18. The International Dyslexia Association. (2002). Retrieved from http://www.interdys.org, April 30, 2011.
19. Knowledge and Practice Standards for Teachers of Reading, The International Dyslexia Association. (2011). Retrieved from http://www.interdys.org, April 30, 2011.
20. Passel et al. (2010).
21. Geva (2006) and Geva (2000).
22. August & Shanahan (2006).
23. Scarcella (2003).
24. Goldenberg, Rueda, & August (2006).
25. Argüelles, Baker, & Moats (2011).
26. Honig, Diamond, & Gutlohn (2008).
27. Vaughn Gross Center for Reading and Language Arts. (2007). *Features of effective instruction.* Austin: University of Texas System/Texas Education Agency.
28. The Common Core State Standards. Retrieved April 10, 2011, from http://www.corestandards.org/
29. The Texas College & Career Readiness Standards. Retrieved April 10, 2011, from http://www.thecb.state.tx.us/collegereadiness/crs.pdf Content and Performance Standards for Alaska Students, revised 2006. Retrieved April 10, 2011, from http://www.eed.state.ak.us/standards/
30. Retrieved April 8, 2011, from http://www.corestandards.org/the-standards
31. International Reading Association Standards for Reading Professionals, Revised 2010. Retrieved April 15, 2010, from http://www.reading.org/General/CurrentResearch/Standards/Professional Standards2010.asp
32. The International Dyslexia Association, Knowledge and Practice Standards for Teachers of Reading. Retrieved April 20, 2011, from http://www.interdys.org/Standards.htm
33. The National Center on Response to Intervention, http://www.rti4success.org/

REFERENCES

Argüelles, M.E., Baker, S., & Moats, L. (2011). *Teaching English Learners: A supplemental LETRS module for instructional leaders.* Longmont, CO: Cambrium Learning Sopris.

August, D., & Shanahan, T. (Eds.). (2006). *Developing literacy in a second language: Report of the National Literacy Panel.* Mahwah, NJ: Lawrence Erlbaum.

Corteilla, C. (2011). *The state of learning disabilities.* New York, NY: National Center for Learning Disabilities.

Content and Performance Standards for Alaska Students. Available at www.eed.state.ak.us/standards

Diamond, L., & Thorsnes, B.J. (2008). *Assessing reading multiple measures.* Novato, CA: Arena Press.

Dynamic Measurement Group. (2010). *DIBELS Next (7th ed.).* Eugene, OR: Author.

Fletcher, J.M., Lyon, G.R., Fuchs, L.S., & Barnes, M.A. (2007). *Learning disabilities: From identification to intervention.* New York, NY: The Guilford Press.

Geva, E. (2000). Issues in the assessment of reading disabilities in L2 children: Beliefs and research evidence. *Dyslexia, 6,* 13–28.

Geva, E. (2006). Second-language oral proficiency and second-language literacy. In D. August & T. Shanahan (Eds.), *Developing literacy in second-language learners: Report of the National Literacy Panel on language-minority children and youth* (pp. 153–174). Mahwah, NJ: Lawrence Erlbaum.

Goldenberg, C., Rueda, R. S. & August, D. (2006). *Sociocultural influences on the literacy attainment of language-minority children and youth.* In August, D. & Shanahan, T. Developing literacy in second-language learners. Mahwah, NJ: Lawrence Erlbaum Associates, Publishers.

Hart, B., & Risley, T. (1995). *Meaningful differences in the everyday experiences of young American children.* Baltimore: Paul H. Brookes Publishing Co.

Hasbrouck, J. (2011). The Quick Phonics Screener 2. St. Paul, MN: Read Naturally.

Honig, B., Diamond, L., & Gutlohn, L. (2008). *Teaching reading sourcebook.* Novato, CA: Arena Press.

International Reading Association. (2010). International Reading Association Standards for Reading Professionals, Revised 2010. Retrieved August 31, 2011 from www.reading.org/General/CurrentResearch/Standards/ProfessionalStandards2010.asp

Passel, J.S., Cohn, D., & Lopez, M.H. (2011). *Hispanics account for more than half of nation's growth in past decade.* Pew Hispanic Center. Retrieved April 20, 2011 from http://pewhispanic.org/reports/report.php?ReportID=140

Scarcella, R. (2003). *Accelerating academic English: A focus on the English learner.* Oakland, CA: Regents of the University of California.

The Common Core State Standards Initiative. (2010). Retrieved August 31, 2011 from http://www.corestandards.org

The International Dyslexia Association. (2010). *Knowledge and practice standards for teachers of reading.* Baltimore: International Dyslexia Association. Available from www.interdys.org/Standards.htm

Texas Higher Education Coordinating Board. (2008). The Texas College & Career Readiness Standards. Retrieved August 31, 2011 from http://www.thecb.state.tx.us/collegereadiness/crs.pdf

Vaughn Gross Center at the University of Texas. (2007). *Best practices in reading instruction for English language learners: Modules 1 & 2.* Austin, TX: Author.

Vaughn Gross Center for Reading and Language Arts. (2007). *Features of effective instruction.* Austin: University of Texas System/Texas Education Agency.

2

The Critical Components of Effective Reading Instruction

by Martha C. Hougen

"Oh no, not more to do," the first-year teacher groaned as she was told she had to test all her students, again. "I don't have time for one more thing. I am going to have to teach less, I guess, and test more."

It is true that teachers are asked to do more—more testing, more counseling, more parent conferences, more supervision, and on and on. Your day can be filled with activities other than teaching. Because of these high demands, it is important that you are cognizant of the most important things to teach so that you make efficient use of the time available.

This chapter will help you make instructional decisions by providing an overview of what research has determined are the most critical components of reading you must teach young students. Without these skills, students are unlikely to learn to read well. The components will be defined and briefly discussed; subsequent chapters in the book delve into more detail about how to teach and assess each component.

The chapter concludes with a discussion of the features of effective instruction, or how to teach the critical components. Examples are provided, illustrating the integration of the critical components of reading and the features of effective instruction.

Objectives: After studying this chapter, you will be able to do the following:

1. Define and describe the critical components of reading instruction.
2. Define and describe the features of effective instruction.
3. Explain the research base for the components of reading instruction.
4. Explain what is meant by scaffolding instruction and provide three examples.
5. Explain the model of teaching: I do, you do, we do, and provide an example.
6. Explain the differences among phonological awareness, phonemic awareness, and phonics.
7. Discuss the relevant Common Core State Standards (or the Texas College & Career Readiness Standards).
8. Explain the Reading Rope figure.
9. Explain the background and major findings of the National Reading Panel Report.
10. Share your plans for your first tutoring session.

WHAT THE RESEARCH SAYS

Over the years, several seminal reports have been published and all reached similar conclusions. Marilyn Adams wrote *Beginning to Read: Thinking and Learning about Print* in 1994.[1] She stated that young students needed to be taught to read in a systematic way that included the critical components of reading instruction. In 1995, Jeanne Chall wrote *Learning to Read: the Great Debate* emphasizing the importance of instruction in phonics.[2] In 1998, Catherine Snow and colleagues, supported by the National Research Council, wrote *Preventing Reading Difficulties in Young Children*.[3] Shortly after, the federal government commissioned a panel to study relevant research in reading and to provide recommendations. This resulted in the Report of the National Reading Panel Report, published in 2000.[4] Since then, others have continued researching how children learn to read, and their conclusions have supported the recommendations of the National Reading Panel.[5] The Panel concluded that there are five essential components that students must master to be able to read efficiently. These five components are phonemic awareness, phonics, fluency, vocabulary, and comprehension.

It is important to note that the Panel did not review the research nor provide recommendations on several topics crucial to literacy development, including early childhood education (birth to age 5), oral language and listening skill development, English language learners, writing instruction, and how to motivate students to read. However, these topics are addressed in this text, and supporting research is provided for the recommendations cited.[6]

Throughout the text, these components will be revisited, deepening your understanding about how to assess student progress and how to design instruction so that all students become capable readers.

THE CRITICAL COMPONENTS OF READING INSTRUCTION

Developing oral language and listening skills are important precursors to learning to read. In Chapter 3, you will learn how to support the development of these skills in young children in preschool (Pre-K) and kindergarten. Of course, students in all grades need to be encouraged to continuously develop their oral language and listening skills. However, it is essential that very young children develop a sound foundation so that they have the linguistic basis to learn to read.

I. Phonemic Awareness

Phonemic awareness is an awareness of the individual sounds in words, the phonemes. Phonemes are the smallest unit of sound. The sounds of phonemes are indicated with slashes, such as /a/ and /t/. The letter name is indicated by the italicized letter, such as *t*. Whole words and parts of words used as examples are italicized. For example, in the word *sit,* there are three phonemes: /s/ /i/ /t/. In the word *ship*, there are also three phonemes: /sh/ /i/ /p/. The word *ball* has three phonemes: /b/ /a/ /l/. The word *fox* has four: /f/ /o/ /k/ /s/ (the letter *x* makes two sounds, /k/ and /s/). Phonemes are not the same as letters, though the sound of a phoneme can be matched to one or more letters. There are 44 phonemes in the English language.

Phonemic awareness is part of a larger umbrella of skills students must learn to master reading. The larger concept is called phonological awareness and includes several skills involving the sounds of our language, culminating in the most difficult skill, phonemic awareness. Most young children intuitively understand phonological awareness skills by age 3 or 4.

Phonological awareness includes the following continuum of skills:

1. **Listening skills** include the ability to differentiate natural sounds from speech sounds (i.e., a door slamming from a bell ringing from a spoken word).
2. **Rhyme and alliteration** are the ability to tell when words rhyme (cake, lake) and which words start with the same sound (busy bees buzz).
3. **Sentence segmentation** is the ability to tell when one word stops and another begins. Students should be able to count the words in a spoken sentence and determine that the

sentence, "The school bus came early," consists of five separate words. If you have learned a foreign language, you know that differentiating individual words in a sentence can be difficult as words tend to run together when spoken.

4. **Syllable blending and segmenting** is the ability to blend and segment syllables into words. A syllable is a word or part of a word made with one opening of your mouth. A syllable makes one vowel sound. Every syllable has a vowel sound. Examples of blending syllables are taking "home" and "work" and forming "homework" or "ta" and "ble" into "table." Segmenting words into syllables means breaking the word apart into syllables, such as "cowboy" into "cow" and "boy," or "reading" into "read" and "ing."

5. **Onset rime blending and segmenting** is the ability to differentiate the beginning consonant of a one-syllable word (the onset) and the vowel and letters that come after the vowel (the rime). The onset in the word *cat* is *c* and the rime is *at*. The rime of a word always contains a vowel.

6. **Phonemic awareness** is the ability to segment, blend, and manipulate phonemes in one-syllable words. Students should be able to hear *cat* and segment it into /k/ /a/ /t/, and to hear /c/ /a/ /t/ and blend the sounds together to say *cat*. Manipulating phonemes is even more difficult and involves such activities as saying *man*, then substituting the /m/ for a /p/, and saying *pan*, changing the /n/ to /t/ and saying *pat*, or changing the medial sound /a/ to /i/ and saying *pit*. Another exercise is removing some sounds, such as taking away /s/ from *slip* and saying the word *lip*. Note that when doing this exercise, you say the sounds of the letters, not the name of the letters (Figures 2.1 and 2.2).

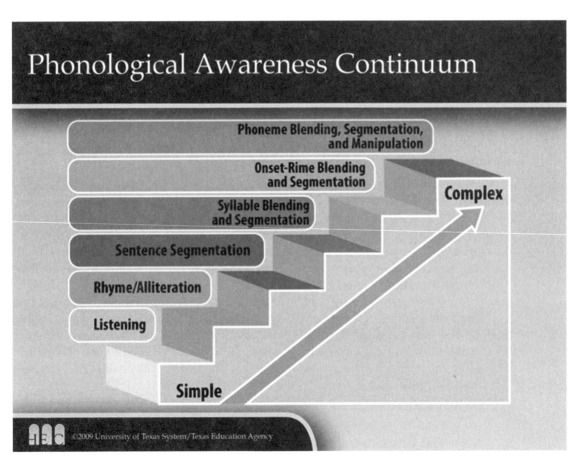

Figure 2.1. Phonological awareness continuum. (From Vaughn Gross Center at The University of Texas at Austin. [2009]. Module 4: Phonological awareness. In *Foundations of reading instruction presentations and print files.* Austin, TX: Vaughn Gross Center [Texas Reading First Higher Education Collaborative]; reprinted by permission.)

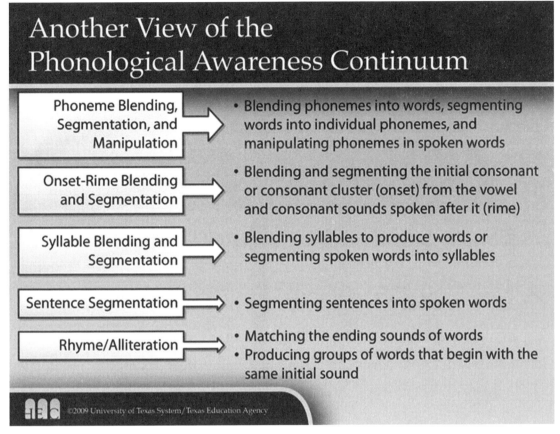

Figure 2.2. Another view of the phonological awareness continuum. (From Vaughn Gross Center at The University of Texas at Austin. [2009]. Module 4: Phonological awareness. In *Foundations of reading instruction presentations and print files.* Austin, TX: Vaughn Gross Center [Texas Reading First Higher Education Collaborative]; reprinted by permission.)

Try this exercise to help you remember the components of phonological awareness. Hold up your hand. Bend it at the wrist. You are making an umbrella with your hand. Each finger represents a stay in that umbrella. The back of your hand is phonological awareness and listening skills, or the all-encompassing concept. Each stay represents one aspect of phonological awareness. Your thumb is the biggest component, rhyming and alliteration. Each finger is another one of the components, with your little finger representing phonemic awareness (Figure 2.3).

Phonemic awareness is essential for learning to read and is one skill that predicts whether a young student will learn to read. The good news is that phonemic awareness can be taught, usually with minimal instruction. Proficiency in phonemic awareness also helps students with spelling as they become aware of the sounds in words.

Phonemic awareness is typically taught with no print; it is a listening skill. Students can close their eyes and practice phonemic awareness skills. Some teachers wear rabbit ears when they teach phonemic awareness to remind students to listen carefully. As students become aware of the sounds, the sounds are quickly mapped to print letters. This will be explained in depth in Chapter 4.

II. Phonics (Decoding, Word Study)

The next essential element of reading is phonics. Phonics is teaching students that the squiggles on a page actually mean something and represent a sound or sounds. Phonics is the relationship between the letters (graphemes) of written language and the sounds (phonemes) of spoken language. Phonics instruction teaches students these letter–sound relationships.

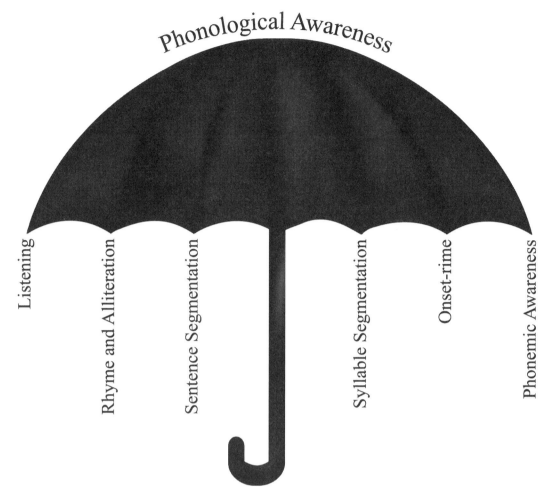

Figure 2.3. Phonological awareness umbrella. (From Vaughn Gross Center at The University of Texas at Austin. [2009]. Module 4: Phonological awareness. In *Foundations of reading instruction presentations and print files.* Austin, TX: Vaughn Gross Center [Texas Reading First Higher Education Collaborative]; adapted by permission.)

Phonics is sometimes referred to as decoding words (reading the words), but phonics is actually more than that. When taught well, phonics teaches students the relationship of letters, sounds, patterns of letters, even the origin of words. In Chapter 5, you will learn how best to teach phonics, suggestions about which letters to teach when, and how spelling supports phonics and vice versa.

III. Fluency

Fluency means being able to read text effortlessly so that you can concentrate on the meaning. It means reading accurately and quickly, but it also entails using appropriate phrasing, reading with expression, and attending to punctuation (called prosody). It does *not* mean reading as quickly as you can, ignoring prosody and reading without comprehension. Fluent reading is highly related to early reading comprehension. In Chapter 8, you will learn how to assess and support your students' ability to read with fluency.

IV. Vocabulary

Vocabulary refers to the words that one must know to communicate effectively by listening, speaking, reading, and writing. Often, students learn to decode well and to read fluently, but they do not understand what they are reading. The problem may be because they do not understand what the words mean. English language learners must learn the complex English vocabulary. All students must focus on increasing their vocabulary.

In Chapter 10, you will learn how to select words to directly teach students, specific strategies to ensure in-depth learning of selected words, and how to create a language-rich environment that motivates students to learn new words.

V. Comprehension

The goal of reading is comprehension, making meaning of the text. Teachers often confuse *assessing* comprehension (asking questions after a reading) and *teaching* comprehension skills. In Chapter 11, you will learn how to teach comprehension skills to young students, in grades K–2, and in Chapter 12, comprehension strategies appropriate for grades 3–6 will be presented.

THE COMPONENTS OF READING ARE INTERWOVEN

Though the critical components of reading are separated in this text to teach you the elements of each component, in the classroom they are interwoven. You may emphasize selected components in certain lessons, but to read well, the components work together. Hollis Scarborough (2001) compared the components of reading to the strands of a rope. Individually, the strands are weak, but when woven tightly together, the strands become a strong rope. Figure 2.4 below displays the separate components of reading and illustrates how they need to be woven together.[7] The concept of the reading rope will be referred to throughout the text.

The Many Strands that Are Woven into Skilled Reading
(Scarborough, 2001)

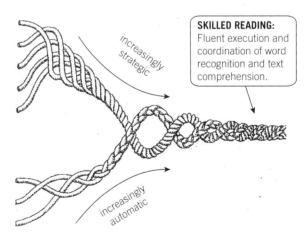

LANGUAGE COMPREHENSION

BACKGROUND KNOWLEDGE
(facts, concepts, etc.)

VOCABULARY
(breadth, precision, links, etc.)

LANGUAGE STRUCTURES
(syntax, semantics, etc.)

VERBAL REASONING
(inference, metaphor, etc.)

LITERACY KNOWLEDGE
(print concepts, genres, etc.)

WORD RECOGNITION

PHONOLOGICAL AWARENESS
(syllables, phonemes, etc.)

DECODING (alphabetic principle, spelling-sound correspondences)

SIGHT RECOGNITION
(of familiar words)

increasingly strategic

SKILLED READING:
Fluent execution and coordination of word recognition and text comprehension.

increasingly automatic

Figure 2.4. Scarborough rope. (Republished by permission of Guilford Press, from Scarborough, H. [2001]. Connecting early language and literacy to later reading disabilities: Evidence, theory, and practice. In S.B. Neiman & D.K. Dickinson [Eds.], *Handbook of early literacy research* [pp. 97–110]; permission conveyed through Copyright Clearance Center, Inc.)

FEATURES OF EFFECTIVE INSTRUCTION

When you are teaching, you will often wonder why students did not learn a concept because you know you taught it to them. "Why didn't they do better on the test? I taught them that!" are comments often heard in faculty lounges. Obviously, you thought you taught the students the concepts, but the teaching did not "stick"—the students did not learn the concept well enough to remember it and generalize it to other contexts, such as tests. The following five features of effective instruction provide a guide to improve your teaching. If you include these features in every lesson you teach, your students will retain more. These features will be referred to throughout this text.[8]

I. Explicit Instruction with Modeling

When teaching, instructors must be clear about what they are sharing with their students so that the students understand exactly what the instructors are saying and what they expect of the students. Think about a time when you were learning something new. Were you ever confused? Have you ever given up on a new task out of frustration?

When instructors teach in a confusing way, students often give up in frustration. It is not their fault that they do not "get it"—it is the instructor's responsibility, as the teacher, to present the material in a way students can understand.

Explicit instruction involves modeling exactly what is required of your students. They are shown how to do it, whether it is differentiating sounds or decoding words. Each step is modeled, checking frequently to determine if the students understand what is being modeled.

Concepts are explained in ways that are concrete and visible; this has been referred to as "making the invisible, visible." Many examples and consistent directions and wording are necessary.

This part of instruction is sometimes referred to as "I do it"—meaning you, the teacher, are doing the task you expect students to do. During this part of the instruction, teachers use clear language, visual aids, and concrete objects that help make the point. Students are actively engaged. Note examples of explicit instruction with modeling throughout this text.

II. Systematic Instruction with Scaffolding

This feature of effective instruction refers to the organization of the instruction, the sequence in which you present the new content. The goal is to clarify the instruction and to provide the necessary prerequisite skills so that the students can learn the new information. To do this, teachers are thoughtful in their planning and move from easier, more concrete skills to more difficult, more abstract skills. Each task is broken down into a series of little tasks, called task analysis. Think about brushing your teeth! There are 25 small skills to learn that lead up to finally being able to brush your teeth![9]

When reading is taught, it is required to first teach letter names and sounds, then small decodable words, and finally multisyllabic words. Students are not expected to pick up a book and start reading as soon as they turn 5 years old! While some students do seem to learn to read "on their own," the majority of students need excellent instruction from a knowledgeable teacher to learn to read.

Scaffolding is an important concept in teaching. Think of a scaffold that surrounds a building being painted. It is a series of wooden platforms that are removed once the painting is done. Those platforms provide temporary support for the painters to stand on while they paint the building.

An instructional scaffold is temporary support to help a student until the student can complete the task independently. You, the teacher, provide enough instructional support to permit the student to make progress toward the academic goal, but only when the student needs the support. Once the student can perform independently, the scaffold is removed.

Examples of instructional scaffolds that you will note in this text are additional modeling, providing more examples, breaking the task down into smaller parts, providing part of the answer, reinforcing an easier skill, using physical movements to reinforce a skill, providing additional practice, and providing instruction in a small group or one-on-one. There are many other ways to scaffold instruction.

This part of the lesson is often referred to as "we do" as you, the teacher, are modeling the skill and the students are following your model, working with you.

III. Frequent Opportunities for Practice

To truly learn something well enough to use the information, students need to practice the new skill. This part of the lesson is often referred to as "you do," or the time students practice the skill independently. Some students need more practice than others. Providing sufficient opportunities for practice that students require is a challenging task for the teacher.

Throughout this text, you will note numerous examples of how to provide additional practice for students. You will *not* see the use of rote worksheets. Rather, students will engage in active, engaging, and meaningful activities to practice their new skills.

Two ways to increase opportunities for practice are to maximize student participation and to increase the number of student responses.

Maximize Student Participation

When a teacher maximizes student participation, there are more opportunities for the student to practice the new skill. Incidentally, when students are participating, there are fewer behavior problems. When students participate and are reinforced for participating, they tend to continue to participate, especially when you have scaffolded the instruction so that the students are confident they will succeed.

Envision a typical classroom. The teacher asks a question and hands go up. One student answers the question. What are the other students doing? They typically tune out the answer, are disappointed they were not called on, or are relieved that they were not called on because they had no idea of the answer. The teacher does not know which students know the information. Contrast that scene with this scenario. All students have a wipe-off white board. The teacher poses a question: "Write the beginning sound of the word moon. Mmmmoon." All students write the letter *m* on their white board and hold it up. The teacher can glance around the room and immediately see who knew the answer and who needs more help.

Another technique is to have the students use a pinch paper. A piece of paper is folded in two. The students write the numbers 1 and 2 on the paper. The teacher reviews vocabulary words, asking the students to pinch the 1 if the word is used correctly in the first sentence and to pinch the 2 if the word is used correctly in the second sentence. For example, the word is hubris, and the sentences are

1. Mother Theresa exhibited much hubris when she worked with the poor.
2. Politicians have a lot of hubris when they say they can save the world.

The students pick #2, the correct use of the word hubris (hubris refers to overly excessive pride, arrogance, something Mother Theresa did not exhibit but some politicians may). Again, all students are involved and responding.

Increase the Number of Student Responses

There are many ways to increase student responses. One thought to keep in mind is the 3:1 rule: For every three statements a teacher makes, the students respond at least once.[10] For example, the teacher says, "Today we are going to learn about the letter *m*. What letter?" Students: "M!" Teacher: "Yes, *m*. The letter *m* makes the sound /m/. What sound?" Students: "/m/." Teacher, "Yes, /m/. If I say some words that start with /m/, you say /m/. If the word does not start with /m/, shake your head no. First word: moon." Students: "/m/." Next word: tree. Students shake their heads no. The lesson continues. This example is for young students learning their letter sounds. The same principle can be applied to all instruction. As you read this text, look for ways to increase student participation. You will find many examples!

IV. Immediate Corrective Feedback

Providing feedback to students is essential for efficient and accurate learning. You do not want students guessing or practicing incorrect responses. It does not hurt students' feelings or inhibit their learning when they are corrected objectively and kindly. It is worse for the students to be allowed to continue making mistakes and then be embarrassed by those mistakes. Imagine the frustration of a sixth-grade student still writing *wen* for *when* or *sed* for *said* merely because a teacher, probably with good intentions, did not want to "inhibit his or her writing" by correcting his or her spelling mistakes. However, it is important to know when and how to provide corrective feedback and when you can expect students to know certain skills.

Teachers need to inform students if they are correct or not and explain why. This can be done indirectly, such as providing a minilesson to several students on how to spell irregular words, such as *was* and *said*. The targeted student may be provided more opportunities to practice.

Another way is to have the entire class repeat the correct answer. In the example used earlier, when students were asked to identify the beginning sound of *moon*, pretend a couple of students said /n/ instead of /m/. The teacher can state the correct answer very explicitly, demonstrating to all students how her lips form to say /m/. All students repeat the sound. The teacher calls on a few students to say the sound aloud while the others whisper the sound. The targeted students receive extra practice.

It is important to correct errors before the student repeats the errors, making learning the correct responses even more difficult for students.

In addition to correcting students' mistakes, accurate performance must be acknowledged and praised. The more specific the feedback, the more likely the student will continue with that practice. For example, when a student has learned the sounds for /ĭ/ and /ĕ/, the teacher may say, "You know how to read words with the vowel sounds /ĭ/ as in *bit* and /ĕ/ as in *met*. Knowing the most common sounds for *e* and *i* will enable you to read more and more words. Good job!"

V. Ongoing Progress Monitoring

Teachers must be aware of where their students are in the learning process. It is easy to assume students are learning what you present, and sometimes students can fool us! For example, some students memorize a story after hearing it read aloud just once and can "read" it verbatim while not actually decoding any of the words.

It is crucial that teachers determine when a student is struggling to learn a new skill so that the student can receive additional, more targeted instruction immediately. It is important not to wait until the student fails before intervention instruction is provided. Therefore, teachers must check their students' understanding often.

The best way to do this is by administering quick, short assessments, frequently. When students are struggling, their progress should be assessed every week or two. Typically, these assessments take about 1 minute. You can use standardized, published assessments such as those provided by DIBELS,[11] AIMSweb,[12] TPRI, or Tejas LEE.[13] You can also create informal assessments based upon what you are teaching (curriculum-based assessments). For example, you can present a short list of words in a certain pattern and ask the student to read the words. Let us pretend that you noticed a student confuses short /ĭ/ and /ĕ/. You reteach both sounds (separate the teaching of the different sounds by 2–3 weeks), then you assess whether or not the student can correctly read words with /ĭ/ and /ĕ/. On a note card, you write *met, mit, bet, bif* (the words do not have to be real words because you are assessing whether or not the student understands the patterns). If the student does well, check again in a couple of days. If the student continues to demonstrate mastery of the targeted sounds, you do not have to do the progress monitoring again, though you continue to observe the student to ensure he or she does indeed know those sounds in various contexts.

One of the easiest, most effective, and most reliable ways to assess progress in reading instruction is to conduct a fluency assessment. Typically, during the second semester of first grade, you can start assessing students by asking them to read a first grade passage for 1 minute. Compute how many words per minute the student reads correctly. By the end of first grade, students should be reading 50 to 60 words correctly per minute. First grade students gain about two or three words per week, so you can compute how many words your targeted students should be reading each week to read 60 words per minute by the end of first grade. This process will be explained in detail in Chapter 7 on fluency instruction.

Each chapter in this text presents methods to assess the progress of your students in each of the essential components of literacy instruction. You will be expected to administer progress monitoring assessments while tutoring your student. You will learn how to set goals, chart progress, and work with your student to ensure the goals are met. You will be surprised by how assessing and charting student progress helps you plan your instruction while motivating students to work hard to reach their goals.

Let us look at how the critical components of reading instruction and features of effective instruction can be integrated. Table 2.1 gives brief examples of each critical component and how it can be taught, applying the features of effective instruction. More examples are provided throughout the text.

Tutoring Component

By now, working with an instructor, you have selected a student with whom to work this semester. You have gathered the required materials for your tutoring toolbox.

At your first meeting with your student, it is important to establish rapport. Explain that you are learning to teach and appreciate that he or she is willing to help you learn to be a good teacher. Ask about the student's interests, what he or she enjoys reading, and what he or she enjoys doing when not in school.

From a selection of fiction and expository books you bring to the tutoring session or that the student's teacher recommends, ask the student to select one for you to read aloud. You proceed to read the book (or part of it) with prosody. Quickly explain vocabulary words the student may not know. At this point, you are modeling how to enjoy the book while getting to know the student.

Ask the student to select a book to read to you. Provide assistance as necessary. If the student is reluctant to read or clearly struggles, do not insist that the student continue. Rather, you can finish that part of the text.

If your instructor has taught you how to administer a basic reading assessment, you may administer it with your student. One research-based assessment that is available to download at no cost is the DIBELS (Dynamic Indicators of Basic Early Literacy Skills) in English and the IDEL (Indicadores Dinámicos del Éxito en la Lectura) in Spanish, grades K–6. Be sure to study the administration guide and watch the videos provided online. The DIBELS is available at https://dibels.uoregon.edu/. Another assessment available at no cost is the San Diego Quick Assessment found at http://www.homeschooling.gomilpitas.com/articles/060899.htm.

Table 2.1. Features of effective instruction and the critical components of reading instruction: A powerful combination

	Phonemic awareness	Phonics	Fluency
Systematic instruction with scaffolding	Listen: The word is *cat*. The first sound is /c/. What sound?	The sound /c/ is written like this (write letter). The letter name is *c*. The sound is /c/.	This is a period. It is like a stop sign. When you see a period, you stop reading as it is the end of the sentence. Let us find all the periods on this page and mark them with the highlighter.
Explicit instruction with modeling	Let us substitute the first sound with another sound. My turn. The word is *cat*. Take away /c/ and put /s/ at the beginning. The new word is *sat*. Your turn.	I am going to read this word as I know all the sounds. /c/ /a/ /t/. Cat. Let us read it together.	Listen while I read this story two ways. Tell me which one you like better? (Read dysfluently and then fluently, using expression. Discuss why one was more interesting.)
Opportunities for practice: active engagement	Let us sing "My Bonnie." When you hear /b/, stand up!	Here is a list of words you know. With a partner, practice reading them.	I will read a sentence fluently. Then, you read the same sentence. Go practice with your partner.
Feedback	The sound is /b/. What sound? Say "Bonnie." What sound does Bonnie start with? Yes, /b/. Stand up!	The sound of this letter is /c/. You said the name, *c*. What letter? Yes, *c*. What sound? Yes, /c/. You have got it!	Yes! You read with expression. You paused at the periods. You did not read too fast or too slowly. You read just right!
Progress monitoring	(In small groups of two to three students, assess their ability to identify the initial sounds of words.)	(Given a list of letters taught, have students read the name and provide the sounds.)	(Have students read for 1 minute, aloud. Count the number of words read correctly and graph.)

	Vocabulary	Comprehension
Systematic instruction with scaffolding	The word is *timid*. What word? It means to be shy and tentative. (Look timid.) I am timid when I enter a room where I do not know anyone. A kitten is timid around dogs.	Listen while I read an article. I am going to determine who or what the article is about. (Usually, the who or what is the person or object that is mentioned most often.)
Explicit instruction with modeling	Think of a time when you felt timid. I was timid the first day I taught. Complete this sentence: I was timid…. (Elicit examples.)	When I read, I ask myself questions to help me understand. Listen while I "think aloud" and share my thoughts with you. (Proceed to model, asking questions such as, "I wonder why the character did that?" "I think I missed something—I am going to reread that paragraph.")
Opportunities for practice—student engagement	I am going to give you examples and nonexamples of timid. When you hear an example of timid, say "timid"! When it is a nonexample, shake your head no. Listen: The new student was timid the first day of school. Yes! Timid! The big dog was timid when he jumped all over me. No, not timid. The dog was not shy or tentative.	With a partner, read this article and think aloud your thoughts as you read. Take turns.
Feedback	Some of you thought the dog was timid. Imagine a dog running up to you and licking your face. Is that dog afraid of you? Is he uncomfortable? No, he is not timid.	Let us share some of your think alouds. (Rephrase the comments if necessary. Note which students were able to apply the strategy and which need more instruction and practice.)
Progress monitoring	(Ask students to use the new vocabulary words while speaking and writing. Create a "Word Wizards" board, and put student names under the word when they use it correctly.)	(In small groups, ask students to think aloud while reading aloud. Note their comments. Give them a short quiz on the content to determine if they comprehend the reading selection.)

Many districts use the Texas Primary Reading Inventory (TPRI), Tejas LEE (Spanish version), or AIMS Web. You will need to ask someone at your student's school to obtain these and to teach you how to use the assessments.[13]

Some districts use assessments they have designed to reflect what their students are being taught. These are called curriculum-based assessments or benchmark assessments. These may be available for you to administer or to analyze if already administered.

The Quick Phonics Screener[14] can be used with students who have begun to learn how to read to determine exactly what skills they need to learn.

You will learn more about how to assess each critical component of reading when you study that component. You will learn how accurate and frequent assessment data are used to help design instruction, making you an efficient and effective teacher while motivating your students to achieve.

APPLICATION ASSIGNMENTS

In-Class Assignments

1. With your classmates, discuss what you noted while observing a reading class. Make a list of the activities observed and the presumed objectives of each. Discuss how the teacher differentiated instruction for students.

2. Form expert groups for each of the five components, and discuss the main ideas of what you read in Chapter 2 and in Put Reading First[15] (i.e., phonemic awareness, phonics, fluency, vocabulary, and comprehension). Then, separate into groups that contain an expert for each component. Share your new learning, and create a list of questions, comments, and concerns to share with the entire class.

3. Reflect upon the lesson format of "I do, we do, you do." Did the teacher you observed follow this format? What did the teacher do for the "I do" component, the "we do" component, and the "you do" component?

Tutoring Assignments

1. Meet with your student to establish rapport and ascertain interests.

2. As suggested in this chapter, read a book to your student, and ask the student to read to you.

3. If you have the permission of the school and you have been trained in its administration, give an early reading assessment (as described earlier in this chapter).

Homework Assignments

1. Explore one of the following web sites, and read about the critical components of reading instruction: Reading Rockets: http://www.readingrockets.org; Florida Center for Reading Research: http://www.fcrr.org; The University of Oregon, Big Ideas in Beginning Reading: http://reading.uoregon.edu/

2. Read Chapter 3 in this text and one additional reading from the resources provided.

ENDNOTES

1. Adams (1994).
2. Chall (1996).
3. Snow, Burns, and Griffin (1998).
4. National Institute of Child Health and Human Development (2000).
5. Brady 2011.
6. Denton and Mathes (2003); Mathes, Denton, Fletcher, Anthony, Francis, and Schatschneider (2005); Burns, Griffin, and Snow (1999).
7. Scarborough (2001).
8. Meadows Center for Preventing Education Risk (2007).

9.   Wehman and Kregal (2004).
10.   The 3:1 rule was shared by Don Deshler, The University of Kansas, in a personal communication.
11.   Information about the DIBELS is available at: https://dibels.uoregon.edu/
12.   Information about AIMSweb is available at http://www.aimsweb.com/

13.   Information about the TPRI Early Reading Assessment is available at http://www.tpri.org/index.html and the Tejas LEE at: http://www.tejaslee.org/
14.   Hasbrouck (2011).
15.   Armbruster, Lehr, & Osborn (2006).

REFERENCES

Adams, M. (1994). *Beginning to read: thinking and learning about reading*. Boston, MA: Massachusetts Institute of Technology.

Armbruster, B.B., Lehr, F., & Osborn, J. (2006). *Put reading first, 3ʳᵈ edition*. Washington, DC: National Institute for Literacy. Available for download from http://www.nichd.nih.gov/publications/pubs/upload/PRFbooklet.pdf

Brady, S.A. (2011). Efficacy of phonics teaching for reading outcomes: Indications from post-NRP research. In Brady, S.A., Braze, D., & Fowler, C.A. Explaining individual differences in reading: Theory and evidence. New York: Psychology Press.

Burns, M.S., Griffin, P., & Snow, C. (1999). *Starting out right: A guide to promote student reading success*. Washington, DC: National Academy Press.

Chall, J. (1996). *Learning to read: The great debate*. Orlando, FL: Harcourt Brace & Company.

Denton, C.A., & Mathes, P.G. (2003). Intervention for struggling readers: Possibilities and challenges. In B.R. Foorman (Ed.), *Preventing and remediating reading difficulties: Bringing science to scale* (pp. 229–251). Timonium, MD: York Press.

Hasbrouck, J. (2011). *The Quick Phonics Screener 2*. St. Paul, MN: Read Naturally.

Mathes, P.G., Denton, C.A., Fletcher, J.M., Anthony, J.L., Francis, D.J., & Schatschneider, C. (2005). The effects of theoretically different instruction and student characteristics on the skills of struggling readers. *Reading Research Quarterly, 40*(2), 148–182.

Meadows Center for Preventing Education Risk. (2007). *Features of effective instruction*. Austin, TX: Texas Education Agency/University of Texas System.

National Institute of Child Health and Human Development. (2000). *Report of the National Reading Panel. Teaching children to read: an evidence-based assessment of the scientific research literature on reading and its implications for reading instruction: Reports of the subgroups* (NIH Publication No. 00-4754). Washington, DC: U.S. Government Printing Office.

Scarborough, H.S. (2001). Connecting early language and literacy to later reading (dis)abilities: Evidence, theory, and practice. In S. Neuman & D. Dickinson (Eds.), *Handbook for research in early literacy* (pp. 97–110). New York: Guilford Press.

Snow, C., Burns, M.S., & Griffin, P. (Eds). (1998). *Preventing reading difficulties in young children*. Washington, DC: National Academy Press.

Wehman, P., & Kregal, J. (2004). *Functional curriculum*, Second Edition. Austin, TX: Pro-Ed, Inc.

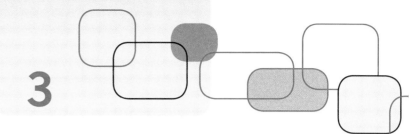

3

Oral Language and Listening Skill Development in Early Childhood

by Christie L. Cavanaugh

"I teach 10 children in a Pre-K class. They're all very different, but I notice major differences in their language. Some seem to pay attention when I give directions or read to them, while others don't seem like they're listening. When I ask questions, a few respond, while others look confused and don't respond at all. Some are talking clearly while others are hard to understand—even the other children don't understand a few. Some children confuse words and mix sounds in words, saying things like 'cyclemotor' instead of 'motorcycle' or 'pasghetti' for 'spaghetti,' while others aren't talking at all. How do I support all my students in developing language?"

If you are reading this chapter, you either have the opportunity to impact a child's life or are interested in learning more about how to do so as an effective teacher, specifically through building oral language. While there is a great deal of knowledge and skill you must possess as an effective teacher, your abilities to enhance a child's oral language development will contribute significantly to children's acquisition of literacy skills and future academic success. What you learn in this chapter will connect to other content in this book and will help solidify the connections among language, vocabulary, and literacy. You will learn to contribute positively to a child's oral language development through the process of providing children opportunities to talk, building upon children's verbal expressions by using language facilitation strategies, and creating an environment that invites children to continue practicing and developing their oral language skills.

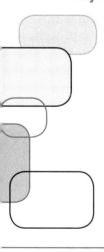

Objectives: After studying this chapter, you will be able to do the following:

1. Define and describe oral language and its components.
2. Articulate the importance of oral language for a young child's development of emergent and early literacy.
3. Identify examples of different types of vocabulary that comprise a young child's repertoire of oral language skills.
4. Name three basic strategies to prompt language or "invite children to talk."
5. Demonstrate the ability to respond to children's responses using research-based language facilitation strategies and rich language models.
6. Implement environmental arrangement strategies to encourage language use.
7. Create a physical environment that reflects your knowledge and abilities to promote oral language.

(continued)

WHAT IS ORAL LANGUAGE?

Oral language is what is used to express ourselves verbally and is the ability to understand language produced by others. It is comprised of the words and how these are combined in phrases and sentences while one is communicating verbally. Oral language is dependent on vocabulary as well as other language components. If you consider that vocabulary is both expressive and receptive and is required in written and oral form for speaking, listening, writing, and reading, then it is easy to see the connections between vocabulary and oral language. Oral language relies on expressive use and receptive understanding of words in oral form for speaking and listening. While oral language does not directly involve reading and writing of the printed form, it contributes to the development of language for reading and writing. If a child knows the meaning of a word in oral form, he or she will understand it in print. For example, a young child learns to use the word "dog" for labeling a dog, first a specific dog and then all dogs. The concept of a dog for which the young child has learned the label is developed enough so that when the child encounters the printed word "dog," he or she is able to link the oral word and the concept of a dog to the written form and, thus, comprehends written language through this linkage.

To understand oral language, it is important to know a bit about all the components of language—of any language. Every language is defined by five components: phonology, morphology, semantics, syntax, and pragmatics. The general forms of language, oral or written, can be described using these five components. Each will be defined and specific examples as they relate to oral language will be provided.

Phonology

Phonology relates to the sounds of a language and the rules that govern how they are combined to form words. Because the focus of this chapter is on oral language specifically, it is important to note that a language cannot be presented in an oral form if phonology is absent. In other words, language requires sounds in order to communicate orally. Phonology has a strong connection to the development of phonological and phonemic awareness skills. Phonological and phonemic awareness are considered essential for early reading success (see Chapter 4). Children need to have the awareness of the sounds of our language and the ability to discriminate and isolate the sounds so they can connect them to print for reading, spelling, and writing. There are about 44 different sounds in our language and only 26 letters to represent all these sounds in various combinations. For example, the sound for /f/ can be represented by these letters or combinations: *f* as in *fan*, *ph* as in *phone* or *graph*, *gh* as in *cough*, *ff* as in *stiff*, *lf* as in *half*. In addition, it is important to know that word meanings can change just by changing one sound (e.g., *receipt and receive* have different sounds at the end of the word and have different meanings, while *mop* and *map* have different middle sounds to differentiate between the two word meanings).

Morphology

Morphology relates to the meanings of individual word parts and how they are combined to create words. Words and word parts are morphemes, or units of meaning. There are two different types of morphemes—free morphemes or bound. Free morphemes are units that have meaning independent of other units (in other words—a stand-alone word). The words *happy, dog, run,* and *home* are all examples of free morphemes. Bound morphemes are units of meaning that are attached to free morphemes and therefore change the meaning and usage of words. The words *unhappy, dogs, running,* and *homeless* all contain both free and bound morphemes and thus have different meanings than the original free morphemes. The most common way to understand bound morphemes is to understand affixes (prefixes and suffixes). Morphology influences the areas of phonics, word study, and, of course, vocabulary.

Semantics

Semantics is knowledge of word meanings for specific words in various contexts and how to select appropriate words to communicate. Understanding that words have multiple meanings and that the meaning changes based on the context, position of the word in a phrase or sentence, or the form is all part of the language component of semantics. Semantics knowledge helps us relate words to each other and categorize and choose the appropriate word to fit the situation (e.g., *happy* vs. *ecstatic, pouting* vs. *bawling, dog* vs. *Golden Retriever puppy*).

Syntax

Syntax relates to the rules that govern word order and how words are combined in phrases and sentences. Another word for syntax is grammar. This component of language influences comprehension of both oral and written language. As young children develop oral language, they learn how words are combined. They often understand words they hear before they can integrate grammatical structures or rules into their spoken language. It is important to know that children learn much about language from listening to it so that we understand how valuable adult language models can be for impacting children's development of syntax. Some more sophisticated forms of syntax, such as complex clauses or embedded phrases, may require frequent modeling and scaffolding for children to comprehend.

Pragmatics

Pragmatics relates to the use of language and the knowledge of the functions of various forms of language—knowing when to use a word or expression for a particular purpose. Young children develop the functions of requesting, protesting, and seeking clarification very early, and they learn how speaking to their teacher and speaking to a sibling may vary.

WHY IS ORAL LANGUAGE IMPORTANT?

Oral language plays a key role in children's development of literacy, but it also impacts other domains such as cognition and social–emotional areas. This brief section will focus on the specific contribution of oral language to written language and comprehension. Oral language develops before written language. However, oral language development and written language development contribute reciprocally to each other and impact the ability to read and write. This reciprocal interaction continues throughout life. In other words, the more knowledge and use of oral language one acquires, the more language one is able to access for writing and reading comprehension. Conversely, the more one reads and engages in writing activities, the more one will be able to understand words in the context of oral language for both listening comprehension and speaking.

The following statements highlight important concepts of oral and written language and their connection to understanding, speaking, reading, and writing:

- Receptive understanding of oral language contributes to listening comprehension.
- Expressive use of oral language contributes to the ability to speak.

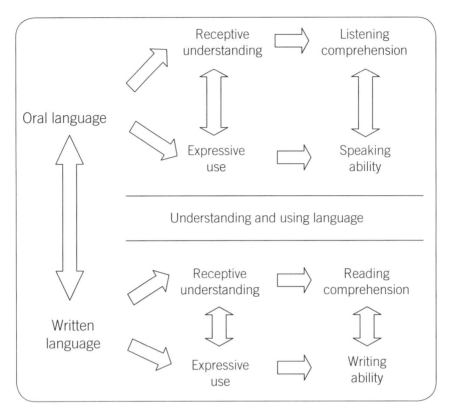

Figure 3.1. The connections between oral and written language.

- Receptive understanding of written language contributes to reading comprehension.
- Expressive use of written language contributes to the ability to write.

Figure 3.1 illustrates the important connections between oral and written language and the contributions to language comprehension and use.

ORAL LANGUAGE DEVELOPMENT IN THE EARLY CHILDHOOD YEARS

Oral language begins to develop in infancy. Young children are introduced to oral language the moment they begin to hear people talking to them. Babies begin to develop their own oral language when they vocalize and babble, making word approximations. Babies eventually begin to develop a single-word vocabulary toward the end of their first year of life. Generally, as soon as a young child has about 50 single words in his or her vocabulary, he or she begins to combine words to form multiword phrases. These phrases grow in length and complexity rapidly, and by the time a child is 3 years old, he or she can truly be considered a conversational partner. Throughout the early childhood period of development, oral language continues to grow rapidly as children encounter new vocabulary, concepts, experiences, and opportunities to use complex language for a variety of purposes. This period of rapid growth represents our golden opportunity to impact a child's oral language abilities in important ways.

A young child's vocabulary consists of nouns, action words, and position words at first (dog, cat, mommy, car, go, eat, up, down, etc.). When children begin to combine words, the early two-word combinations reflect some relationship between the words such as object/action (e.g., car go), person or agent/action (e.g., mommy eat), or object/object (e.g., dog car). The adult who is building oral language (parents and teachers) interprets the child's meanings based on the context and "fills in the blanks" to provide language models (e.g., Yes, the dog is in the car). Once children begin to combine more words, their vocabulary increases to support the development of syntax to be able to use complex language, such as expressing cause and effect, asking questions, embedding clauses to provide more description, or expressing a negative statement (e.g., I can't eat that anymore).[1] Adult language models play a key role in building children's sophisticated language. Thus, your role as a teacher is critical.

RESEARCH-BASED PRACTICES TO PROMOTE ORAL LANGUAGE DEVELOPMENT

In this section, you will learn about two research-based practices that are effective for promoting oral language development in young children: Language facilitation strategies and interactive reading using dialogic reading strategies. These two broad sets of practices are related to each other in that dialogic reading is dependent upon the ability to use language facilitation strategies to elaborate children's language. However, language facilitation strategies should be integrated throughout a child's day in the context of many activities and routines—basically, anytime that language is involved.

LANGUAGE FACILITATION STRATEGIES TO PROMOTE ORAL LANGUAGE DEVELOPMENT

Language facilitation refers to the ways that children are encouraged and invited to use oral language. Language facilitation strategies are specific actions taken to support young children's language development and use of oral language. The following vignette contains language interaction between a pre-K teacher and her young students during center time. Notice that Ms. Takeisha prompted the children to talk and then she responded to them by modeling language and vocabulary that elaborated the children's language. By using specific strategies, it is ensured that children are exposed to rich language models so that they eventually embed them into their oral language.

Vignette: Conversation between Ms. Takeisha and Her Students During Center Play

Ms. Takeisha used several strategies during her interaction with the children (see Box 3.1). Each one and its purpose will be identified. The important point to remember about Ms. Takeisha's interaction is that she was deliberate about her word choices and language use so that she could model and prompt while enjoying the time to play with her children. This interaction illustrates how easy it is to teach during play for the purpose of building oral language.

It is important to use language facilitation strategies for several reasons. Research conducted during the past 40 years has shown that children's language improves when the adults and teachers in a child's life encourage children to talk and respond in a way that provides children more opportunities to hear and use words that add to their current language.[2–5] Improving children's language improves their listening comprehension and, thus, their ability to learn to read and succeed in school.

These key terms are necessary to understand so you may use language facilitation strategies effectively to teach and assess children's oral language development.

Prompt: A verbal action that the adult uses to invite children to respond verbally. A prompt can be considered as an "invitation to talk." There are three main types of verbal prompts: questions, completion prompts, and comments. For example, Ms. Takeisha prompted with a comment and a question in line 2 of the vignette.

Utterance: The amount of language a child produces in one breath or statement. The length of an utterance can range from one word to several words or even a couple of phrases or sentences if they are produced in one connected utterance. The number of words (and morphemes) in children's utterances are counted to monitor their language development.

BOX 3.1. CONVERSATION BETWEEN MS. TAKEISHA AND HER STUDENTS

1. Ms. Takeisha, the lead pre-K teacher, was playing with a small group of children in the cooking show center. Dominique and Cassandra, two 4-year-olds, were pretending to mix some ingredients in a bowl. Here is part of the conversation that occurred during this play scene.

2. **Ms. T:** Oh, I can see that you're creating something that's going to be delicious! Tell me the ingredients. What did you put in your bowl?

3. **D:** Well, first we put-ed in five spoons of that white powder and we mixed in this.

4. **Ms. T:** You are quite the chefs! This looks so scrumptious that I want to write down the recipe. Then I'll have directions for making it myself. Do you mind?

5. **C:** That's okay.

6. **Ms. T:** Okay. First, you put in five spoonfuls of flour. That's this powdery white ingredient that many chefs, or cooks, use for baking.

7. **C:** Don't forget that we used some of that shaker stuff and eggs and chocolate cookies and . . .

8. **Ms. T:** Then you added a stick of butter. Next you added salt from the shaker, two or three shakes?

9. **C:** I think five shakes!

10. **Ms. T:** It will be a salty treat! You also blended in some eggs and crumbled chocolate cookies—yum! This will be a salty AND sweet treat. I can't wait to sample your creation.

11. **D:** It will be ready soon.

12. **Ms. T:** Terrific! Now I have the ingredients, but tell me the next steps?

13. **D:** Well, you just mix it and then put it in the stove.

14. **Ms. T:** Will I place it on the stove to cook or in the oven to bake?

15. **C:** In the oven 'cause it is like a cake. You have to keep it in there for a long time.

16. **Ms. T:** I guess we should set the timer so it won't overcook.

17. **D:** We need to put it in a pot.

18. **Ms. T:** That's an important step—we need to pour the batter in a cake pan and then place it in the oven to bake. I think we'll be able to smell the flavors as they bake and that will make our mouths water and want to devour it—eat it quickly.

19. **C:** It's good!

20. **Ms. T:** Oh, it's going to be more than good! It will be scrumptious. That means really, super yummy to eat. Let me hear you say "scrumptious."

21. **C and D:** Scrumptious!

22. **Ms. T:** Now, while it's baking, tell our friends that you baked a scrumptious treat to share!

23. **C and D:** We made a scrumptious treat!

24. **Ms. T:** You made a scrumptious treat to share with everyone!

For example, in line 11, D's utterance length was five words (It will be ready soon). As you recall, morphemes are the smallest unit of meaning, and words contain either free or bound morphemes. Free morphemes are words that stand alone and have meaning without being combined with other morphemes (e.g., cat, walk, in, happy). Bound morphemes, also units of meaning, are combined with free morphemes to change meaning. For example, "plural s" is added to indicate more than one (e.g., cat). The past tense marker, -ed, is also a bound morpheme (e.g., walked). Words that contain a free and bound morpheme count as two or more morphemes (e.g., walked, cats, happiness). In line 3, D used the word "mixed," which is two morphemes, and his use of this word indicates correct usage. In the same line, he also added -ed to the word "put" to indicate past tense. Because he combined the bound morpheme (-ed) incorrectly with a free morpheme (put), this is incorrect usage. These early combinations are important for understanding children's language development and for providing opportunities for us to model correct forms.

In addition to counting the numbers of words, we also notice the types of words and how children combine them to convey their thoughts. For example, in line 15, C's utterance includes a connecting word (because) to show a comparison. She also demonstrates appropriate use of several examples of position words or prepositions.

Elaboration: An adult's verbal response to a child that builds upon what the child said by increasing the number of words *and* inserting vocabulary to build a child's oral vocabulary knowledge. For example, Ms. Takeisha elaborated D's utterance in line 6 by increasing the number of words and using different vocabulary words to provide a rich language model.

Dialogic reading, as you will learn in the next section, incorporates the strategy of elaboration as a form of expansion for building and scaffolding children's language and vocabulary development.

Expansion: An adult's verbal response to a child that builds upon what the child said by increasing the number of words. The goal of using expansions is to increase the amount of language a child is using or "expanding" their utterances. For example, Ms. Takeisha expanded the last statement by adding a few more words, "to share with everyone" (line 24). The complete statement is not only an expansion, but it offers another opportunity for the children to hear the word "scrumptious" used again. Dialogic reading incorporates expansion as a purposeful strategy for building and scaffolding children's language and vocabulary development.

Model: The use of a model is a purposeful way for adults to provide an example of a word, phrase, or sentence with the expectation that the children will to attempt to imitate it. Models are extremely important for much of what is done with young children and are a powerful way that children acquire and develop language. For very young children, the model may be single words or two-word phrases and may include a prompt, such as "Say 'milk'" or "Say 'more please.'" The prompt that follows a model should be explicit so children know that they're expected to repeat the model. Lines 20 and 21 illustrate the powerful use of models. Ms. Takeisha first modeled a new vocabulary word and embedded the meaning in her statement. She followed this with a prompt for the children to say the word, "scrumptious." This step is particularly important when modeling words that children are not accustomed to saying or words that may be difficult to say because they have several syllables or chunks or different combinations of letter sounds. In dialogic reading, the adult provides models frequently when responding to children's responses and conversing about the book.

Narrative: A narrative is basically a retelling or describing of an activity that children are doing. The adult narrates what a child is doing with a specific purpose—to model the words that help a child acquire the language to talk about what he or she is doing, hearing, or seeing. Many of the other language facilitation strategies are embedded within a narrative, especially modeling vocabulary. Lines 6, 8, and 10 all contain examples of narratives. Narratives are important for scaffolding children's abilities to participate in the storytelling as part of dialogic reading. Sometimes, these can be considered as "think alouds" when narrating what is being done to provide children with the language models. "Think alouds" allow us to talk without expecting a response.

Here are a couple more examples to illustrate a few of these strategies:

Child (points to flowers): Flowers are pretty.

Teacher (following child's lead: Yes, those flowers are colorful and gorgeous. Elaboration and extension, instead of "Yes, the flowers *are* pretty" [repetition and slight extension]).

Child (chooses the bakery center for play): I want to cook something.

Teacher (again, following child's lead after arranging an inviting center): Great! Let's create something delicious together. Do you have a special recipe in this cookbook to guide us [elaboration, embedded vocabulary with support]? Tell me how we will make it [open-ended prompt, instead of "I want to cook with you."].

The teacher continues to converse, narrate, and model vocabulary and syntax during play and also uses opportunities for the child to say key vocabulary words using mands, or prompts, and models (to emphasize the important connection between phonology and semantics). For example, the teacher might prompt by saying, "These chocolate-flavored biscuits you created are scrumptious! Scrumptious is another word for delicious. Say 'scrumptious.'" (model). The teacher might scaffold by allowing the young child to first say the word in two parts by syllable and then model putting it together. Later, the teacher might prompt by saying, "This cake is not only delicious, it's _____" (mand or prompt), waiting for the child to insert the new vocabulary word.

Language Facilitation Practice

Read the following examples of prompts and children's responses followed by the adult's responses (Table 3.1). Using what you just learned about language facilitation, determine if the adult response is strong or weak for building children's oral language. For any responses you identified as weak, create an improved oral language-building response. Try to identify the specific language facilitation strategy used for the strong examples and the ones you embedded into the improved responses.

Now, for those adult responses that you determined to be weak, put your new knowledge to work! In Table 3.2, write an improved adult response that would qualify as a strong language model and would likely have a positive impact on a child's oral language development. Try to identify the type of language facilitation strategies you incorporated in the improved response.

Table 3.1.   Language facilitation practice

Prompt	Child	Teacher	+ or - ?
Who do you think they're going to find at the zoo?	Animals	That's right—animals!	
What do you think he's going to do?	Fly home.	He might fly away to return home to his family.	
Why is she laughing?	It's funny.	Oh, she's laughing because she thinks he's amusing.	
They didn't know what happened, so they _____.	Called someone.	They called for help because they didn't know what happened to the injured dog.	
I wonder when he might be able to go back to school.	When he's better.	That's right, when he's better.	
How can he reach it?	Jumping up.	Yes, he can jump or leap or stretch. He might be able to use a ladder if there's someone to assist him.	

Table 3.2. Language facilitation improvements

Previous adult response	Improved adult response	Type(s) of language facilitation strategies applied
Example: While reading aloud, a teacher pauses, and asks, "What is he doing?" (The illustration depicts a boy walking down the street). One of the children responds, "He's walking." The teacher responds, "Yes, he's walking."	*"Do you think he's walking or strutting?" (The teacher demonstrates the action 'strutting.') When the children respond, "Strutting," the teacher then says, "Yes, he's strutting confidently. Strutting is a better word for what he's doing because he looks like he's proud and confident."*	**Model (within a scaffold):** The teacher provided an alternative word choice along with a demonstration so that children could hear and understand the meaning of a different word to describe the boy's action. **Expansion:** The teacher expanded the children's response by adding more words in the context of a sentence. **Elaboration:** The teacher provides support for the meaning of the word *'strutting'* based on the story and illustration.
Another Example (from Table 3.1): In response to the child's response, "*animals,*" the adult said, "*That's right—Animals!*" (This is considered a **weak** response because it represents a mere repetition of what the child said and does not provide an elaborated language model).	*"Yes, they'll find a variety of, or different, animals and they might even see the zookeeper who tends, or takes care of, the animals."*	**Expansion:** The adult added more words to expand the child's response to include more words in the context of a compound sentence. **Elaboration:** The adult inserted the word "variety" to indicate that they'll find different animals. The word "tends" was also inserted and paired with the meaning.

Interactive and Dialogic Reading

Reading to young children presents multiple opportunities to build language. Books provide language that is decontextualized, or does not rely on the immediate or present context to understand meaning.[6] Understanding decontextualized language contributes to listening comprehension because young children begin to understand language that is beyond the "here and now." Preschoolers experience a rapid period of growth in their ability to interpret meaning of decontextualized language, and shared reading experiences contribute greatly to this development. Books provide background knowledge and context that support children's ability to use and comprehend decontextualized language through use of word meanings (semantics) and grammatical structures (syntax) that may be beyond a child's current repertoire or understanding and, thus, help build these areas. While there are many ways to enjoy reading to young children, the intentional use of scientifically validated interactive and dialogic reading approaches significantly impact the development of oral language.

Interactive reading is a general approach that focuses on engaging children in book reading through commenting and asking questions.

Dialogic reading is a specific type of interactive reading that relies on a systematic and explicit set of strategies. There are two acronyms associated with dialogic reading, and both of these help teachers plan for using dialogic reading purposefully to build children's oral language. The acronym PEER (Prompt, Evaluate, Expand, Repeat) is used to create a conversation with children and to help them take an active role in storytelling. The acronym, PEER, serves as a reminder for teachers to use the strategies and prompts systematically. These also require specific action on the teacher's part. **P** represents *prompt,* and the acronym CROWD relates to the types of prompts (described later). The teacher prompts children to engage them in dialogic reading. **E** serves as a reminder for the teacher to *evaluate* the child's response and then immediately *expand* (also **E**) the child's response to provide a more elaborate model. This is what is most beneficial for using dialogic reading for oral language development. Teachers are expected to evaluate the child's response in order to acknowledge the child's response and language use, but also to scaffold, or support, higher-level language development. The final letter of the PEER acronym is **R** for *repeat,* and this action serves as a reminder for the teacher

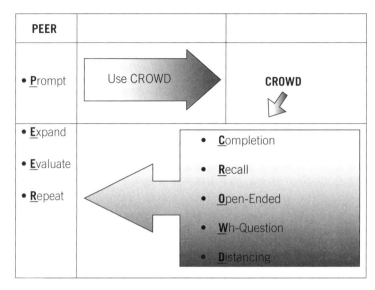

Figure 3.2. Dialogic reading strategies.

to encourage the child to repeat the expanded or elaborated response. This important step provides the child with additional opportunity to practice the new language model (an important feature of effective instruction). Dialogic reading is conversational, intentional, and effective for assessing and building oral language and vocabulary in young children.[7]

With dialogic reading, there are five specific prompts, which are typically posed in the form of a question. The prompts have a specific purpose—to prompt children to respond. Whereas a comment is an implicit "invitation to talk," question prompts, however, are explicit in that the adult who poses them waits for and provides scaffolds so that children respond. Figure 3.2 illustrates the connection between the PEER and CROWD strategies, illustrating the specific prompts, which are defined with examples.

Dialogic Reading Prompts (CROWD):[8–10]

- *C* stands for *completion prompts*. The reader (teacher) makes a statement and purposefully pauses (similar to a time-delay prompt) so that the children can provide the missing word or words. For example, "Mary had a little _____." The children provide the missing word. The completion prompt serves as a scaffold to support understanding and recall, but also provides an easy way for children to participate using language. The reader may challenge the children by using completion prompts that match their particular needs.

- *R* stands for *recall questions*. The reader plans questions to pose at appropriate points in the book reading that encourage children to recall details or sequential events. For example, "What three materials did the three little pigs use to build their houses?" "What were some things that worried Wemberly?" The reader may pose these questions during and after the book is read.

- *O* stands for *open-ended questions*. The reader prepares questions that elicit more than a one-word response and may also elicit more than one correct answer. The reader poses these questions to provide the children more opportunity to respond using multiword responses. For example, "Why do you think Chrysanthemum didn't like her name?" "How did Petunia feel when she first arrived on the farm?" "How did Duck and Goose figure out that the soccer ball was not an egg?"

- *W* stands for *Wh- questions*. The reader asks a variety of Wh- questions and puts more emphasis on those that may be challenging for children to answer (giving more opportunities for children to practice responding and for the reader to provide more scaffolding). For very young children, Wh- questions are more basic than for older children with higher-level language skills. The teacher encourages labeling of objects, actions, and concepts to build basic vocabulary and children's abilities to use these basic words while talking about the book. It is generally recommended that the teacher address at least one vocabulary word that may be unknown to most children. For example, "What do you think *drowsy* means?" "Why did the author use the word *extraordinary*?"

- *D* stands for *distancing questions*. The reader prepares questions that prompt children to make connections with the book. The connections may be related to the children's personal experiences or earlier knowledge. For example, "Tell me about a time when you felt worried like Wemberly." This is an open-ended prompt also and is preferred over asking, "Did you ever feel worried like Wemberly?" because children would likely respond with one word—yes or no—and require additional prompting to expand. Another example is, "Tell us about a place you've visited where you might have seen other animals like this."

While ongoing opportunities to use and understand language contribute to children's developing listening comprehension, dialogic reading specifically targets both oral language and listening comprehension through the use of specific prompts.

Vocabulary Support Strategies during Read-Alouds

While reading to young children and focusing on both oral language and vocabulary development, there are many opportunities to provide explicit support for children to understand and learn new vocabulary. Research-based practices include the use of "child friendly" or "student friendly" definitions or explanations.[11] Sentence stems (see Table 3.3) are helpful for creating simple explanations of words that provide meaning. They also provide an additional model of the word used in the context of a sentence (sometimes in a different form or tense). These strategies are useful for embedding vocabulary support before, during, and after reading aloud to young children. This type of practice benefits semantic and syntactic development. Table 3.3 illustrates examples of using sentence stems to create explanations of words that young children can understand.

Table 3.3. Sentence stems for vocabulary support

Key word for strategy	Sentence stem	Example
Something	If something is ___, it is ____.	If something is gigantic, it is really big, like a giant.
Someone	If someone is ___, he or she is ___.	If someone is exhausted, he or she is tired.
Describe	____ is a word that can be used to describe ____.	Delighted is a word to describe a happy or pleased feeling.
Type (or kind)	___ is a type of ___ that ___.	A vest is a type of sweater or shirt that doesn't have sleeves.
Another word for	___ is another word for __.	Vehicle is another word for car or automobile.

These are additional ways to embed vocabulary support while reading and after reading.

Sentence stem	Example word in text	Example of meaning
That means ____.	Irritable	That means crabby.
That's the same as ____.	Flock (of sheep)	That's the same as a group of sheep.
It's kind of like _____.	Drowsy	It's kind of like sleepy.
It's something that ____.	Ladle	It's something that is used to scoop or serve soup or stew.
When someone is (selected word), they are ___.	Elated	When someone is elated, they are really happy and excited about something.
That word tells about or describes something that is _____.	Scrumptious	That word describes something that is really yummy or delicious.
If you are (selected word), you are _____.	Approaching	If you are approaching someone, you are going toward them or getting near them.

Table 3.4.   Synonym substitutions

Text from book	Text with paired synonym
"I think it's a beautiful name," commented Daisy.	"I think it's a beautiful name," commented/said Daisy.
He tried to lift the enormous watermelon.	He tried to lift the enormous/huge watermelon.
The gallant young sailor turned the boat around and headed home.	The gallant/brave young sailor turned the boat around and headed home.
She felt fortunate that day.	She felt fortunate/lucky that day.

Another key strategy for providing vocabulary support and building oral language is called synonym substitution. While reading aloud using synonym substitution, you embed synonyms children are likely to understand and pair these with the new vocabulary word in a way that children can hear a slight pause or change in intonation. Table 3.4 illustrates some examples.

Practice Activity

Select a book that you would consider reading to your group of young children. Be sure to select one that provides opportunities to build language and vocabulary as you are reading. Preview the book to identify opportunities to embed dialogic reading prompts using Figure 3.3, CROWD Strategy Planning Template. Create the prompts and write them on sticky notes to place in the book in preparation for reading. Then, look for opportunities to provide vocabulary support using any of the previously mentioned strategies. Use Figure 3.4, Embedded Vocabulary Support for Building Oral Language, to write the words you would teach, the child-friendly explanations you will provide using the sentence stems, and/or the synonyms

---

Title: *A Girl and Her Gator*

Author: *Sean Bryan*   **Illustrator:** *Tom Murphy*

C – Completion questions (e.g., *Lily's purse is _____ and she brings it _____.*)

A girl named Claire had a gator on _____.

R – Recall questions (e.g., *What happened when Jose went back to school? What was missing from Corduroy's overalls? How did Stephanie wear her hair?*)

What were some of the things that the Gator was trying to convince Claire she could do with a "gator up there?"

O – Open-ended questions (e.g., *Why was Alexander having a bad day? How did the cat get his whiskers? What do you think his friends thought when they heard he moved?*)

Why was Claire worried about having a gator on top of her hair?

W – Wh-questions (*Creating and asking a "What" question referring to word meaning or vocabulary is a good choice to ensure that you are embedding specific vocabulary instruction; e.g., What do you think shy means? What does it mean to be embarrassed? What are braids?*)

What do you think "gossip and stare" means?

D – Distancing question (e.g., *Tell me about a time when you felt lost or lost something. How did you feel when your friend moved away? Do you have something that is very special to you like Owen's blanket?*)

Tell your friend next to you about something that was embarrassing to you but turned out to be okay in the end. How was this like Claire's feelings?

Figure 3.3.   Example of a completed CROWD Strategy Planning Template for *A Girl and Her Gator*.[12]

Book title: _____ Author: _____ Illustrator: _____

Word	Child-friendly explanation (Refer to the sentence stems)	Synonyms for substitution	Before, during, after?

Figure 3.4. Embedded vocabulary support for building oral language.

you will provide using synonym substitution, and determine when you will emphasize these words—before, during, or after you read the book or a combination.

Create at least three prompts or questions for each category that you can use to prompt and build upon children's language during a read aloud. Include the page number that corresponds to the appropriate opportunity to use each prompt. Use these to prompt dialogue and interaction and then evaluate, expand, and repeat while reading.

C—Completion questions (e.g., Lily's purse is _____ and she brings it _____.)

R—Recall questions (e.g., What happened when Jose went back to school? What was missing from Corduroy's overalls? How did Stephanie wear her hair?)

O—Open-ended questions (e.g., Why was Alexander having a bad day? How did the cat get his whiskers? What do you think his friends thought when they heard he moved?)

W—Wh- questions (Creating and asking a "What" question referring to word meaning or vocabulary is a good choice to ensure that you are embedding specific vocabulary instruction; e.g., What do you think shy means? What does it mean to be embarrassed? What are braids?)

D—Distancing question (e.g., Tell me about a time when you felt lost or lost something. How did you feel when your friend moved away? Do you have something that is very special to you like Owen's blanket?)

ENVIRONMENTAL SUPPORT FOR BUILDING ORAL LANGUAGE

There are many ways that you can engineer your classroom environment to support oral language development. Arranging theme-based centers is a way to build vocabulary and concepts around a specific topic. Not only does this build language, but it also helps build background knowledge. Building background knowledge for children will contribute to the development of listening and reading comprehension. Planning purposefully to bring more language opportunities into your classroom will benefit your children now and in the future. Each opportunity they have to learn words, relate them to concepts and experiences, and use them as part of their oral language means that they will be able to comprehend those words and concepts when they encounter them in print. When you provide rich language at the oral level when children are young, they will likely develop a rich vocabulary—a key ingredient for reading comprehension.

If you plan carefully to create a language-rich classroom, you will be successful. In other words, it will not just happen without your thoughtful actions! Paying attention to the physical arrangement in your classroom, materials you select, environmental prompts you create, and the words you choose to talk about the experiences you provide, are valuable and necessary for having a language-rich classroom.

The physical arrangement should include space for large group activities, such as read-alouds and circle time. Small group areas should be well-defined and include furniture appropriate to the activity or routine. For example, if you provide opportunities for children to work on puzzles together, a tabletop surface with children sitting next to each other is more conducive to interaction and collaborative efforts than floor space. Areas that accommodate dramatic play of all types should be large enough so that children have space and access to materials that relate to the center. For example, a grocery store requires shelves with labels and a check-out area and walls to display ads and pictures that encourage verbal interaction. Each area in the classroom can display pictures, photos, or items that prompt oral language. As teachers, it is important for you to provide interesting topics, cues, and models for children to practice their language.

The decisions you make for the selection of materials is similar to that of the physical arrangement. The key is to extend what children already know or have experienced so that they acquire the language to build upon their background knowledge. If you think beyond what children might have experienced and include talk that expands upon their experiences, you are providing opportunities to build oral language and add a whole new vocabulary to their repertoires.

A simple tool for you to use as an environmental prompt or cue to assist in modeling efforts is "The Teacher's Word Wall" (Table 3.5). This word wall serves as a reminder for you to use sophisticated language or expressions in place of common, routine comments produced in the child's environment or your classroom. The table provides examples of alternate ways to say common expressions, like "great job" or "thank you." Because some of these alternatives may not be part of your typical vocabulary when conversing with young children, you and others talking to young children can easily glance at the word wall and select an option to insert into a comment or dialogue. Over time, as the common expressions are replaced

Table 3.5. Example of a teacher word wall (reminders to use sophisticated language in place of common expressions)

Great job!	Thank you	I'm happy	Please . . .
Awesome!	I really appreciate what you did.	I am so delighted!	I would appreciate it if you . . .
Fabulous!	We are grateful.	I am elated!	Will you charm us with your great listening?
Kudos to you!	I admire your kindness.	We are so pleased.	I would relish your willingness to participate.
Stupendous!	I treasure your cooperation.	I am tickled pink!	Por favor (Spanish for "please")
Impressive!	Muchas gracias! (Spanish for "many thanks" or "thank you")	I am impressed with your effort.	S'il vous plait (French for "please")

with more sophisticated options in a fluent manner, the children will hear them used multiple times and eventually will weave them into their own speaking vocabulary. The idea is to replace the expressions often to continue building on children's vocabulary.

An extension of the "Teacher's Word Wall" includes vocabulary, anchors for conversation or conversation starters, prompts (questions and comments), and actions that relate to a specific theme (Table 3.6). The example in Table 3.6 relates to a flower shop–themed center. Again, these cues serve as reminders for you and other adults to embed the language into the context of interacting with children during center play or other classroom routines.

Table 3.6.   Example of a theme-based teacher's word wall

Center theme: The flower shop			
Vocabulary	Conversation starters	Prompts (questions or comments)	Actions to model and narrate
embellish convenient arrange bouquet	The location of your shop is so convenient—it's so close to everything.	How would you like me to embellish or decorate this vase of flowers?	I'm selecting several different colored flowers to arrange a colorful bouquet.
schedule a delivery bouquet single exquisite bud vase	I'd like to schedule a delivery for a bouquet of flowers. Can you send it soon?	That is one beautiful bouquet you've arranged for someone special!	This single rose looks exquisite in this bud vase, don't you think?
decorate clip stems stay fresh wither examples creations	May I look at examples of your creations in your catalogs?	I wonder how I can use this ribbon to decorate this basket. I might try to weave it through the openings.	I always clip the ends of the stems so the flowers will stay fresh longer. This way, they'll last for days and won't wither quickly.
houseplants include dish garden nice touch celebrations attractive combination	I think the combination of flowers and houseplants is attractive—I like how they look together.	Which houseplants would you like to select to include in this dish garden?	I'm adding flowers as a nice touch to this dish garden that usually has only houseplants. A celebration is not complete if it does not include flowers somewhere!
message include greeting card variety purchase	Oh, I didn't know that you also included a variety of greeting cards to purchase in your shop! There are so many to buy!	What message will you include on your greeting card?	I'm trying to find the perfect words to include in my special message.
fortunate locate blooming floral arrangement	How fortunate for me to locate your shop! I am lucky that I don't have to walk far.	Who's the fortunate, or lucky one, to receive this floral arrangement?	I'm fortunate to have all these flowers blooming in my garden behind the shop. It makes it very easy to create all of these floral arrangements like this one.

THE FEATURES OF EFFECTIVE INSTRUCTION AND ORAL LANGUAGE

Table 3.7 illustrates some examples of how each of the features of effective instruction can be addressed through efforts to build oral language and listening skill development in young children. Try to apply what you know to think of others that may not be represented in this table.

Refer to Table 3.8, and review the examples of how oral language, vocabulary, and other language-related skills are embedded throughout the course of a typical day and are embedded into routines. As a teacher, you will want to identify activities or opportunities to address each of the major areas of emergent literacy that are integrated throughout the day. Planning for a minimum of three opportunities for each area will ensure sufficient attention and will likely result in more language skills practiced than planned. This planning will illustrate how you attend to an important feature of effective instruction providing multiple opportunities for students to respond and practice.

Differentiation

Differentiating instruction for students at any age will become a commonplace occurrence in your classroom. While it is common, it is not easy! You may have interacted with enough children at this point to know that all children are different and have varying needs at multiple time points. The opening of this chapter illustrated a teacher's concern about the vast language differences between children within a small group. These differences require knowledge and practice to be able to meet children's needs and support their development appropriately.

Your ability to differentiate successfully depends on your ability to assess your children and identify their needs. When you are able to do this, you can adjust what you do within an activity to meet varying needs. When you are considering developing language skills in the context of talking with children during center activities or read-alouds, it becomes a simple matter of adjusting your language to match children's needs. The tricky part is knowing what they need! Understanding language needs means that you must know where children are in their language development *and* what comes next. Your role as a teacher is to provide support for what comes next so that children are working toward developing more advanced language.

Here are a couple of examples of how you can differentiate easily in the context of conversation during center play. Let us consider that you have one child who is still developing his single-word vocabulary and has about 50 words in his lexicon (oral vocabulary repertoire). Another child is beginning to embed descriptive words to tell about experiences and feelings. Most of the children speak in phrases or short sentences, but there is one child who is quite verbose—she can talk in complete sentences, take conversational turns in excess of four turns, and she has a pretty sophisticated vocabulary for a 4-year-old, using words like *actually, enormous, exhausted,* and *finally.* What a wonderful opportunity *and* responsibility to differentiate by varying your language and models to match the next steps for these children. For the child who uses primarily single words, your models and prompts would target his or her ability to combine words. Your models would emphasize words that he or she uses in appropriate combinations (e.g., *You have a* **red car.***; Do you want* **more crackers?***; What would you like to do,* **ride bikes** *or* **play ball?***). For most of the children, you would extend and elaborate using descriptive words, linking words or conjunctions (e.g., *and, but, because, then,* etc.) and modeling sophisticated vocabulary for everyone, especially your most verbal child. Use alternatives like, *What do you* **prefer** *to do right now?* or **If** *we all choose to play ball together* **then** *we'll have to* **remain** *inside because it looks like the* **weather's about to change!**

In addition to the children that were described in the previous example, you may also have a child who is learning English as a second language. He or she may be similar to the child with a single-word vocabulary or one who is beginning to use more descriptive words, but how you differentiate may vary. A child who is learning English as a second language

Table 3.7. Features of effective instruction and oral language

	Explicit instruction with modeling	Systematic instruction with scaffolding	Frequent opportunities for practice	Immediate corrective feedback	Ongoing progress monitoring
Phonology (Providing practice for children to say and use three-syllable words.	Tell children that you are going to say a word slowly and in parts because it's hard to say.	Provide part of the word when children have difficulty saying multisyllable words.	Prompt children to use new words many times throughout the day.	Provide the model and prompt child to say it again.	Identify specific sounds or multi-syllable words to monitor.
Morphology		Provide sentence stems that allow children to create different word forms to fit the context. For example, "If you're not happy, you might be ___."	After talking about words we use to talk about things that already happened, provide story starters that prompt children to embed past tense and use the –ed marker.		Listen to sponta-neous language during free play and note new combinations of word parts. Chil-dren may begin to create their own words.
Semantics				When children use a descriptive word, use it as an opportunity to model a different word or synonym.	
Syntax		Provide a prompt that creates a forced opportunity for a child to combine the right word forms. *The dog barks, and yelps, and ___ (cries—child usually uses first-person verb for third-person noun).*		Provide the correct model using slight elaboration and have the child repeat it with you the next time.	
Pragmatics	This is an exam-ple of when we might use this word when we greet someone . . .			Provide a simple rationale for us-ing certain words when expressing feelings.	
Language facilitation				Expand and elaborate children's language using correct forms.	Identify specific language goals and create data sheet to docu-ment progress (see the example of the progress monitoring data sheet in this chapter).
Read aloud with dialogic reading	I'm going to use these three words to help me retell the story in order—first, next, finally.		Use higher-level questions throughout the read-aloud to provide many opportunities to process and respond.	Let's see if we can find the words the author used to tell us about that. If we're answering a "Who" question, we'll answer with a person or a character.	

Table 3.8. Planning matrix for embedding vocabulary and other emergent literacy skills throughout the day

Week of: (EXAMPLE) Theme: Bugs and Creepy Crawlers

Vocabulary Words to Model or Prompt: This week: invisible, mystery, camouflage, Previous words: amazed, delighted, magnify

	Arrival	Circle	Centers	Free play	Outside play	Snack/meal time	Story time	Dismissal	Transitions or other
Oral language (vocabulary and listening comprehension)	Use previous vocabulary words to greet children	Read *Dot & Jabber and the Big Bug Mystery*	Use magnifying glass to find hidden objects (invisible)	Model elaborated language as children play	Look for bugs that might be examples of camouflage	Provide topics and opportunities for children to converse	Retell using pictures and props		"I am delighted that you had fun."
Phonological awareness	Call children's names by syllables	Sing "bug-theme" fingerplays (e.g., "Baby Bumble Bee")	Find objects that begin with same sound as "bug"		Play "I Spy" by segmenting words		Read "bug poems"	Call children's names by deleting last sound or syllable	"You moved so quietly, I thought you were invisible."
Concepts of print	Have children "sign in"	Names visible, song titles	Centers labeled many ways	Label toys and play areas	Look for print and signs	Menu/sign showing food items	Focus on parts of book.	Put name badges away	
Alphabetic principle	Children place name on word wall	Show letters that start names	Some letter stencils available for tracing			Talk about foods, show shopping list	ID letters on each page		
Opportunities to model vocabulary (from read-alouds)	"I'm delighted to see everyone today."	"Is someone absent or invisible?"	"I'll be amazed when I see you clean up."	"It's a mystery! The balls have disappeared."	"You're wearing green so are you in camouflage?"	"If you can see your raisins, they're not invisible."	Focus on selected words.	"I can't wait to see how you'll amaze me tomorrow."	"Your voices seem magnified—ouch my ears hurt."

may require additional support from illustrations, objects, or demonstrations in order to understand concepts or new vocabulary. What is most critical, however, is that you provide many opportunities for children learning other languages to actually say the words and practice the oral language you are modeling. While this is important for all young children developing oral language, it is even more important for English language learners.

Differentiating during read-alouds is easy to achieve through the use of various prompts and questions followed by the elaborated responses you provide.

Assessment

As a teacher, you will have the responsibility of assessing your young children in several areas, including oral language. In addition, as a teacher, you will also have the opportunity to engage in self-reflective practice. First, we will discuss ways that you can assess children's oral language skills. Next, you will be introduced to a tool that you will use for self-evaluation of your skill for reading aloud to young children and incorporating strategies that will lead to enhanced oral language development.

Progress Monitoring of Children's Oral Language

When you introduce new concepts or words into a child's vocabulary, the easiest way to assess progress is to listen for the child's spontaneous use of new language and then document it in the form of notes or checklists that you created to match the aspect of language you have targeted. You might also ask specific questions that would likely solicit specific words or complex sentences. For example, if you have taught and modeled words presented in the flower shop center, you might listen as children play in the center and document episodes when children use the words. You might also consider asking specific questions that invite children to use new words. For example, "What do you recommend for me to send to a friend for her birthday?" If children are having difficulty recalling words such as *bouquet* or *floral arrangement*, you could provide them as models embedded in a question such as, "Do you suggest a floral arrangement or a bouquet or a dish garden?" A child would have to select one and say it, and you could follow up by having them show you the difference.

Another way to monitor children's progress is during read-alouds. Figure 3.5 can be used to identify specific goals for specific children and to provide opportunities for children to respond to the prompts that you generated for use during a read-aloud. You may consider asking all children to respond to a few prompts and pose specific prompts to children who need additional practice or varying levels of support, modeling, or increased challenge.

When planning a read-aloud, think about specific children in your class who need help on targeted oral language skills. In the chart below, write the child's name and specific skills you want to focus on during the read-aloud. Then, make a checkmark in the box for which CROWD prompts you will use during the read-aloud to address those skills.

Next, during the read-aloud, when you ask the child the question, put a + or a − next to the checkmark depending on whether the child successfully completed the prompt or not. After the read-aloud, add appropriate comments and next steps to continue the assessment and progress monitoring. This information can also be documented on sticky notes placed in the back of the book you are reading and later transferred to this chart. Please note that it may not be necessary or feasible to progress monitor all students during a read-aloud, but this is a way to plan for differentiated lessons to meet individual children's needs *and* to monitor their progress to see if what you are doing is working.

Self-Reflection Activity

Earlier in this chapter as part of a practice activity, you selected a book to read aloud to a group of young children. You also planned to read it using dialogic reading strategies and created

Teacher Name: _____   Classroom: _____

Date	Child	Specific Skills to Work On	CROWD Prompts to Use					Comments/Next Steps
			C	R	O	W	D	
2/3	Nina	- Understanding sequencing in a story - Being able to make predictions		☐+		☐−		Needs more help in making predictions, continue to ask "what do you think will happen next" type of questions
	Julian	- Responding with more than two or three word utterances - Recalling details		☐−	☐−			Provide additional modeling and scaffolds for three-word phrases; use sentence stems

Figure 3.5.   Progress monitoring tool for use during read-alouds.

prompts to embed during the reading. In addition, you planned to embed vocabulary support. Now, it is time to actually read the book to a group of young children and record yourself so that you can engage in self-reflection. If recording is not an option, you may want to pair with a classmate so that you can observe each other and provide feedback using the tools available.

You can use the *Read Aloud Tool for Evaluation (RATE)*[13] to improve your skill with reading to young children by learning all the components of a valuable read-aloud and maximizing its potential for enhancing oral language and listening skill development for young children. The RATE is divided into five components of a read-aloud:

1. Book selection: This component addresses the quality of the book selection for meeting the objectives associated with dialogic reading, oral language development, and other specific goals within emergent literacy.

2. Book introduction: The quality of the introduction relates to *how* the book is introduced and goes beyond the identification of the title, author, and illustrator. Rating this component allows you to strengthen this area if needed so that you identify an objective or indicate a specific purpose related to why you chose the book to read. This also helps children focus on the purpose while listening and participating in the read-aloud.

3. The read-aloud: This component represents a significant part of the entire read-aloud and includes your attention to features such as eye contact and use of voice, management of the flow, posing appropriate questions, responding to children, facilitating interaction, and embedding vocabulary support

4. Specific dialogic reading strategies: This portion of the RATE allows you to reflect and evaluate your skill in using the dialogic reading strategies systematically and purposefully.

5. Book closure: The way that a teacher closes the book and supports children's understanding and ability to connect the book to other knowledge or concepts is what contributes to a high-quality book closure. During the closure, the teacher engages children in conversation

about the book using guiding questions that relate specifically to the intended purpose of selecting the book as well as important oral language skills.

For each component, a rating of 1 (low score) to 5 (high score) is assigned, and the individual component ratings are summed for a total score out of a maximum of 25. Anchor descriptions are provided for a rating of 1 (Needs much attention), 3 (Needs some attention), and 5 (Best). While the overall score allows for a general idea of the quality of a read-aloud and progress monitoring of your read-aloud skill, the individual component ratings allow you to identify areas of strength and those in need of additional attention.

For self-reflection, read the *Read Aloud Coding Guidelines* provided and familiarize yourself with the RATE. Once you feel prepared to conduct your read-aloud by planning appropriately, make arrangements to do the read-aloud and record yourself. After you have recorded, use the RATE to evaluate your read-aloud and identify particular strengths and areas in need of further practice. Remember to evaluate yourself with an informed, knowledgeable lens based on the information you have learned in this chapter.

When you have finished evaluating yourself, develop a plan for strengthening the areas you feel needed more attention. Then, plan for the next read-aloud and focus on improving all parts, particularly the ones you identified for yourself. Providing yourself with multiple opportunities to practice is another illustration of the features of effective instruction. Multiple practice opportunities help you improve while also building children's oral language.

CONCLUSION

There exists a strong research base that has validated some simple, effective strategies to build oral language in young children.

These translate to simple actions:

- Talk to children, converse.
- Plan for the opportunity for children to use their language.
- Use read-alouds systematically.
- Follow children's leads. (You can build upon their interests and experiences, but you must create an environment that will prompt more language and curiosity.)
- Model, model, model!
- Prompt (comments and questions).
- Use rich vocabulary.
- Build background knowledge.
- Continuously make connections among words, concepts, and topics.

If you do all of this purposefully and consistently, you will set your young students on a path toward success in learning to read.

ENDNOTES

1. Owens (2008).
2. Campbell & Ramey (1994).
3. Hart & Risley (1995).
4. Hutinger & Bruce (1971).
5. Lever & Senechal (2011).
6. Pence & Justice (2008).
7. Whitehurst & Lonigan (1998).
8. Morgan & Meier (2008).
9. Briesch, Chafouleas, Lebel, & Blom-Hoffman (2008).
10. Zevenbergen & Whitehurst (2003).
11. Beck, McKeown, & Kucan, 2002.
12. Bryan & Murphy, 2006.
13. Cavanaugh (2011).

REFERENCES

Beck, I., McKeown, M., & Kucan, L. (2002). *Bringing words to life: Robust vocabulary instruction*. New York: Guilford.

Briesch, A.M., Chafouleas, S.M., Lebel, T.J., & Blom-Hoffman, J.A. (2008). Impact of videotaped instruction in dialogic reading strategies: An investigation of caregiver implementation integrity. *Psychology in the Schools, 45*, 978–993.

Bryan, S., Murphy, T. (2006). *A girl and her gator*. New York: Arcade Pub.

Campbell, F.A., & Ramey, C.T. (1994). Effects of early intervention on intellectual and academic achievement: A follow-up study of children from low-income families. *Child Development, 65*(2), 684–698.

Cavanaugh, C.L. (2011). *Read Aloud Tool for Evaluation (RATE)*. Chapel Hill, NC: University of North Carolina, FPG Child Development Institute, Doing What Works Implementation Project and CONNECT (Center to Mobilize Early Childhood Knowledge).

Hart, B., & Risley, T. (1995). *Meaningful differences in the everyday experience of young American children*. Baltimore: Paul H. Brookes Publishing Co.

Hutinger, P., & Bruce, T. (1971). The effects of adult verbal modeling and feedback on the oral language of Head Start children. *American Educational Research Journal, 8*(4), 611–622.

Lever, R., & Senechal, M. (2011). Discussing stories: On how a dialogic reading intervention improves kindergartners' oral narrative construction. *Journal of Experimental Child Psychology, 108*, 1–24.

Morgan, P.L., & Meier, C.R. (2008). Dialogic reading's potential to improve children's emergent literacy skills and behavior. *Preventing School Failure, 52*, 11–16.

Owens Jr., R.E. (2008). *Language development: An introduction* (7th ed.). Boston: Pearson, Allyn & Bacon.

Pence, K.L., & Justice, L.M. (2008). *Language development from theory to practice*. Boston: Pearson, Allyn & Bacon.

Zevenbergen, A.A., & Whitehurst, G.J. (2003). Dialogic reading: A shared picture book reading intervention for preschoolers. In A. Van Kleeck, S.A. Stahl, & E.B. Bauer (Eds.), *On reading books to children: Parents and teachers* (pp. 177–200). Mahwah, NJ: Lawrence Erlbaum.

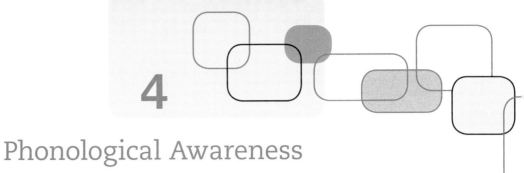

4

Phonological Awareness

A Critical Foundation for Beginning Reading

by Stephanie Al Otaiba
and Martha C. Hougen

Andrew's family loved playing word games and reading books to Andrew and his younger brother. One day when Andrew was 3 years old, he asked his mom for a cookie. She replied, "I'm sorry Andrew, we don't have any cookies, but I can give you a banana." Andrew paused for minute, looked up at his mom, smiled, and said, "Okay, I'll have a banana fofana!"

It is likely that you have similar memories or family stories from growing up. Making up words or even languages such as pig Latin[1] were favorite pastimes. Explicit instruction in manipulating sounds (phonemic awareness) is crucial for learning to read and spell effectively and efficiently. In fact, knowledge of phonemic awareness is an essential skill for learning to read in all alphabetic languages. Phonemic awareness supports reading even in languages, such as Spanish, in which syllables are more often the basis of oral language. Therefore, when young children have early experiences with phonemes in Spanish and other languages, their phonemic awareness ability transfers to English and makes learning to read and write in English easier.[2]

In the vignette above, Andrew's comment showed that he was developing an awareness of playing with words, that words can rhyme, that he could make up words, and that it was fun! His ability to rhyme and his awareness about initial sounds in words are in stark contrast to many of the young students with whom you will work during your teaching career, children for whom this awareness does not develop so easily. Andrew is developing phonemic awareness, a skill critical for learning to read and write.

This chapter addresses the most effective ways to assess and teach overall *phonological awareness*, and the discrete skill known as *phonemic awareness*.

Objectives: After studying this chapter, you will be able to do the following:

1. Explain and provide examples of phonological awareness.
2. Explain and provide examples of phonemic awareness.
3. Identify the number of syllables and phonemes in words.
4. Explain the stages of phonological awareness.
5. Model a routine to teach phonemic awareness.
6. Assess a child's progress toward developing phonemic awareness.
7. Plan general and intervention instruction in phonemic awareness.
8. Teach the student whom you are tutoring to segment and blend three phoneme words.
9. Evaluate the progress of your student and plan a follow-up lesson.
10. Explain to parents the role of phonemic awareness in identifying students with dyslexia.

WHAT IS PHONOLOGICAL AWARENESS? WHAT IS PHONEMIC AWARENESS? WHY ARE THESE SKILLS IMPORTANT? WHAT DOES THE RESEARCH SAY?

Both phonological and phonemic awareness are related to *phonology*, defined as the sound system of language. It may help you to think about a phone as a key word to cue you to remember that phonemes are speech sounds. (The morpheme *phone* refers to sound.) Phonological and phonemic awareness are initially taught only with sounds, no print. Children can learn to discriminate (hear and process) individual sounds in words with their eyes closed!

This chapter describes how to systematically introduce phonological skills in a continuum, from easy to more difficult, to increase your students' reading achievement. Knowing how to teach phonological awareness explicitly is vital given research findings about the importance of this skill for beginning reading achievement. To be an effective teacher, you need to be knowledgeable about why and how to scaffold instruction for children who struggle to develop phonological awareness.

Phonological Awareness and Phonemic Awareness: What is the Difference?

The term *phonological awareness* refers to a global awareness of large chunks of speech.[3] Phonological awareness encompasses an awareness of rhyming and alliteration, the number of words in a sentence, syllables within words (e.g., *cupcake* is made up of *cup* and *cake)*, and onset and rime. The onset of a one-syllable word is the beginning consonant(s), and the rime is the vowel and all that comes after (i.e., *dog* begins with /d/, the onset, and ends with /og/, the rime).

Phonemic awareness is the ability to think about, combine, or segment *individual* sounds in speech. This understanding of individual sounds, or phonemes, undergirds the ability to read.[4] This discrete set of skills helps children understand that a word like *dog* can be separated, or segmented, into three individual sounds: /d/ /o/ /g/, and that, inversely, these three sounds can be combined, or blended, into a single word, *dog*. One day when testing a kindergartener early in September, his teacher asked him to tell her the sounds in *dog*, and he answered "woof-woof." Clearly, he did not yet know how to attend to the qualities of the individual sounds in the word, rather than the literal meaning of the word. This student needed intensive instruction to develop phonemic awareness.

Figure 4.1 is an illustration of the continuum of phonological skill development, beginning with oral language and listening skills. Typically, the skills are taught following this sequence, though children may be exposed to several stages at a time. Do not wait, for example, for a child to master rhyming before you introduce syllable segmentation. Examples of how to provide instruction in each stage are discussed later in this chapter.

There is an extensive research base that has shown *why* the concept of phonemic awareness is a vital step in understanding how children learn to read and to spell. This research base describes important pathways for how phonemic awareness undergirds early reading development[5] and spelling development.[6] Phonemic awareness supports development of the alphabetic principle, or letter–sound correspondence.[7] Unless students can hear the individual sounds in words and can blend them together, it will be difficult for them to decode, or sound out, words. Therefore, phonemic awareness plays an important role in *fast mapping*, or the process children develop of forming grapheme–phoneme (i.e., letter–sound) representations for words in their memory.[8] (Some people also use the term phoneme-grapheme correspondences for this concept of letter–sound connections.)

Thus, through fast mapping, phonemic awareness supports the ability to decode unknown or novel words through phonetic decoding. It is not, therefore, surprising that the National Early Literacy Panel reported important predictive relationships between very young children's phonological awareness and decoding and between phonological awareness and spelling.[9] Similarly, the National Reading Panel found that the most effective phonological

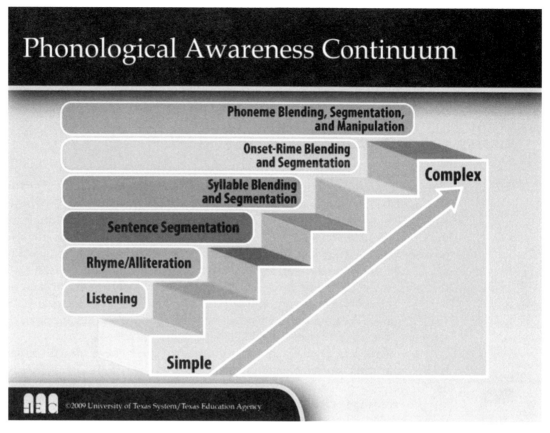

Figure 4.1. Phonological awareness continuum. (From Vaughn Gross Center at The University of Texas at Austin. [2009]. Module 4: Phonological awareness. In *Foundations of reading instruction presentations and print files.* Austin, TX: Vaughn Gross Center [Texas Reading First Higher Education Collaborative]; reprinted by permission.)

awareness instruction incorporated letter–sound work (Box 4.1).[10] The ability to translate print to speech, phonological recoding, is dependent upon phonological skills and is necessary for learning to spell (orthographic learning).[11]

Interestingly, the failure to develop phonological processing skills (which includes phonological and phonemic awareness) is the primary correlate of dyslexia. Students with dyslexia typically have a history of not being successful segmenting and blending phonemes (sounds) to form words. In fact, one component of a dyslexia evaluation is a phoneme awareness test. And as the research above suggests, students who do not have intact phonemic awareness skills struggle to learn letter–sound correspondences or phonics. Also, word recognition is poor. These students tend to read slowly, and their comprehension is negatively impacted. So what may have started out as a phonemic awareness problem in a young child ends up, unless identified and remediated early, affecting reading comprehension and, in most cases, spelling as well. It is important to note that dyslexia frequently occurs with language

BOX 4.1. A large amount of research has demonstrated that explicit training of phonological and phonemic awareness leads to stronger phonological outcomes and to stronger reading and spelling outcomes, too.[9,10]

impairments and attention deficit/hyperactivity disorder. Recent research considers dyslexia as a developmental disorder the severity of which may depend upon co-occurring conditions and other factors.[12] Though students with dyslexia may also have other conditions such as attention deficits and oral language impairments, the majority of students with dyslexia have phonological deficits that must be addressed.

WHAT PHONOLOGICAL SKILLS SHOULD STUDENTS KNOW AT VARIOUS GRADE LEVELS?

Preschool children who have had early book reading experiences with family members and early childcare providers will likely have an awareness of rhyme and alliteration. Children as young as 3 years old are typically aware of when words rhyme and begin with the same letter, such as the alliteration in "busy bees buzz." Consider the earlier example that was provided about Andrew. By age 3, he was making up a word based upon his knowledge of how to combine chunks of sounds, in his case syllables, to make up a word (i.e., *banana* and *fofana*). Children who are read to frequently, or who watch educational media that emphasize reading, may be aware of initial sounds in words that start with the same sound. Andrew's brother, Thomas, was very proud that he shared his name with the ever-popular Thomas the Tank Engine, a book series that features alliteration in the title including two words that start with the /t/ sound: "Thomas" and "Tank."

By around 4 years of age, most children who have book reading experiences will be able to fill in the blank when a parent or teacher reads to them and pauses at the end of a line such as: "Brown bear, brown bear, what do you **see**?"[13] They likely will have heard and sung simple songs or recited nursery rhymes that incorporate rhyme, such as "Twinkle, twinkle little **star**, how I wonder what you **are**." Some children appear to learn these early phonological skills incidentally, without direct instruction but through exposure as they listen and then as they fast map or connect sounds to words.

By the end of kindergarten, children should have mastered phonemic awareness. They should be able to segment and blend the individual sounds in one-syllable words. Once they can segment three- or four-phoneme words into individual phonemes, you can be assured that they have mastered this concept, and you no longer have to address it on a daily basis. Next, children will begin to use this knowledge to support decoding and encoding (spelling) of real words.

However, some children will continue to need instruction in phonemic awareness in first and second grades, sometimes even later. A substantial number of young children, particularly children who have had less exposure to print associated with growing up in poverty or who may be at risk for reading difficulties, will need explicit and systematic instruction in order to master these concepts. You will want to closely monitor children for phonological weaknesses, particularly those with speech and language impairments and children who are learning English as a second language. Still other children just seem to struggle to hear and manipulate sounds in words; some may have a family history of dyslexia or learning disabilities, but, for others, it may seem surprising or unexplainable. Whatever the cause, it is essential these young students receive specialized instruction (remediation) to prevent or ameliorate potential reading disabilities.

You will need to model and explain in child-friendly terms to your students how to rhyme, pronounce sounds, match first sounds, segment, and blend sounds. Your students may be instructionally naïve or struggling to develop this awareness and may be at high risk for reading disabilities. Your systematic, explicit instruction in phonemic awareness will make a tremendous difference in whether these struggling students learn to read and spell.

Here are a few examples for delivering explicit instruction:

"Listen carefully while I say the first sound in Thomas; /t/."

You will also need to know how to follow modeling with guided practice:

"Our turn, let's try one together; let's say the first sound in 'Thomas' together after I tap my finger. Ready? (Tap) /t/."

In addition, you will need to know how to test for understanding and provide independent practice:

"Your turn to tell me the first sound in Thomas." "Does it sound the same as the /t/ in 'tank'"?

At the start of kindergarten, you will find considerable variability in students' skills, and that variability may be associated with a lack of exposure to these concepts. Through instruction that is systematic and explicit and at the students' instructional level, students can learn these skills. For example, you will notice which children can learn to identify the first sound in their own name, and then you teach them to hear the onset and rime and begin to blend and segment chunks of speech at the onset–rime size. For example, if asked what animal sounds like /g/ /oat/, they could answer "goat." By the end of kindergarten, optimally, most children, will be able to blend and segment one-syllable words with two, three, and four phonemes.

At the start of first grade, as students learn to read, these blending and segmenting skills help students learn to sound out words. By the end of first grade, some students may learn to manipulate sounds and be able to know that "cowboy" without the "cow" leaves "boy"; but complex phonemic skills, such as understanding that "tack" pronounced backwards is "cat," may not develop until later.

For many children, including children with learning disabilities, these phonological skills do not develop so easily or efficiently. Given the strong and significant correlation between the ease at which students master these emerging phonological skills and their subsequent reading and spelling development, it is important for teachers to know how to assess phonological skills and recognize when to be concerned about a child's progress.[14] It is particularly challenging to distinguish an early lack of exposure from true difficulties in hearing and manipulating sounds in words. Therefore, teachers should know how to screen for weaknesses, how to determine who needs intensive small group intervention, and how to monitor students' response to the intervention instruction.

HOW DO YOU ASSESS THE ACQUISITION OF PHONOLOGICAL SKILLS?

As a teacher, you will learn to have an eye and an ear poised to informally collect data about your students' acquisition of phonological skills. In time, you will have enough experience to say to yourself, "Should I be worried? Why is this child on my radar screen?" Your inner dialog might sound something like the following:

"Hmm, it is winter and I am worried about Selina, who is 5 and a half now. She started kindergarten having some problems pronouncing and remembering her classmates' names that seemed unusual relative to her peers'. She seems to persist in confusing blends as when she asked for 'psgetti' rather than spaghetti, even when corrected."

Your next bit of data might come from observing her more carefully in a small group book reading that might uncover more concern; for example:

"Uh-oh, Selina is much less sensitive to rhyme and can't tell me the first sound in her own name. I think I had better do some assessments to look into this more systematically."

Fortunately, there are many measures of phonological skills so it is important for you to select an assessment or assessments that will help you "piece" together a picture of a student's strengths and weaknesses. These include both criterion-referenced and norm-referenced assessments. The purpose of norm-referenced tests is to provide a standard score and a percentile that allows you to compare a child's performance to other students her age or in her grade based upon a large national sample. Examples of norm-referenced tests that assess various phonological skills include the Comprehensive Test of Phonological Processing[15] (for children aged 5 and older) and the Test of Preschool Early Literacy.[16]

In contrast, the purpose of criterion-referenced tests is to help you determine whether a child has mastered a specific skill. Many districts use benchmark assessments several times a year. These are a type of criterion-referenced test because the tests measure an individual student's mastery of specified criteria, generally material that has been covered in the classroom.

Universal screening assessments are a type of criterion-referenced assessment and are designed to be teacher friendly so that you can quickly administer them to all children in your class several times per year. The screening assessments help you determine which students are achieving as expected and which are at risk in specific components of reading. Most states require that teachers in K–2 administer universal screening assessments to identify children who are at risk for having reading difficulties.

Progress monitoring assessments are quick checks of student mastery of specific skills and can be used frequently (perhaps once a week) to learn whether students are improving their skills and responding to your instruction. Some examples of criterion-referenced tasks that you can use for progress monitoring include the alliteration or rhyming tasks from the Individual Growth and Development Indicators (IGDIs; 2001),[17] suitable for children ages 3–5 and available from http://ggg.umn.edu/get/procedures_and_materials/Alliteration/index.html. [18] Assessments that are designed for students in kindergarten and first grade include the Initial Sounds Fluency from the Dynamic Indicator of Basic Early Literacy Skills (DIBELS)[19] and the Phonological Awareness Literacy Screening (PALS; http://pals.virginia.edu).[20]

HOW DO YOU USE ASSESSMENTS TO PLAN INSTRUCTION?

Phonological skills do develop rather hierarchically, and you can use your assessment data to plan instruction in order to target areas of weakness. Your data can guide you as you think about grouping students for instruction. For example, you might work with a homogenous group of students who are all struggling to blend onset and rimes (i.e., /m/ /an/ combines to make *man*). While you do so, you might have center time set up with children grouped heterogeneously (mixed abilities) so that the students who have strengths in blending could assist their partners. You know that the ability to segment and blend onset rimes will support phonemic awareness, the next critical skill in phonological awareness.

Note: Throughout this chapter, letter sounds will be denoted between slashes, like this: /a/. Words used as examples will be in italics, *like this*. The phonetic alphabet or dictionary system will be used to illustrate sounds, not the International Phonetic Alphabet (IPA). The IPA represents all the sounds of all the world's languages, and it is too detailed for our purposes at this time.

HOW DO YOU TEACH PHONOLOGICAL AWARENESS EFFECTIVELY, EFFICIENTLY, AND IN A MANNER THAT IS APPROPRIATE TO STUDENTS' AGE AND GRADE LEVEL?

Given the variability in student skills, it is vital for you to understand what instructional strategies are at an appropriate phonological level (i.e., syllables, onset–rime, individual phonemes) to best scaffold phonological awareness instruction to meet your students' diverse needs.[21] Extensive research has concluded that knowledge of phonemic awareness is a strong predictor of which students will learn to read easily and that explicit instruction in phonemic awareness is effective in improving students' achievement.[22]

Knowing that it is important to teach phonological awareness, you will want to do so in a manner that is effective, efficient, and age appropriate. For many of you, you may need to learn to correctly pronounce phonemes, or sounds, yourself. In far too many classrooms, teachers incorrectly add a schwa or "uh" sound to consonant sounds. For example, Mrs. Smith might say that the sounds in "cat" are /kuh/ /a/ /tuh/ instead of correctly pronouncing /c/ /a/ /t/ (Table 4.1).

As you select phonemes to teach, keep in mind that just as some letters are visually confusing (such as *b* and *d*, which may easily be reversed), sounds may be confusing because the sounds may be pronounced (articulated) in the same part of the mouth and sound similar. For example, if you say *fox* and *victory* the first sound is pronounced in the same part of your mouth because /f/ and /v/ are voiced and voiceless pairs. Another voiced and voiceless pair is the /p/ in *pat* and the /b/ in *bat* (see Table 4.2). You can hear the voiced/voiceless difference

Table 4.1. Guide to pronunciation of English sounds

Sound	Key word	Most frequent spelling	% of the time	Other spellings
/ĭ/	it	i	66%	y
/t/	tip	t	97%	tt, ed
/p/	pig	p	96%	pp
/n/	nose	n	97%	nn, kn, gn
/s/	see	s	73%	c, ss
/ă/	at	a	96%	ae
/l/	lip	l	91%	ll
/d/	did	d	98%	dd, ed
/f/	fly	f	78%	ff, ph, lf
/h/	him	h	98%	wh
/g/	get	g	88%	gg, gh
/ŏ/	on	o	79%	aw, augh, ough
/k/	kit	c	73%	cc, k, ck, lk, q
/m/	man	m	94%	mm
/r/	rat	r	97%	rr, wr
/b/	bin	b	97%	bb
/ĕ/	elm	e	91%	ea, e_e
/y/	yet	y	44%	l
/j/	jar	g	88%	j, dg
/u/	us	u	92%	o, ou
/w/	wet	w	92%	u
/v/	vet	v	99.5%	f (of)
/z/	zoom	z	23%	zz, s
/th/	that	th	100%	--
/ch/	chill	ch	55%	t
/sh/	shop	sh	26%	ti, ssi, s, si, sci
/zh/	sure	si	49%	s, ss, z
/hw/	wheel	wh	100%	--
/ng/	song	n	41%	ng
/oi/	boil	oi	62%	oy
/ou/	house	ou	56%	ow
/oo/	soon	oo	38%	u, o, ou, u_e, ew, ue
/oo/	book	oo	31%	u, ou, o, ould
/ā/	aim	a	45%	a_e, ai, ay, ea
/ē/	ear	e	70%	y, ea, ee, ie, e_e, ey, i, ei
/ī/	ice	i_e	69%	i, igh, u, ie, y_e
/ō/	oat	o	100%	o_e, ow, oa, oe
/yoo/	use	u	69%	u_e, ew, ue
/th/	the	th	100%	--
/ô/	ball	o		a, au, aw, ough, augh
/û/	bird	er	40%	ir, ur
/ä/	car	a	89%	aw, aa, ah
/a/	alarm	a	24%	e, i, o, u
/â/	chair	a	29%	are, air

Source: *Research-Based Methods of Reading Instruction Grades K—3 (p. 36-37)*, by Sharon Vaughn & Sylvia Linan-Thompson. Alexandria, VA: ASCD. © 2004 by ASCD. Adapted with permission. Learn more about ASCD at www.ascd.org

Table 4.2. Voiced and unvoiced letter sounds

Voiced	Unvoiced
/b/	/p/
/v/	/f/
/d/	/t/
/z/	/s/
/k/	/g/
/th/ (this)	/th/ (think)
/zh/	/sh/
/j/	/ch/

in at least two ways. First, you can put two fingers gently on your Adam's apple as you say these words. Second, you can cover your ears and feel that the sound /b/ in *bat* has more of an explosion in your head. Keep in mind the guiding principle: teach the sounds that are similar at least 3 weeks apart, and when you do teach them, teach how the sounds differ. Explicitly model how the formation of the mouth is different for individual sounds, where the tongue is placed, whether or not the mouth is open or closed, and if the sound is voiced or unvoiced.

For example, think of the short vowel /ĕ/, as in *Ed*. Look in a mirror and say /e/. Notice how your mouth forms a tight smile, similar to how a horse looks with a bit in its mouth. All these associations help students distinguish the sound of /ĕ/ from /ĭ/ and other vowel sounds. Louisa Moats has a helpful demonstration of the way the mouth forms various sounds. The Speech Sounds of English video is available from http://store.cambiumlearning.com. You can watch an abbreviated video of Dr. Moats working with a kindergarten teacher pronouncing letter sounds at http://www.readingrockets.org/teaching/reading101/soundsofspeech.[23]

You will also use your informal classroom observations and formal assessment data to help you know what level of phonological awareness children have mastered in order to provide instruction at the "just right" level in the phonological hierarchy of skills. This notion of "just right," which is akin to the Goldilocks principle, is essential in scaffolding instruction. In other words, if the activity is too easy, a child may be bored; if it is too difficult, a child may not be able to complete the task and may become frustrated. Instruction might just be right.

One group of children (with weaker skills) may sort objects or pictures into only two categories: words that start with /sss/ or words that start with /mmm/. (So, Sally might be the "boss" of all things that start with /sss/, and Mary might be the "boss" of all things that start with /mmm/.) Another group might be sorting pictures into four or five categories, such as those words with the same initial sound, final sound, medial sound, or by number of phonemes. Another group of children might be playing a more open-ended game like an "I spy treasure hunt" in the classroom. "I spy with my eye something starting with /p/—what is it?"

BOX 4.2. A good place to start is to teach children to sort words by starting sounds. This concept should involve activities that address a continuum from easier to more difficult skills.

Their objective would be to find as many things (paint, pencil, paper, etc.) in the classroom that start with the target sound.

Prominent researchers in the area of phonological awareness consistently recommend using a systematic and explicit direct instruction approach, which leaves little to chance.[24] You should clearly state in your lesson plan the objective for your instruction in measurable terms. In other words, "By the end of this week, Selina will correctly blend all five of the following words when presented orally in onset rime (/c/ /at/; /d/ /og/; /g/ /oat/; /b/ /ear/; and /b/ /ug/)." Of course, you will want to sequence your phonological skills from easiest to more difficult so the first steps will involve larger chunks of words, such as the onset rimes rather than individual phonemes, and you can provide pictures to support the memory of the animals. Your lesson plans should also include a cycle of scaffolding that includes modeling (I do), guided practice (We do), and finally independent practice (You do).[25] This cycle includes multiple exposures for practice and cumulative review, and the last step allows you to monitor and give immediate corrective feedback to ensure mastery.

Foorman and Torgesen[26] argued persuasively that small group instruction is a better vehicle for systematic instruction than a whole class setting because interventions can be more targeted, or individualized, to the students' needs. You can group your students homogenously so that groups have similar levels of skills (revisit Figure 4.1). That way, your students will not only learn, but also practice skills, at the "just right" level.

Catts (1995)[27] offers guidance about what makes activities, or tasks, easier or more difficult. The first factor related to difficulty is now familiar to you; it is the **size of the spoken sound(s).** The bigger the chunk of text, the easier it is to segment, blend, or delete. For example, it is much easier to blend *cow* and *boy* to make *cowboy* than it is to blend the /c/ and /ow/ to make *cow*.

The second factor should also be familiar; it is the **complexity of the linguistic skill** required. As you see in the phonological continuum in Figure 4.1, manipulating phonemes is the hardest task because it requires more memory. For most children, rhyming is the easiest. For example, it is challenging to think that *tack* said backwards is *cat*: it is much easier to rhyme *cat* and *hat*.

The third factor that makes an activity more difficult is the **number of units in the word.** For example, you are when teaching phonemic blending and segmenting, it is easier to segment a two-phoneme word such as *at* /a/ /t/, than a five-phoneme word, such as *scratch* /s/ /c/ /r/ /a/ /tch/. A silly example of a very challenging syllabic segmentation task would be to segment the word *supercalafragalisticexbealadocious*. That is obviously much harder than to segment the syllables in *popcorn* or *birthday*. So, how many syllables are there in that long word above? There are 14 syllables in /su/ /per/ /cal/ /a/ /frag/ /a/ /lis/ /tic/ /ex/ /be/ /al/ /a/ /do/ /cious/.

A fourth factor that impacts task difficulty is the **position of the sound within a word.** It is developmentally easiest to hear the first sound in a word, next is the last sound, and most challenging is the medial sound. Of course, hearing the individual sounds within a blend, as in the /s/ /t/ /r/ in *street*, is also complex.

A fifth factor that impacts difficulty of blending, and segmenting particularly, is whether the **sound is a continuous or is a stop sound.** Continuous sounds may be held or hummed (e.g., the /mmm/ or /sss/ sounds), whereas a stop sound may not (e.g., /t/ or /c/). So you can see for yourself that it is easier to blend continuous sounds like the /mmm/ /aaa/ /nnn/ than it is to blend /t/ /o/ /p/. Say each sound in *man* as you hold up a finger; then close your three fingers as you blend them together to pronounce the whole word *man*. Now try *top*.

BOX 4.3. The National Reading Panel found that phonemic awareness training combined with letter–sound training was most effective.[28]

Because working with sounds requires a child to remember the sounds and may tax short-term memory, the last factor that reduces difficulty is to make the sounds and words, or the process, more *concrete*. Having children choose between two objects is easier than having them provide examples on their own (e.g., Which word starts with the last sound in *bus*? Is it *sun* or *moon*?). Selecting from pictures and objects simplifies the task further: "Show me a picture of a word that rhymes with cat; is it hat or ball?" Using manipulatives to demonstrate is also a good strategy to reduce the working memory load. "Pick the object that starts with /f/. Yes, *fork* begins with /f/."

Finally, once students understand the concept of phonological awareness, it is time to use letters to stand for sounds that are being blended and segmented.

Let us consider now how you might keep these factors in mind while you learn how to use Elkonin boxes or Say-It-Move-It Cards (see Figure 4.2) to support students' ability to blend and segment.[29] We will use the term Benita Blachman and others have used for this strategy: "Say it and move it."[30]

You do: As you teach your students to blend and segment sounds in a word, you model exactly how to move an object, such as a plastic chip or Unifix cube, for each sound. For the lowest performing students in a first-grade classroom, the boxes might initially reflect onset–rime blending and segmenting at their independent level. You might have picture cards to help the children remember the words. Then, during the last 5 minutes of the lesson, you might want to introduce individual boxes to teach phonemic blending and segmenting. Because this is more difficult, you should anticipate doing a lot of modeling. If needed, this activity could be also further scaffolded, or supported, by providing a limited set of pictures of the animals so that students are selecting words from a set number of known objects. This is an example: "Here is a pig and here is a cow. Let's see if you can name my animal. Ready? /c/ /ow/. Good, you heard *cow*. Now watch me use my blocks to show each sound in *cow*. (Move one block to the line to represent /c/ and another block as you say the sound /ow/.) Your turn to try with me. Now, girls, do it by yourselves. Boys, your turn to do by yourselves."

In contrast, for a higher performing first-grade group, the activity with the say-it-move-it boxes might begin with phonemic blending and segmenting, and students might not need picture supports. Instead, you provide clue words from a particular category—for example, animals. "Let's see if you can move a cube for each sound you hear me say. Then, when I ask you and give the sign, you can say my word. Ready? /p/ /i/ /g/."

Working with small homogenous groups will allow you to provide more intensive and supportive activities than you could during whole-group instruction. In working with a small group, it is easier to see and hear if a child is struggling. In a whole group, children who do not know the answer may "sponge" or wait until someone else answers and then copy. Some children mumble, and you may not hear them well enough to distinguish the correct from incorrect pronunciations during group responses. Finally, when you give corrective feedback in a small group, it is easier to do so in an emotionally supportive fashion and to allow an individual child to practice with you until he or she masters the sound on his or her own. You may also "catch" a partially correct answer. For example:

"Selina, say the sounds in pie." Selena says the letter name P. You could say, "that's almost right, the first letter in pie is P and its sound is /p/. Say it with me /p/. Now listen to me say each sound in pie. /p/ /i/. Let's try it together…. Good and your turn…."

This cycle of my turn, our turn, your turn, or I do, we do, you do, is the scaffolding of direct instruction.

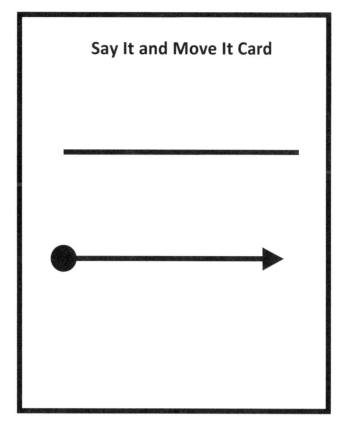

Figure 4.2. Say-It-Move-It card. (From Blachman, B., Ball, E.W., Black, R., & Tangel, D.M. [2000]. *Road to the code: A phonological awareness program for young children.* Baltimore: Paul H. Brookes Publishing Co.; reprinted by permission.)

You might be asking yourself, what activities might the other students be able to do independently while I work with a small group at a teacher table? Successful teachers use a variety of grouping strategies. You could strategically pair a high- and low-performing child for peer practice, or you could form small same-ability groups and vary the activities that you assign to them during center times. Be sure that the activities in the learning centers provide practice for concepts already introduced. Avoid creating center content that the children do not already understand. One recommended resource for center activities and for improving instructional routines may be found at the Florida Center for Reading Research web site (http://www.fcrr.org).[31] An example of a simple phonological awareness game is "Go fish." Introduce this first at a teacher table, and then place in a student center. Students have cards with pictures and try to collect other pictures of objects that start with the same sound. For example, you ask: "I have a picture of a bus. Do you have a picture of anything that starts with /b/ like bus?"

For older students who have still not developed phonemic awareness, you may look for programs that are multisensory or that offer supportive manipulatives such as color-coded squares to help students distinguish vowel and consonant sounds as they practice blending and segmenting. Teaching how to name and write letters and to decode and write simple words will reciprocally contribute to understanding how to hear, manipulate, read, and write the sounds in spoken language.

HOW DO YOU DEVELOP INSTRUCTIONAL PLANS THAT INCORPORATE STANDARDS AND EVIDENCE-BASED STRATEGIES?

This section illustrates sample lessons for several aspects of phonemic awareness development. These brief samples will give you an idea of what instruction in phonemic awareness should look like and sound like. For most students, 10–15 minutes a day in kindergarten and

1. Explicit instruction with modeling.
2. Systematic instruction with scaffolding.
3. Multiple opportunities for students to respond and practice.
4. Ongoing progress monitoring.
5. Immediate corrective feedback.

Figure 4.3. Features of effective instruction. (*Source*: Vaughn Gross Center for Reading and Language Arts, 2007.)

the beginning of first grade is sufficient. If you are teaching students who need intensive work in this area, it is suggested that you obtain more information by selecting an evidence-based program, watching videos of teachers and students completing phonemic awareness activities, and observing other teachers. A list of resources that can support you in this area is in Appendix C.

It is known that children learn best when the five features of effective instruction are utilized. Look for these as you review the following activities (Figure 4.3).

Note, this is a good time to wear your rabbit ears!

Skill: Identifying Initial Sounds

Same or Different: Thumbs UP if the same, Thumbs DOWN if different.

Say a pair of words, emphasizing the first sound. Ask the student to indicate if the sounds are the same or different. Sample words: *sun* and *sat, man* and *me, lip* and *loss, tip* and *lip, song* and *sang, cap* and *nap.*

You Do: *Listen: I am going to say some words. If they start with the same sound, I will put my thumb up, like this. If they start with different sounds, I will put my thumb down.* Model. *Here are the words: ssssssun, sssssssat. My thumb is up! They both start with ssss. Say the words after me: ssssun, ssssat. Do they start with the same sound? Yes! Thumbs up! What sound? Sssss.*

Skill: Identifying Final Sounds

You can do the same activity as above but concentrate on the end sounds, using words such as *dog* and *bag, walk* and *talk, ran* and *rat, sip* and *sock, match* and *catch.*

You can vary the activity by having the students sort objects or pictures by their initial sound or the final sound. For example: A final sound sort basket for /p/ and /n/ could contain: *top, cup, cap, clip, car, jar, can, pan.*

Skill: Identifying Medial Sounds

Prepare a list of words that you say to the students. The students indicate if the medial sound is the same or different. They could use a phone to amplify the sounds of letters.

When they have learned all the short vowel sounds, you can play a sorting game. Have the short vowels posted on the board (you can use the sticky board for this activity, see Appendix A).

Start with a review of the sounds. Use the reminding word used in your program. Say the letter name, the reminding word or key word, and letter sound.

Let us review the short vowel sounds. Ready? All together: a apple, /ă/, e Ed, /ĕ/, i igloo, /ĭ/, o octopus, /ŏ/, u up, /ŭ/.

Listen for the vowel in the middle of these words. Baaat. What word? Yes, bat. What sound? Yes, /ă/. Put the word *bat* in the /ă/ column. Continue with additional words, including *lap, slap, cap, pest, bell, pet, bit, sit, mitt, sock, cot, mop, sun, gum, pun.* Be sure to mix up the words!

Skill: Blending Phonemes into Words (You Will Need a Turtle Puppet for this Version!)

Tell me, boys and girls, how does a turtle walk? Slowly or quickly? Yes, very slowly. If a turtle could talk, how do you think it would talk? Yes, very slowly. We're going to talk slowly like a pretend turtle might talk, and Tommy Turtle, my puppet friend, is going to help us.

Listen. Tommy Turtle is going to say three sounds. Listen for the beginning sound, the middle sound, and the final sound. See if you know the word Tommy is saying. Tommy will talk very slowly.

Mmmmmmmooooommmmmm. What word? Yes, mom! Let's try another one. Tommy says: /p/ /i/. What word? Yes, pie! Continue with additional words. If a student has difficulty, repeat the exercise, more explicitly. Use an easier word. For example: *Listen, Johnny. The sounds are mmmm-mmmaaaaaannnnn. What word? Yes, man! Everyone, what word! Yes, man.*

Skill: Segmenting Words into Phonemes

This time, let's help Tommy learn some new words. We have to say the words very slowly, enunciating each sound, so Tommy can understand. Then, we'll say the word fast. Let's try one.

The word is man. What word? Yes, man. Say it slowly: mmmmmaaaaannnnn. Say it fast! Man! Let's try another one: seat. What word? Yes, seat. Say it slowly: sssseeeeeet. Say it fast! Seat!

Continue with additional words, allowing students to take individual turns as well as responding all together.

Skill: Elision (Eliminating Sounds)

This is a more difficult skill as it requires a higher level of phonemic awareness. When you are doing these exercises, be sure you say the letter sounds, not the names.

Today, we're going to play a game. I'll say a word and then ask you to take away a sound. Listen as I do it first: man. I'll take away the /m/ [say the sound, not the letter name]. What's left? Yes, /an/. Let's try another one. Say slip. Take away the /s/. What word is left? Yes, lip! Continue with additional words such as *gold/old, mast/mat.*

Skill: Substituting Sounds

This activity uses all the skills your students have practiced. Usually, it takes kindergartners about 6–8 weeks to be able to do this skill.

Listen. I'm going to say a word, and then I'll ask you to substitute, or use a different sound, for some sounds. Let's try it. Everyone, say man. Say it again, slowly: mmmmaaaaan. Take away the /m/ and put /p/ [say the sounds, not the letter names]. What word? Yes, pan. Say pan again. Take away the /n/ and put /t/. What word? Yes, pat! Now be careful with this one. Say pat. Take away the /a/ and put /i/. What word? Yes, pit! Great job listening!

Figure 4.4 is a sample lesson plan incorporating these features with the "I do, we do, you do" model of instruction. You may use this lesson, adjusted for your student, when you tutor.

Kindergarten or first grade small group intervention

Note: The text in italics is what you could say verbatim. When you first begin teaching, you may want to write down every word you are going to say. Later, once you have learned the patterns and routines, you do not need to write down each word.

Date: <u>1/10/12</u>   Teacher: <u>Ms. Wilson</u>

Target students: Five students—Jimmy, Kaitlin, Meagan, Beth, Wilber

(Whole class or small group? Identify specific students who need differentiated instruction.)

Objective of the lesson: The students will be able to blend and segment three-phoneme words using Say-It-Move-It charts. Targeted words: *dog, cat, bird, top, sun.*

Required resources: Chips and Say-It-Move-It charts for each student; list of words to teach.

Review of previous learning: Review of segmentation of two-phoneme words: *at, it, in, so.*

Let's review words that we segmented yesterday. Remember, to segment means to pull apart. Everyone, say at. Yes, at. Now let's say the sounds of at. Fingers up. Say /a/. Raise one finger. Now say /t/. Yes, /t/. Second finger up. Let's say both sounds in at. /a/ /t/. Yes! Now blend the two sounds together to form a word. What word? Yes! At.

(Continue reviewing the next three words *it, in, so* at a faster pace.)

I do: Segmenting and blending three-phoneme words.

Teacher models skill to be taught using

• explicit instruction with modeling

• systematic instruction with scaffolding

Today, we are going to learn how to blend and segment words with three sounds. Listen: cat. Now, I am going to say the sounds in cat slowly, and for each sound, I slide one chip down onto this line. Watch me. /c/ [slide a chip]. /a/ [slide a chip]. /t/ [slide a chip]. Now I'll say the word fast: cat.

We do: Students blend and segment words with teacher guidance.

Teacher guides instruction focusing on

• Immediate corrective feedback

• Providing multiple opportunities for students to respond and practice

(Present each child with an Elkonin or "Say-It-Move-It" card and three chips.)

Try one with me. Everyone, say this word: cat. Yes, cat. What is the first sound you hear in cat, Jimmy? Yes, /c/. Slide one chip down to the line. Let's say the word again: cat. What is the next sound, the middle sound, of cat? Meagan? Yes, /a/. Everyone, say /a/ and slide a chip down. Say the word one more time, listening for the very last sound: cat. What is the last sound in cat, everyone? Yes! /t/ is the last sound in cat. Slide a chip down to the line. What word? Cat.

Corrective feedback: [Wilber said *kit.*] *Let's try that word again. Listen. The word is cat* [emphasize the /a/]. *What word? Yes, cat. Wilber, what word? Yes! Cat. Wilber, try this word: /d/ /o/ /g/. What word? Yes! Dog. Great job, everyone! Let's try some more words.*

Figure 4.4. Lesson plan template: example.

Figure 4.4. *(continued)*

(Follow the model for two more words, *bird* and *top*.)

You do: Students practice blending and segmenting.

Students practice skill independently, in pairs, or in small groups.

Practice words: *sun*, *leaf*, *road*.

Try the next one by yourself. The word is sun. What word? Yes, sun. Say the word quietly and move a chip down for each sound.

If the children are doing well, add additional words such as leaf and road.

Differentiation

Challenge words for accelerated students (provide them an additional chip): *tree* (3), *slip* (4).

English language learners: Avoid confusing sounds.

(When first teaching the concept of blending and segmenting phonemes, avoid letters and sounds that may be pronounced differently in the child's first language. For example, most Spanish speakers pronounce *ll* as /y/ and /v/ as /b/, so avoid words that contain the letters v, ll, and y and the sounds /v/ and /y/. Also, be cognizant that vowels in other languages may represent different phonemes. For example, the /a/ as in apple does not exist in Spanish. You can say to the child, *"In your first language* [or home language or whatever term you are to use in your district], *you pronounce the letter **a** differently than it is pronounced in English. In English the letter **a** is pronounced /a/, as in apple.*

However, if your objective is ensuring the child knows how to segment words into phonemes, do not be too concerned if the phonemes are mispronounced as long as he or she is aware of how many phonemes there are and can segment them. That is your instructional objective. Later, you can focus on the correct pronunciation of the sounds.

Additional scaffolding:

Provide a "Say-It-Move-It" card with circles for the chips and dotted lines from the circle to the bottom line so that students know exactly how to move the chips.

Try hand over hand: place your hand on the child's and guide the movement of the chips as the child says the sounds.

If the child has difficulty with identifying the sounds, go back to the first sound and ask the child to identify the first sound only. When the child has mastered identifying the first sound, ensure the child can identify the last sound and, finally, the median sound before asking the child to identify all the sounds in a three-phoneme word.

Verbally recast the procedures, and model again.

Provide additional guided practice.

Progress monitoring: Students segment and blend two out of three words.

Teacher conducts a quick assessment of student progress.

(One by one, give students a word and ask them say the individual phonemes, then to blend it into a word. Note which children are still struggling and attend to them in a 1:1 format later in the day.)

Objectives for the Next Lesson

The students will match the sounds to letters in three-phoneme words and will blend the letters to form a word.

SUMMARY

Phonological awareness and especially phonemic awareness are precursors to effective reading and writing acquisition. Generally, a few minutes a day of direct instruction in phonemic awareness in grades PreK–1 is sufficient for most children to acquire the necessary skills. Once children can segment and blend three-phoneme words, begin to match the sounds to letters. Spending time on these skills in the early grades may prevent reading and spelling difficulties later.

When older students are not reading on level, teachers may need to assess whether the students' early skills in phonological and phonemic awareness are developed. It is not uncommon in intensive or remedial classes for fourth-, fifth-, or sixth-grade students to spend some time going back to this very early stage in reading development and building the missing concepts. You will want to teach it differently, of course, and associate letters with the sounds.

Students who are English language learners must understand phonemic awareness also. Whether or not they learn the concept in their home language or in English, knowledge of phonemic awareness will transfer to reading English and will support their reading achievement.

Finally, remember that difficulty with phonological skills, particularly phonemic awareness, is generally the most challenging for students with dyslexia and reading disabilities. It is crucial that these children learn this skill so that they can to learn to read.

APPLICATION ASSIGNMENTS

In-Class Assignments

1. With a partner, explain the concepts phonological awareness, phonemic awareness, and phonics. Clarify how they are different and provide examples of each.
2. Find a list of the 44–45 phonemes in the English language (the number differs depending on whether or not the schwa is included). Write the phonemes on sticky notes, and sort them into various combinations as follows: voiced and unvoiced sounds; continuous and stop sounds; sounds that are different in Spanish than English and sounds that are the same in both languages. A list of English phonemes is available at http://www.lancsngfl.ac.uk/curriculum/literacy/lit_site/lit_sites/phonemes_001/. A comparison between English and Spanish sounds is available at http://www.colorincolorado.org/background/capitalizing?theme=print.
3. Go to the Florida Center on Reading Research web site (www.fcrr.org) and download an activity that teaches phonemic awareness in kindergarten. Make the activity, and practice it with a partner.

Tutoring Assignments

1. Assess your student on his or her ability to segment and blend three-phoneme words using a list of words from the core reading program or from an assessment your instructor provides.
2. Select, prepare, and teach phonemic awareness using an activity found on the FCRR web site that is appropriate to the needs of your student. Assess your student's progress, and plan what you need to do next in phonemic awareness.
3. Create a word sort for older students who struggle to hear sounds in words because they confuse voiced and voiceless pairs (e.g., /f/ and /v/).
4. Select a children's book with rhyming words and/or alliteration that you could read aloud. Make a list of all the rhyming words and all the alliterative phrases. Read the story to your student, emphasizing rhymes and alliteration.
5. Plan a follow-up lesson systematically and explicitly, teaching the concept of rhyming and the concept of alliteration, using the lesson plan format provided. Be prepared to share the lesson plan and your reflections about the lesson you taught in class.

Homework Assignments

1. Create a graphic organizer illustrating the relationship of phonological awareness and phonemic awareness (Hint: you may NOT use the umbrella concept!).
2. Go to the web site of The International Dyslexia Association, and read the Fact Sheet on the definition of dyslexia (http://www.interdys.org/FactSheets.htm). Write a two-paragraph explanation for parents of the role phonemic awareness plays in dyslexia.

ENDNOTES

1. Pig Latin is a language game of alterations played in English. To form the pig Latin form of an English word, the first consonant (or consonant cluster) is moved to the end of the word, and an *ay* is affixed (for example, *pig* yields *ig-pay* and *computer* yields *omputer-cay*). The reference to Latin is a deliberate misnomer, as it is simply a form of jargon, used only for its English connotations as a "strange and foreign-sounding language" (http://en.wikipedia.org/wiki/Pig_Latin).
2. Yopp & Stapleton (2008); Gerston et al. (2007); August & Shanhan (2006).
3. Al Otaiba, Kosanovich, & Torgesen (2012).
4. Ehri (2000); Snow, Burns, & Griffin (1998); National Early Literacy Panel (NELP) (2008); National Reading Panel (NRP) (2000).
5. Adams (1990); Snider (1995); Snider (1997).
6. Torgesen (2000).
7. Moats (2005/2006).
8. Ehri (2000); Apel, Wolter, & Masterson (2006); Ehri, (2002).
9. NELP (2008); Lonigan, Schatschneider, & Westberg (2008).
10. NRP (2000).
11. Share (2011).
12. Snowling (2011); Catts & Adlof (2011).
13. Martin & Carle (1967).
14. NELP (2008).
15. Comprehensive Test of Phonological Processing (CTOPP): Wagner, Torgesen, & Rashotte (1999).
16. Test of Preschool Early Literacy (TOPEL); Lonigan et al. (2007).
17. Carta, Greenwood, Walker, & Buzhardt (2010).
18. Missal & McConnell (2004).
19. Good et al. & Kaminski (2002).
20. Phonological Awareness Literacy Screening (PALS) (1997): http://pals.virginia.edu
21. Fuchs, Fuchs, Thompson, Svenson, Yen, Otaiba et al. (2001).
22. Juel & Minden-Cupp (2000); Snider (1997).
23. The video made by L. Moats illustrating correct sound pronunciation is available from: http://www.readingrockets.org/teaching/reading101/soundsofspeech
24. Foorman & Torgesen (2001); Brady (2011).
25. Archer & Hughes (2011).
26. Foorman & Torgesen (2001).
27. Catts, Wilcox, Wood-Jackson, Larrivee, & Scott, (1997)
28. National Reading Panel Report (2000).
29. Elkonin (1973).
30. Blachman et al. (2000).
31. Florida Center for Reading Research, http://www.fcrr.org

REFERENCES

Adams, M.J. (1990). *Beginning to read: Thinking and learning about print.* Cambridge, MA: MIT Press.

Al Otaiba, S., Kosanovich, M., & Torgesen, J. (2012). Assessment and instruction in phonemic awareness and word recognition skills. In: A.G. Kamhi & H.W. Catts *Language and reading disabilities,* 3rd edition. Needham Heights, MA: Allyn & Bacon.

Apel, K., Wolter, J.A., & Masterson, J.J. (2006). Effects of phonotactic and orthotactic probabilities during fast mapping on 5-year-olds' learning to spell. *Developmental Neuropsychology, 29,* 21–42.

Archer, A. & Hughes, C. (2011). Explicit instruction: Effective and efficient teaching. New York: The Guilford Press.

August, D., & Shanahan, T. (Eds.). (2006). *Developing literacy in second-language learners. Report of the National Literacy Panel on Language-Minority Children and Youth.* New York: Routledge.

Blachman, B., Ball, E.W., Black, R., & Tangel, D.M. (2000). Road to the code: A phonological awareness program for young children. Baltimore: Paul H. Brookes Publishing Co.

Brady, S.A. (2011). *Efficacy of phonics teaching for reading outcomes: Indications from post-NRP research.* In Brady, S.A., Braze, D., & Fowler, C.A. Explaining individual differences in reading: Theory and evidence. New York: Psychology Press.

Carta, J., Greenwood, C., Walker, D., &, Buzhardt, J. (2010). *Using IGDIs: Monitoring Progress and Improving Intervention for Infants and Young Children.* Baltimore: Paul H. Brookes Publishing Company

Catts, H.W. & Adlof, S. (2011). Phonological and other language deficits associated with dyslexia. In S.A. Brady, D. Braze, & C.A. Fowler. Explaining individual differences in reading: Theory and evidence. New York: Psychology Press.

Catts, H.W., Wilcox, K.A., Wood-Jackson, C., Larrivee, L.S., & Scott, V.G. (1997). Toward an understanding of phonological awareness. In C.K. Leong & R.M. Joshi (Eds.), *Cross-language studies of learning to read and spell: Phonologic and orthographic processing.* Dordecht, The Netherlands: Kluwer Academic Press.

Ehri, L.C. (2000). Learning to read and learning to spell: Two sides of a coin. *Topics in Language Disorders, 20,* 19–36.

Ehri, L.C. (2002). Phases of acquisition in learning to read words and implications for teaching. In: R. Stainthorp, & P. Tomlinson (Eds.), *Learning and teaching reading* (pp. 7–28). Leicester, UK: The British Psychological Society.

Elkonin, D.B. (1973). Reading in the U.S.S.R. In J. Downing (Ed.), *Comparative reading.* (pp. 68–88). New York: MacMillan.

Foorman, B.R., & Torgesen, J. (2001). Critical elements of classroom and small-group instruction promote reading success in all children. *Learning Disabilities Research & Practice, 16*, 203–212.

Fuchs, D., Fuchs, L.S., Thompson, A., Svenson, E., Yen, L., Otaiba, S.A., et al. (2001). Peer assisted learning strategies in reading. *Remedial and Special Education, 22*(1), 15–21.

Gerston, R., Baker, S.K., Shanahan, T., Linan-Thompson, S., Collins, P., & Scarcella, R. (2007). *Effective literacy and English language instruction for English learners in the elementary grades: A practice guide* (NCEE: 2007-4011). Washington, DC: National Center for Education Evaluation and Regional Assistance, Institute of Education Sciences, U.S. Department of Education. Available online at http://ies.ed.gov/ncee.

Good, R.H., & Kaminski, R.A. (Eds.). (2002). *Dynamic indicators of basic early literacy skills* (6th ed.). Eugene, OR: Institute for Development of Educational Achievement.

Invernizzi, M. (1997). *PALS: Phonological Awareness Literacy Screening.* Charlottesville, VA: PALS Marketplace.

Juel, C., & Minden-Cupp, C. (2000). Learning to read words: Linguistic units and instructional strategies. *Reading Research Quarterly, 35*, 458–492.

Lonigan, C.J., Schatschneider, C., & Westberg, L. (2008). Identification of children's skills and abilities linked to later outcomes in reading, writing, and spelling. In: *National Early Literacy Panel, Developing early literacy: Report of the National Early Literacy Panel* (pp. 55–106). Washington, DC: National Institute for Literacy. Retrieved June 12, 2011, from http://www.nifl.gov/earlychildhood/NELP/NELPreport.html

Lonigan, C.J., Wagner, R., Torgesen, J.K., & Rashotte, C. (2007). *TOPEL: Test of preschool early literacy.* Austin, TX: ProEd.

Martin, B., & Carle, E. (1967) *Brown bear, brown bear, what do you see?* New York: Harcourt Brace & Co.

Missal, K.N., & McConnell, S.R. (2004). *Psychometric characteristics of individual growth & development indicators: picture naming, rhyming, and alliteration.* Technical Report for U.S. Department of Education, Improving Preschoolers' Reading Outcomes by Measuring Instruction and Classroom Environments. University of Minnesota, Center for Early Education and Development.

Moats, L.C. (Winter 2005/06). How spelling supports reading: And why it is more regular and predictable than you think. *American Educator*, 12(22), 42–43.

Moats, L.C. The sounds of speech. Reading 101: What you should know. Retrieved August 18, 2011, from http://readingrockets.org/teaching/reading101/soundsofspeech/

National Early Literacy Panel. (2008). *Developing early literacy: Report of the National Early Literacy Panel.* Washington, DC: National Center for Family Literacy.

National Reading Panel. (2000). *Teaching children to read: An evidence-based assessment of the scientific research literature on reading and its implications for reading instruction* (National Institute of Health Pub. No. 00-4769). Washington, DC: National Institute of Child Health and Human Development.

Share, D.L. (2011). On the role of phonology in reading acquisition: The self-teaching hypothesis. In S.A. Brady, D. Braze, & C.A. Fowler. Explaining individual differences in reading: Theory and evidence. New York: Psychology Press.

Snider, V.E. (1995). A primer on phonemic awareness: What it is, why it's important, and how to teach it. *School Psychology Review, 24*, 443–455.

Snider, V.E. (1997). The relationship between phonemic awareness and later reading achievement. *Journal of Educational Research, 90*, 203–211.

Snow, C.E., Burns, M.S., & Griffin, P. (Eds.) (1998). *Preventing reading difficulties in young children.* Washington, DC: National Academy Press.

Snowling, M.J. (2011). Beyond phonological deficits: Sources of individual differences in reading disability. In S.A. Brady, D. Braze, & C.A. Fowler (2011). Explaining individual differences in reading: Theory and evidence. New York: Psychology Press.

Torgesen, J.K. (2000). Individual differences in response to early interventions in reading: The lingering problem of treatment resisters. *Learning Disabilities Research & Practice, 15*, 55–64.

Vaughn Gross Center for Reading and Language Arts. (2007). *Features of effective instruction.* Austin: University of Texas System/Texas Education Agency.

Vaughn, S., & Linan-Thompson, S. (2004). *Research-based methods of reading instruction, grades K–3* (p.90). Alexandria, VA: Association for Supervision and Curriculum Development.

Wagner, R.K., Torgesen, J.K., & Rashotte, C.A. (1999). *CTOPP: Comprehensive test of phonological processes.* Austin, TX: PRO-ED Publishing, Inc.

Yopp, H., & Stapleton, L. (2008). Offering or limiting opportunities: Teachers' roles and approaches to English-language learners' participation in literacy activities. *The Reading Teacher, 61*, 216–225.

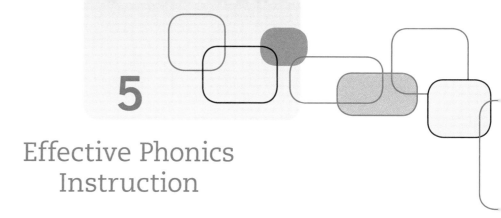

5

Effective Phonics Instruction

by Martha C. Hougen

In January, a local elementary school analyzed middle-of-the-year student benchmark data. They discovered some interesting patterns. One involved two first-grade teachers, Ms. Jones and Ms. Smith. Both teachers work hard, staying late planning lessons together. Both use the same reading program and feel they are following it as intended. Both care for their students and have created welcoming classrooms. However, the performance of their students differs greatly. Ms. Jones' students are meeting expectations, and all but one student did well on the recent benchmark test. The student who is still developing in phonics recently moved from another school.

On the other hand, most of Ms. Smith's students are at risk for reading difficulties. Two thirds are not yet phonemically aware of the sequence of sounds in words. Very few are reading basic, regular words.

What, the teachers and their principal wondered, could be the difference?

The second pattern that came to light was the performance of fifth- and sixth-grade students. Most of the students performed adequately in earlier grades, but in the upper grades, their reading scores plummeted. The students had difficulty comprehending grade-level texts, and their vocabulary was deficient. The teachers and principal wondered why these students lost ground in reading.

This chapter addresses a probable reason for the disparate reading scores in the first grade classrooms and why the reaching achievement scores of older students dropped. The students did not have a strong foundation in phonics.

In 2001, Jim Collins wrote a book entitled *Good to Great: Why Some Companies Make the Leap and Others Don't.*[1] This chapter addresses a related conundrum in education: what makes some teachers merely good while others are truly great? This text wants to help you become a good, effective beginning teacher who can develop into a truly great, super-effective teacher! The ability to teach phonics well is an important step to becoming a truly great teacher of literacy.

Note: Throughout this chapter, letter sounds will be denoted between slashes, like this: /a/. Words used as examples will be in italics, *like this*. The phonetic alphabet or dictionary system will be used to illustrate sounds, not the International Phonetic Alphabet (IPA). The IPA represents all the sounds of all the world's languages, and it is too detailed for our purposes at this time.

Objectives: After studying this chapter, you will be able to do the following:

1. Assess the phonics skills students have learned and identify what they need to learn next.
2. Describe the stages of word recognition.
3. Explain terms such as grapho-phonemic correspondence, digraphs, diphthongs, and blends.
4. Demonstrate how to explicitly and systematically teach phonics.
5. Define and provide examples of words or word parts that illustrate the six types of syllables.
6. Explain and provide examples of how knowledge of morphology enhances word reading.
7. Apply basic rules to divide words into syllables.
8. Demonstrate how to teach an effective phonics lesson, implementing the features of effective instruction.

WHAT IS PHONICS? WHY IS IT IMPORTANT? WHAT DOES THE RESEARCH SAY ABOUT IT?

Phonics is the study of the relationships between grapheme (letter combinations) and phoneme (individual sounds) relationships. It is a method of teaching students to decode words, learning how to take print and convert it to its spoken form and to take the spoken form and convert it to the written form (encoding).[2]

The Report of the National Reading Panel (NRP) reviewed the relevant scientifically based research on how to teach beginning reading skills and concluded that systematic and explicit phonics instruction is most effective for young children and for older students who struggle to learn to read.[3] Such instruction prevents reading failure and improves comprehension for all students. The research since the publication of the NRP supports the conclusion that systematic, explicit instruction in decoding is more effective than other approaches, for all students.[1]

Phonics is important because, as researchers have demonstrated, most students who enter school with limited phonological awareness and weak initial alphabetic awareness, such as print awareness and an understanding of how letters stand for sounds, have a more difficult time acquiring reading skills.[4] Sadly, more than a third of fourth graders performed below basic on the reading portion of the 2009 National Assessment of Educational Progress, and minority students demonstrated the most difficulty (e.g., 58% of Blacks and 54% of Hispanics at fourth grade performed below basic).[5] Many students, primarily those from poor and minority homes, enter school with significant deficits in vocabulary and background knowledge that make it difficult for them to comprehend text that places heavy demands in these areas.[6] As will be discussed later in this text, one reason older students experience deficits in vocabulary and comprehension skills is because they do not read very much. The primary reason many students do not read very much is because it is so hard for them to decipher the words—they have not mastered phonics—and reading is hard and not enjoyable for them. Therefore, it is our responsibility as teachers to ensure that our students master the basic code of their language early in their school careers.

Many students struggle to acquire early word reading skills because of insufficient experience with letters, print, and language in their preschool environment. This lack of exposure to the prerequisites of reading limits the ability of these students to make the most of their early reading instruction.[7] Far too often, this early gap only increases across the years. Therefore, as a future teacher, you can assume that at least one in three (and likely more) of your students will struggle to learn to read proficiently. It is vital that you know how to help all of your students acquire a firm foundation in phonics so that they can learn to read well.

WHAT SHOULD STUDENTS KNOW AND BE ABLE TO DO AT SPECIFIC GRADE LEVELS?

Some students will enter your class knowing some or all of the letters and sounds; other students will know none. It is up to you to teach the letter names and sounds during kindergarten. Once students have the concept of phonemic awareness and can segment and blend three-phoneme words, they are ready to put the sound with the appropriate letter.

The University of Oregon, Center on Teaching and Learning, has outlined which skills students need to learn at each grade, K–3.[8] Study this chart; each skill will be discussed and an instructional model provided in this chapter (Figure 5.1).

The Common Core State Standards (CCSS), as well as other standards referenced in the resources, provide a guide to teaching phonics. Figure 5.2 lists some of the Common Core State Standards for first-grade phonics.[9] The CCSS emphasize phonics in first grade as it is considered the most crucial year to learn basic phonics. Indeed, future reading achievement depends upon students receiving a strong phonics foundation in first grade.[10]

As each step in teaching phonics is discussed, examples are provided to help you "see" and "hear" exactly how to teach the skill. Videos and other texts that illustrate how to teach these skills are referenced. Note how the features of effective instruction are applied in each lesson.

To develop the alphabetic principle across grades K–3, students need to learn two essential skills:

1. **Letter-sound correspondences**: comprised initially of individual letter sounds and progresses to more complex letter combinations.
2. **Word reading**: comprised initially of reading simple CVC words and progresses to compound words, multi-syllabic words, and sight words.

Kindergarten Skills

- **Letter-sound correspondence**: identifies and produces the most common sound associated with individual letters
- **Decoding**: blends the sounds of individual letters to read one-syllable words.
  - When presented with the word fan the student will say "/fffaaannn/, fan."
- **Sight word reading**: Recognizes and reads words by sight (e.g., I, was, the, of).

First Grade Skills

- **Letter-sound and letter-combination knowledge**: produces the sounds of the most common letter sounds and combinations (e.g., th, sh, ch, ing).
- **Decoding**: sounds out and reads words with increasing automaticity, including words with consonant blends (e.g., mask, slip, play), letter combinations (e.g., fish, chin, bath), monosyllabic words, and common word parts (e.g., ing, all, ike).
- **Sight words**: Reads the most common sight words automatically (e.g., very, some, even, there).

Second and Third Grade Skills

- **Letter-Sound Knowledge**: produces the sounds that correspond to frequently used vowel diphthongs (e.g., ou, oy, ie) and digraphs (e.g., sh, th, ea).
- **Decoding and Word Recognition**:
  - Applies advanced phonic elements (digraphs and diphthongs), special vowel spellings, and word endings to read words.
  - Reads compound words, contractions, possessives, and words with inflectional word endings.
  - Uses word context and order to confirm or correct word reading efforts (e.g., does it make sense?).
  - Reads multi-syllabic words using syllabication and word structure (e.g., base/root word, prefixes, and suffixes) in word reading.
- **Sight word reading**: increasing number of words read accurately and automatically.

Figure 5.1. Alphabetic principle and phonics skill development. (Content reprinted with permission from the University of Oregon Center on Teaching and Learning. Copyright © University of Oregon Center on Teaching and Learning. All rights reserved. For original source see: http://reading.uoregon.edu/big_ideas/au/au_what.php)

- Know and apply grade-level phonics and word analysis skills in decoding words.
- Know the spelling–sound correspondences for common consonant digraphs (two letters that represent one sound).
- Decode regularly spelled one-syllable words.
- Know final -e and common vowel team conventions for representing long vowel sounds.
- Use knowledge that every syllable must have a vowel sound to determine the number of syllables in a printed word.
- Decode two-syllable words following basic patterns by breaking the words into syllables.
- Read words with inflectional endings.
- Recognize and read grade-appropriate irregularly spelled words.

Figure 5.2. Common Core State Standards: Grade 1 phonics. (Reprinted from http://www.corestandards. org Copyright © 2010. National Governors Association Center for Best Practices and Council of Chief State School Officers. All rights reserved.)

Phases of Word Recognition Development

Teaching phonics consists of several phases. Ehri describes five phases of word recognition development as illustrated in Table 5.1.[11]

Pre-Alphabetic Phase: This is considered by most to be the first phase of reading. During this phase, children can "read" environmental print, recognizing their favorite fast food restaurant, the grocery store, or a gas station. They are attending to outstanding features, such as golden arches or a wiggly pigly. Some children appear to read when they have memorized a book often read to them and use the pictures to help them tell the story. Most children in kindergarten enter school "reading" at this phase.

Partial Alphabetic Phase: Gradually, children move into the partial alphabetic phase. They know some letters, including the letter with which their name begins, and some sounds. Children at this phase will guess at words, using only the first letter. For example, almost every word that starts with a *d* is *dog* or *dad.* Students need to learn more letter sounds before they can decode words with any reliability.

The Full Alphabetic Phase: Students in this phase know the letters of the alphabet and the sounds of the letters. Reading may be slow and laborious, but, given time and words with regular phonetic patterns, students can decode words. This is an exciting phase as students have "unlocked" the key to reading! Typically, this occurs during first grade. Students with reading disabilities such as dyslexia may take longer to reach this stage. Students who are English language learners generally achieve this stage rather easily, given explicit instruction in the letter names and sounds. Students at this stage should be encouraged to read independently and often, reading a wide range of genres and text structures.

Table 5.1. Phases of word recognition development

Pre-alphabetic Pre-K–K	Partial alphabetic K–1	Full alphabetic K–1–2	Consolidated alphabetic 1–2	Automatic word reading 1–2–3
Makes visual connections: logos, familiar signs	Has limited knowledge of letters and sounds; utilizes context: pictures, first letter	Recognizes all letters and sounds; decodes each letter in a word; begins independent reading; less reliance on context to aid decoding	Recognizes patterns; increase in sight words; retains words in memory	Has automatic word recognition; uses strategies to decode unfamiliar words; fluency and comprehension increase

Adapted and republished by permission of Taylor & Francis Ltd, from Ehri, L.C., & McCormick, S. (1998). Phases of word learning: Implications for instruction with delayed and disabled readers. Reading and Writing Quarterly, 14, 135–163; permission conveyed through Copyright Clearance Center, Inc..

During this stage, the use of pictures and context to decode words should be discouraged. Rather, encourage your students to sound out words. Soon, students can read words that they have practiced automatically, no longer needing to sound out each letter. They have merged the orthographic (written form) characteristics of the word to its phonetic patterns. Context and pictures can be used to confirm meaning, or comprehension of the text, but should not be relied upon for decoding words.

Consolidated Alphabetic Phase: Students are reading with more automaticity and increased comprehension. They are remembering word patterns, syllables, and other units so they can recognize words more quickly. Because they are reading more efficiently, they are reading more and acquiring more vocabulary words. They can read by analogy, recognizing parts of words they know to help them decode new words. Their sight word knowledge increases. Sight words are any words a person can read automatically without having to stop and decode each letter.[12]

Automatic Phase: This is the goal for all students—to be able to read automatically, rarely having to stop to decode individual words because they automatically recognize the words. If a difficult word appears in the text, students at this phase have strategies to decode it. At this stage, all the reading processes are working together, efficiently and seamlessly. Students can begin to focus completely on comprehension.

Marilyn Adams conceptualized the development of reading skills a bit differently. She explains the ability to read as series of connections that strengthen as skills develop.[13] Speech is processed by the phonological processor, and print stimulates the orthographic processor. They both influence the semantic processor, accessing meaning of the word. These lead to the context processor to fully comprehend the text. As you gain more knowledge and experience teaching reading, read Adams' work for a deeper insight into how skilled reading is developed.

However, there is a caveat. Not all students follow these phases easily and thoroughly. That is why you must know how to teach the skills so that all students can master them. Most students master these skills by the end of second grade. However, you must be prepared to teach older students who, for myriad reasons, have not learned phonics.

The essential skills and concepts students must understand include the following:

- The alphabetic principle, enabling students to transition from phonemic awareness to acquiring phonics skills
- Automaticity naming letters (upper and lower case) and producing letter sounds
- Grapheme–phonemic relationships (sound to symbol correspondence)
- Single consonants and vowels
- Consonant digraphs and blends
- Vowel patterns including digraphs, *y* as a vowel, and variant vowel digraphs and diphthongs
- Silent consonants
- The types of syllable patterns
- Common syllable division patterns
- Multisyllabic words
- Morphemes, including prefixes, suffixes, roots, and combining forms
- Irregular words

Phonics instruction should be taught in a sequence of skills, each building upon the other, from simplest to more complex. The remainder of this section describes those discrete skills, illustrates how to teach them, and provides sample instructional scripts to illustrate several lessons. But first, we have to know what our students know so we can determine what to teach them.

HOW DO YOU ASSESS WHAT STUDENTS KNOW AND HOW MUCH THEY ARE LEARNING?

Knowing how to assess decoding, sight word reading, and fluency will be an instrumental part of your effective teaching practice. You will learn to put these assessment "pieces" together to begin to understand the strands of students' strengths and weaknesses. Refer again to the reading rope figure discussed in Chapter 2 for a visual representation of how all these strands must work tightly together to produce an effective and efficient reader.

Informal Assessments

Informal assessments and observations are invaluable. While teaching, you notice how your students are reading and informally take notes to accumulate information about their reading abilities. For example, if you are a second-grade teacher, you might note that Sally enjoys when you read to her, but that she does not seem to enjoy reading herself. She might wait to answer the teacher's question until she has heard the answer, in essence, "sponging" the answer from her classmates. You might also notice that she has begun to sit in the back of the room and avoid your eye contact when you begin to teach and to ask the class questions. Sally's behavior will trigger a part of your diagnostic radar that something is amiss. It is time to work with Sally individually, to listen to her read, and to conduct more formal assessments as appropriate.

Formal Assessments

Let us consider what type of formal assessments would help you understand more about Sally's reading behavior, her stage of reading development, and her level of performance on specific subskills of reading. It is beneficial to assess all of your students using brief screening assessments to determine who is and who is not reading on grade level.

One brief screening assessment is oral reading fluency. Fluency measures become important in about second to third grade when students have acquired a fund of word recognition skills they can be expected to apply with reasonable accuracy. You could, for example, use an assessment such as the DIBELS Oral Reading Fluency measure to learn whether Sally reads more slowly than her peers and to compare her performance to cut-points or benchmarks that correlate with risk for future reading problems.[14]

If the screener confirms that Sally is struggling, you can administer informal reading inventories, such as the Quick Phonics Screener (Figure 5.3)[15] or a spelling inventory such as the one in *Words Their Way*.[16] Criterion-referenced assessments, such as presented in the *ABCs of CBM*,[17] could provide you with specific data about the level of Sally's word reading skills so you can focus your instruction. Keep in mind that students like Sally who cannot recognize the words in text accurately and fluently are less able to focus on the meaning of the text and may be confused why their peers do not need to stop to laboriously "decode" words that are new.[18] Sally may start to guess at words, using pictures for clues. You do not want to encourage guessing! Rather, teach Sally how to sound out each letter or groups of letters to decode the word. Pictures and other context clues are useful to help with comprehension but not for initial word decoding. For example, Sally may be slow to read because she cannot decode certain syllable types or because she does not have an adequate number of grade-level sight words in her working memory, or both. Perhaps you would even use a simple inventory to test which letter–sound correspondences she does and does not know, whether she can sound out words with certain patterns, or if she is challenged by multisyllable words. You can create your own inventory or use commercial inventories such as those found in *Core Assessing Reading Multiple Measures*, 2nd edition (2008)[19] or in *Next STEPS in Literacy Instruction* (2010).[20] This knowledge will help you individualize or differentiate instruction for Sally. It is important to monitor her progress (e.g., oral reading fluency) on a weekly or biweekly basis to

---

FORM A

Skill Set 5: CVCC and CCVC Words

gosp   rimp   mant   jast   sund   clof   trin   snaf   prem   slun

Glen **sw**am pa**st** the ra**ft** in the po**nd**.

The **fr**og can **sp**in and ju**mp** and **fl**op in the sa**nd**.

Skill Set 9: Vowel Digraphs, Diphthongs, and Advanced Vowel Sounds

kray   fraw   chout   koe   poid   galt   kigh   nauf   toam   moy

The t**all** ship cr**ea**ks as it s**ai**ls on the gr**ay** waves in the storm.

He t**old** us that the wind s**oo**n bl**ew** so hard they had to sh**out**.

Can you j**oi**n us on the b**oa**t to go fishing today?

Skill Set 12: Three-Syllable Words

amputate   liberty   dominate   elastic   entertain   practical   innocent   electric   volcano   segregate

Figure 5.3. Sample items from the *Quick Phonics Screener*. (From Hasbrouck, J. [2011]. *The quick phonics screener 2*. St. Paul, MN: Read Naturally; reprinted by permission.) *Key:* CVCC, consonant–vowel–consonant–consonant; CCVC, consonant–consonant–vowel–consonant.

determine whether she is responding to your instruction. Progress monitoring using fluency measures is discussed fully in Chapter 8.

Standardized Assessments

There are also standardized tests that you will administer. Although the type of assessment will depend on the grade level you teach, generally, you should have at least four types of reading assessments in your arsenal: 1) word reading accuracy, reading lists of real words and nonsense words and both in-context reading of text and out of context, such as lists of words; 2) phonemic decoding and encoding (sounding out words with regular patterns and encoding skills, i.e., spelling from dictation); 3) oral fluency (the number of words read correctly per minute); and 4) reading comprehension at the sentence and paragraph level.

You might wonder why it would be important to include measures that assess reading nonsense words and reading words in lists rather than words in the context of sentences. Reading nonsense words ensures that students have internalized the phonics patterns and supports reading individual word parts in multisyllabic words. The measures that assess out-of-context word reading address the kinds of specific word recognition skills that are particularly problematic for children with reading difficulties who may over-rely on contextual support (e.g., guessing words from picture clues).

HOW DO YOU USE ASSESSMENTS TO PLAN INSTRUCTION?

As you keep in mind the "pieces" of your assessment puzzle related to word reading skills, recall the sequence of phonetic skill development. You will also want to determine whether an underlying weakness involves phonemic awareness as discussed in Chapter 4 or vocabulary and oral language skills as discussed in Chapters 3 and 10. For example, if a student cannot hear the rime that is common in the words *cat* and *mat*, it will be difficult for him or her to blend an onset and rime to read the word. If a student does not know that the word *mat* means a small rug or that *sand* is on a beach, then even if he or she reads the words, he or she will not understand a sentence such as, "We saw sand on the beach, and we sat on mats."

In addition, you must consider whether a child's difficulties appear related to either limited English proficiency or to non-mainstream dialect use.

You will use your assessment data diagnostically to plan targeted instruction and to group children with similar instructional needs for small group individualized instruction. Remember Ms. Smith? Even though she followed her core reading program, students were having difficulty. Ms. Smith had to determine why. After she examined her data, it was clear that many students demonstrated letter sound confusion. They needed an extra 10–15 minutes in a teacher-directed small group to receive direct instruction on letter–sound correspondences and in blending and segmenting common short vowel CVC (consonant–vowel–consonant) words like *dad, mom, cat, dog*.

You will be able to get some helpful information from your screening assessments. For example, if a student has been given the Nonsense Word Fluency test from DIBELS NEXT, you can evaluate his or her responses to determine if more work is needed on short vowels and specifically which short vowels warrant targeted instruction.[21] If your student reads "wap" for "wup" and has other similar errors, you may conduct additional testing to see if your suspicion of difficulty with short vowels may in fact be true.

Sometimes, students who are learning English appear to have reading difficulties when, in fact, they are struggling to learn the language. Consider providing these students with specific support in learning common English vocabulary words, and clarify the different meanings of false cognates: English words that mean very different things in Spanish. Examples are *area* means *sand*, *pie* means *foot*, and *red* means *net* in Spanish.

HOW DO YOU TEACH PHONICS EFFECTIVELY, EFFICIENTLY, AND IN A MANNER APPROPRIATE TO THE AGE/GRADE LEVEL OF YOUR STUDENTS?

This section addresses exactly *what* phonics skills should be taught and *how* to teach the specific skills. The teacher edition of your core reading program provides a scope and sequence, the curriculum that outlines what you will teach and when you will teach it. However, often the teacher editions do not provide enough guidance about how to teach the skills explicitly and systematically, nor how to adjust instruction for those students who need acceleration, more intensive support, or for English language learners.

As how to teach phonics is discussed, keep in mind the features of effective instruction:

1. Explicit instruction with modeling
2. Systematic instruction with scaffolding
3. Frequent opportunities for practice
4. Immediate corrective feedback
5. Ongoing progress monitoring

Teaching the Alphabetic Principle, Letter Names and Sounds: Knowledge of the alphabetic principle refers to the understanding that squiggles on a page actually represent a sound and the squiggles have names. Students also learn that words are read from left to right, every letter or letter pattern makes a sound, the sounds of spoken words are ordered in a specific, temporal way, and there are spaces between the words.

Understanding the alphabetic principle means perceiving phonemes and the ability to manipulate the phonemes, as discussed in the previous chapter. When students can segment a three-phoneme word, such as *mop* into /m/ /o/ /p/, they are ready to match the sounds to letters and to begin decoding simple, regular words. Begin with one-syllable words with short vowel sounds.

What to teach: Teach letter names and sounds, manipulating the sounds, and mapping the sounds to letters. The term "short vowel sound" should be introduced and the short vowel sounds taught first, before the long vowel sounds. Short vowels occur more frequently and therefore have more utility.

How to teach: Once students understand the concepts of phonemic awareness and can segment words into individual phonemes and blend phonemes into words, begin to add letters to your instruction.

While working on phonemic awareness, teach your students the alphabet. Students should be able to recite the letters in order, not only when they sing the alphabet song. There are a variety of ways you can practice saying the alphabet other than singing it. For example, have the girls say one letter and the boys the next; whisper two letters and shout the third; start in the middle of the alphabet. Try a variety of games to encourage your students to learn the alphabet.

Students must develop automaticity when naming letters, first upper-case letters, then the lower-case letters. One kindergarten teacher was proud that all of his students could name the letters of the alphabet. He wanted to demonstrate the skills of one of his students. He presented her with cards with letters written on them. He showed her an F and asked, "What letter is this?" The little girl thought for awhile, then sang the alphabet out loud, "A, B, C, D, E, F!" The next letter was T, and the girl sang the alphabet all the way to T. She could not recognize the letters automatically. This student would have a terrible time working her way through a word at such a slow pace.

Students need to recognize letters immediately. As you teach them to "read" letters and words, teach them to form the letters. Practicing writing the letter while saying its name reinforces their letter naming knowledge. (You will learn more about teaching beginning writing in the next chapter.) Begin with the upper-case letters, then teach the lower-case letters.[22] Most reading programs have key cards that associate a word and picture with each letter sound. Usually, students practice by saying the letter name, the word association, then the letter sound: a, apple, /ă/.

Alphabet arcs are helpful for students to learn the shape of the letters and to name them with automaticity. Students are given plastic alphabet letters that they place over an outline of the letter on an alphabet arc. They should be able to complete this task in 2 minutes or less by the end of kindergarten.

As the students place the letters, ask them to name the letter. When you have taught the letter sound, they can both name the letter and say its most common sound. As the students clean up after completing the activity, again ask them to name the letters as they place them back in the container.[23]

Students are transitioning from an instructional emphasis on phonemic awareness to mapping the sounds to letters. They are beginning the progression of reading regular words (Figure 5.4).[24]

Before how to teach the sounds of the vowels is discussed, let us ensure we know how to pronounce them ourselves! Louisa Moats has made a diagram of how the mouth moves when it produces the different sounds. The letters closest together on this diagram are the ones students most often confuse. Study this diagram (Figure 5.5), and keep it in mind as you read about the guidelines to teaching letter sounds.[25]

Research has not concluded that there is a prescribed order to best teach the letters and sounds. However, research has determined guidelines that ensure better learning. As you follow the order presented in your core reading program, be aware of the guidelines. Some

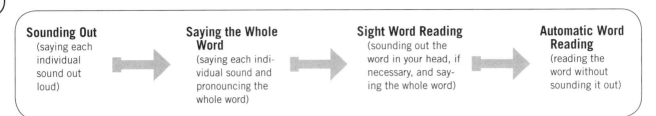

Figure 5.4. Progression of regular word reading. (From Carnine, D., Silbert, J., Kame'enui, E.J., & Tarver, S.G. [2004]. *Direct instruction reading* [4th ed.]. Upper Saddle River, NJ: Pearson Prentice Hall. Content reprinted with permission from the University of Oregon Center on Teaching and Learning. Copyright © University of Oregon Center on Teaching and Learning. All rights reserved. For original source see: http://reading.uoregon.edu/big_ideas/au/au_what.php)

reading programs do not follow the guidelines so you will need to make adjustments. The guidelines include the following:

1. Teach the most common sounds first, such as *m* rather than *x*; hard /k/ sound for the letter *c* as in *can* before the soft sound as in *cent*.

2. Begin with letter–sound correspondences that can be combined to make words that students can read and understand. For example, *m, t, s, a* can be combined to form many words: *mat, mast, tam, Sam, sat, at, am.* Teach students the words *the* and *on*, and they could read this silly sentence: *Sam sat at the mast on a mat.* Within a short time, your students are reading!

3. Begin with continuous sounds as they are easier for young students to discern. Continuous sounds are those that you can continue to make as long as you can breathe, such as *m, n, s.* Stop sounds (or clipped sounds) are those that are stopped by your teeth or tongue, such as *t, d, k.* They are more difficult for young students to discriminate.

   It is often helpful to provide small mirrors for the students and teach them how to watch the positions of their tongue and lips when they say selected letter sounds. That will help them distinguish /m/ from /n/, for example, and /d/ from /b/.

   Arlene Cox has created a musical scale to help teachers and students recall how to pronounce vowel sounds. Study Figure 5.6.

   Some students find it helpful to put their fingers on their vocal chords and feel the difference between voiced and unvoiced sounds. Several sounds look the same when pronounced but feel differently. One is voiced (your vocal chords vibrate), and the other is unvoiced (Table 5.2).

4. When asking students to identify sounds in a word, stretch the words, like you stretch a rubber band. You want to be sure the students hear every sound. Have the students repeat the word, then select letters that spell the word. If you have taught them how to write the letters in the words, allow them write the words on white erasable boards, sounding them out letter by letter. For example, say *mmmmmaaaat.*

5. Separate letters that sound alike or look alike, such as /m/ and /n/; /ĕ/ and /ĭ/; /d/, /b/, and /p/. Teach them about 3 weeks apart, after students have truly learned one of the confusing sounds.

6. Teach only two or three sounds per week.

7. Provide multiple opportunities for students to practice their new letter names and sounds. One way to provide extra practice for students who may be struggling with these concepts is to use "pocket children" (Figure 5.7).[26] Most teachers have pockets or wear a tool apron that has pockets. Identify the students who are having trouble learning the new sounds; start with two students. You can include more once you learn the system. For each student, write on cards the new letter the student is learning as well as up to five sounds the student knows well. Place the cards in your pocket. Show the cards to the student whenever you

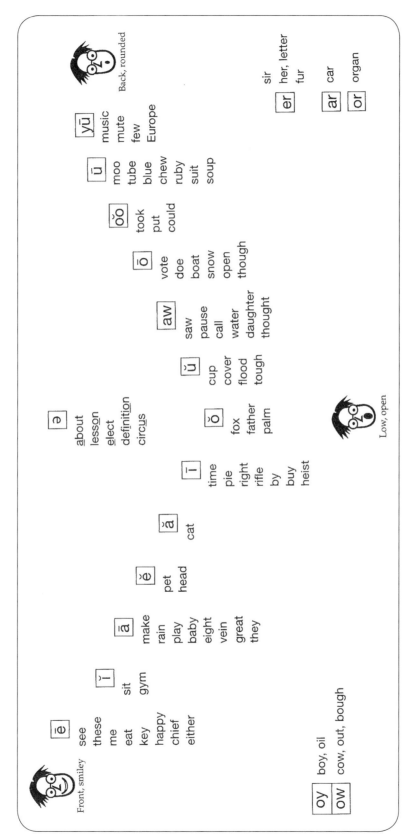

Figure 5.5. Moats vowel chart. (From Moats, L.C. [2010]. *Speech to print: Language essentials for teachers, second edition* [p. 96]. Baltimore, MD: Paul H. Brookes Publishing Co.; reprinted by permission.)

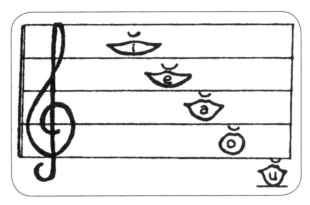

Figure 5.6. Mouth position short vowel. (From Cox, A.R. [1992]. *Foundations for literacy: Structures and techniques for multisensory teaching of basic written English language skills* [p. 129]. Cambridge, MA: Educators Publishing Service; reprinted by permission. Copyright © 1992. Used by permission of School Specialty Inc., [800] 225-5750, http://eps. schoolspecialty.com)

can, prompting the student to read the letter names and sounds. You can provide seven to 10 extra practice opportunities throughout the day, greatly increasing the student's learning. The following script is a sample script.

Show your student the letter to be learned and say its sound. *This letter says /ŭ/ as in up. Let's say it together, /ŭ/. Now you say it.* The student says /ŭ/. If the student does not say the correct sound, provide immediate correction. *Listen, /ŭ/ as in up. What sound?* Once the student says the correct sound, proceed with letters the student knows well, inserting the new letter among the known letters several times.[27]

Demonstration of a Lesson

All students have a copy of a Say-It-Move-It chart, blank chips, and chips with the letters *s, t, a, m* written on the chips, and a whiteboard.

Today we're going to learn to read words! First, let's review our phonemic awareness. You will need three chips for this lesson. Using your charts, when I say a letter sound, you repeat the sound and move a blank chip to the line.

Mmmm. What sound? Yes, mmmmm. Next sound: aaaaa. What sound? Yes, aaaa. Move a chip to the line. What sounds do we have now? mmmmmaaaa. Listen. The next sound is /t/. What sound? Yes, /t/. Move a chip down. What sounds do we have? Say them slowly. Mmmmmaaaaat. Now, say it fast (move your chips closer together). Mat. What word? Yes, mat! Good work.

What letter makes the sound mmmm? Yes, the letter m. Find the chip with the letter m written on it. Put that chip on the line. What letter makes the /a/ sound? Yes, a! Find the letter a and place it on the line. Finally, what letter makes the /t/ sound? Yes, t makes the /t/ sound. Place it on the line. Let's read this word, letter by letter. Mmmmaaaat. Now, read it quickly. mat. Yes, mat. Sometimes, you rest on a mat in our room.

Table 5.2. Voiced and unvoiced letter sounds

Voiced	Unvoiced
/b/	/p/
/v/	/f/
/d/	/t/
/z/	/s/
/k/	/g/
/th/ (this)	/th/ (think)
/zh/	/sh/
/j/	/ch/

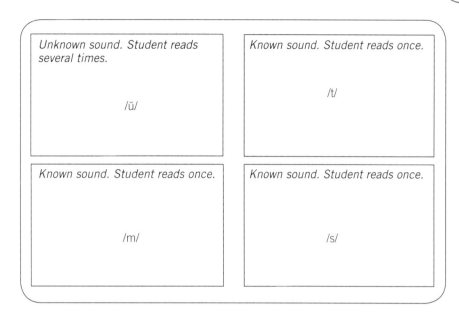

Unknown sound. Student reads several times.	Known sound. Student reads once.
/ŭ/	/t/
Known sound. Student reads once.	Known sound. Student reads once.
/m/	/s/

Figure 5.7. Pocket children cards.

Add the letter *s* and have students work with a partner, creating new words with the four letters they know: *sat, mats, at, tam, am, Sam,* etc. Later in the week, you might begin to teach your students how to write these letters. Then, they can encode words as you dictate, further reinforcing the letter–sound correspondences.

Such instruction is generally best done in a small group so you can monitor the performance of each student. Once students have learned these letters and sounds, they can practice with a partner or in a center.

You will practice saying the alphabet every day, but you will study only a few letters each week. Begin teaching letters that occur most frequently and ones that the name is associated with the sounds, such as b /b/ and t /t/.

Although there is no one best sequence for teaching the letter sounds, do not teach a letter of the week, starting with *a* and finally getting to *z* about the time school ends.

Teaching Letter Combinations and Patterns

Once your students have a grasp of the alphabetic principle and that letters correspond to sounds, you can begin teaching them more complex letter combinations.

This diagram illustrates which word patterns are the easiest to learn and which are more difficult.[28] Remember, it is best to start with the easier patterns (Table 5.3).

There are several terms you should know and that you can teach to your students to help them understand common phonetic patterns. Study the explanations below.

Consonant digraphs are two adjacent letters that make one sound, such as *sh, th, wh,* and *ch*. When a student segments a word into phonemes, digraphs are one phoneme because they make one sound. For example, the word *ship* would be segmented into /sh/ /ĭ/ /p/.

Vowel digraphs or vowel teams consists of two adjacent vowels, usually in the middle of a word. Two adjacent vowels are also called vowel pairs. Examples include *oa, ee, ie, ai,* and *ea*. Examples of words containing vowel teams or vowel diagraphs include *maid, sweet, bean, boat, pie*. Sometimes, there is more than one pronunciation of the vowel pairs. Consider *beat* and *great*. The vowel pair in *beat* makes a long /ē/ sound, while the *ea* in *great* makes a long /ā/ sound. The good news is that there are only four words in English in which *ea* makes a long a sound: *great, break, steak,* and *yea*. You can remember these four words with this sentence: "Yea! Steak is great but it will break the budget."

Table 5.3. Simple regular words—listed according to difficulty

Word type	Reason for relative ease/difficulty	Examples
VC and CVC words that begin with continuous sounds	Words begin with a continuous sound	it, fan
VCC and CVCC words that begin with a continuous sound	Words are longer and end with a consonant blend	lamp, ask
CVC words that begin with a stop sound	Words begin with a stop sound	cup, tin
CVCC words that begin with a stop sound	Words begin with a stop sound and end with a consonant blend	dust, hand
CCVC	Words begin with a consonant blend	crib, blend, snap, flat
CCVCC, CCCVC, and CCCVCC	Words are longer	clamp, spent, scrap, scrimp

Content reprinted with permission from the University of Oregon Center on Teaching and Learning. Copyright © University of Oregon Center on Teaching and Learning. All rights reserved. For original source see: http://reading.uoregon.edu/big_ideas/au/au_what.php
Key: V, vowel; C, consonant.

Diphthongs are vowels that slide in the middle. Examples are the glide-like sounds such as *oy (boy), ow (now), oi (boil),* and *ou (cloud).*

Variant vowel digraphs are two vowels making one sound; they are not classified as either long or short. Examples include *aw, au, oo (book), oo (moo).*

Silent consonants: Thanks largely to the contributions of Anglo-Saxon and Norske languages, there are several silent consonants students need to learn. Only one of the two consonants is heard; the other is silent. Examples include *kn (knee)* and *wr (write).*

R-controlled vowels: When the letter *r* follows a vowel, the sound of the vowel is affected. Examples include *er, ir, ur, ar,* and *or.*

Long vowels with silent e: The pattern for this category is vowel–consonant–e, or v_e. The final *e* is silent, and the vowel is long. Some teachers call the *e* a "magic e" because it makes the vowel say its name (it is a long vowel). Examples include *lake, bake, bike, cute,* and *hate.* An effective activity to reinforce this pattern is to ask students to decode a word such as *cut,* then add the *e* and read the new word, *cute.*

Types of Syllables

There are six syllable patterns. A syllable is a word or part of a word (a unit of pronunciation) that includes one vowel sound and requires one opening of the mouth (Table 5.4).

Begin teaching the types of syllables in first grade. Typically, begin with closed syllables as they are easiest to learn. Provide direct, explicit instruction. A sample routine follows.[29] Please note that students must understand the concepts of vowels, consonants, and syllables before you teach them about the types of syllables. Students should understand the difference between long and short vowels.

I do:
There are six types of syllables. The first one we are going to learn about is a closed syllable. What type of syllable? Yes, a closed syllable. There are three rules that define a closed syllable. How many rules? Yes, three.

1. *The closed syllable ends in one or more consonants. A closed syllable ends in what? Yes, in at least one consonant.*
2. *The second rule is that a closed syllable contains only one vowel. How many vowels? Yes, a closed syllable contains just one vowel.*
3. *The vowel is short. Is the vowel long or short? Yes, short.*

   Turn to your partner, and repeat the three rules.
   Look at this word: met. Does it end in a consonant? Yes, it does. How many vowels does it have? Yes, one. Is it a closed syllable? Yes! It ends in the consonant t. So, the vowel is short. (Point to the e). What sound? Yes, /e/. What word? Yes, met.

Table 5.4. Types of syllables

Syllable type		Rules	Examples
Closed	1. 2. 3.	Ends in at least one consonant Contains one vowel The vowel is short	*met, sat, wig*gle
Open	1. 2.	Ends in one vowel The vowel is long	*me, go, bu*gle
Vowel-Consonant-e VCe or CVCe	1. 2. 3.	A vowel followed by one consonant A final silent *e* The vowel is long	*lake, like, bake, bike*
Vowel-r R-controlled	1. 2.	The letter *r* follows the vowel The vowel sound is changed	*car, stir, park, lurk*
Vowel pairs	1. 2.	Two adjacent vowels Sounds must be learned individually	*pail, steep, great, meat*
Final stable syllable or C-le	1. 2.	A final consonant-*le* combination or a nonpho- netic but reliable unit such as *tion (shun)* Accent usually on the preceding syllable	bu*gle*, wig*gle*, sta*tion*

We do:

Proceed, following the same instruction with two other words: *sun* and *bat* as examples. Allow the students to work with a partner and analyze a final word, *cat*.

You do:

Once the students grasp the concept, give them examples and nonexamples of closed syllables to examine with a partner.

Turn to your partner and discuss why this word is a closed syllable. Look at these words? Discuss, are they closed? Yes or no?

Examples include *cat, dog, mat, nod, sit, sled, cut*. Nonexamples include *meat* (there are two vowels), *dove* (ends in a vowel), and *me* (ends in a vowel).

Over the course of several weeks, teach the remaining types of syllables. Provide ample opportunities for students to practice iden-tifying the different types of syllables, starting with simple sorting activities, such as sorting closed syllables in one stack and open syllables in another. Gradually add words representing different types of syllables until students are sorting them all correctly.

Most students can learn the types of sylla-bles and can identify them in one-syllable words by the end of first grade. However, older strug-gling readers also may need this instruction, with ample practice provided.

When students recognize the types of syllables, it is easier for them to decode multi-syllabic words. Examine the word *bugle*. How do you know it is *bu-gle* and not *bug-le*? Because you know *-gle* is a final stable consonant-*le* syl-lable. That makes *bu-* an open syllable, and the vowel is long. Easy! The word is *bugle!*

High-Frequency Irregular Words

Irregular words are those that are not phonetically regular; that is, the words do not follow the typical or expected letter–sound correspondences (e.g., *cough*). Students must learn these words by examining them and practicing reading them. Suzanne Carreker, a contributor to this text, has a memorable way of calling attention to these words. She will snap her fingers, open her eyes wide, and proclaim: "These letters make an unexpected sound" (snap).

Said is a very common word. What letters make an unexpected sound? The letters *ai* are a vowel team, and the most typical sound they make is a long /ā/, as in *paid*. In the word *said*, the *ai* sounds like a short /ĕ/ as if word is pronounced *sed*. Have your students circle the *ai* in *said* with a bright color. Ask them to stand, placing their right hand on their left shoulder (if right-handed) or left hand on their right wrist. Then, spell the word, tapping down their arms (or up their arms if left-handed) and, as they do so, say the letters: "s-a-i-d." Then, they slide their hands down their arms, saying the word, "said." This is a multisensory technique to help students remember how to read and spell irregular words. Next, have the students write the word *said* on a white board, circling the unexpected letter sounds, *ai*. Write the word again, spelling and saying the word out loud.

Follow the same routine when teaching other irregular words, such as *was, son, put, to,* and *there.* When a word cannot be decoded phonetically, it must be learned as a unit. Do not ask students to try to sound out words that are irregular. In subsequent chapters, you will learn about the most common words in the English language, and you are encouraged to teach these words to your students. Students should decode the words that have regular sound–letter associations you have taught. Also, carefully teach the irregular words as units. A sampling of irregular words that are among the 50 most commonly occurring words are *the, your, of, was, their, said, have, were, they, one,* and *do.*

Common Syllable Division Patterns

When students are confronted with long words, they need to be taught how to begin to attack that word in a systematic way. Knowing a few syllable division patterns can help them. Teach the students the following steps:

1. Look for prefixes and suffixes. Circle them.
2. Count the number of vowels in the base or root word. Remember, a syllable has one vowel sound.
3. Count the consonants between two vowels and identify the syllable pattern. Remember, vowel digraphs and consonant digraphs count as one sound.
4. Apply the rules of syllable division (these usually work but not always):
   a. VC-CV: When two consonants are between vowels, divide between the consonants. Examples: *napkin, velvet, campus.*

b. V-CV: When one consonant is between vowels, the word is usually divided before the consonant. Examples: *open, over, music.*

There are several other rules you will want to examine. Also note where the word is accented, as the syllable divisions are influenced by the accent: di/*vide* **versus** *mod*/ern. An excellent source is Birsh, 2012.[30]

Finally, remind the students to ask themselves these questions:

c. Is this word a real word? (English language learners may need help determining if the target word is, indeed, a real English word.)

d. If the word is not a real word, have the students try accenting a different syllable or saying a word that sounds like the target word. For example, *secret.* If this word is divided between the consonants, as the first rule suggests, it would be pronounced *sec/ret.* Is this a real word? No, so try again. Usually students are close enough to the real pronunciation to try *secret.*

e. Does it make sense? If yes, continue reading! If not, examine the word again.

Reading Multisyllable Words

Teaching students to read multisyllabic words provides them with tools to tackle those long, difficult words they will encounter in the upper grades. Some techniques have been discussed already, including how to divide words into syllables, separating prefixes and suffixes, and categorizing syllables so it is clear how the vowels are pronounced.

A strategy that has been utilized successfully with students who struggle with decoding multisyllabic words is called The Word Identification Strategy and uses the mnemonic DISSECT. It was developed by the Center for Research on Learning at the University of Kansas to help students remember the steps of the strategy.[31] This strategy takes about 8 weeks to teach to students with reading difficulties, and teachers need to be trained in how to teach it with fidelity. However, the steps used in the strategy will help you understand how to teach a strategy well (Figure 5.8).

This strategy instructs students how to systematically examine a word, dissect it into manageable parts, and then use their phonics skills to decode the smaller parts.

There is another set of rules to support the strategy. Once a student has isolated the prefix (circled it) and separated the suffix (circled it), it is time to examine the stem, or root word. The rules of twos and threes helps students figure out that stem word (Figure 5.9).

Step 1:   Discover the context

Step 2:   Isolate the prefix

Step 3:   Separate the suffix

Step 4:   Say the stem

Step 5:   Examine the stem

Step 6:   Check with someone

Step 7:   Try the dictionary

Figure 5.8.   Steps of the DISSECT Strategy. (From Lenz, B.K., Schumaker, J.B., Deshler, D.D., & Beals, V.L. [1996]. *Learning strategies curriculum: The word-identification strategy.* Lawrence, KS: University of Kansas; reprinted by permission.)

> Rule 1
>
> If a stem or part of the stem begins with:
>   * A vowel, divide off the first two letters.
>   * A consonant, divide off the first three letters.
>
> Rule 2
>
> If you can't make sense of the stem after using Rule 1, take off the first letter of the stem and use Rule 1 again.
>
> Rule 3
>
> When two different vowels are together, try making both of the vowel sounds (diet).
>
> If this does not work, try pronouncing them together using only one of the vowel sounds (believe).

Figure 5.9. Rules of twos and threes. (From Lenz, B.K., Schumaker, J.B., Deshler, D.D., & Beals, V.L. [1996]. *Learning strategies curriculum: The word-identification strategy.* Lawrence, KS: University of Kansas; reprinted by permission.)

Let us try this strategy to decode the word *unconstitutional.* First isolate the prefixes and separate the suffixes (there are two of each in this word).

un con stitu tion al

Examine Figure 5.9 using the rules of twos and threes, let us look at the stem. The first letter is a consonant, *s*, so we count by 3 and divide. un con sti/tu tion al

Let us sound out all the parts: *un-con-sti-tu-tion-al.* Easy! If a student knows that *sti* is an open syllable, they may pronounce the *i* as a long /i/. So the students ask themselves, is this a real word? No, but it is close to a real word that I have been hearing about in history class. The word is *unconstitutional!*

The strategy is included here to illustrate how teachers can make explicit and systematic response to a challenging task. If provided multiple opportunities for practice with immediate feedback, students soon use the strategy independently. Finally, they are able to read those long, challenging words.

Challenges and Curiosities

English is a complex language. As you will learn in subsequent chapters, more than 87% of words can be decoded once you know about word patterns and word origins (50% of words are predictable; 37% are predictable except for one sound; 13%, mostly high-frequency words, must be recognized by sight).[32] There are situations, of course, in which students must use context to confirm if they read a word correctly. Let us examine some letter patterns, and then we will have some fun with our language.

Table 5.5. Letter–sound word wall for the letter /ā/

a	C-a open syllable	V-e	ai	ay	ey	eigh	ea
a	table	lake	paid	say	they	eight	great
	sable	bake		pray		sleigh	break
		take		day		neighbor	steak

Table 5.6. Letter–sound word wall for /sh/

When the /sh/ sound comes before a vowel suffix, it is spelled *ti*, *ci*, or *si*.

ti	ci	si
partial	musician	expulsion
patient	physician	pension

The long /a/: Many choices!

You have taught your students the short/ă/; it is the most common sound the letter *a* makes. Now, it is time to teach the other sound the letter *a* makes, the long /ā/ when the letter says its name. Examine these words in which the vowel is pronounced as a long /ā/: *paid, say, cake*. These are patterns you have taught: the vowel teams *ai*, as in *paid*, and *ay*, as in *say*; and the vowel–consonant–*e* pattern as in *cake*. Because you have taught them about open syllables, students will know that the *a* in *paper* is long. But what about the other spellings of /ā/? There are eight ways to spell that sound!

The other spellings are less frequent but must be taught. They are *eigh* as in *eight* and *sleigh*, *ay* as in *tray*, and *ea* as in *great, break*, and *steak*. And let us not forget the irregular *ey* as in *they*.

A way to draw attention to these options for spelling the long /ā/ is to have a letter sound–spelling wall. Many teachers put vocabulary words on a wall in their room, listing the words in alphabetical order. The letter–sound word wall organizes the words by the way they are spelled. See Table 5.5 for an example of a "a letter–sound word wall."

You and your students can make a similar letter–sound word wall for other challenging spellings, such as /sh/ as in *station, confusion*, and *musician* and the /sh/ spelled with the letters *ti* or *ci*: *partial, cautious* (Table 5.6). Put the rule on the word wall: When the /sh/ sound comes before a vowel suffix, it is spelled *ti, ci*, or *si*.

C and G

Most of us learn how to spell words rather easily, relying on the orthographic representations of the words as well as the sounds. However, some children do not easily internalize the patterns to pronounce or spell words. So you must teach them.

Take the letters *c* and *g*. How do we know if the *c* is "soft" as in *cent* or "hard" as in *cat*? What about *goat* and *gem*? When an inquisitive student asks about why those letters are pronounced differently, do not say "because." The reason is that, when the letters *c* or *g* are followed by *e, i*, or *y*, *c* sounds like /s/, and the *g* sounds like /j/. Examine the words *city, central, cyber*, and *gem, giant, stingy*.

If *c* or *g* is followed by *a, o, u*, or a consonant, the sounds are hard, as in *carat, color, cut, clarity* and *gate, gold, gut, group*.[33] In the following chapter, you will learn more about rules to help with spelling.

Carol Tolman has created a diagram that illustrates the skills we have been discussing (Figure 5.10).[34] Notice that when students are first learning about the sounds in spoken language, they learn about big units, such as sentences, then gradually learn about smaller and smaller units. The 1:1 indicates they understand the correspondence between spoken sounds and written letters.

As students learn to read and spell, they learn in small units of letters, gradually increasing to syllables and words.

SUMMARY

Learning phonics and studying word patterns is a lifelong endeavor. However, the most crucial years for students to master these skills are the early elementary years. Once the basic understandings are obtained, students can learn about more complex, sophisticated, and

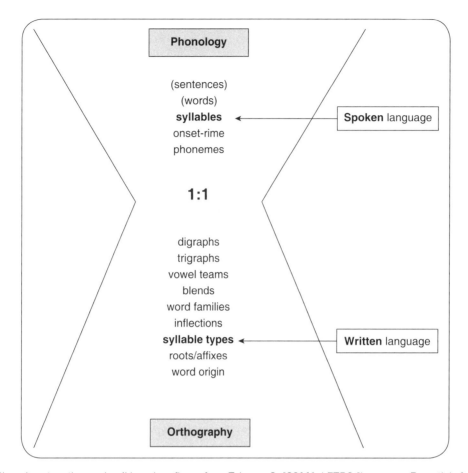

Figure 5.10.   Phonology to orthography. (Hourglass figure from Tolman, C. [2011]. LETRS [Language Essentials for Teachers of Reading and Spelling]. Frederick, CO: Sopris West Educational Services; reprinted by permission.)

interesting facets of English. If you are excited and intrigued about learning English, your students will be, too. And take note, no worksheets were used to teach phonics!

APPLICATION ASSIGNMENTS

In-Class Assignments

1. With a partner, write on note cards 12 one-, two-, and three-syllable words, two words for each syllable category. Join two other sets of partners, for a group of six, and sort all the cards into the correct syllable pattern.

2. Discuss: What words and patterns might be most difficult for students? Make a list of activities you could do to teach the syllable types, and for each activity, explain how you could make it more explicit and systematic to scaffold the learning.

3. With a partner, create a bright ideas paper. Take a brightly colored piece of paper, bright yellow works great, and write down five to 10 things you learned from this chapter that you do not want to forget. This bright ideas paper should be taped in your classroom in a place you can easily see. It will remind you of critical teaching behaviors. Be sure to include the features of effective instruction!

Tutoring Assignments

1. Select a phonics objective appropriate for the student you are tutoring. This objective could range from teaching several letters and sounds to more advanced multisyllabic word

decoding. Write the objective using the following format: Given (describe the task), the student will (conditions) with ---% accuracy (the evaluation). Examples: "Given 10 V-C-e words, Johnny will explain the syllable pattern and read the words with 90% accuracy."

"Given 10 three- and four-syllable words with prefixes and suffixes, Mary will identify the affixes in each, use the rules of syllable division on the root word, determine the vowel sounds using her knowledge of syllable types, and read the words with 90% accuracy."

2. Write and teach a lesson plan, using the template provided, addressing the instructional objective you identified.

Homework Assignments

1. Review the following sets of standards and read the sections addressing phonics. Note how the standard changes from K–6. Be prepared to share your observations during class.

a. Your state standards

b. The Common Core State Standards (http://www.corestandards.org/)

2. Read: *How Spelling Supports Reading* by Louisa Moats, available for download at http://www.aft.org/search/ (search by the title). Write a 1–2 page paper summarizing the gist of this paper, and be prepared to discuss it at the next class.

ENDNOTES

1. Collins (2001).
2. Honig, Diamond, & Gutlohn (2008).
3. National Reading Panel Report (2000).
4. Raynor, Foorman, Perfetti, Pesetsky, & Seidenberg (2001).
5. Rampey, Dion, & Donahue (2009); National Assessment of Educational Progress (NAEP) (2009).
6. Beck, McKeown, & Kucan (2002); Hart & Risley (1995).
7. National Early Literacy Panel (NELP) (2008); Whitehurst & Lonigan (1998).
8. University of Oregon Center on Teaching and Learning.
9. National Governors Association Center for Best Practices and Council of Chief State School Officers (2010).
10. Adams (1990, 2001).
11. Ehri (2002) in Honig et al. (2008).
12. Ehri (2002).
13. Adams (1990, 2001).
14. Good & Kamisnki (2002).
15. Hasbrouck (2011).
16. Bear, Invernizzi, Templeton, & Johnston (2011).
17. Hosp, Hosp, & Howell (2007).
18. Fuchs, Fuchs, Hosp, & Jenkins (2001).
19. Honig (2008).
20. Smartt & Glaser (2010).
21. Good & Kaminski (2002).
22. Birsh & Shaywitz (2011, p. 151).
23. Neuhaus Center (1992).
24. Cox (1992).
25. Moats (2010).
26. Notari-Syverson, O'Connor, Vadasy (2007).
27. O'Connor (2007).
28. IDEA, http://reading.uoregon.edu/.
29. Adapted from *Foundations of reading instruction* (2009).
30. Birsh (2011).
31. Lenz, Schumaker, Deshler, & Beals (1996).
32. Moats (2010).
33. Joshi (2006).
34. Moats & Tolman (2011).

REFERENCES

Adams, M.J. (1990). *Beginning to read: Thinking and learning about print.* Cambridge, MA: MIT Press.

Adams, M.J. (2001). Alphabetic anxiety and explicit, systematic phonics instruction: A cognitive science perspective. In S.B. Neuman and D.K. Dickinson (Eds.), *Handbook of early literacy research* (pp. 66–80). New York: Guilford.

Bear, D.R., Invernizzi, S., Templeton, S., & Johnston, F. (2011). *Words their way: Word study for phonics, vocabulary, and spelling instruction.* Upper Saddle River, NJ: Prentice-Hall.

Beck, I.L., McKeown, M.G., & Kucan, L. (2002). *Bringing words to life: Robust vocabulary instruction.* New York: Guilford.

Birsch, J.R. (2011). *Multisensory teaching of basic language skills.* Baltimore: Paul H. Brookes Publishing Co.

Center on Teaching and Learning. (2011). *Big ideas in reading.* University of Oregon. Retrieved April 3, 2011 from http://reading.uoregon.edu/big_ideas/au/au_what.php

Collins, J. (2001) *Good to great: Why some companies make the leap...And others don't.* New York: HarperCollins Publisher, Inc.

Cox, A. (1992). *Foundations for literacy: Structures and techniques for multisensory teaching of basic written English language skills.* Cambridge, MA: Educators Publishing Service.

Ehri, L.C. (2002). Phases of acquisition in learning to read words and implications for teaching. In R. Stainthorp and P. Tomlinson (Eds.), *Learning and teaching reading* (pp. 7–28). London: British Journal of Educational Psychology Monograph Series II.

Ehri, L.C., & McCormick, S. (1998). Phases of word learning: Implications for instruction with delayed and disabled readers. *Reading and Writing Quarterly, 14*, 135–163.

Fuchs, L.S., Fuchs, D., Hosp, D., & Jenkins, J.R. (2001). Oral reading fluency as an indicator of reading competence: A theoretical, empirical, and historical analysis. *Scientific Studies of Reading, 5*(3), 239–256.

Good, R.H., & Kaminski, R.A. (Eds.). (2002). *Dynamic indicators of basic early literacy skills* (6th ed.). Eugene, OR: Dynamic Measurement Group. Available at https://dibels.uoregon.edu.

Hart, B., & Risley, T.R. (1995). *Meaningful differences in the everyday experiences of young American children.* Baltimore: Paul H. Brookes Publishing Co.

Hasbrouck, J. (2011). *The quick phonics screener 2.* St. Paul, MN: Read Naturally.

Honig, B., Diamond, L., & Gutlohn, L. (2008). *Teaching reading sourcebook.* Novato, CA: Arena Press.

Hosp, M.K., Hosp, J.L., & Howell, K.W. (2007). *The ABCs of CBM: A practical guide to curriculum-based measurement.* New York: Guilford Press.

Joshi, M. (2006, December). *Spelling instruction to support reading: What teachers know and don't know (but should know).* Paper presented at the meeting of the Texas Higher Education Collaborative, Dallas, TX.

Lenz, K., Schumaker, J., Deshler, D., & Beals, V. (1996). *The word identification strategy.* Lawrence, KS: The University of Kansas.

Moats, L. (2010). *Speech to print: Language essentials for teachers.* Baltimore: Paul H. Brookes Publishing Co.

Moats, L., & Tolman, C. (2011). LETRS: The challenge of learning to read (Module 1). Longmont, CO: Sopris West.

National Center for Education Statistics. (2009). *NAEP 2009 National and State Reading Assessments.* Washington, DC: Institute of Education Science.

National Governors Association Center for Best Practices and Council of Chief State School Officers (2010). *Common core state standards.* Retrieved May 3, 2011, from http://www.corestandards.org/the-standards/english-language-arts-standards/reading-foundational-skills/grade-1/

National Institute for Literacy. (2008). *Developing early literacy: A report of the National early literacy panel.* Washington, DC: National Institute for Literacy.

National Reading Panel. (2000). *Teaching children to read: An evidence-based assessment of the scientific research literature on reading and its implications for reading instruction.* Rockville, MD: NICHD Clearinghouse.

Neuhaus Education Center. *Alphabet Arcs.* (1992). Houston, TX: Author. http://www.neuhaus.org/

Notari-Syverson, A., O'Connor, R.E., Vadasy, P. (2007). *Ladders to literacy: A preschool activity book.* Baltimore: Paul H. Brookes Publishing Co.

O'Connor, R. (2007). *Teaching word recognition.* New York: Guilford Press.

Rampey, B.D., Dion, G.S., & Donahue, P.L. (2009). *The nation's report card: Trends in academic progress in reading and mathematics 2008.* Washington, DC: National Center for Education Statistics.

Raynor, K., Foorman, B.R., Perfetti, C.A., Pesetsky, D., & Seidenberg, M.S. (2001). How psychological science informs the teaching of reading. *Psychological Science in the Public Interest, 2*, 31–73.

Report of the National Early Literacy Panel (NELP) (2008). *Developing early literacy: A scientific synthesis of early literacy development and implications for interventions.* Washington, DC: National Institute for Literacy. Available at: http://lincs.ed.gov/earlychildhood/NELP/NELP09.html

Smartt, S.M., & Glaser, D.R. (2010). *Next STEPS in literacy instruction: Connecting assessments to effective interventions.* Baltimore: Paul H. Brookes Publishing Co.

Whitehurst, G.J., & Lonigan, C.J. (1998). Child development and emergent literacy. *Child Development, 60*(3), 848–872.

6

Beginning Handwriting, Spelling, and Composition Instruction

by Suzanne Carreker

Julia is a gregarious third grader who delights in participating in class discussions. She is the first to raise her hand to answer questions or volunteer to give an oral presentation to her classmates. From casual observation, Julia seems to be a bright child with deep knowledge and exemplary language skills. However, Julia's written assignments present a conundrum. Her written work is virtually illegible. The parts that can be deciphered are teeming with spelling errors and lack cohesion. Writing a one-page book report takes her hours to complete. As Julia says, "I would rather scrub the kitchen floor 10 times with my toothbrush than write one sentence!"

It is easy to underestimate how essential foundational skills are to master. Foundational skills seem so mundane, so tedious. Yet, without handwriting, spelling, and sentence construction, it is difficult to become an accomplished writer. An important idea about foundational skills, which are also known as low-level or transcription skills, is that there is research to support the necessity of these skills. A second important idea to remember is that these skills require small investments of instructional time that pay big dividends. A third important idea is that students do not have to master these skills before writing sentences and paragraphs. Explicit instruction of foundational skills and authentic writing experiences occur simultaneously.

This chapter is divided into four sections: three sections for the foundational skills and an assignment section, where you will apply and extend what you have learned in the chapter.

Objectives: After studying this chapter, you will be able to do the following:

1. Understand the importance of instruction in handwriting, spelling, and sentence construction.
2. Delineate the research base for handwriting, spelling, and sentence construction.
3. Explain how to assess student needs and progress in each skill.
4. Describe activities that promote each of these skills.
5. Explain how to incorporate foundational written composition skills in your lesson planning.
6. Be prepared to teach these skills to students.

HANDWRITING

Why Is Handwriting Important? What Does Research Say?

Handwriting instruction teaches students how to form letters correctly, using a style such as manuscript or cursive, and promotes fluent writing. Handwriting instruction may not have been part of your educational experience. More and more, handwriting instruction has been squeezed out of the instructional day because it is not directly part of the accountability system.

Research has demonstrated that handwriting does contribute to achievement in written composition.[1] For example, Virginia Berninger found that handwriting fluency strongly predicts the quality of written composition from first to sixth grade. Steven Graham and colleagues suggested that students with good handwriting tend to get better grades.[2] Deborah McCutchen proposed a capacity theory of writing: that is, if handwriting is automatic, then students have more cognitive resources to attend to ideas, organization, and spelling.[3] Therefore, students produce higher-quality compositions when handwriting is automatic and fluent. In short, fluent handwriting positively impacts written composition.

What Should Students Know and Be Able to Do at Specific Grade Levels?

Automaticity in handwriting is facilitated by understanding how letters are formed.[4] Pre-K and early kindergarten students can sort printed letters by how the letters are formed: with all straight lines, with all curved lines, with straight and curved lines. For example, the letters **A**, **M**, and **T** are formed from all straight lines; the letters **C** and **O** are formed with all curved lines; and the letters **B**, **P**, and **R** are formed with straight and curved lines.

Although there is no consensus about which style of writing is best,[5] manuscript handwriting is usually introduced to students in kindergarten through first or second grade because manuscript letters are similar to letters students see in print. The Common Core State Standards[6] recommend that, in kindergarten, students should know how to form many upper- and lowercase letters. In first grade, students should know how to form all upper- and lowercase letters. Beyond first grade, the standards do not mention handwriting. Your state or school district may have more detailed expectations for different age or grade levels.

A helpful way to teach beginning writers is to use continuous manuscript writing.[7] The idea of continuous manuscript is that while a letter is being written, lines are retraced, and the pencil is picked up as infrequently as possible. Contrast these two descriptions for letter *d*:

1. Continuous manuscript description: "around, up, down."
2. Traditional manuscript description: "around, pick up your pencil, and down."

The first description does not require the student to pick up his or her pencil. In the second description, students must pick up their pencils and then move down, but do students know where to place their pencils after they have picked them up?

Table 6.1 presents stroke descriptions for letter formations using continuous manuscript. For the most part, there is one word for each stroke needed to form a particular letter.

Table 6.1. Continuous manuscript stroke descriptions

a	around, up, down	n	down, hump
b	down, up, around	o	around, close
c	around, stop	p	down, up, around
d	around, up, down	q	around, down
e	across, around, stop	r	down, up, over
f	curve, down, cross	s	curve, slant, curve
g	around, down, hook	t	down, cross
h	down, hump	u	down, curve up, down
i	down, dot	v	slant down, up
j	down, hook, dot	w	slant down, up, slant down, up
k	down, slant in, slant out	x	slant right, slant left
l	down	y	slant right, slant left
m	down, hump, hump	z	across, slant, across

From Carreker, S. (1992). *Reading readiness.* Bellaire, TX: Neuhaus Education Center; adapted by permission.

Table 6.2. Lowercase cursive stroke descriptions

a	under, over, stop, back around, up, down, release
c	under, over, stop, back around, release
d	under, over, stop, back around, up, down, release
g	under, over, stop, back around, up, down, loop left, release
o	under, over, stop, back around, loop, bridge
q	under, over, stop, back around, up, down, loop right, release
i	swing up, down, release. Dot
j	swing up, down, loop left, release. Dot
p	swing up, down, loop left, around, release;
r	swing up, down, across, down, release
s	swing up, around, release
t	swing up, down, release. Cross
u	swing up, down, up, down, release
w	swing up, down, up, down, up, bridge
m	push up, over, down, up, over, down, up, over, down, release
n	push up over, down, up, over, down, release
v	push up, over, down, up, bridge
x	push up, over, slant down, release. Cross
y	push up over, down, up, down, loop left, release
z	push up, over, in, curve down, loop left, release
b	curve way up, loop left, down, curve up, bridge
e	curve up, loop left, down, release
f	curve way up, loop left, down, loop right, release
h	curve way up, loop left, down, up, over, down, release
k	curve way up, loop left, down, up, over, close, slant down, release
l	curve way up, loop left, down, release

From Carreker, S. (1998). *Basic language skills (Books 1–3)*. Bellaire, TX: Neuhaus Education Center; adapted by permission.

Continuous manuscript is closer in its flow to cursive handwriting. Table 6.2 presents stroke descriptions for letters using cursive writing, which is usually introduced in third grade or perhaps in second grade. When you compare the two sets of stroke descriptions, you will notice similarity of the descriptions. For the most part, the predominant differences are the approach and release strokes that are part of the cursive stroke descriptions. Take, for example, the descriptions of continuous manuscript and cursive strokes for letter *d*:

1. Continuous manuscript description: "around, up, down."
2. Cursive description: "under over, around, up, down, release."

Although there may be advantages to different styles of writing and you may have a preference for one style or another, students ultimately will develop their own style.[8] If one particular style of script is not comfortable or appropriate for a student, the student should use what works best for him or her.

How Do You Assess Handwriting?

Examining the students' writing, either manuscript or cursive, is a good way to assess handwriting. As you look at a student's writing sample, ask yourself these questions: 1) is the handwriting legible, 2) do letters seem to be formed correctly, 3) are the letters proportional in size to one another, 4) did the student seem to apply appropriate pressure on his or her pencil, and 5) is the writing well organized on the paper? If the answer to any of these questions is "no," the student may have handwriting difficulties.

For a student who demonstrates difficulties with handwriting, you will want to do more assessment by observing how the student writes letters that you dictate. First, it is prudent to observe the student's pencil grip and writing posture.[9] With a correct grip, the pencil is held with the thumb and the index finger. The pencil may rest on the first joint of the middle finger or the pencil may be perpendicular to the writing surface. The grip is relaxed, not tense or tight. As to writing posture, the student is balanced in his or her seat, with both feet on the floor. The student's paper is slanted, so that the student's writing hand and arm are parallel to the side edges of the paper. The nonwriting hand holds the top of the paper and is parallel to the top edge of the paper. Inappropriate grip or posture, either of which could be a source of handwriting difficulty, should be corrected.

After a check of the student's pencil grip and posture, you will want to observe the student's automaticity and correctness in forming letters. Dictate five or six letters, one at a time. Observe how quickly the student is able to produce the letter. Does he or she stop and think about the letter or is the student able to reproduce the letter instantly? Observe how the student forms the letter. Does the student form the letter in a reasonable and efficient manner, or does he or she write the letter in a haphazard or bizarre manner? Does the student's letter look like it is supposed to look? If the student is forming letters appropriately, you will want to have him or her copy several sentences and then freely write a sentence or two. The goal here is to attain a sense of the student's writing rate. How automatic and fluid is the student's writing? Interestingly, girls are faster than boys in handwriting.[10] First-grade girls average 21 letters per minute versus 17 letters for first-grade boys. By sixth grade, girls average 91 letters per minute, and boys average 78 letters per minute.

How Does Assessment Inform Instruction?

Explicit handwriting instruction should be integrated with opportunities to engage students in authentic writing activities.[11] Your observations will guide your explicit handwriting instruction. For example, if a student can produce a letter correctly but not automatically, the student needs regular review and practice of letters. Activities that provide this review and practice include the following:

- Instant writing—Students are given a pencil and a piece of paper that is appropriate to their writing needs. For example, paper without lines for younger students or with lines for older students. The teacher dictates a letter. Students repeat the letter and write it. In fairly quick succession, the teacher dictates other letters one at a time. Students repeat each letter and write.

- Memory writing—Students are given a pencil and a piece of paper, appropriate to their needs. The teacher dictates a sequence of 2–5 letters. Students repeat the letters in sequence several times. The teacher gives a nonverbal signal, and students write the sequence of letters, naming the letters as they write.

The student who has difficulty forming a letter needs instruction that is focused on the formation of the letter. An activity that is appropriate for this student is presented in Figure 6.1. The student is given a practice page such as the one in this figure. With this activity, you can see the "I do, we do, and you do" feature of effective instruction:

1. On the board, the teacher writes a large letter. The teacher models how to form the letter (*n*, down, hump).
2. The student and teacher write the letter in the air (sky write) as together the student and teacher name the letter (*n*) and describe the letter strokes (down, hump).
3. Using the practice page, the student names the letter (*n*) and traces the letter three times with his or her finger while the teacher and student describe the letter strokes (down, hump).
4. The student names the letter (*n*) and traces the letter three times with his or her pencil while the teacher and student describe the letter strokes (down, hump).

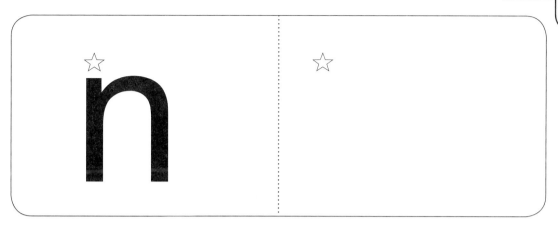

Figure 6.1. A trace-and-copy handwriting practice page.

5. The student puts his or her finger on the star on the right side of the paper.
6. The student names the letter (*n*) and plans the letter with his or her finger three times while the student describes the letter stroke (down, hump).
7. The student picks up his or her pencil. The student covers the model letter or folds the paper so the model letter is not in view. The student names the letter and writes the letter, describing the letter strokes to himself or herself.
8. The student compares his or her written letter to the model and assesses how well he or she has written the letter.
9. The student turns the paper over and writes the letter two more times.

The addition of arrows or numbers to a model like the one in Figure 6.1 to indicate the actions or sequences in forming a letter can further aid the student in writing the letter correctly.

How to Teach?

Beverly Wolf suggested daily instruction of 20 to 30 minutes while students are learning how to form letters in any script.[12] When students know how to form the letters, daily practices of 5 to 10 minutes will help students improve and maintain their automaticity and fluency. The number of letters that is introduced or practiced will be dictated by your students' needs. In addition to practicing letters, students can practice writing phrases and sentences.

A systematic order of letter introductions can be determined by thinking about how letters are formed and by grouping letters that are similar in formation together. For example, look back at Table 6.1. The manuscript letters *a, c, g, o,* and *q* begin with the stroke "around." You might want to teach those letters in a sequence. The cursive letters presented in Table 6.1 are grouped by approach strokes. For example, the cursive letters *a, c, d, g, o,* and *q* share the same "under, over" approach stroke. Uppercase letters should be included in the order of presentation and can be grouped according to starting point.

As you introduce a letter, it is helpful for you to model how the letter is formed, provide a model for students to trace and copy, and provide direction for forming the letter (arrows, number sequences, and/or stroke descriptions). The practice page presented in Figure 6.3 can be adapted for students of all ages and abilities. For example, instead of only one letter on unlined paper, the page could have lines and several letters for practice.

In sum, handwriting is important and does not require much instructional time. When handwriting is automatic and fluent, students have one less thing to think about as they write. Student needs will determine the focus and intensity of your instruction.

SPELLING

Why Is Spelling Important? What Does Research Say?

Spelling, the translation of spoken words into their written counterparts, is the second foundational skill of written composition. If spelling was part of your educational experience, it was probably pretty boring. No doubt you memorized lists of words for the weekly spelling tests. Perhaps you were, like many students, a "Friday speller." You spelled words correctly on a Friday test, but you soon forgot them after the test was over. If your spelling experience in school was just rote memorization, you learned how to spell a prescribed list of words for a test, but you did not experience the full benefit of learning how to spell any word.

Spelling develops in stages or phases. Initially, very young children imitate writing with scribbles or random strings of letters.[13] Children as young as age 4 may begin to demonstrate their rudimentary understandings of how sounds in spoken words can be translated into print. Children at this stage may use only the prominent consonant sounds, as in KT for *cat* or RN for *run*.[14] More precocious children may represent all the sounds phonetically, such as KAM for *came*, BEDR for *better*, or YUZ for *use*.[15] As children learn more about letters and sounds and read more, phonetic spellings give way to a mixture of phonetic and conventional spellings as in ENUGHF for *enough* and WADTER for *water*.[16] Repeated exposures to words and increased knowledge of spelling patterns eventually help children form correct spellings of words and hold those spellings in memory.

Convergent research affirms that spelling is not merely a rote skill.[17] Spelling is a complex linguistic skill that involves understanding of phonology (sounds), orthography (spelling patterns), morphology (word parts), semantics (meaning), and syntax (usage). Spelling is a skill that requires explicit instruction, not just memorization. Students' spelling attempts can provide you with insights as to how well students are learning and internalizing information about the language. When spelling unfamiliar words, students apply their awareness of sounds (phonemic awareness) and knowledge of letter patterns. In their trials of spelling unfamiliar words, students reinforce and enhance their reading skills.[18] Just as is true of fluent handwriting, efficient spelling frees students' attention to focus on their ideas and goals as they write.[19] Lastly, whether it is accurate or fair, spelling is often seen as a reflection of a person's ability, motivation, and attention to detail.[20]

What Should Students Know and Be Able to Do at Specific Grade Levels?

The Common Core State Standards[21] for spelling at each grade level are fairly broad. Your district or state may have guidelines as to specific content for spelling instruction at different ages or grades. Malatesha Joshi and colleagues outlined spelling patterns and other concepts that are appropriate at each grade level.[22]

Pre-K and kindergarten:
- Students engage in activities that heighten awareness of sounds in spoken language.
- Students begin to recognize which letters frequently spell a sound (/b/=b, /k/=k or c).

First grade:
- Students spell one-syllable words with one-to-one letter–sound correspondences (/b/=b, /g/=g, /m/=m).
- Students learn common patterns, such as initial or medial /k/ before *a, o, u,* or any consonant is spelled with *c* (*cap, color, cut, class*) and before *e, i,* or *y* is spelled with *k* (*kept, kite, sky*).
- Students learn that after a short vowel in a one-syllable base word, final /f/ is spelled *ff*, final /l/ is spelled *ll*, and final /s/ is spelled *ss* (*puff, bell, miss*).

Second grade:

- Students spell common inflectional endings (*-s, -ed, -ing*).
- Students learn that if a base word ends in a final *e* and a vowel suffix (a suffix that begins with a vowel) is added, the *e* is dropped before adding the suffix (*hope+ing=hoping, time+er=timer*).
- Students learn that if a base word ends in one vowel, one consonant, and one accent (all one-syllable words are accented) and a vowel suffix is being added, the final consonant in the base word is doubled (*runner, beginning* but *peeked, jumping, opening, gladness*).
- Students learn final /k/ after a short vowel in a one-syllable word is spelled *ck* (*back, sick, duck*), and final /k/ after a consonant or two vowels is spelled with *k* (*silk, desk, look, seek*).
- Students learn final /ch/ after a short vowel in a one-syllable word is spelled *tch* (*catch, pitch*) and after a consonant or two vowels is spelled *ch* (*bench, pouch*)—the words *which, such, rich,* and *much* are exceptions.

Third grade:

- Students learn more spelling patterns, such as medial /s/ is spelled with a *c* after a vowel and before *e, i,* and *y,* as in *grocery* or *recess.*
- Students spell multisyllabic words with an unstressed vowel or schwa (*sofa, alone, ribbon*).
- Students learn additional prefixes (*re-, mis-, ad-*) and suffixes (*-ist, -est, -er*).
- Students learn to change *y* to *i* when a suffix that does not begin with *i* is added to a base word that ends in a consonant and a *y,* such *happy–happiness, baby–babies.*

Fourth grade:

- Students learn Latin-based prefixes and suffixes, and roots such as *port* (*export, import, transport*) and *spect* (*spectacle, spectator, spectacular*).

Fifth and sixth grades:

- Students learn Greek combining forms, such as *photo* (*photography, photosynthesis*) and *philo* (*philosophy, philodendron*).

The outline above provides general guidelines about patterns and concepts students should know or learn at different grade levels. Certainly, when students are writing and demonstrate the need to know a particular pattern or concept, you can teach it to them regardless of their grade level.

Table 6.3[23] presents frequently recurring spelling patterns for sounds in different positions of words. Initial sounds are at the beginning of words. Final sounds are at the end of words. Medial sounds are between the initial and final sounds. For example, in the word /lăst/, /l/ is the initial sound, /ă/ and /s/ are medial sounds, and /t/ is the final sound.

How Do You Assess Spelling?

Traditionally, spelling is assessed with weekly tests, where student spellings are marked as "right" or "wrong." Although this kind of assessment will give you information about which words students know and which words they do not know, the assessment will not inform your instruction. Analyzing students' spellings errors will help you evaluate your students' understanding of sounds, letter patterns, and other spelling concepts.

To analyze your students' spellings, you will need to be aware of the sounds within words. With this knowledge, you can determine whether a student's spelling, although erroneous, demonstrates that the student at least is detecting all the sounds in the target word. For example, one student's spelling of the word *brake* as *brak* demonstrates that the student detected each sound in the word even though another student's spelling of *brake* as *bak* does not demonstrate the same awareness of sounds.

Table 6.3. Reliable spelling patterns

Initial and medial consonant sounds:

/k/ before *e, i,* or *y* is spelled *k* (*keep, kite, sky*)

/k/ before *a, o, u,* or any consonant is spelled *c* (*cat, cot, cut, clap, crash*)

/j/ before *e, i,* or *y* is spelled *g* (*gem, giant, gym*)

/j/ before *a, o,* or *u* is spelled *j* (*jam, joke, junk*)

/s/ after a vowel and before *e, i, or y* is spelled *c* (*grocer, recede*)

Final consonant sounds:

/k/ after a short vowel in a one-syllable base word is spelled *ck* (*pack, sock*)

/k/ after a short vowel in a word with two or more syllables is spelled *c* (*music, public*)

/k/ after a vowel pair or consonant is spelled *k* (*peek, milk*)

/j/ after a short vowel in a one-syllable base word is spelled *dge* (*badge, fudge*)

/j/ after a vowel pair, long vowel, or consonant is spelled *ge* (*scrooge, cage, bulge*)

Initial and medial vowel sounds:

/ā/ before a final consonant sound is spelled *a-consonant-e* (*cake, rotate*)

/ā/ at the end of a syllable is spelled *a* (*table, canine*)

/ē/ is spelled *ee* (*eel, meet, green*)

/ē/ at the end of a syllable is spelled *e* (*even, equal*)

/ē/ before a final consonant sound in a multisyllabic word is spelled *e-consonant-e* (*supreme*)

/ū/ before a final consonant sound is spelled *u-consonant-e* (*cube, infuse*)

/ū/ at the end of a syllable is spelled *u* (*unit, music*)

/oi/ is spelled *oi* (*joint, appoint*)

/ou/ is spelled *ou* (*round, astound*)

Final vowel sounds:

/ā/ is spelled *ay* (*day, decay*)

/ī/ is spelled *y* (*try, reply*)

/ō/ is spelled *ow* (*show, window*)

/ē/ in a one syllable word is spelled *ee* (*see, free*)

/ē/ in a word of two or more syllables is spelled *y* (*candy, ugly*)

/ŭ/ at the end of a word is spelled *a* (*tuba, sofa*)

/oi/ is spelled *oy* (*boy, destroy*)

/ou/ is spelled *ow* (*cow, endow*)

From Carreker, S. (2005). Spelling instruction: Foundation of reading and ornament of writing. *Perspectives, 31*(3), 22–25; adapted by permission.

In addition to understanding the sounds in words, you will need to understand the structures within words, such as prefixes and suffixes. With this understanding, you can assess students' spellings of derivatives (words that have a prefix and/or a suffix). For example, one student's awareness of suffixes, specifically inflectional endings, is reflected in the spelling of the word *pitched* as *piched*, but the same understanding is not demonstrated in a second student's spelling of *pitched* as *picht*.

Assessing errors is often the best way to measure student progress. Table 6.4 presents a student's errors on an initial benchmark measure spelling words with beginning and ending blends and the same student's errors on a second benchmark after 2 weeks of instruction focused on beginning blends. If you look only at the number of words spelled correctly, it seems as if the student has not made much progress from the first benchmark to the second benchmark, in spite of explicit instruction and practice. However, if you analyze the student's errors, her progress is more dramatic. In addition to spelling one more word correctly on the second benchmark measure, the student spelled all beginning blends and vowels correctly. On the initial benchmark measure, the student did not spell all the beginning blends correctly, and she omitted vowels in several words. The student is making progress, although she needs continued instruction and practice with ending blends.

Table 6.4. A student's performance on an initial spelling benchmark measure and 2 weeks later on a second benchmark measure after focused instruction and practice with beginning blends

Benchmark 1				Benchmark 2		
1.	mt	(mast)		1	gap	(gasp)
2.	bewd	(blend)		2.	lat	(last)
3.	stop		*40%*	3.	brush	*50%*
4.	dk	(drink)		4.	chip	
5.	fish			5.	step	
6.	shop			6.	slat	(slant)
7.	tash	(trash)		7.	dish	
8.	lit	(list)		8.	drak	(drank)
9.	chat			9.	shut	
10.	ptn	(plant)		10.	blat	(blast)

How Does Assessment Inform Instruction?

Students' errors on spelling tests, writing assignments, and daily work will inform your instruction. Consider these three spellings of the word *brick* by three different students: *bk*, *prek*, and *brik*. All the spellings are incorrect; however, the spellings tell different stories that necessitate different instruction for each student. For the purpose of thinking about informed or differentiated instruction, let us assume that the error made by each of the three students is representative of the errors each student often makes on spelling tests and when writing.

Student One, who spelled *brick* as *bk*, does not detect all the phonemes or sounds in words. The first need that should be addressed is the student's phonemic awareness. Provide the students with counters or blocks. Dictate a word with three or four phonemes: *mat, last, shop, trip*. The student repeats the word and moves a counter or block for each phoneme. There is no urgency to teach this student how to spell final /k/ until he or she is more secure with phoneme segmentation.

Student Two, who spelled *brick* as *prek*, can detect the correct number of phonemes in words, but, as you can see, does not discriminate sounds well. The sounds /b/ and /p/ are easily confused. Get out a small mirror. When you look in your mirror and pronounce /b/ then /p/, the sounds are similar in how they look when you produce them (your lips are together and then pop open). When you pronounce /b/ and /p/, they feel similar as you produce them (you feel your lips are together and then separate). The only difference in the two sounds is that when you place your fingers on your vocal cords and pronounce /b/, you feel your vocal cords vibrate: But, when you pronounce /p/, your vocal cords do not vibrate. With this information, the student can better determine whether to use *b* or *p*. Similarly, /ĭ/ and /ĕ/ are easily confused. Look in your mirror, and pronounce /ĭ/ as in *itch*. Your mouth is spread out like a grin, and your lips are tight and close together. Now, look in your mirror, and pronounce /ĕ/ as in *echo*. Your chin drops, and your mouth is open. To help the student discriminate these two sounds, teach him or her, "/ĭ/ makes you grin, /ĕ/ drops your chin." As you work with this student on discriminating confusing sounds, you can also present the spelling pattern for final /k/ spelled *ck*.

Student Three, who spelled *brick* as *brik*, can detect all the sounds in words and demonstrates good understanding of letters and letter patterns that reasonably represent sounds in words. Most errors this student makes demonstrate that he or she does not know how to spell sounds that have more than one possible spelling. With the word *brick*, the student just did not know when to use *ck*, which he or she is well poised to learn. As you can see by the three examples, students may misspell the same word in different ways and for different reasons. Each student requires instruction that is sensitive to his or her particular needs.

How to Teach?

Spelling involves translating sounds into letter patterns. Activities and strategies that heighten students' awareness of sounds in spoken words and spelling patterns in written words prepare students for spelling success.[24]

Phonological (phonemic) awareness activities. Pre-K and kindergarten students can be engaged in phonological awareness activities that promote their awareness of sounds. Activities could have students 1) listen to an alliterative sentence and fill in a word that matches the alliteration (*Many muddy monkeys mischievously make messy _____*) or 2) listen and choose the one word out of four dictated words that does not begin with the same sound (*mat, mist, soup, mud*).

Letter tiles. Kindergarten and first-grade students can practice spelling words using letter tiles. For example, students have tiles with letters: *s, m, p, a, i, t, n*. You might ask students to spell the word *sat*. You say the word, emphasizing the sounds as you pronounce the word. Students say the word, move the tiles with *s, a, t* to spell the word, and read the word. Then, you say, "You have spelled the word *sat*. Trade one tile to spell the word *mat*." Students say the word, replace the *s* with an *m*, and read the new word. You can continue to have students spell words by replacing one tile at a time: *mat* to *pat*; *pat* to *pan*; *pan* to *pin*; *pin* to *pit*; and *pit* to *sit*.

Guided discovery. As Malatesha Joshi and colleagues suggested, "The primary mechanism for word memory is not a photographic memory, as many believe; it is insight into why the word is spelled the way it is" (p. 16).[25] Students need to understand the patterns of English spelling. With spellers in first grade and beyond, the use of guided discovery to teach spelling patterns heightens students' awareness of sounds and letter patterns in words.[26] Guided discovery of a spelling pattern might look like this:

Teacher:	**Today you will discover a sound, how to spell the sound, and when to spell the sound that way. Listen as I read some words. Repeat each word after me.** [The teacher reads the words *pick, sock, stack, luck,* and *speck* one at a time as students repeat each word.] **What sound do you hear in each word?**
Students:	**The /k/ sound.**
Teacher:	**Where do you hear /k/—in initial, medial, or final position?**
Students:	**In final position.**
Teacher:	**What kind of vowel do you hear in each word?** [The teacher rereads the words.]
Students:	**The words have short vowel sounds.**
Teacher:	**How many syllables are in these words? In other words, how many times does your mouth open when you say each word?** [The teacher rereads the words and students repeat each word.]
Students:	**They all have one syllable.**
Teacher:	**Yes, all the words have one syllable.** [The teacher writes the words on the board.] **Look at the words. What do you see in each of these words?**
Students:	**All the words have *ck*.**
Teacher:	**Right, you have learned when /k/ is spelled *c* and when /k/ is spelled *k*. Now, tell me when you think /k/ is spelled *ck*. Think about all the different things you discovered.**
Students:	**When /k/ is at the end of a word, /k/ is spelled *ck* after a short vowel in a one-syllable word.**
Teacher:	**Now, you will apply what you have learned.** [Students spell *duck, lock, deck, black,* and *stick*.]

Notice in the introduction of the pattern that the students first discover information auditorily, what they hear. Students then discover the information visually, what they see. The students verbalize the pattern and apply their new learning by spelling words with the pattern.

Sorting words. Word sorts[27] can be used to heighten students' awareness of spelling patterns. On separate index cards, write words that share a common sound although the sound may not be spelled with the same letter patterns in all the words. For example, you could use these words: *pitch, rich, bench, catch, pouch, blotch, such, sketch, lunch, mulch, which, much, approach clinch, speech, entrench.* Tell students that all the words have /ch/ in final position. When students sort the words by a common spelling pattern, they will sort them as words that end in *ch* and words that end in *tch.* Then, students will discover when to use *ch* versus *tch.* All the words that end in *tch* are one-syllable words and have short vowels. The words that end in *ch* have a consonant or two vowels, except for the words *which, rich, such,* and *much.* These four words have short vowels but are not spelled with final *tch.* The patterns that students will discover are 1) final /ch/ in a one-syllable word is spelled *tch,* 2) final /ch/ after a consonant or two vowels is spelled *ch,* and 3) the words *which, rich, such,* and *much* do not follow the patterns. Students generate other words that follow the patterns they have discovered.

Irregular words. Words that do not follow the recurring patterns of English are irregular words and are more difficult to learn to spell. These words must be held in memory because they cannot be spelled by sounding them out. You can use different strategies to help students permanently memorize irregular words.[28]

1. Some words can be given a spelling or exaggerated pronunciation, such as /fră gīl/ for *fragile* or /wĕd nĕs dā/ for *Wednesday.* A spelling pronunciation creates a more vivid image of a word.

2. Words that share the same irregular pattern can be grouped together in a sentence: *Which rich people have so much money and drive such fast cars* or *The bright light at night is just right.* If students remember the spelling of one of the words, it increases the likelihood that they will remember the spelling of the others.

3. A trace-copy-spell-write page as presented in Figure 6.1 can be used, sparingly, for words that are particularly vexing to students.

   a. Students fold the page on the dotted line, so the model of the word is in view.

   b. Students look at the irregular word (*enough*) and circle the letter or letters that make the word irregular (*ough*).

   c. Students trace the model of the word three times, and then copy the word three times with the model in sight.

   d. Students spell the word with their eyes closed three times.

   e. Students turn the page over and write the word three times from memory, with no model in view.

   f. Students say the word and name the letters each time they spell the word.

Noah Webster once wrote, "Spelling is the foundation of reading and the greatest ornament of writing."[29] When students learn sounds and spelling patterns, they become better spellers. This same information reinforces and improves their decoding skills. In this way, spelling is the foundation of reading. Students who know how to spell have more cognitive resources available as they write. Students are also better able to use the most appropriate words to express their ideas when writing instead of settling for the simple words that are easy to spell. Students' attempts to spell more sophisticated words may not always be correct, but the usage of these words embellishes their writing.

SENTENCE CONSTRUCTION

What Is Sentence Structure and What Does Research Say?

Sentence construction is your knowledge of grammar, word order, and punctuation. Sentences are the building blocks for writing paragraphs, essays, and other forms of written discourse. Parts of speech are the building blocks for sentence construction. When sentence construction skills, like handwriting and spelling, are automatic, students have more cognitive resources for ideas and organization.[30] However, research suggests that when parts of speech and other aspects of sentence construction are taught in isolation, there is scant transfer or application of these skills to authentic writing experiences.[31] The trick is balancing the explicit instruction of effective teaching with the real-world application of these skills.

What Should Students Know and Be Able to Do at Specific Grade Levels?

Expectations for grammar and punctuation are found in the language section of the Common Core State Standards[32] for each grade level, beginning with kindergarten. The language standards for writing and speaking include the following:

Kindergarten. Students use frequently occurring nouns, verbs, and prepositions; form plural nouns (with -s as in *hats* and -es as in *dresses*); and produce and expand complete sentences.

First grade. Students demonstrate noun–verb agreement; use personal (*I, me*), possessive (*mine, ours*), and indefinite pronouns (*everything, everyone*); use articles (*the, a, an*) and frequently occurring adjectives, conjunctions, and prepositions; use past, present, and future verb tenses; use appropriate end punctuation in sentences; and write using simple and compound declarative, interrogative, imperative, and exclamatory sentences in response to a prompt.

Second grade. Students use collective nouns (*group, staff*), irregular plural noun forms (*geese, mice*), irregular verbs (*told, ran, said*), adjectives, and adverbs; produce and expand simple and compound sentences.

Third grade. Students understand the functions of nouns, pronouns, verbs, adjectives, and adverbs; form and use regular and irregular plural nouns and verbs; confirm subject–verb (*the dog barks* rather than *the dog bark*) and pronoun–antecedent agreement (*each student reads her paper* rather than *each student reads their paper*); use coordinating and subordinating conjunctions; use quotation marks in dialogue; form possessives; and produce simple, compound, and complex sentences.

Fourth grade. Students use relative pronouns (*who, which, that*) and adverbs (*when, where*); correctly order adjectives and use prepositional phrases; use model auxiliaries (*can, must*); use quotation marks and commas appropriately with coordinating conjunctions; and recognize and correct incomplete sentences and run-on sentences.

Fifth grade. Students explain the function of all parts of speech; use verb tenses to convey time, condition, and sequence; demonstrate conventions of capitalization and punctuation when writing; and use correlative conjunctions (*either/or*).

Sixth grade. Students can recognize nonstandard conventions, such as a shift in pronoun number and person and vague pronouns.

How to Assess Sentence Construction?

There are tests that measure different aspects of written composition, for example, the *Test of Written Language-Fourth Edition* (TOWL-4).[33] However, just as with your assessments of handwriting and spelling, a student's writing sample is a useful assessment tool. The questions you might ask that are specific to sentence construction are 1) are all sentences complete, 2) does the student order words in sentences correctly, 3) does the student use proper agreement (subject–verb or pronoun–antecedent), 4) does the student use appropriate capitalization and punctuation, 5) does the student use parts of speech correctly (*the child did well* rather than *the child did good*), and 6) does the student's variety of sentence structures match the expectations for his or her grade level?

How Does Assessment Inform Instruction?

Examining students' writing samples informs instruction for written composition. Consider a fourth-grade student whose teacher has evaluated one of her writing samples. The teacher's assessment: the student uses only simple sentences. The teacher knows this student must learn conjunctions, so she can write compound and complex sentences. Here is the student–teacher conference that might ensue to teach the student conjunctions:

Teacher:	Martinique, your story about your birthday party was hilarious! I felt as if I had been there. How is that cute puppy that helped open your presents?
Martinique:	Best birthday present ever!
Teacher:	You have great ideas and a wonderful voice. One thing to think about when you write is to combine sentences. Combining sentences will make your writing really smooth and clear. For example, you wrote these three sentences: Daddy chased the pup. Mama screamed. The kids went crazy. You might combine these sentences using the words *while* and *and*. For example: *While Daddy chased the pup, Mama screamed, and the kids went crazy.* The words *while* and *and* are conjunctions. Conjunctions join two words, phrases, or sentences together. When you combine your sentences with conjunctions, the reader has a really good sense of what happened!

As you can see in this conference, the teacher has assessed the student's needs using a writing sample, affirmed the student's efforts, and taught conjunctions in an authentic manner.

How to Teach?

Students' writing samples inform your instruction and can be used as an integral part of your instruction. For example, parts of speech can be explicitly taught in a clear and concrete manner to younger students and then linked to their writing samples. An example of teaching parts of speech in this manner will be presented. An effective activity for older students is writing summary paragraphs of passages students have read. This activity, which helps students learn about writing conventions, will also be presented.

Parts of speech. The eight parts of speech are tied to sentence construction. Some parts of speech are essential for a sentence to be complete. Other parts of speech add additional information to help convey the writer's precise message or viewpoint to the reader. A solid understanding of nouns (and pronouns), verbs, and articles can give a solid foundation for writing sentences. As you look at these examples of teaching the parts of speech, notice that the function of each part of speech is emphasized.[34] Students do not just memorize a definition, they understand *why* the part of speech is important.

Nouns (and pronouns). Nouns name a *person, place, thing,* or *idea*. To establish the need to know nouns, present four yellow objects and ask a student, *"Can you give me the yellow?"*[35] That student and two other students you ask will be unable to choose the "correct" yellow object. Their "failure" to choose the correct object will lead to an understanding of the function of nouns and why nouns are important. If there were no nouns, it would be difficult to know who or what someone is talking about. It would have been easier for the students to choose the correct object if it you had given the object a name. Nouns are color-coded yellow. Because pronouns take the place of a noun, pronouns are also color-coded yellow. Students can look at a sample of their writing and underline the nouns in yellow. In this way, explicit instruction of nouns is linked to their writing.

Articles. There are three words in English that are called *articles—a, an, the*. If you were given this traditional definition, "an article modifies a noun," you probably would not think the definition helpful in understanding what an article was and why it was necessary. Now, think about the function: an article warns that a noun is coming. Much better! Articles are color-coded red, which is a warning color. In a writing sample, students can underline articles and draw an arrow from an article to the noun it modifies or describes. Examples follow:

The dog barks.

An elephant eats peanuts.

Verbs. Verbs show action, being, or state of being. Write this sentence on the board:

I can _____. Students generate words that complete the sentence. The generated words (*dance, read, sing, play, hop, work*) show action. Verbs are necessary; without verbs, no one could do anything. Verbs are very important; every sentence must have a verb. Other verbs include linking verbs (*appear, be, become, feel, prove, remain, seem*) and auxiliary or helping verbs (*be, can, do, have, may, must, should, will, would*). All verbs are color-coded orange. Students can look at one of their writing samples or writing samples of other people and underline all verbs in orange.

Subject and predicate. The *subject* tells who or what the sentence is about, or in other words, the subject is the subject noun and all the words that go with it, so the subject can be highlighted in yellow. The *predicate* tells what is said about the subject, or in other words, the predicate is the verb and everything that comes after it, so the predicate can be highlighted in orange. A complete sentence, which is also an independent clause, has a yellow part (the subject) and an orange part (the predicate). If a group of words does not have a yellow part and an orange part, it is not a complete sentence. As students learn more parts of speech, the lengths of their sentences grow as well as the lengths of the subjects and the predicates within the sentences.

Understanding that a complete sentence (independent clause) must have a subject and a predicate helps students know if their sentences are complete. Knowing that the subject is tied to a subject noun will help them identify the subject. Knowing that the predicate is tied to a verb will help them identify the predicate.[36]

Summarization. A very effective strategy for writing is to have students summarize a passage or part of a text that they have read.[37] That might seem strange to you, but summarization of reading materials teaches students to be concise in their writing endeavors. Figure 6.2 presents a comprehension passage and a third-grade student's summarization of that passage. Notice how the student uses fewer words and still captures the essence of the original passage. Summarizing a passage or text gives students something to write about and exposes them to new vocabulary words. The reading materials also provide models of sentence structure, capitalization, and punctuation.

SUMMARY

Louisa Moats captured the importance of foundational or transcription skills in this quote, "writing is a mental juggling act that depends on automatic deployment of basic skills such as handwriting, spelling, grammar, and punctuation, so that the writer can keep track of such concerns as topic, organization, word choice, and audience needs" (p. 12).[38] To make written composition less of a juggling act, teachers must make all the foundational elements of written composition so automatic that there is but one focus—the purpose of the composition. When writers are freed from the foundational skills, the purpose is clearly evident and appreciated by the reader!

Passage:

Elephants

Elephants are the largest of all land animals and can weigh more than 12,000 pounds! The average height at the shoulder is 10 feet. At birth, an elephant calf is 3 feet tall and weighs about 200 pounds.

The two kinds of elephants are African and Asian elephants. African elephants are generally heavier and taller than Asian elephants. African elephants have much larger ears, which are shaped somewhat like the continent of Africa and weigh about 110 pounds each.

Elephants feed mainly on roots, leaves, fruit, grasses, and sometimes, tree bark. An adult elephant eats as much as 300 pounds of food a day, but it only digests half of the food it eats. Elephants sometimes walk hundreds of miles in search of water and food.

The elephant's trunk is very versatile. The elephant inhales and exhales through two nostrils at the end of its trunk. It can swim long distances using the trunk as a snorkel. There are fingerlike parts at the tip of the trunk, enabling the elephant to grasp objects as small as a single blade of grass. An elephant calf sucks its trunk just as a human baby sucks its thumb.

Student Summary:

Here are facts about elephants. They stand 10 feet and can weigh 12,000 pounds. Baby elephants stand 3 feet and weigh 200 pounds. African elephants are larger and heavier than Asian elephants and have ears shaped like Africa. Each day elephants eat 300 pounds of food such as roots, grasses, leaves, and fruit. Their trunks are used for breathing, snorkeling, and grasping. Babies suck their trunks.

Figure 6.2. Sample comprehension passage and a third-grade student's summary of the passage. (From Neuhaus Education Center. [2003]. *The colors and shapes of language: Units for developing oral language and listening comprehension.* Bellaire, TX: Neuhaus Education Center; adapted by permission.)

APPLICATION ASSIGNMENTS

In-Class Assignments

1. Try this simulation to see how difficult writing can be.
   - On a blank sheet of paper, draw a five-pointed star that is about the size of your fist.
   - Take a small mirror and, with the hand you write with, hold it perpendicularly to the star on your paper, making sure that your star is completely visible in the mirror.
   - Place your pencil in your nondominant hand, the hand you do not write with.
   - While looking only in the mirror and as fast as you can, trace the star, making sure that you stay on the lines. Go ahead, try it!

     Undoubtedly, you found it difficult to trace the star with your nondominant hand while looking only in the mirror. You probably traced your star very slowly, had to stop and start several times, fell off the lines, and concentrated really hard on which way you needed to move your hand. Welcome to the world of poor handwriting! Imagine that you are trying to write a composition under a similar condition. You are a student with great ideas, but how do you compose and remember your ideas and think about sentence construction and how to spell the words you want to use when all your attention is focused on how to form a particular letter? With a partner, share thoughts about this experience.

2. Teaching handwriting
   - Prepare a handwriting model of a letter. Use Figure 6.1 as a guide.
   - Teach the letter you have chosen to your partner.

3. Spelling—Using the sample script provided in this chapter as a guide and using Table 6.3 for information, introduce that the pattern final /j/ after a short vowel in a one-syllable word is spelled *dge*.

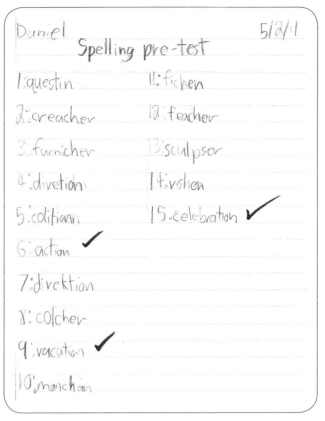

Figure 6.3. Spelling test 1.

4. Examine the spelling test inserted above (Figure 6.3). Determine what this second-grade student knows about spelling. Make a list of patterns he needs to learn. Determine what you will teach him first and how you will teach him. Describe specific activities you could use to reinforce spelling for this student.

5. Sentence construction—Read the passage presented in Figure 6.2. Do not look at the student summary. Write your own summary using about 60 words.

Tutoring Assignments

1. Handwriting—Examine a student's writing sample. Assess his or her handwriting. Using the information from the chapter, determine if handwriting might be a deficit area for the student. Describe why you think your student does or does not have difficulties with handwriting.

2. Spelling—Prepare the word sort with final /ch/ that was outlined in this chapter. Have your student sort the words and verbalize the patterns he or she discovers.

3. Sentence structure—In the context of authentic writing, teach the concepts of nouns, verb, subject, predicate, and complete sentence to your student using the information in this chapter.

Homework Assignments

1. To teach the foundational skills of written composition requires considerable knowledge and skill. The International Dyslexia Association has established Knowledge and Practice Standards for Teachers of Reading. The standards are available as a PDF at https://dyslexiaida.org/. View the document on the site. Identify all the standards that apply to the knowledge and skills teachers need to teach the foundational skills of written composition.

2. As you teach spelling, it is important for you to understand the frequently recurring patterns of English and to be reflective about the language. Review Table 6.3. Write 10 words for each spelling pattern that exemplify the pattern. You can include the example words used in Table 6.3.

3. There are five rules that determine when a letter in the spelling of a word should be doubled, dropped, or changed. View the webinar at http://library.readingteachersnetwork. org/webinars/five-spelling-rules. Write the checkpoints for each of the five rules, and give five examples and five nonexamples for each spelling rule.

4. Examine the spelling test inserted below (Figure 6.4). It is the same test you examined in an earlier assignment. This was the result after the student received instruction. What is the good news? Look what can happen with effective instruction!

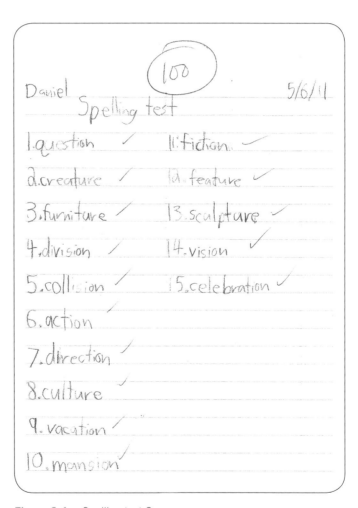

Figure 6.4. Spelling test 2.

ENDNOTES

1. Berninger (2009).
2. Graham, Harris, & Fink (2000).
3. McCutchen (1996).
4. Graham & Weintraub (1996).
5. Graham (2009/2010).
6. Council of Chief State School Officers & National Governors Association (2010).
7. Carreker (1992).
8. Graham & Weintraub (1996).
9. Graham & Weintraub (1996).
10. Graham (2009/2010).
11. Graham, Berninger, Abbott, Abbott, & Whitaker (1997).
12. Wolf (2005).
13. Gentry (1982).
14. Moats (1995).

15. Read (1971).
16. Treiman (1993).
17. Joshi, Treiman, Carreker, & Moats (2008/2009).
18. Moats (2005/2006).
19. Graham et al. (1997).
20. Carreker (2011).
21. Council of Chief State School Officers & National Governors Association (2010).
22. Joshi, Treiman, Carreker, & Moats (2008/2009).
23. Carreker (2005).
24. Joshi et al. (2008/2009).
25. Joshi et al. (2008/2009).
26. Carreker (2011).
27. Bear, Invernizzi, Templeton, & Johnson (2008).
28. Carreker (2011).
29. Venezky (1980).
30. Hillocks (1986).
31. Graham & Perin (2007).
32. Council of Chief State School Officers & National Governors Association (2010).
33. Hammill & Larsen (2009).
34. Carreker (2002).
35. Carreker (2006).
36. Carreker (2006).
37. Graham & Perin (2007).
38. Moats (2005/2006).

REFERENCES

Bear, D.R., Invernizzi, M., Templeton, S., & Johnson, F. (2008). *Words their way: Word study for phonics, vocabulary, and spelling instruction.* Upper Saddle River, NJ: Pearson Education.

Berninger, V. (2009). Highlights of programmatic, interdisciplinary research on writing. *Learning Disabilities Research & Practice, 24*(2), 69–80.

Carreker, S. (1992). *Reading readiness.* Bellaire, TX: Neuhaus Education Center.

Carreker, S. (1998). *Basic language skills (Books 1–3).* Bellaire, TX: Neuhaus Education Center.

Carreker, S. (2002). *Multisensory grammar and written composition.* Bellaire, TX: Neuhaus Education Center.

Carreker, S. (2005). Spelling instruction: Foundation of reading and ornament of writing. *Perspectives, 31*(3), 22–25.

Carreker, S. (2006). The parts of speech: Foundation of writing. *Perspectives, 32*(2), 8–12.

Carreker, S. (2011). Teaching spelling. In J.R. Birsh (Ed.), *Multisensory teaching of basic language skills.* Baltimore: Paul H. Brookes Publishing Co.

Council of Chief State School Officers & National Governors Association. (2010). Common core standards for English language art and literacy in history/social studies, science, and technical subjects. Retrieved May 1, 2011, from http://www.corstandards.org/the-standards.

Gentry, J.R. (1982). An analysis of developmental spelling in GYNS at WRK. *The Reading Teacher, 36,* 192–200.

Graham, S. (2009/2010). Want to improve children's writing? Don't neglect their handwriting. *American Educator, 36*(Winter), 20–26, 40.

Graham, S., Berninger, V.W., Abbott, R.D., Abbott, S.P., & Whitaker, D. (1997). Role of mechanics in composing of elementary school students: A new methodological approach. *Journal of Educational Psychology, 89,* 17–182.

Graham, S., Harris, K., & Fink, B. (2000). Is handwriting causally related to learning to write? Treatment of handwriting problems in beginning writers. *Journal of Educational Psychology, 92,* 620–633.

Graham, S., & Perin, D. (2007). A meta-analysis of writing instruction for adolescent students. *Journal of Educational Psychology, 99*(3), 445–476.

Graham, S., & Weintraub, N. (1996). A review of handing research: Progress and prospects from 1980 to 1994. *Educational Psychology Review, 8*(1), 7–87.

Hammill, D.D., & Larsen, S.C. (2009). Test of written language—fourth edition (TOWL-4). Austin, TX: Pro-Ed.

Hillocks, G. (1986). *Research on written composition: New directions for teaching.* Urbana, IL: National Conference on Research in English.

Joshi, R.M., Treiman, R., Carreker, S., & Moats, L. (2008/2009). How words cast their spell: Spelling instruction focused on language, not memory, improves reading and writing. *American Educator, 32*(4), 6–16, 42–43.

McCutchen, D. (1996). A capacity theory of writing: Working memory in composition. *Educational Psychology Review, 8*(3), 299–235.

Moats, L.C. (1995). *Spelling: Development, disabilities, and instruction.* Timonium, MD: York Press.

Moats, L.C. (2005/2006). How spelling supports reading: And why it is more regular and predictable than you may think. *American Education,* Winter, 12–43.

Neuhaus Education Center. (2003). *The colors and shapes of language: Units for developing oral language and listening comprehension.* Bellaire, TX: Neuhaus Education Center.

Read, C. (1971). Pre-school children's knowledge of English phonology. *Harvard Educational Review, 41*(1), 1–34.

Treiman, R. (1993). *Beginning to spell.* New York: Oxford University Press.

Venezky, R.L. (1980). From Webster to Rice to Roosevelt. In: U. Frith (Ed.), *Cognitive processes in spelling* (pp. 9–30). London: Academic Press.

Wolf, B. (2005). Teaching handwriting. In J.R. Birsh (Ed.), *Multisensory teaching of basic language skills.* Baltimore: Paul H. Brookes Publishing Co.

The Common Core State Standards and Text Complexity

by Elfrieda H. Hiebert

For a long time, educators have asked questions about what makes a text difficult. Why is it harder for students to read some books than others? How can we help students select texts that will promote their reading while not frustrating them? What type of texts will increase reading achievement most effectively? What texts will motivate students to read more and reinforce skills they need to learn and to develop a life-long enjoyment of reading?

Determining text difficulty is complex. Any reading act involves a text—something with written language on it. That is what makes reading different from getting information from oral language. But the reading of any text is also influenced by the characteristics of readers (What does the reader know? How well does the reader recognize new words or think strategically) and context (Is the reader given assistance in pronouncing words?). For a long part of the history of American reading education, determining text complexity has been either to rely on people's judgments (typically those of editors in publishing houses and expert consultants that they hire) or quantitative formulas (numbers that rate the relative difficulty of a text, e.g., readability formulas).

The question of text complexity is especially important at the present time because of the expectations established in the Common Core State Standards (CCSS).[1] In the near future, the view of text complexity is going to be powerful in terms of the assessments that students are given, and it is going to determine how the students' accomplishments are viewed and the kinds of texts that are given to them.

Objectives: After studying this chapter you will be able to do the following:

1. Describe the emphasis on text complexity within the Common Core State Standards (CCSS).
2. Explain three overall approaches to text difficulty.
3. Implement informed choices of text using a combination of the three approaches.

TEXT COMPLEXITY AND THE CCSS

Beginning in the middle to late 1980s, states began to develop standards that describe what students should know at particular grades. Typically, the guidelines for reading and language arts of many states have simply described the kinds of strategies and knowledge that readers should have at particular grades. The level of text to which that knowledge was to be applied was not prescribed. The typical phrase in a state standards document was "on-grade-level" text. It was not clear how "on-grade-level" was determined nor how complexity of text was defined. Another challenge was that "on-grade-level" could mean texts were determined to be on varying grade levels depending on the expectations of different schools and communities.

This situation changed with the CCSS. The CCSS has an entire standard devoted solely to text complexity. Standard 10 defines a grade-by-grade "staircase" of increasing text complexity that rises from beginning reading to the college and career readiness level. The reading standards place equal emphasis on the sophistication of what students read and the skill with which they read.

The CCSS Initiative takes a perspective on text complexity that is similar to one that scholars have taken for almost 100 years.[2] According to this view, three factors need to be considered in determining the difficulty of a text:

1. *Quantitative:* To get a sense of the difficulty of government documents and also school texts, scholars have worked hard for almost 100 years to get quantitative measures of the difficulty of a text. You probably have such a measure on your computer such as the Flesch-Kincaid.[3,4] Application of the software indicates that, at least at this point, this chapter has a difficulty that is estimated to be at the first month of grade 10.

2. *Qualitative:* It is hard to say that a classic such as *To Kill a Mockingbird*[5] is "three times" harder than the latest John Grisham novel[6] but even a fairly quick overview of these two books leaves a reader with the sense that these books are different in some important ways. Such differences are described as qualitative and, while identifying qualities that distinguish a classic and a simple "good read" can be difficult, literary and education experts have identified features such as the levels of meaning required (e.g., readers need to make inferences to understand a character's motive).

3. *Reader–task components*: The system also recognizes that features of those who are reading a text, such as their motivation and prior knowledge, will influence comprehension of a text. For example, someone who knows a great deal about World War II will respond quite differently to the bestseller *Unbroken*[7] than someone who does not have any background knowledge about World War II. This part of the equation also recognizes that there are ways in which teachers and situations can influence how comprehensible a text is for a reader. For example, listening to an audiotape of a text or having the support of an instructor in understanding a text are likely to influence readers' comprehension.

Such a three-part system of text complexity fits with what is known about texts and readers. But even though this three-part system is a reasonable one, examples of all of the system's components were not available when the standards were released. In its final form, the CCSS gives explicit guidance for determining only the quantitative component, and, even for that component, it describes only one scheme—Lexiles, a recent form of a readability formula.[8] The term "Lexiles" will be explained extensively in subsequent parts of this chapter. But, at this point, what is important to know is that Lexiles are a recent type of readability formula that uses digital technology to apply a quantitative formula to thousands and thousands of texts. In fact, Lexiles have been applied to all of the books available on sale at the Barnes & Noble web site. If you want to check out titles of books that you are reading, you can find their Lexiles at http://www.lexile.com.

Within the CCSS, the Lexiles have been recalibrated from longstanding recommendations for particular grade levels to a grade-by-grade "staircase" from beginning reading to the college and career readiness level. Beginning with the grade 2–3 band, Lexiles have been increased to ensure that high school texts have the difficulty of texts assigned in college classes and used in many careers. The specific Lexiles by grade bands, the ease of obtaining Lexile scores, and the lack of ready access to validated qualitative rubrics mean that considerable weight could be placed on Lexiles in choosing texts for instruction and assessment in schools over the next decade (if not beyond that).

Much of this weight could be laid on the shoulders of teachers who could be asked to have their students read texts that are simply too difficult for them. Giving students texts that are too difficult for them does not support their growth in reading capacity—the central goal of the CCSS. As professionals, you need to be able to evaluate the data on Lexiles. You also need to be able to supplement these data with qualitative information on the texts as well as on your knowledge of students and the situations in which you are asking students to read texts. The next section gives you additional background to understand the appropriate uses and shortcomings of quantitative measures such as Lexiles and also ways in which quantitative data need to be evaluated in relation to professional wisdom about the features and content of texts, the capabilities and interests of students, and the contexts in which students are reading the texts.

THREE PRIMARY APPROACHES TO TEXT COMPLEXITY

Quantitative Information

For almost a century, readability formulas have been used in American schools to describe the difficulty of texts. An estimate is that more than 200 readability formulas have been developed.[9] With few exceptions, readability is established through formulas that use information on two features of texts: the complexity of the sentences and the complexity of the vocabulary in the text. The first component is almost always measured in number of words in sentences. There is a little more variability in how vocabulary complexity is measured. Some readability formulas like the Dale-Chall (1948)[10] compare the words in a text to those on a list of words that have been identified as appropriate for different grade levels. One very popular readability formula developed by Fry (1968)[11] counts the number of syllables. Fry's view was that the more syllables in a word, the harder it is.

Lexiles are based on a third system of measuring vocabulary complexity. Words in samples of a text are compared to a database that began with a group of approximately 135,000 unique words and now has expanded to include many more unique words (although likely not all of the approximately 750,000 words in the British National Corpus).[12] A log of the mean frequency of the words in the text is used in a formula with the mean sentence length. The computation produces a Lexile that can be placed on a scale, which spans 0 (easiest texts) to 2000 (most complex texts). For example, the Lexile for a well-loved and award-winning book, *Sarah, Plain and Tall,*[13] is 430, while *Green Eggs and Ham*[14] has a Lexile of 30 and *Pride and Prejudice*[15] is given a Lexile of 1030. These numbers are consistent with a general direction that makes sense to most educators acquainted with these texts. *Green Eggs and Ham* is easy; *Sarah, Plain and Tall* is somewhat harder; and *Pride and Prejudice* is the most complex of the three.

When an individual text is examined for purposes of instruction and independent reading, however, particular features of a text can mean the Lexile is not sufficient to predict how well a student may be able to read a particular text. For example, *Harry Potter and the Chamber of Secrets*[16] and *The Old Man and the Sea*[17] have the same Lexile: 940. While the Harry Potter book is by no means a simple one, it has a style and content that likely make it more comprehensible to a sixth grader than the Hemingway text.

Scholars have long been aware of the problems with readability formulas, many of which were summarized in a national report in the 1980s.[18] One problem is that sentence length can influence the readability level. Narratives (i.e., stories) often have dialogue, and the sentences of oral language are often short. Short sentences do not necessarily make a text easy to read. The presence of dialogue and typically shorter sentences in narratives than in informational texts mean that readability formulas such as Lexiles typically *underestimate* the difficulty of a text.

There are also several problems with the ways in which vocabulary is computed that means that the difficulty of informational texts is often *overestimated*. One reason is that the writers of informational texts typically repeat words often because terms in social studies and science are precise and do not have synonyms (e.g., *photosynthesis*). Because many of these words are rare, that means that the vocabulary of a text will be rated as very difficult. Readers, however, pick up a word after several uses of it, and it becomes "easier" to read. The readability formula, however, does not take this into account. The repetition of the infrequent words can be an aid to comprehension and vocabulary learning. Further, the words in an informational text usually relate to a theme that also can make words easier to comprehend.

The "rare word" phenomenon that leads to a high (i.e., more difficult) readability is not limited to informational texts. Often, names of characters or places in stories are rare and are repeated often, such as *Mudge* in *Henry and Mudge*,[19] increasing the purposed difficulty of the text. *Mudge* is a very infrequent word, and its repetition (30 times in the entire text) means that the text is rated harder than *Sarah: Plain and Tall* even though *Henry and Mudge* is a very straightforward book appropriate for second graders.

What professionals need to be bear in mind is that readability formulas give an overall indication of the difficulty of a text relative to thousands of other texts. Once a book has been established to be in a particular grade span, the teacher's difficult task begins—understanding the demands of the book for students.

Qualitative Measures

Benchmark Texts. One way of establishing whether texts are appropriate for particular students is to do a "comparison" with a text that educators agree represents the demands of a particular grade level. These are often referred to as benchmark texts. The CCSS provides exemplar texts but these have not been validated by either teachers or through a variety of analyses, so at this time they cannot be considered benchmark texts. Jeanne Chall, with a group of colleagues, identified a set of texts almost two decades ago and validated them with teachers and school administrators.[20] Table 7.1 provides a list of benchmark texts that includes some from Chall's list, others identified by the CCSS writers, and an additional set that I and my colleagues chose to represent the diversity among American students.[21] These texts have been analyzed and correlated with particular developmental levels.

A comparison of *The Birchbark House*[22] to the book benchmarks in Table 7.1 makes it clear that it is very similar to the benchmark texts for grade 5, even though it has a Lexile of 860, which places it in grade 4, according to the new levels in the CCSS. Its content is very similar to *Island of the Blue Dolphins*,[23] which, for several generations, has been a book enjoyed by fifth and even sixth graders. The heroine of *The Birchbark House* must deal with the challenges brought on by the appearance of Europeans, different in form but similar in their dilemmas as the heroine of *Island of the Blue Dolphins*.

Qualitative dimensions. As described earlier, educators and literary experts work to define dimensions that describe features of texts that move from simple to more complex features. The CCSS identified four such dimensions, and Table 7.2 provides a fleshed out description of each of those dimensions at three points in time—the beginning, middle, and end of the elementary years. These dimensions will be applied to several books shortly, but, before doing that, it is also important to understand ways of describing readers and the tasks they are asked to do with texts.

Readers and Tasks

Standards such as the CCSS can be viewed as a type of map that points educators to the goal for high school graduates to be reading texts used in colleges and careers. All students may not be at the same point at the same time (they never are) but they are all moving toward attaining the same capacities. What teachers need are milestones along the way to let them and their students check in to see where they are in relation to the goal. Once again, I turn to the

Table 7.1. Benchmark books (narrative)

Grade level	Benchmark books	Description
1	*Green Eggs and Ham*[a] End of first grade/beginning of second grade: *The Fire Cat*[b] *Frog and Toad*	Structure of text is simple. Illustrations play a central role in enhancing story content.
2	Middle: *The Treasure*[b] *Henry & Mudge* End: *The Bears on Hemlock Mountain*[a] *Tops & Bottoms*[b]	Straightforward development of a theme.
3	Middle: *The Stories Julian Tells*[b] *Grandfather's Story* End: *The Magic Finger*[a] *The Lighthouse Family*[b] *Beezus & Ramona*	Themes can deal with challenging concepts (e.g., decimation of rain forest) but story structure and development of characters are straightforward.
4	*Soup and Me*[a] *The Black Stallion*[b] *Because of Winn-Dixie*	Feelings and motivations of characters are a focus of text and are multifaceted; characters face personal, family, school-related challenges.
5	*The Light in the Forest*[a] *Higgins the Great*[b] *Island of the Blue Dolphins*	As with previous level, feelings/motivations are central but the challenges encountered by characters include societal/environmentally complex circumstances/issues.

From Chall, J.S., Bissex, G.L., Conard, S.S., & Harris-Sharples, S. (1996). *Qualitative assessment of text difficulty.* Cambridge, MA: Brookline Books; reprinted by permission.
[a]Chall, Bissex, Conard, & Harris-Sharples (1996)
[b]Common Core State Standards (2010)

work of Jeanne Chall, a premiere reading researcher of the past century. Chall[24] identified six milestones or stages, one of which I have subdivided to create an additional stage, resulting in the seven stages in Table 7.3.[25]

Table 7.2. Qualitative dimensions of text complexity

Dimension	Stage 1	Stage 3	Stage 5
Levels of meaning/purpose	Single level of meaning (often supported by illustrations) Aims/themes explicitly stated	More than one level of meaning (e.g., *Great Kapok Tree* where an individual's choices relate to the choices of many) Inferencing of characters' motives and/or how features of context may influence plot	Multiple levels require drawing extensively on reading/experiences from other sources Implicit purpose may be hidden or obscure
Structure	Texts follow structure of common genres (e.g., simple narrative, enumerative expository)	Texts include less common genres (e.g., autobiography, cause–effect expository)	Traits specific to a content-area discipline or use of unique chronologies/perspectives (literary)
Language conventions & clarity	Literal	Figurative; some irony (e.g., Dahl)	Literary: high level of figurative, metaphorical language (e.g., Hemingway)
Knowledge demands	Simple theme	Complex ideas interwoven	Interconnected theme

From Hiebert, E.H. (2011). *The text complexity multi-index.* Santa Cruz, CA: TextProject, Inc.; reprinted by permission.

Table 7.3. Developmental stages of reading

Stage	Primary task	Grade span
0	Prereading	Through kindergarten
1	Initial reading or decoding	Grades 1–2
2	Confirmation, fluency, ungluing from print	Grades 2–3
3	Reading for learning new content and developing basic background knowledge	Grades 4–6
4	Reading for increasing content knowledge	Grades 7–8
5	Reading for multiple viewpoints	High school
6	Construction and reconstruction: A world view	College

The stages are an adaptation and extension of Chall, J.S. (1983). *Stages of reading development.* New York: McGraw-Hill Book Co.

Readers are not always easy to place in stages because growth can be erratic, and content can influence readers' actions. For example, young children love informational texts (and need to have an abundance of them), which seems somewhat at loggerheads with the distinction of learning content in stages 3 and 4. However, before readers can devote considerable attention to *new* content for which they do not have background knowledge, they need to be sufficiently automatic with the "code" of written language. Chall's stages give a sense of the primary milestones that readers face in becoming proficient through the school years.

The tasks of reading, just as is the case with readers and texts, are also complex.[26] For purposes of an initial analytic scheme, however, task dimensions have been limited to three: 1) the social configuration, 2) form of response, and 3) the allocation of time. Each of these dimensions is represented in Figure 7.1. As this figure shows, each dimension of a task does not lend itself to a scale where one end represents "easy" and the other "difficult." Rather, the critical component of these dimensions is the degree to which students are asked to be independent in the reading task and the level of open-endedness there is in both the kinds of response that are required from reading and in the time period that students have for the task. At one extreme, students are guided in every act of reading with time prescribed and the teacher monitoring their every response. At the other extreme, students are free to respond in whatever way they want to what they read (or even not to respond at all), with little guidance from their teacher and with few time constraints. Neither of these extreme scenarios is typical of classroom life where the features of tasks shift from lesson to lesson. The elements in Figure 7.1 simply point to the features of decisions that teachers need to make in designing reading tasks in their classrooms.

How to Use the Three Forms of Information: The Text Complexity Multi-Index

This section demonstrates how professionals use the three forms of information to make choices about which texts to use with which students in a process labeled the Text Complexity Multi-Index (TCMI).[27] You can think of the TCMI process much like making an online purchase in which you have to go through specific steps of selecting a product, entering your billing information and address, and confirming the purchase. Similarly, when you are considering which text to use with which students, you are analyzing a text through a series of steps—beginning with the quantitative, moving to the qualitative, and then considering the readers and task/context. The process is illustrated in Table 7.4 with three texts that were identified within the CCSS as exemplifying the grade 2–3 grade band but without information as to where during this period the texts should be used.

The first step in the process is to examine the quantitative data on Lexiles. The information on the Lexiles places the texts in this order of difficulty: *The Fire Cat*[28] (480L), *Henry and*

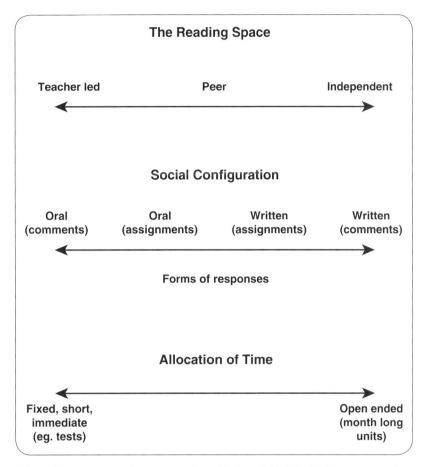

Figure 7.1. The reading space. (From Hiebert, E.H. [2011]. *The text complexity multi-index*. Santa Cruz, CA: TextProject, Inc.; reprinted by permission.)

Mudge (460L), and *Sarah: Plain and Tall* (430L). *Fire Cat* and *Henry and Mudge* have Lexiles that are within the first part of the Lexile range for grades 2–3. The Lexile for *Sarah* falls below the grade 2–3 band into the K–1 levels.

But, you will remember the cautions that were raised about relying just on the overall Lexile. It is also important to look "inside" the Lexile at the two measures that are used in the formula: sentence length (Mean Sentence Length or MSL) and vocabulary/word frequency (Mean Log Word Frequency or MLWF). From the examination of sentence length and vocabulary/word frequency, a different picture emerges. *Sarah* has the most common words, while *Henry and Mudge* has more uncommon words, which can be traced to the 30 appearances of *Mudge* in the text. The situation with *Fire Cat* is similar—the names of characters appear frequently. Rare words in *Sarah* typically appear once or twice in the chapter or even the whole book. But when these words appear, they are challenging (e.g., *hearthstones, wretched, holler*).

From the quantitative analysis, it is uncertain as to the appropriateness of assigning *Sarah: Plain and Tall* to beginning second graders and the other two books to slightly more able readers. The next step of the TCMI process where the texts are compared with benchmark books gives additional direction. *Fire Cat* looks very similar to a prototypical beginning second grade book—*Frog and Toad*. In fact, when the cover of *Fire Cat* is examined, it is evident that it is from a commercial reading program with a similar designation as *Frog and Toad*. *Henry and Mudge* is even easier to classify in that, through a series of analyses with teachers (and of existing reading programs), *Henry and Mudge* is a clear choice for a mid–second grade book. Because *Sarah: Plain and Tall* received a Newbery award and is similar to the *Little House*[29] series, a classification as a third-grade book is appropriate.

Table 7.4. The Text Complexity Multi-Index process

Step	Sarah: Plain & Tall	Henry & Mudge	The Fire Cat
1. Quantitative indices	*Lexile:* 430 MLWF: 3.84 MSL: 8.44	*Lexile:* 460 MLWF: 3.65 MSL: 7.98	*Lexile:* 480 MLWF: 3.76 MSL: 8.68
2. Qualitative benchmarks	Middle of grade 3 (*Grandfather's Story*)	Middle of grade 2 (*The Treasure*)	End of grade 1 (*Frog & Toad*)
3. Qualitative dimensions			
Levels of meaning/purpose	Numerous levels of meaning: pioneer story but also story of a motherless family	Single level of meaning that is easy for children to grasp (similar to television sitcoms)	Characters are straightforward and follow the pattern of many simply written books
Structure	Follows a fairly conventional narrative sequence	Follows a fairly conventional narrative sequence	Follows a fairly conventional narrative sequence
Language conventions and clarity	Use of language is simple but elegant. Some archaic words (e.g., *hearthstones*).	Very straightforward	Very straightforward
Knowledge demands	High: Knowledge of pioneer life and effects on life of geography	Little, if any	Little, if any
4. Reader and tasks	Appropriate for teacher-led discussions with third graders (i.e., early Stage 2 readers)	Appropriate for repeated and independent reading for most readers in Stage 2	Appropriate for repeated and independent reading for most readers at end of Stage 1

From Hiebert, E.H. (2011). *The text complexity multi-index.* Santa Cruz, CA: TextProject, Inc.; reprinted by permission.

Key: MLWF, mean log word frequency; MSL, mean sentence length.

The conclusion at this point in the process is that *Henry and Mudge* and *Fire Cat* are appropriate for second-grade readers and that *Sarah: Plain and Tall* is appropriate for third graders (or very advanced readers in a second-grade class at the end of the school year). These evaluations are verified by looking at the qualitative dimensions. Indeed, *Henry and Mudge* and *Fire Cat* both have straightforward plots that are similar to those of many of the cartoons and/or sitcoms on television that second graders might watch. *Sarah,* however, is much more than a simple recitation of facts about pioneer times or a sitcom. It requires students to use background knowledge on geographic differences (Maine and the prairie) as well as understanding the need for acceptance of a motherless family. The conclusions made after the match to benchmark books seem appropriate.

But now, the teacher needs to decide exactly with whom and how the texts will be used—the final step of the TCMI process. The analysis of vocabulary/word frequency in step 1 served as a reminder of vocabulary that would be good to pre-teach in both *Henry and Mudge* (e.g., *Mudge, pointy, curly, milky*) and *Fire Cat* (e.g., *Pickles, Goodkind, fireman/firemen*). Because the books are so straightforward in their content, these are good books for students to do some independent and partner reading but with a follow-up in a small-group session where students read aloud a favorite page from these books.

For *Sarah: Plain and Tall*, the choices would be quite different. A third-grade teacher might choose to have students read particular chapters on their own, followed by small-group or whole-class discussions. This book has many layers of meaning, but also has language that is accessible enough to give students the chance to read chapters on their own, allowing them to develop their stamina in independent reading.

CONCLUSIONS AND RECOMMENDATIONS

Selecting appropriate text for students to read is of crucial importance. By guiding students to read text that "fits" them, which stretches their reading capabilities while not frustrating them, teachers can promote high expectations and gratifying reading experiences for students. The CCSS have prompted a renewed examination of how teachers select text and a critical awareness of the means available to evaluate the difficulty of texts. The TCMI provides a means for ensuring that students have the right texts to read and, in the process, grow their capacity.

APPLICATION ASSIGNMENTS

In-Class Assignments

1. With a partner, review the CCSS, English Language Arts and Literacy in History/Social Studies, Science, and Technical Subjects. Write 1–2 paragraphs summarizing your understanding of text complexity. Share your understanding with another set of partners. Reconcile your differences, and write 1–2 paragraphs reflecting the understandings of all four of you.

2. Review the CCSS, English Language Arts and Literacy Appendix B: Text Exemplars and Sample Performance Tasks. Choose a sample performance task for Stories and Poetry and Informational Text. With a partner, create a lesson plan using the sample performance task as your final evaluation.

Tutoring Assignments

1. Review the text selections listed in the CCSS, Standard 10, Texts Illustrating the Complexity, Quality, & Range of Student Reading, K–5. Choose two that are appropriate for your student.

2. Develop and teach a lesson that utilizes the texts you selected. Specify the CCSS addressed (or the standards used by your state), the objectives of the lesson, and how you plan to deliver and differentiate instruction. Use the lesson plan provided in this text.

Homework Assignments

1. Reflect upon the lesson you taught, and write 1–2 paragraphs about what went well and what you would change next time you teach this lesson. Also, discuss the following questions: Were the texts you selected appropriate for your student? Was the level of complexity what you expected or was the text too easy or too difficult for your student? If the text was too easy or too difficult, how could you adjust your instruction?

2. Examine the CCSS, Standard 10, Staying on Topic Within a Grade and Across Grades. Using the exemplar texts as a guide, select a topic or a theme and plan how you might systematically develop the knowledge base of your student. Obtain five nonfiction texts on that theme. Write a short paper including the texts, the identified topic or theme, and the objectives you plan to address. Be prepared to discuss your selections and instructional objectives in class.

ENDNOTES

1. Common Core State Standards Initiative (2010).
2. Gray & Leary (1935).
3. Flesch (1948).
4. Kincaid, Fishburne, Rogers, & Chissom (1975).
5. Lee (1960).
6. Grisham (2010).
7. Hillenbrand (2010).
8. Smith, Stenner, Horabin, & Smith (1989).
9. Klare (1984).
10. Dale & Chall (1948).
11. Fry (1968).
12. Leech, Rayson, & Wilson (2001).
13. MacLachlan (1985).
14. Geisel (1960).
15. Austen (1813).
16. Rowling (1998).

17. Hemingway (1952).
18. Anderson, Hiebert, Scott, & Wilkinson (1985).
19. Rylant (1987).
20. Chall, Bissex, Conard, & Harris-Sharples (1996).
21. Hiebert (2011).
22. Erdrich (1999).
23. O'Dell (1960).

24. Chall (1983).
25. Hiebert (2011).
26. Hiebert & Martin (2009).
27. Hiebert (2011)
28. Averill (1960).
29. Wilder (1935).

REFERENCES

Anderson, R.C., Hiebert, E.H., Scott, J.A., & Wilkinson, I.A.G. (1985). *Becoming a nation of readers: The report of the Commission on Reading.* Champaign, IL: The Center for the Study of Reading, National Institute of Education, National Academy of Education.

Austen, J. (1813). *Pride and prejudice.* Accessed on October 20, 2008 at http://www.authorama.com/pride-and-prejudice.

Averill, E. (1960). *The fire cat.* New York: HarperCollins.

Chall, J.S. (1983). *Stages of reading development.* New York: McGraw-Hill Book Company.

Chall, J.S., Bissex, G.L., Conard, S.S., & Harris-Sharples, S. (1996). *Qualitative assessment of text difficulty.* Cambridge, MA: Brookline Books.

Common Core State Standards Initiative. (2010). *Common Core State Standards for English Language Arts & Literacy in History/Social Studies, Science, and Technical Subjects.* Washington, DC: CCSSO & National Governors Association.

Dale, E., & Chall, J.S. (1948). A formula for predicting readability and instructions. *Educational Research Bulletin, 27*(January 21 & February 18), 11–20, 28, 37–54.

Erdrich, L. (1999). *The birchbark house.* New York: Hyperion.

Flesch, R. (1948). A new readability yardstick. *Journal of Applied Psychology, 32,* 221–233.

Fry, E. (1968). A readability formula that saves time. *Journal of Reading, 11*(7), 513–516, 575–578.

Geisel, T.S. (1960). *Green eggs and ham.* New York: Random House.

Gray, W.S., & Leary, B. (1935). *What makes a book readable.* Chicago: University of Chicago Press.

Grisham, J. (2010). *The confession.* New York: Doubleday.

Hemingway, E. (1952). *Old man and the sea.* New York: Scribner.

Hiebert, E.H. (2011). The Text Complexity Multi-Index. Santa Cruz, CA: TextProject, Inc. Retrieved August 11, 2011 from http://www.textproject.org/teachers/benchmark-texts-stepping-up-complexity/the-text-complexity-multi-index/

Hiebert, E.H., & Martin, L.A. (2009). Opportunity to read: A critical but neglected construct in reading instruction. In E.H. Hiebert (Ed.), *Reading more, reading better: Solving problems in the teaching of literacy* (pp. 3–29). New York: Guilford.

Hillenbrand, L. (2010). *Unbroken. A World War II story of survival, resilience, and redemption.* New York: Random House.

Kincaid, J.P., Fishburne, R.P. Jr., Rogers, R.L., & Chissom, B.S. (1975). Derivation of new readability formulas (Automated Readability Index, Fog Count and Flesch Reading Ease Formula) for Navy enlisted personnel, Research Branch Report 8–75, Millington, TN: Naval Technical Training, U. S. Naval Air Station, Memphis, TN.

Klare, G. (1984). Readability. In P.D. Pearson, R. Barr, M.L. Kamil, & P. Mosenthal (Eds.), *Handbook of reading research* (pp. 681–744). New York: Longman.

Lee, H. (1960). *To kill a mockingbird.* New York: Harper.

Leech, G., Rayson, P., & Wilson, A. (2001). *Word frequencies in written and spoken English based on The British National Corpus.* London: Longman.

MacLachlan, P. (1985). *Sarah, plain and tall.* New York: HarperCollins.

O'Dell, S. (1960). *Island of the blue dolphins.* New York: Sandpiper.

Rowling, J. (1998). *Harry Potter and the sorcerer's stone.* New York: Scholastic.

Rylant, C. (1987). *Henry and Mudge: The first book of their adventures.* New York: Atheneum.

Smith, D., Stenner, A.J., Horabin, I., & Smith, M. (1989). *The Lexile scale in theory and practice: Final report.* Washington, DC: MetaMetrics. (ERIC Document Reproduction Service No. ED 307 577).

Wilder, L.I. (1935). *Little house on the prairie.* New York: Harper.

8

Fluency Instruction

by Jan Hasbrouck
and Martha C. Hougen

"I don't get it. Sam knows all his letters and sounds and can read most any word in the second-grade books. But he doesn't seem to understand what he reads, though his listening comprehension is on grade level. I have noticed that he reads very slowly, probably because he wants to be accurate. It seems to take forever for him to finish one sentence! How can I help Sam?"

"There is no comprehension strategy that compensates for difficulty reading words accurately and fluently."[1]

This teacher has aptly described a student, Sam, who may have problems with his reading fluency: the ability to read accurately yet quickly, with expression and comprehension. Sam may have other reading challenges that the teacher will want to investigate, but lack of reading fluency appears to be Sam's biggest obstacle. This chapter will provide an overview of fluency and how you can help students like Sam.

Objectives: After studying this chapter you will be able to do the following:

1. Identify and define the three primary components of reading fluency.
2. Explain why it is important for students to become fluent readers.
3. Explain the difference between fast reading and fluent reading.
4. Explain the role that both accuracy and rate play in text comprehension.
5. Explain how the statement, "The rich get richer and the poor get poorer," relates to reading fluency.
6. Describe the different levels of text: independent, instructional, and frustrational.
7. Explain how curriculum-based measures of oral reading fluency can be used to identify students who might need help with reading and to evaluate or monitor their progress in reading.
8. Identify the differences between benchmark/screening and progress monitoring assessments.
9. Identify and explain four instructional strategies to improve students' reading fluency.
10. Explain this statement: "Teaching students to read faster is not the answer."

READING FLUENCY: WHAT IS IT? WHY IS IT IMPORTANT? WHAT DOES THE RESEARCH SAY?

Reading fluency has long been considered an essential skill that must be developed by readers to facilitate the comprehension of what has been read and to motivate engagement in the act of reading. The concept of reading fluency has been discussed in professional literacy circles since 1886![2] Since the 1970s, there has been a flurry of research about fluency and its relationship to comprehension.[3] It has been confirmed that the human brain has the capacity to perform tasks such as reading at an automatic, nearly unconscious level, once sufficient learning has occurred. Readers who have achieved automaticity, immediately and effortlessly recognizing words in print, can allocate their cognitive processes (thinking) to the meaning of what is being read, rather than thinking about how to decode the words. When readers have to devote a significant amount of their cognitive resources to simply decoding and recognizing words, the cognitive resources available for paying attention and for processing information are limited, resulting in impaired comprehension. Therefore, it is important that students become fluent readers, reading text with minimal effort so that they can concentrate on the meaning of the text.

Many reading professionals refer to the Report of the National Reading Panel as being a modern watershed in terms of reading fluency. In the section on fluency in the summary document, it was stated: "Fluency is one of several critical factors necessary for reading comprehension. Despite its importance as a component of skilled reading, fluency is often neglected in the classroom."[4] This strongly worded proclamation was a wake-up call to educators to learn more about the importance of fluency and how to provide instruction in the classroom.

Defining Reading Fluency

Even though reading fluency has been a topic of discussion for more than a century, there are still many questions surrounding the definition of the term, in part because fluency has many subtle components that are interdependent and, therefore, difficult to separate.[5] Although there may not be a firm consensus on a single definition of reading fluency, most definitions include three components: rate, accuracy, and prosody.

Rate. Reading rate is sometimes mistakenly used as a synonym for fluency, but rate technically refers only to the speed with which students read text. Most teachers have had experience with students who read quickly but still may not have good comprehension. Speed alone is not sufficient to facilitate comprehension, and a fast reader is not necessarily a fluent reader. In fact, fast readers may be reading inaccurately, or perhaps are reading too quickly to think about what they are reading. The rate or speed at which text is decoded and identified is clearly one aspect of fluency. How-

> Fluency is reading at an appropriate rate, with accuracy and prosody.

ever, reading fast is not the same as reading fluently. Some teachers encourage their students to "read as fast as they can"—this is *not* good practice. Rather, students should do their "best reading." This will be addressed further when the instructional strategies to improve fluency are discussed.

Accuracy. A second essential component of fluent reading is accuracy. In fact, accuracy may be considered to be the foundation of fluency. In order for a reader to understand what is being read, the text must be read with a certain level of accuracy; that is, reading words correctly. It is not known exactly how accurate a reader must read to obtain adequate or even minimal comprehension. However, there seems to be general consensus that comprehension is impaired when text is read with less than 95% accuracy. This means students should be able to correctly read at least 95 out of every 100 words.[6] Fluent readers should read text at an appropriate rate for the task while maintaining a reasonable level of accuracy.

Prosody. There is one additional component that is commonly considered a characteristic of a fluent reader: the ability to read with good expression. The technical term for this is *prosody*. Prosody refers to the pitch, tone, volume, emphasis, and rhythm in speech or oral reading. Teachers also talk about "chunking" words together into appropriate phrases as being another element of good expression. There is far less research on the contributions of prosody to comprehension than has been conducted on rate and accuracy, but emerging findings suggest there is some relationship. At this point, it is unclear whether prosody is a cause or an outcome of comprehension or if the relationship is in fact reciprocal. However, the extent to which a student uses correct expression while reading orally can indicate how well a reader comprehends the text being read.[7] If the reader does not know what he is reading about, it is difficult to phrase the words appropriately and to emphasize the correct words to obtain meaning.

What Research Says about the Role of Reading Fluency

As the National Reading Panel report made clear, reading fluency is an essential component of reading because it is necessary for comprehension. The ultimate goal of reading is to understand what has been read. To understand the role that fluency plays in reading comprehension, it is helpful to know how the brain processes information.

The human brain processes information (such as the visual images of printed text) using a complex, interconnected system that begins with working memory.[8] The working memory of the brain temporarily stores and manages information that will be used to complete the complex cognitive tasks involved in learning, reasoning, and comprehending. Scientists acknowledge that, although individual brains differ in their function and capacity, the models of working memory embrace the idea that, in order to function, all brains need to process information in a manner that is manageable. If too much information comes into the brain at once, the working memory becomes overloaded, and comprehension is impaired. Conversely, if information comes into the brain too slowly, the working memory cannot devote sufficient attention to the information to identify a pattern or see a relationship to previous learning. Because of this, a rate of reading that is appropriate to the task (neither too fast nor too slow) must be utilized by the reader in order for comprehension to be facilitated. Of course, the brain must process information that is reasonably accurate in order for comprehension to occur. Thus, comprehension is impaired or limited by reading too fast, too slowly, or inaccurately and is facilitated by reading at an appropriate rate for the task with reasonable accuracy. In other words, fluent reading assists comprehension.

Reading at a rate appropriate to the task acknowledges that different types of material are read at different rates. Think of how quickly you read a novel with a great story. Compare that to how you read a physics text. Most of us read the novel quickly and accurately, without thinking about decoding individual words. In contrast, if you are not knowledgeable about physics and you are reading a physics textbook, you are likely to read much slower, taking time to decode difficult words and to contemplate their meaning.

Levels of text difficulty for individual students are often described as being at an instructional level, an independent level, or frustrational level. When you are working with students on building fluency, the text should be at the instructional level. When the students are working independently, the text should be at the independent or instruction level; the student should be able to read the text with no support (Table 8.1).

Another way that poor fluency skills can impede comprehension has to do with what Dr. Keith Stanovich famously referred to as the "Matthew effect."[9] The term is taken from the Biblical passage describing the phenomenon in which it seems that in life the rich get richer and the poor get poorer. Stanovich applied this concept to struggling readers, who early on in the process of learning to read begin to lag behind their peers, and throughout the subsequent years often fall even further behind, in part because they simply are reading far less text.

Table 8.1. Levels of text difficulty

Independent-level text	The reader makes no more than one error in 20 words (95% and higher accuracy) and shows good comprehension.
Instructional-level text	The reader has 90%–94% accuracy and satisfactory comprehension. This type of text is used with teacher or peer support and is appropriate for fluency practice.
Frustrational-level text	The reader makes more than one error per 10 words, less than 90% accuracy, and shows poor comprehension. Do not require students to read at this level.

From Betts, E.A. (1946). *Foundations of Reading Instruction, With Emphasis on Differentiated Guidance.* New York: American Book Company.

The good readers get "richer" because they are reading significantly more text than their less capable peers and, thus, deepening their decoding and word-recognition skills and increasing their vocabulary.[10] These same researchers also found that the act of reading helps create motivated or "avid" readers, and they even go so far as to state that their data indicate that those who read a lot enhance their verbal intelligence—that is, reading actually makes them smarter!

Figure 8.1 illustrates the vicious cycle that occurs when students struggle with fluency.

It is helpful to think of fluency as a link in a chain connecting beginning decoding skills and comprehension skills. Fluent reading enables students to link from word-by-word decoding to being able to read with automaticity and to concentrate on the meaning of the text.

If readers do not develop adequate levels of fluency, the chain link will break, and the student may not be able to decode accurately and quickly enough to adequately understand what they are reading (Figure 8.2). These students typically become our reluctant readers, often with dire consequences for themselves, their future families, and society.[11]

Researchers have noted that the role of fluency changes across the developmental stages of reading. For emergent readers, the accuracy of reading, rather than the rate, should be the focus. Accuracy plays the most important role in comprehending in kindergarten and early first grade. Once students are reading connected text with reasonable accuracy—typically by the middle of first grade—the rate and accuracy of their reading is strongly tied to their overall reading skill, including comprehension.[12] Some researchers have noted that, once a student's reading level is around the sixth-grade level, factors other than fluency become more important in the overall reading process, including vocabulary and background knowledge.[13]

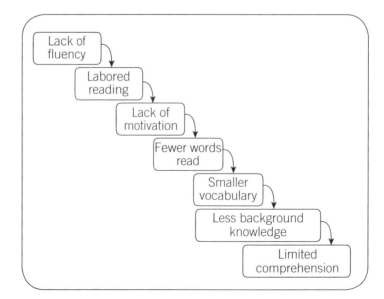

Figure 8.1. The vicious cycle.

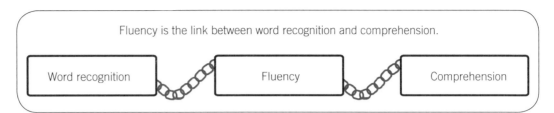

Figure 8.2.   Links to comprehension.

WHAT SHOULD STUDENTS KNOW AND BE ABLE TO DO AT SPECIFIC GRADE LEVELS, Pre-K–6?

General guidelines for the number of words students are expected to read correctly in 1 minute are in Tables 8.2 and 8.3. These numbers represent what typical students should be reading when they are on track in reading. More detailed norms are provided in Table 8.2. Note that the assessment of students' oral reading fluency of connected text does not generally start before second semester of first grade.

If students can read the expected words per minute fluently (accurately, with comprehension), they should learn to read as expected. However, if they struggle reaching these expectations, they may have a problem with fluency or some other reading difficulty. Poor fluency tells us there may be a problem, but what is causing the problem cannot be known until further diagnostics are done.

HOW DO YOU ASSESS READING FLUENCY?

It should be clear from the information presented so far that assisting students to become fluent readers also plays an important role in helping them become motivated readers who enjoy the process of reading and who can understand and learn from what they read. The process of assisting all students to become fluent readers logically starts with identifying which students are already sufficiently fluent and which students would benefit from fluency instruction or intervention.[14] Stahl and Kuhn suggest that when fluent readers read aloud, their reading sounds like normal speech.[15] This implies that simply listening to students read text aloud might be a way to start the process of identifying fluent and dysfluent students.

Table 8.2.   National oral reading fluency norms

	50th Percentiles		
Grade	Fall WCPM	Winter WCPM	Spring WCPM
1		23	53
2	51	72	89
3	71	92	107
4	94	112	123
5	110	127	139
6	127	140	150
7	128	136	150
8	133	146	151

GREEN Zone ≥10 to -4; YELLOW Zone -5 to -10; RED Zone >10 below

From Hasbrouck, J., & Tindal, G. (2006). ORF norms: A valuable assessment tool for reading teachers. *The Reading Teacher, 59*(7), 636–644; reprinted by permission.

Key: WCPM, words correct per minute.

Table 8.3. National oral reading fluency norms

Grade	Percentile	Fall WCPM	Winter WCPM	Spring WCPM	Grade	Percentile	Fall WCPM	Winter WCPM	Spring WCPM
1	90		81	111	5	90	166	182	194
	75		47	82		75	139	156	168
	50		23	53		50	110	127	139
	25		12	28		25	85	99	109
	10		6	15		10	61	74	83
2	90	106	125	142	6	90	177	195	204
	75	79	100	117		75	153	167	177
	50	51	72	89		50	127	140	150
	25	25	42	81		25	98	111	122
	10	11	18	31		10	68	82	93
3	90	128	146	162	7	90	180	192	202
	75	99	120	137		75	156	165	177
	50	71	92	107		50	128	136	150
	25	44	62	78		25	102	109	123
	10	21	36	48		10	79	88	98
4	90	145	166	180	8	90	185	199	199
	75	119	139	152		75	161	173	177
	50	94	112	123		50	133	146	151
	25	68	87	98		25	106	115	124
	10	45	61	72		10	77	84	97

From Hasbrouck, J., & Tindal, G. (2006). ORF norms: A valuable assessment tool for reading teachers. *The Reading Teacher, 59*(7), 636–644; reprinted by permission.

Key: WCPM, words correct per minute.

In addition to this initial and informal assessment, there are tools available to teachers to systematically and objectively identify students at various levels of need for assistance with reading fluency. Teachers who are responsible for teaching students to become successful readers should know about these assessments and how to use them appropriately to both identify students who might need special assistance with fluency, and then assess their progress—or lack of progress—once instruction has started. There are reliable, valid, and classroom-useful assessments that help teachers accomplish these important tasks by targeting the three primary components of fluency: rate, accuracy, and prosody. Here, they will be discussed in reverse order.

Assessing reading prosody. Researchers, including Ron Cole and his colleagues at Boulder Language Technologies in Boulder, Colorado, have developed voice recognition and evaluation software that may someday allow teachers to objectively and precisely rate a student's oral reading expression and eventually be able to compare it with some normative standards or expectations.[16] However, at the present time, there are no tools available to classroom teachers to objectively score for students' expression or prosody. Instead, qualitative rubrics or rating scales developed by researchers to guide the assessment process are commonly used to evaluate expression and assign a grade or performance level. A widely used rubric is the four-level scale from the National Assessment of Educational Progress that ranges from well-phrased, expressive reading at Level 4 to word-by-word, monotonic reading at Level 1 (Figure 8.3).[17] Other scales have been created for assessing prosody that allow teachers to rate a student's pace, smoothness, phrasing, expression, and intonation.[18]

Level 4: Reads with expressive interpretation

Level 3: Reads primarily in three- or four-word phrase groups

Level 2: Reads primarily in two-word phrases that are awkward and haphazardly grouped

Level 1: Reads primarily word-by-word

Figure 8.3. National Assessment of Educational Progress descriptors of prosody. (From Institute of Education Sciences, 2002.)

Assessing rate and accuracy. One of the procedures for assessing students' rate and accuracy is based on a body of research conducted over the past 25 years called curriculum-based measurement (CBM). Numerous CBM studies have used measures of rate and accuracy to assess students' skill development and progress in reading, math, writing, and spelling.[19] The CBM assessment process for oral reading fluency (ORF) assessments requires using standardized procedures that involve having a student read aloud from unpracticed, grade-level passages or lists of letters, letter sounds, or words for 1 minute, while an examiner identifies errors. At the end of 1 minute, a score of words correct per minute (or letters or sounds correct) is calculated. That score can then be compared with an established benchmark that indicates proficiency. Students at or above the designated benchmark are considered at low risk (or are likely on track with their skill development); students below benchmark are considered possibly at risk (if they are slightly below the benchmark) or likely at risk (if significantly below benchmark).

Norms for ORF. In 2006, Jan Hasbrouck and Jerry Tindal published a set of national norms for oral reading fluency.[20] These norms were created to provide educators with guidelines for what reading fluency scores would be appropriate for students in grades 1–8 across the school year. A student's score from a 60-second assessment on an unpracticed, grade-level passage would be compared to the Hasbrouck and Tindal chart for his or her grade level and the time of the school year in which the assessment was administered. They recommend that if a student's ORF score is more than 10 words below the 50th percentile, the teacher can flag that student as one who might need some additional instructional support. The percentile number indicates the percentage of scores that fell at or below that score. In other words, the 20th percentile is the score below which 20% of all the scores from the assessment can be found.

Researchers generally agree that performance at the 50th percentile serves as a reasonable benchmark for fluency performance. However, some states and districts across the country have set their state standards for reading fluency at the 75th percentile or even higher. This decision possibly comes from the belief that it is better to set higher standards for students' performance or perhaps from the notion that "our state's students are all above average, so everyone else's average is not good enough for us." Although setting high standards for our students is usually a good thing to do, in this case, it is a mistake. There is absolutely no research or theory to support this idea. There is ample empirical evidence that it is essential for students to read fluently at least at the 50th percentile, but there is no research to suggest that pushing students to read above the 50th percentile has any benefit. Very few students will be able to achieve such levels, so they and their teachers may become frustrated with the attempt. More importantly, there is no research to indicate there is a significant benefit to their reading if they do achieve this higher fluency level. In other words, students need not read as fast as possible to become good readers. Students who read in the average range are on target to become effective readers.

Using ORF as benchmark/screening assessments. Curriculum-based measurements of oral reading fluency may be used as benchmark or screening assessments. Benchmark assessments are widely used these days, especially in elementary schools, and are often administered three times each year to all students in a school, a process referred to as universal screening.

Table 8.4.   Expected fluency gains

Words correct per minute gains per week	
Grade 1:	2–3 words
Grade 2:	1.5–2 words
Grade 3:	1–1.5 words
Grade 4:	0.85–1.1 words
Grade 5:	0.5–0.8 words
Grade 6:	0.3–0.65 words

Source: Fuchs, Fuchs, Hamlett, Walz, & Germann (1993).

Well-known examples of benchmark/screening assessments include DIBELS, DIBELS-Next, AimsWEB, the Texas Primary Reading Inventory (TPRI), and the Reading Fluency Benchmark Assessor (RFBA).[21] Although the reliability and validity of these assessments have been well-documented, teachers should be cautioned to use results from benchmark/screening assessments as only one indicator or snapshot of a student's performance. Teachers should always consider other relevant sources of evidence about a student's reading ability, including daily performance in class work, language proficiency levels, and other assessment results.

Table 8.4 is a research-based guide to the expected word gains for students reading at various grade levels.[22] Teachers can use this chart to help set fluency goals for students. You will note that students reading at the first-grade level make more gains per week than older students. As students reach their optimum fluency rate, the number of words gained levels off.

Confusion about ORF Assessments

The labeling of these CBM measures as ORF implies these assessments measure the complete skill of reading fluency, and that has led to a lot of confusion in the ranks of educators.[23] Some think that ORF is a measure of rate only or that using CBM benchmark/screening measures implies that fluency is the only reading skill that needs to be assessed and considered for making instructional decisions about students. Many mistakenly conclude that students who read fast are good readers and that if students who read slowly are simply taught how to read faster, they will become better readers overall!

Because rate and accuracy are used in ORF measures, and because rate and accuracy are two key components of the skill of reading fluency, this confusion is understandable. However, when used for benchmark/screening decisions, CBM assessments are not simply measures of fluency skill levels and were never intended to be interpreted that way. Instead, the assessments must be used as highly efficient and reasonably accurate indicators of general reading ability. Numerous studies conducted over the past several decades have clearly established that these fluency-based measures are strongly correlated with measures of reading comprehension and overall reading proficiency.[24]

It is most accurate and appropriate to think of these benchmark/screening measures as "thermometers" that help determine students' general academic (reading) health or wellness. They cannot provide a specific diagnosis or imply an appropriate treatment plan, but scores can be used to raise a red flag of concern about a student. Once a student has been identified as

BOX 8.1. Measures of rate and accuracy have been identified as strongly predictive indicators of overall reading performance, including comprehension.

possibly or likely at risk of reading difficulty, a teacher should next look at another category of assessments that will help diagnose specific skill deficits in all the key areas of reading including oral language development, phonemic awareness, phonics and decoding, vocabulary, and comprehension.[25]

Monitoring Students' Progress in Fluency

The purpose of progress monitoring is to help teachers determine if their students are benefitting sufficiently from instruction or intervention and when that instruction should be adjusted. CBM assessments can be used to help provide this important information for students who are receiving on-level instruction in Tier 1 programs, as well as those students receiving extra assistance in Tier 2 or Tier 3.[26] Because they involve the assessment of rate and accuracy, these assessments are also useful to monitor the progress of students' fluency skill development.

Tier 1 progress monitoring. For students who are on level or above and appear to be succeeding with their Tier 1 classroom instruction, systematic progress monitoring involves simply repeating the CBM benchmark/screening assessments that were conducted in the beginning of the school year. These assessments should be administered three to four times a year for all students, at least in the primary and intermediate levels of elementary schools. Results can then be routinely analyzed each time they are administered across a single school year and from grade to grade to help make sure that no student falls behind in those early, critical years of reading instruction. Because these measures do involve assessing rate and accuracy, when students continue to perform at the 50th percentile or higher on fluency norms, a teacher can also safely assume that their fluency skill progress is adequate. Additional checks of prosody should also be taken periodically as a more complete assessment of fluency skill development. For students above a sixth-grade reading level, using assessments other than ORF including the multiple choice cloze or maze may be more appropriate.[27] A maze assessment utilizes a variation of the cloze format. Every fifth or sixth word in the text is omitted. Students are given a choice of three words to replace the omitted word: the original word and two other words that do not fit in the sentence. The reader selects which of the three options makes the sentence meaningful.

Tier 2 and Tier 3 progress monitoring. Students receiving Tier 2 (supplementary instruction) or Tier 3 (more intensive intervention) assistance should also participate in the repeated benchmark/screening assessments conducted across the school year along with their classmates. And, of course, their teachers will also be carefully observing them during their daily instruction and will administer appropriate in-program assessments and quizzes. However, for students who are struggling and/or receiving extra instruction or intervention, additional data will need to be collected to monitor their progress on a more frequent basis. This is because of the fact that, even when academically challenged students are making progress, gains can be small and difficult to detect. Teachers responsible for teaching these students simply cannot afford to wait to determine if their students are benefitting from their Tier 2 or Tier 3 instruction. For students at these levels, many educators find that the progress monitoring assessments based on the previously discussed CBM research can yield valuable useful information for making key instructional decisions.

CBM for Progress Monitoring Versus Benchmark Assessments

CBM assessments utilized for monitoring students' progress use most of the same standardized procedures that are used with benchmark/screening assessments, but with four differences. 1) Perhaps the most significant variation between the two types of assessment is that, for progress monitoring, students' performances are compared with individually set goals and previous performance, rather than being compared with a set of grade-level norms and benchmarks. 2) A second difference is that progress monitoring is conducted at more frequent intervals than benchmark/screening. Depending on the severity of student need,

Table 8.5. Differences between curriculum-based measurement benchmark/screening assessments and progress monitoring assessments

Benchmark/screening	Progress monitoring
Scores compared to established norms or *benchmarks*.	Scores compared to individually set *performance goals*.
Administered *three or four times per year*.	Administered as often as *two times per week, once per week, bimonthly, or monthly* depending on services student is receiving.
Scores recorded as *numbers*.	Scores recorded on individual student *graphs* for visual analysis of data trends.
Assessment passages are always at the student's *current grade level* (e.g., all second-grade students read second-grade passages).	Assessment passages are either at the student's *current instructional level or one level above* (goal level; e.g., a fourth grader reading at the second-grade level uses either second-grade or third-grade passages).

current recommendations suggest that assessments can be administered once or twice a month, or as often as once a week. However, newer emerging research suggests that less frequent monitoring, perhaps using two passages every 3 weeks, may be the most appropriate.[28] More research in this area is needed so that more precise guidance can be provided.

3) The third difference between the benchmark and progress monitoring assessments is that a student's results from progress monitoring assessments are recorded on graphs so that teachers and specialists can easily evaluate an individual's progress—or lack of progress—over time (Table 8.6). These graphs provide easy-to-interpret visual displays of student progress when compared with a predetermined individual performance goal. Most important, when a graph indicates less than expected progress, immediate adjustments can be made in the student's instruction. Students can be taught to graph their own progress, a highly motivating activity.

4) The final difference between CBM benchmark/screening and progress monitoring assessments is the level of difficulty of the passages. The passages used for benchmark/screening are always at the student's grade placement level, even when it is clear the student is reading well above or well below their current grade, while the level of the passages for progress monitoring varies. When progress monitoring, students can be assessed using passages that are easier or more difficult than their current instructional level or one level above their current instructional level, also called "goal level," and the technical adequacy of the measures is not affected.[29] For example, if an eighth-grade student is currently reading at about the third-grade level, she can have her progress monitored using either third-grade passages (instructional level) or fourth-grade passages (goal level).

HOW DO YOU TEACH THIS COMPONENT EFFECTIVELY, EFFICIENTLY, AND IN A MANNER APPROPRIATE TO THE AGE/GRADE LEVEL OF YOUR STUDENTS?

It is well established that readers with inadequate fluency skills often struggle with comprehension, and it is rare that students with poorly developed fluency are highly motivated readers who eagerly look forward to opportunities to read. However, simply increasing a student's levels of rate and accuracy and improving their prosody cannot guarantee that the student's comprehension will also increase. In other words: Fluency is necessary but not sufficient for reading comprehension. Teachers must keep this concept in mind when designing appropriate fluency instruction or interventions for students. As Kuhn, Schwanenflugel, and Meisinger state: "It is critical that we establish…instruction that assist(s) learners in becoming truly fluent readers rather than just fast ones."[30] Other researchers have also warned teachers not to expect that if students simply read more, they will achieve adequate levels of fluency.[31] They point out that research and theory strongly suggest that at least some students will require systematic instruction and teacher guidance in order to become skillful and motivated fluent readers.

Findings from Fluency Research

From the numerous studies that have been conducted over recent decades, some key points should be considered when one is designing fluency instruction and intervention for students.[32] Below are some of these key findings from fluency studies:

- The National Reading Panel reported that guided, oral reading practice improves fluency for typically developing students, but that silent reading and independent practice is likely not sufficient to improve students' fluency skill.[33]

- Repeated reading remains the "gold standard" of fluency interventions, but providing feedback or having the student reading along with a model as part of repeated reading is more effective that independent repeated reading.[34]

- For some students, the same amount of time spent engaged in "wide reading" (sustained reading of a variety of texts) has as much positive impact on fluency as rereading a single piece of text,[35] but other researchers found that wide reading must be monitored and students held accountable for attending to what they read.[36]

- Structured partner reading can improve reading fluency.[37]

- Cueing students to attend to their accuracy and rate while reading can increase students' fluency.[38]

- Students can improve their fluency when the passages used for instruction are very challenging, even at a frustration level of 85% accuracy (15 out of 100 words are unknown or read incorrectly), if teachers monitor the process closely and provide sufficient support including feedback.[39]

- Instructional strategies that combine 1) reading with a model of skillful reading, 2) repeated reading of a single text, and 3) providing progress monitoring feedback before and after practice can improve students' fluency and comprehension and has a positive impact on motivation to read.[40]

- Although there has been little research specifically focused on improving prosody, some researchers have concluded that prosody develops from acquiring efficient word and text reading skills[41] and that it is likely improved by guided and assisted reading activities where feedback on expression is provided.[42]

Research Applied to Classroom Settings

The type and amount of instruction that students will need to become fluent readers will of course vary depending on their general reading skill level. For students who are receiving instruction solely in the general education classroom (Tier 1) and successfully making progress in reading, there are some techniques that a teacher can use to support the development of fluency. For those students who can read grade-level text with sufficient accuracy (91% to 97% or higher words read correctly) and generally understand what they are reading but whose fluency rates are below expected levels, more systematic and explicit fluency instruction should be provided, perhaps as part of a Tier 2 intervention. For students whose fluency levels are low and they also struggle with deficits in phonics and decoding, word recognition, vocabulary, or other skill areas, a more comprehensive intervention will likely need to be developed and provided in a Tier 2 or Tier 3 setting. In these cases, explicit and systematic fluency instruction should be provided as one component of a more multifaceted instructional program.

Tier 1 fluency instruction. Research is clear that many—if not most—students will develop adequate fluency levels by simply engaging in reading, especially if they also hear models of fluent reading and receive feedback about their reading rate, accuracy, and prosody. Two commonly implemented but less effective ways teachers try to encourage reading are round robin reading and silent sustained reading; neither is an effective method to increase comprehension.

In round robin reading, students take turns reading aloud from unpracticed text, often in a whole-class, large-group setting. Teachers use this technique with varieties of text genres including novels, social studies, or science texts. Note only one student is reading at a time while the others are typically losing interest and not paying attention. Sustained silent reading (SSR), sometimes called drop everything and read (DEAR), requires students to read silently in self-selected texts for a designated period of time, sometimes up to 20 or 30 minutes or more daily. Often, students choose books that are either too easy or much too difficult for them, so they are not improving their reading skills. Also, too much time can be wasted as students choose their books, and typically students are not accountable for what they are reading. Although some students might benefit from these activities, neither of these methods provides the amount of practice that at-risk or struggling readers will need to develop their fluency, and both activities limit the amount of modeling and opportunities for specific feedback that are also critical.

Teachers can consider replacing round robin reading with choral reading or cloze reading.[43] In choral reading, students read text aloud in unison along with the teacher—all students are participating. Cloze reading involves having the teacher read text aloud while students follow along silently in their own copies of the text or from a shared text such as on an overhead or whiteboard. From time to time, the teacher randomly pauses before reading a word, and the students read that "omitted" word aloud in unison.

Another alternative to SSR or DEAR is structured partner reading where assigned partners read together and provide each other feedback including pointing out errors and supporting the correct pronunciation and decoding of words. Structured partner reading can take several forms, including simultaneous oral reading, taking turns reading a sentence, paragraph, or page aloud, sharing one book, or each student having his or her own copy of the text.[44] Students can be taught even more explicit feedback techniques that extend the practice to vocabulary and comprehension development.

Tier 2 or 3 fluency instruction. For students who need a more targeted intervention to improve their fluency skills, the three-component strategy developed by Candyce Ihnot known as Read Naturally (RN)[45] has been shown to be successful.[46] In this strategy, students are first assessed to determine an appropriate level of text in which to receive instruction. Using the RN placement guidelines, students will typically be placed in text that is at or close to their frustration level (below 90% accuracy). The placement guidelines also help a teacher establish a specific fluency goal for each student, which is usually set at 30 words above the assessed baseline ORF score for students in grades 1–4 and 40 words above the ORF baseline for grades 5 and higher.

The RN intervention itself begins with having a student complete a 60-second "cold read" of a self-selected passage at his or her designated skill level. The purpose of this step is to establish a score that the student can use as an indicator of his or her unpracticed score. This serves as a motivator for the student to try to increase that score by practicing. During this cold read, the student marks words that cause him or her to "stop, stumble, or skip" and then calculates a score of words correct per minute. This score is recorded on the student's graph.

The next step involves having the student quietly read the same passage again from the beginning, but this time reading aloud along with a narrator (on a CD or computer) or a skilled reader. The purpose of this step is to help the student learn how to identify and correctly pronounce all the words of the passage and also provides a model of appropriate prosody. Students typically read the entire passage (from 80 to 350 words in length, depending on the grade level of the passage) three times with the skilled reader or narrator. Once the student feels he or she knows all the words, he or she next engages in repeated reading practice by reading aloud from the practiced text for 60-second intervals until his or her designated ORF goal has been achieved. For each practice, the student returns to the start of the passage. This step often takes three to 10 attempts. This step helps build the student's reading rate while maintaining accuracy.

Table 8.6. Reading fluency WPM.

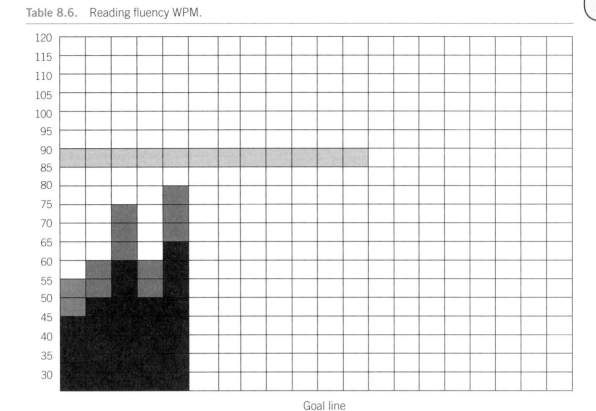

Goal line

Story	1		2	4	6	7																
Page#	9		5	8	11	15																

Name _____ Teacher _____

Date _____

Key: WPM, words per minute.

Finally, the teacher listens to the student read aloud for 60 seconds from the now well-practiced passage. If the student is able to read the passage with no more than three errors, reads with appropriate expression, and reaches his or her designated goal, he or she is allowed to record the practiced score on his or her graph, alongside the original cold read score. Comparing the original "cold" score to the usually much-higher practiced score is clear proof that practice makes a difference! This process is repeated with the next passage. The RN strategy also incorporates prediction, retell, and question answering to hold students accountable for comprehending the content of the passages used for practice (Table 8.6).

There are many other commercially available programs and materials that address reading fluency. Matching the materials to the student's reading level is the biggest challenge for teachers, so you should carefully examine the various materials and determine which would be best for your students.

Examples of Fluency-Building Activities for Grades K–3[47]

Kindergarten and beginning of first grade: Students improve their speed and accuracy of letter names and sounds through the following activities:

- Alphabet arc: Students place plastic letters on top of the written letters. Gradually, the written letters are removed, and students put the plastic letters in alphabetical order within 2 minutes.
- Letter recognition: Students point to the letter the teacher names.
- Letter naming: Students name the letters when the teacher points to them.
- Letter–sound correspondence: Students name and provide the sounds of the letters.
- Reading high-frequency words: Students read a list of 50 high-frequency words.
- Reading words: Students read lists of decodable and high-frequency irregular words.
- Phrase reading: Students read short phrases.
- Chunking phrases: Students read chunks of text with prosody.

Second semester first grade through third grade: Students gain speed and accuracy reading connected text.

- Repeated reading: Students read and re-read text at their independent or instructional level.
- Partner reading: Students read and re-read text with a partner. Words correct per minute are charted.
- Prosody: Students read connected text with appropriate expression and phrasing.

SUMMARY

Reading fluency is a skill that must be adequately developed in order for a reader to be able to comprehend what he or she has read and to enjoy and benefit from the act of reading. But, like other reading skills—including phonemic awareness, phonics and decoding, word recognition, and vocabulary knowledge—fluency alone is not sufficient to help students comprehend. Teaching students to read faster is not the answer. Fluency is a complex and interrelated set of skills that includes rate but also involves accuracy and expression. Reading well includes reading fluently—with appropriate rate, accuracy, and prosody. Teachers must assess students to determine who might need assistance in becoming fluent readers and then effectively provide the instruction and intervention necessary to help everyone achieve success. For students who are already sufficiently fluent, pushing them to read ever faster and faster is a futile effort and has no instructional value. As Marilyn Adams said, "If we want to induce children to read lots, we must teach them to read well."[48]

APPLICATION ASSIGNMENTS

In-Class Assignments

1. As a class, practice a strategy to improve reading fluency. The strategy is repeated reading. Follow the directions below.
   a. Choose two pages of this text or another adult-level text. It should be a text that is unfamiliar to you and challenging.
   b. Pair up with a partner. Decide who will be Partner A and who will be Partner B.
   c. Your instructor or a classmate should be the timer and time the first reading for 1 minute.
   d. When given the signal, Partner A begins to read the text aloud. Partner B follows along. When the timer goes off, Partner A marks the last word read.

e. When given the signal to begin, Partner B reads the same material. Partner A follows along. When the timer goes off, Partner B marks the last word read.

f. Both partners count the number of words they read, including prepositions, etc. On the line graph, color in the line with a blue pencil or marker up to the number of words read correctly.

g. Now, both partners take turns again, each reading the same material for 2 minutes. You should be able to read much further.

h. It is time for the "hot" reading. Again, Partner A reads for 1 minute while being timed. When the timer goes off, mark the last word read.

i. Partner B reads for 1 minute and, at the end, marks the last word read.

j. Both partners count the words read and chart the totals on the graph, using a red pen or marker, directly on top of the blue line. This system will clearly indicate how much growth you made.

k. Did you increase the number of words you read per minute? You will learn that students typically will increase about 25%–40%, and they will feel great about their progress!

Note: When using partner reading with your students, obtain materials with the word totals already counted out and the number of words indicated in the margins. There are many sources for such materials, as listed in the appendixes.

Tutoring Assignments

1. Partner read with your student. The material should be at your student's instructional level, meaning your student can read at least 95% of the words. You be Partner A, reading first while your student follows along. Then your student reads it "cold" and graphs the number of words read correctly using a blue marker. Allow your student to practice reading the passage, untimed, about two or three times. Assist your student as needed. Finally, your student reads the passage again for the "hot" reading score and graphs those results with a red marker. Celebrate the progress made!

    A reminder: Do NOT encourage your student to read as quickly as possible. Do NOT tell him or her to begin with a phrase such as, "get ready, set, go!" Rather, calmly ask your student to do his or her best reading. Then calmly set the timer and say, "Begin."

2. Implement another fluency-building activity with your student. You may choose which one. It could be as easy as asking your student to select a favorite page or a favorite sentence and reading it several times with prosody, like an actor would practice reading lines for a movie.

Homework Assignments

1. Read Teaching Reading Is Rocket Science: What Expert Reading Teachers Should know and Be Able to do, by Louisa Moats, 1999, available to download from http://www.readingrockets.org/guides/teaching-reading-rocket-science.

    Write a one-page essay discussing the major points of the article, what you have learned about those points, and topics about which you need additional information.

ENDNOTES

1. Torgesen (2007).
2. Huey (1908/1968).
3. Rasinski, Reutzel, Chard, & Thompson (2011).
4. NRP Summary (2000). Retrieved September 26, 2011 from:http://www.nichd.nih.gov/publications/nrp/findings.cfm
5. Kuhn, Schwanenflugel, & Meisinger (2010).
6. Rasinski, Reutzel, Chard, & Thompson (2011).
7. Hudson, Lane, & Pullen (2005).
8. Miyake & Shah (1999).
9. Stanovich (1986).
10. Cunningham & Stanovich (1998).
11. Baer, Kutner, & Sabatini (2009).
12. Wayman et al. (2007).
13. Fuchs, Fuchs, Hosp, & Jenkins (2001).
14. Hasbrouck (2010a).
15. Stahl & Kuhn (2002).
16. Personal communication, Ron Cole, Boulder Language Technologies (www.blt.com).
17. National Assessment of Educational Progress. The Oral Reading Fluency Scale (2002).
18. Rasinski (2004).
19. Hosp, Hosp, & Howell (2006).
20. Hasbrouck & Tindal (2006).
21. For more information on specific benchmark/screening assessments you can go to these web sites: DIBELS, DIBELS-Next: http://www.dibels.org/next.html; AimsWEB: http://www.aimsweb.com; The Texas Primary Reading Inventory (TPRI): http://www.tpri.org/index.html; Reading Fluency Benchmark Assessor (RFBA): http://www.readnaturally.com.
22. Fuchs, Fuchs, Hamlett, Walz, & Germann (1993).
23. Rasinski & Hamman (2010); Hasbrouck (2010b).
24. Fuchs, Fuchs, Hosp, & Jenkins (2001); Wayman et al. (2007).
25. Information on diagnostic assessments is widely available including from *Educators as physicians* by Jan Hasbrouck and *Assessing reading: Multiple measures* from the Consortium of Reading Excellence.
26. Fuchs et al. (2001).
27. Wayman, Wallace, Wiley, Tichá, & Espin (2007).
28. Jenkins & Terjeson (2011).
29. Wayman et al. (2007).
30. Kuhn, Schwanenflugel, & Meisinger (2010).
31. Pikulski & Chard (2005).
32. Rasinski et al. (2011).
33. NRP (2000).
34. Kuhn, Schwanenflugel, Morris, Woo, Meisinger, Sevcik, et al. (2006).
35. Reutzel, Jones, Fawson, & Smith (2008).
36. Osborn, Lehr, & Hiebert (2002).
37. O'Shea & Sindelar (1984).
38. Stahl & Heuback (2005).
39. Hasbrouck, Ihnot, & Rogers (1999).
40. Kuhn, Schwanenflugel, & Meisinger (2010).
41. Schreiber (1991).
42. Hasbrouck (2006).
43. Hasbrouck (2006).
44. Fuchs, Fuchs, Mathes, & Simmons (1997).
45. The multistep strategy described here is referred to as "the Read Naturally strategy" or RN.
46. Hasbrouck, Ihnot, & Rogers (1999).
47. See the Florida Center for Reading Research for specific activities and materials to address fluency; http://www.fcrr.org.
48. Adams (1990).

REFERENCES

Adams, M.J. (1990). *Beginning to read: Thinking and learning about print*. Urbana-Champaign, IL: University of Illinois, Reading Research and Education Center.

Baer, J., Kutner, M., & Sabatini, J. (2009). *Basic reading skills and the literacy of America's least literate adults: Results from the 2003 National Assessment of Adult Literacy (NAAL) supplemental studies* (NCES 2009-481). Washington, DC: National Center for Education Statistics, Institute of Education Sciences, U.S. Department of Education.

Betts, E.A. (1946). *Foundations of Reading Instruction, With Emphasis on Differentiated Guidance*. New York: American Book Company.

Consortium of Reading Excellence (CORE). (2008). *Assessing reading: multiple measures* (2nd ed.). Novato, CA: Arena Press.

Cunningham, A., & Stanovich, K.E. (1998). What reading does for the mind. *American Educator, 22*(1–2), 8–15.

Dynamic Measurement Group. (2010). Dynamic Indicators of Basic Early Literacy Skills—NEXT (7th ed.). Eugene, OR: Institute for Development of Educational Achievement.

Fuchs, L.S., Fuchs, D., Hamlett, C.L., Walz, L., & Germann, G. (1993). Formative evaluation of academic progress: How much growth can we expect? *School Psychology Review, 22*, 27–48.

Fuchs, L.S., Fuchs, D., Hosp, M.K., & Jenkins, J.R. (2001). Oral reading fluency as an indicator of reading competence: A theoretical, empirical, and historical analysis. *Scientific Studies of Reading, 5*, 239–256.

Fuchs, D., Fuchs, L.S., Mathes, P.G., & Simmons, D.C. (1997). Peer-Assisted Learning Strategies: Making classrooms more responsive to diversity. *American Educational Research Journal, 34*, 174–206.

Hasbrouck, J. (2006). Drop everything and read: But how? For students who are not yet fluent, silent reading is not the best use of classroom time. *American Educator*, Summer, 22–31, 46–47.

Hasbrouck, J. (2010a). *Educators as physicians: Using RTI data for effective decision-making*. Wellesley, MA: Gibson Hasbrouck & Associates.

Hasbrouck, J. (2010b). Response to Raskinski and Hamman. *Reading Today, 28*(2).

Hasbrouck, J., Ihnot, C., & Rogers, G. (1999). Read Naturally: A strategy to increase oral reading fluency. *Reading Research and Instruction, 39*(1), 27–37.

Hasbrouck, J., & Tindal, G. (2006). ORF norms: A valuable assessment tool for reading teachers. *The Reading Teacher, 59*(7), 636–644.

Hosp, M., Hosp, J., & Howell, K. (2006). *The ABCs of CBM: A practical guide to curriculum-based measurement.* New York: Guilford Press.

Hudson, R.F., Lane, H.B., & Pullen, P.C. (2005). Reading fluency assessment and instruction: What, why, and how? *The Reading Teacher, 58*(8), 702–714.

Huey, S.E. (1908/1968). The psychology and pedagogy of reading. Cambridge, MA: MIT Press.

Jenkins, J., & Terjeson, K.J. (2011). Monitoring reading growth: Goal setting, measurement frequency, and methods of evaluation. *Learning Disabilities Research & Practice, 26*(1), 28–35.

Kuhn, M.R., Schwanenflugel, P.J., & Meisinger, E.B. (2010). Aligning theory and assessment of reading fluency: Automaticity, prosody, and definitions of fluency. *Reading Research Quarterly, 45*(2), 230–251.

Kuhn, M.R., Schwanenflugel, P.J., Morris, R.D., Woo, D.G., Meisinger, E.B., Sevcik, R.A., et al. (2006). Teaching children to become fluent and automatic readers. *Journal of Literacy Research, 38*(4), 357–387.

Miyake, A., & Shah, P. (Eds.) (1999). *Models of working memory: Mechanisms of active maintenance and executive control.* New York: Cambridge University Press.

National Institute of Child Health and Human Development (NICHD). (2000). Report of the National Reading Panel. *Teaching children to read: An evidence-based assessment of the scientific research literature on reading and its implications for reading instruction* (NIH Publication No. 00-4769). Washington, DC: U.S. Government Printing Office.

Osborn, J., Lehr, F., & Hiebert, E. (2002). *A focus on fluency.* Honolulu, HI: Pacific Resources for Education and Learning.

O'Shea, L.J, & Sindelar, P.T. (April, 1984). *The effects of repeated readings and attentional cuing on the reading fluency and comprehension of third graders.* Paper presented at the 68th Annual Meeting of the American Educational Research Association, New Orleans, LA.

Pikulski, J.J., & Chard, D.J. (2005). Fluency: Bridge between decoding and comprehension. *The Reading Teacher, 58*(6), 510–519.

Rasinski, T.V. (2004). *Assessing reading fluency.* Honolulu, HI: Pacific Resources for Education and Learning.

Rasinski, T., & Hamman, P. (2010). Fluency: Why it is "not hot." *Reading Today, 28*(1), 26.

Rasinski, T.V., Reutzel, D.R., Chard, D., & Thompson, S.L. (2011). Reading fluency. In M. Kamil, D. Pearson, E. Moje, & P. Afflerbach (Eds.), *Handbook on reading research,* (Vol. IV, pp. 286–319). Philadelphia, PA: Routledge.

Reutzel, D., Jones, C.D., Fawson, P.C., & Smith, J.A. (2008). Scaffolded silent reading: A complement to guided repeated oral reading that works! *The Reading Teacher, 62*(3), 194–207.

Schreiber, P.A. (1991). Understanding prosody's role in reading acquisition. *Theory Into Practice, 30*, 158–164.

Stahl, S.A., & Heuback, K. (2005). Fluency-oriented reading instruction. *Journal of Literacy Research, 37*, 25–60.

Stahl, S.A., & Kuhn, M.R. (2002). Center for the Improvement of Early Reading Achievement: Making it sound like language: Developing fluency. *The Reading Teacher, 55*(6), 582–584.

Stanovich, K.E. (1986). Matthew effects in reading: Some consequences of individual differences in the acquisition of literacy. *Reading Research Quarterly, 21*, 360–407.

Texas Education Agency. (1998). Texas Primary Reading Inventory (TPRI). Austin, TX: Author.

Torgesen, J.K. (2007, March). Research Related to Strengthening Instruction in Reading Comprehension: Comprehension strategies and other methods. Presentation to state level Reading First Leaders. San Francisco, CA.

U.S. Department of Education, Institute of Education Sciences, National Center for Education Statistics, National Assessment of Educational Progress (NAEP), 2002 Oral Reading Study.

Wayman, M.M., Wallace, T., Wiley, H.I., Tichá, R., & Espin, C.A. (2007). Literature synthesis on curriculum-based measurement in reading. *The Journal of Special Education, 41*(2), 85–120.

9

What Is Important to Know About Words of Written Language

by Elfrieda H. Hiebert

Hi. *Namaste. Konnichiwa.* You'll recognize that first word as an informal way English speakers greet one another. The second word will be familiar to Hindi speakers and yoga aficionados, while Japanese speakers will recognize the third. All of these words mean the same thing, but their spellings and sounds have developed independently and distinctly as a function of their respective languages. English is an unusual language in that it has assimilated patterns and words from multiple languages. The language source influences how a word is constructed (its orthography or spelling), and it also influences how a word is related to other words (its morphology or meaning). Understanding the language sources of English helps in teaching students to read and will also improve your own comprehension.

This chapter develops three ideas about how the origins of English words influence reading: 1) knowing about a word's origin helps in understanding its structure and meaning, 2) English has many words, a small number of which are used often and many of which are used rarely, and 3) the often-used words have some special features that can challenge beginning readers and English language learners.

Objectives: After studying this chapter, you will be able to do the following:

1. Describe a brief history of the English language and the primary sources of its vocabulary.
2. Explain the relationship of the origin of a word to its morphology or structure.
3. Teach students the words that occur most frequently in English and recognize words that are rarely used.
4. Understand characteristics of words that can challenge beginning readers and English language learners, including polysemy, parts of speech, and idioms.

THE ORIGINS OF ENGLISH

Linguists have followed large groups of languages back to their common Indo-European roots. About 130 languages are of Indo-European origins, including Latin, French, Norwegian, Dutch, and Spanish. But the commonalities of many of these languages are only visible to the experts. From the point of view of modern speakers, it is fair to say that languages, such as English, Hindi, and Japanese, are completely separate systems. One derives no advantage in English for knowing Hindi or Japanese. Other languages are related in ways that can be seen and heard. They may have developed in close physical proximity or may have been derived from the same source. That is why people who speak Spanish can often understand people who speak French. These two languages, along with Italian and Portuguese, are part of the

Romance language family. This family of languages is derived from Latin. When Italian speakers say *buon giorno* and French speakers say *bonjour,* they can easily understand each other.

Likewise, when German speakers say *guten tag* and Dutch speakers say *goededag,* they understand each other. German and Dutch are considered West Germanic languages. Although you might not find it easy to understand German or Dutch, English is in fact part of the West Germanic family of languages. If you have doubts about the relationship, listen to the resemblance between *guten tag, goededag,* and *good day.*

The pyramid in Figure 9.1 has been developed to convey the story of English. The history of English begins from the bottom of the pyramid and moves upward.

More than 2,000 years ago, the English Isles were populated by tribes of Celts. Their language, Celtic, was not part of the Indo-European language family but was a unique language. For the next 1,000 years, the island was subjected to a series of invasions, and, each time, the invaders left part of their language and culture in England. In 54 C.E. the Romans, led by Julius Caesar, invaded, departed, then returned, and stayed in England for about 400 years, speaking Latin. Many of the old English towns were named after the Latin word for camp, *castr,* such as Manchester, Rochester, and Lancaster.[1]

German Base

West Germanic tribes, the Jutes, Angles, and Saxon, moved into the British Isles as the Romans were withdrawing around 410 A.D. The Germanic groups terrorized England, driving the Celts to the northern and western edges of the island (currently Ireland, Scotland, and Wales). The Germanic invaders spoke Anglo-Saxon, often referred to as Old English. Their vocabulary consisted of everyday words to suit their daily agrarian life: *sheep, earth, plough, dog, wood, field,* and *work* as well as basic words such as *the, is,* and *you.*[2]

Early English was very close to German. There are still many other English words that are similar in meaning, sound, and orthography to German words such as *heart/Herz, house/*

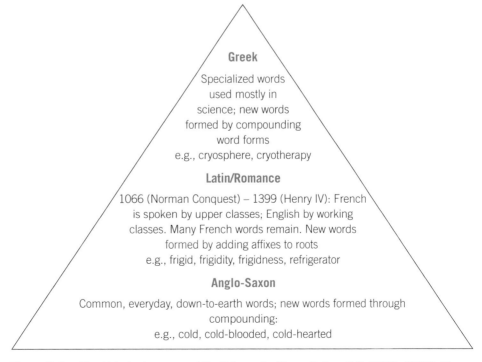

Figure 9.1. The historical sources of English words. (From Calfee, R.C. [1981–1984]. *The book: Components of reading instruction* [Unpublished manuscript]. Palo Alto, CA: Stanford University; adapted by permission.)

Haus, and *bear/Bär.* The most common words in English continue to be derived from this German base.

Between 750 and 1050, England was once again invaded, this time by the Scandinavians called Vikings. Although extremely destructive, sacking and plundering monasteries, they blended in with the Anglo-Saxons and, rather than obliterating the language, added to it. The ancient poem *Beowulf*[3] and the language of "middle-earth" in the *Lord of the Rings* series by J.R.R. Tolkien[4] illustrate this blend of the Nordic and Anglo-Saxon languages.

French Accoutrement

The English language went through a massive transformation as a result of the Norman Conquest in 1066 when William the Conqueror defeated England. William was French and insisted that French be the official language. During the 350 years that France dominated England, French was spoken by the upper classes, high-ranking members of the clergy, the leaders of fashion and haut cuisine, and members of the legal profession. The working classes continued to speak Anglo-Saxon. More than 10,000 French words entered the English vocabulary, and most are still in use today.[5] Examples of these words include *gentleman, faithful, parliament, and prologue.*

In 1399, Henry IV ascended to the throne of England. After a series of successful wars against the French, Henry IV declared that English was to be the official language. However, English had changed in some important ways from the original language spoken by the Anglo-Saxons because of the many French words that had been added to the lexicon. This change can be seen in the middle of the pyramid where words of French origin are located. For the most part, French enriched the areas of literature and academe, while having less effect on everyday conversation. That is why many of the words that are called "academic" are recognizable to speakers of Romance languages.

Latin and Greek

Latin, the language of the early Roman invaders and also the basis for Romance languages, again entered the English lexicon during the Renaissance. Scholars turned to Latin when they were developing ways to categorize and describe information such as the physical environment. Evidence of how these scholars used Latin terms can be seen in the system for classifying birds. Consider, for example, the name for a wonderful (but not exotic) bird—the white-breasted nuthatch. This bird is classified as *Animalia* (kingdom), *Chordata* (phylum), *Aves* (class), *Passeriformes* (order), *Sittidae* (family), *Sitta* (genus), and *Carolinensis* (species).

Europe was also undergoing a great revival of classical learning during the Renaissance. Scholars who wanted to show their classical training often drew on the original sources of words in Greek to name new inventions (e.g., *telescope, microscope*). Medical and musical terminology was often derived from Greek, including words such as *chorus* and *physician*. The number of Greek-origin words may be small but these words are central to learning in the sciences and social sciences. The Greek influence can be seen at the top of the pyramid.

This short history is not just of academic interest. Knowledge of the origin of a word assists readers of English in understanding how new words are generated and also the formation or structure of words. The history of English has resulted in many English words that have similar meanings; the simple everyday words are Anglo-Saxon, and the more sophisticated and nuanced words are from the Romance languages. Take, for instance, ways of describing the feeling of a driver who was cut off on a highway. The driver might be described as *mad* or *upset* (Anglo-Saxon words) or as *infuriated* or *irate* (Romance words). As teachers, we want to move our students' vocabulary beyond *mad, glad,* and *sad* to *infuriated, joyful*, and *miserable.* To guide students in extending their vocabularies, professionals need knowledge about how words with different language origins are formed (morphology) and how words are connected to one another (semantic clusters). The language source of a word also helps figure out spelling and pronunciation. But, with three languages that each has its unique letter–sound patterns, the story of English letter–sound correspondences is sufficiently complex that I will leave that topic to other authors in this book.

Morphology

Morphology refers to the ways in which words are formed in a language. Words with both German and Roman origins add inflected endings (e.g., *happens, happening, happened*). Inflected endings serve grammatical functions but do not change the fundamental meaning of the word. Inflected endings are part of the topic of morphology but the ways in which words for unique concepts are formed in a language is the essence of morphology. All three of the languages that contribute to English generate words in different ways, as was evident with the examples related to the word *cold* (which is the Anglo-Saxon word) in the language pyramid in Figure 9.1.

Anglo-Saxon has a large group of root words, many of which are relatively short words (e.g., *cat, cow, coat, creek, church, sheep, earth, plough, wood, field, work*). Some Anglo-Saxon words add endings (suffixes) such as *–less* or *–ful* to Anglo-Saxon words (e.g., *hopeless, handful*) and an even smaller group of prefixes, among them *a- (alike), un- (unlike),* and *dis- (dislike).*

When a new object or event enters into a Germanic language, it is often represented by a compound word. Evidence comes from the many new words that have been generated as part of the World Wide Web (itself a compound phrase): *firewall, bandwidth, bookmark, home page, listserv.* In Germanic languages, two root words can combine to form a new word that has a related but unique meaning from the root words. In German, a long string of words can be fused together to form a new word such as *Windschutzscheibewaschanlage* (which means *windshield wiper squirting device)* but, typically, only two words are used to form a new English word.

Some of the words spawned by the World Wide Web are compound words made by adding an Anglo-Saxon word to a word of Greek origin (e.g., *hyperlink*) or of Romance origin (e.g., *Internet).* But such compounding with Romance words is not how new words are formed in Romance languages typically. When new words themselves are generated in Romance languages, it is done through adding prefixes and/or suffixes around a meaning base, often called a root word. Anglo-Saxon words do have, as already noted, some derivational morphology (e.g., *"un"* in *unchecked* or *"a"* in *asleep*), but those constructions are vastly outnumbered by the prolific Romance derivational morphologies (e.g., *attend, attention, attentive, inattentive*). Thus, once students know the meaning of a root word and several prefixes and suffixes, they can usually figure out what the new word means. For example, if a student knows that the root word *dict* refers to saying words, he or she can use context clues to determine the meaning of words such as *diction, dictate,* and *dictionary.*

In Greek, two root words of equal weight form a new word. While this process resembles the Anglo-Saxon way of compounding, the Greek root words retain their distinctive meanings in the new word; that is not usual with compound words with Anglo-Saxon roots. The two Greek roots that make up the word *cryotherapy* retain the meaning of cryo (cold) and therapy (cure). In cryotherapy, low temperatures are used as a means of treatment for a disease or pain. In the compound word with Anglo-Saxon origins—*cold-hearted*—an individual's heart has not been subjected to low temperatures. The expression is figurative, implying that someone lacks feeling or sympathy. The Greek contribution to English is much smaller than that of Romance or Anglo-Saxon words, and its word formations follow straightforward rules. Greek roots traditionally do not function independently.

Semantic Clusters

Semantic clusters are words with similar though nuanced meanings. The example on the pyramid of *cold* and *frigid* illustrates how, to this day, our language is divided into parallel vocabularies. Many words overlap in meaning, which allows for us to make subtle distinctions that include but are not limited to connotation (good/bad), register (formal/informal), and intensity (high/low). Words derived from Anglo-Saxon (*church, clothes, food,* and *law*) exist alongside similar words that are derived from French (*religion, fashion, cuisine,* and *attorneys*). A challenging activity to do with your students is to ask them the difference between words that have similar, yet different meanings. What is the difference among *hungry, famished,* and *starved? Thin, emaciated,* and *slender? Tired, fatigued,* and *exhausted?*

Romance words, such as *religion* and *cuisine,* tend to be more formal and appear more frequently as part of our written language as the vocabulary of content areas and literature. This is not surprising when you consider that French was the language of the ruling class in England after the Norman Conquest, as was Latin when Britain was under Roman rule. All the while, Anglo-Saxon remained the language of the people. Romance words are many, but the Anglo-Saxon words continue to make up the bulk of the words of English texts and conversations—the topic of the next section.

ALL ENGLISH WORDS ARE NOT USED EQUALLY

The pyramid's tapering rise suggests the distribution of total English words according to their language of origin. Anglo-Saxon words outnumber the Romance words, not only in terms of sheer vocabulary size but also with regard to frequency of usage. For example, among the 25 most frequent words in English (which account for 33% of the words that appear in written language), all are Anglo-Saxon in origin. With few exceptions, the other 75 words that are on the list (Table 9.1) can be traced to their Anglo-Saxon roots. This group of 100 words accounts for around half of the words in written English.[6] This percentage holds for texts that children read as well as those read by adults in chapters such as this one.

The English lexicon has been stocked with vocabulary from two distinct language sources, which means English has more words than most other languages. This presents both an embarrassment of riches for writers and an Everest-like climb for second-language learners. However, there is good news for the latter group. This overwhelming mass of English verbiage can be boiled down to a very small group of words that does most of the heavy lifting. This is a form of linguistic efficiency that is described by Zipf's[7] Law, which can be summarized thusly: The most frequent words are used many times more often than the least frequent words.

The words in written English can be clustered into four groups.[8] The first group consists of highly frequent words. The number of words in this group is relatively small—approximately 1,000 words. These words are likely to occur at least 100 times per 1 million words of text. They contain the many functional words that help us form grammatical statements without regard to content, such as articles, pronouns, auxiliary verbs, prepositions, etc. This very small group of words accounts for almost two thirds of the words in a text, including this chapter. In the previous sentence, for example, numerous words are in this group: *this, very, small, group, of, words, for, almost, two, the, that, in, a.*

A second group—fairly frequent words—form an appreciably larger group of approximately 4,900 words. We can expect to encounter these words at a rate that varies from 10 to 99 times per 1 million words. This group of words is full of names and basic concepts that would be known by an average fifth–grader. Examples of words that fall into this group in this paragraph are *million, average,* and *fifth.*

The words in the third group appear with moderate frequency. Approximately 14,000–15,000 words are in this group. These words appear from one to nine times per million words of texts—words such as *reflect, infrequent,* and *zone.*

The remaining words fall into the fourth group—rare words. This group includes literally thousands of words. These words are the "specialty" words of English and appear less than once per million words of text. These are words such as *usage, gradations,* and *functional.* The British National Corpus[9] put the number of unique words in English as 750,000 words, most of which fall into the last zone where words occur less than once per 1 million (or even 10 million) words. Many of these words are archaic ones that are not used in written text anymore (e.g., *alack, thole, forby*) or the inflected endings of archaic words (e.g., *tholes*).

Table 9.1.   100 most frequent words in written English

1–25	26–50	51–75	76–100
the	they	when	come
be	we	make	its
to	say	can	over
of	her	like	think
and	she	time	also
a	or	no	back
in	an	just	after
that	will	him	use
have	my	know	two
I	one	take	how
it	all	person	our
for	would	into	work
not	there	year	first
on	their	your	well
with	what	good	also
he	so	some	even
as	up	could	new
you	out	them	want
do	if	see	because
at	about	other	any
this	who	than	these
but	get	then	give
his	which	now	day
by	go	look	most
from	me	only	us

Source: Wikipedia, most common words in English (2011).

This analysis of words begs the question of what is a word and how it should be counted. Think of a word rich in multiple meanings, such as the word "set." I can set the table, set you right, build a set, buy a bedroom set, collect a set, set the glue, create a set, do things in a set way, etc. The first thing that might be noticed is that the various meanings would not be used at the same frequencies. Another issue involves derivations, words that are made by adding suffixes and prefixes to a word base (e.g., *preset, reset*).

Derivations were mentioned previously as primarily a feature of the words that have come into English from French. The number of words created by derivations gets increasingly larger as the language continues to grow. An estimate is that, in the middle grades and beyond, more than 60% of the new words that readers encounter have relatively transparent morphological structure—that is, they can be broken down into parts.[10] When students realize that large, challenging words may be made up of smaller words that they know, students are able to break the large word into the smaller words and determine its meaning.

The vastness of English vocabulary raises the question of what should be taught. The rare words are often the ones that give a text its unique meaning, such as *sponges, rubbish, weird, dolphins, flicked, cove, swords,* and *snouts* in the children's book *Turtle Bay*.[11] There are also many words that are unique to academic texts such as *focus, majority, communication,* and *extension*. Content, literary, and academic words are, in fact, typically the focus of lessons in guidebooks for teachers. In Chapter 10 on vocabulary, you will learn how to thoughtfully choose which words to teach students, when to teach the words, and how to teach the new words.

Authors of books for children and teachers often expect that readers know the highly frequent words or the words that are easy to learn. However, this is not always true with students who are learning to read, whether they are young children or English language learners who are recent immigrants. Teachers and tutors need to be aware of some features of the high-frequency or core vocabulary that can create challenges in comprehension and word recognition.

THE FEATURES OF THE CORE VOCABULARY

The words within core vocabulary are the most frequently used words, and one reason they are used so frequently is because they make themselves very useful. Part of their usefulness is a result of their versatility (i.e., they can be used in multiple ways). This versatility is a product of three characteristics, namely 1) polysemy, 2) parts of speech, and 3) idiomatic language. These characteristics create challenges for striving learners. In teaching and tutoring, an awareness of these characteristics can go a long way toward supporting student growth as strong readers and effective communicators.

Polysemy

Many of the most common words in a language have multiple meanings, a feature that is called polysemy (from Greek *polus□mos* having many meanings). Consider the word *set*, which has 464 definitions according to the *Oxford Unabridged Dictionary*. That is an unusually high number, but quite a few everyday words (e.g., *find, change, good, check, play*) have a surprising number of nuanced, or distinct, meanings.

Polysemy has been identified as a factor that inhibits word learning. Words that share the same root but have different meanings (e.g., *comprehensive* and *comprehensible*) can be particularly challenging to learn.[12] When English language learners have been asked to guess the meanings of English words, they have had trouble with polysemous words. It is possible that exposures to a word with multiple meanings do not create the conditions for meaning to be inferred. The definition of a word with a single meaning can be reinforced over a variety of contexts, even if the sense of the word's meaning remains vague and cannot be articulated. Furthermore, researchers[13] found that readers who were familiar with one meaning of a polysemous word tended to cling to that known meaning during reading, even when it was clear it did not make sense in that particular context. In this way, the known definition prevented other definitions from being considered, leaving these readers worse off than if the word had been completely unknown to them.

There are several delightful books that have been written to highlight the polysemous nature of words. One is a series about a maid called Amelia Bedelia[14] who consistently interprets a request on the part of her employers with the wrong meaning of a word. When asked to *dust* the living room, she finds a jar of face powder and covers the surfaces in the living room with it, and when asked to *dress* a chicken for dinner, Amelia painstakingly dresses the bird in a little suitcoat and a tie. Fred Gwynne (who was also famous as a character in the *Munsters*) has written several books that even high-school students find humorous (and can use as the impetus for creating cartoons and illustrations). Gwynne's books—with titles such as *The Sixteen-Hand Horse*[15]—are illustrations of a child's perceptions of the expressions that she hears. Some of the child's confusion comes from polysemous words, while others are words that have similar pronunciations but different spellings (e.g., *The king who rained*). The content reinforces the need to recognize that the most common words in English are not necessarily straightforward in their meaning.

Parts of Speech

Polysemous words often take on different parts of speech as well as meaning changes. For example, some meanings of the word *set* function as verbs, as in *set an example* or *set the vase down*. In other situations, the word *set* functions as a noun, as in *a set of dishes* or *a TV set*. These words are considered homonyms because they are spelled and pronounced the same way, but they mean different things.

In addition to the homonyms mentioned in the previous paragraph, there is a particular group of homographs (same spelling, different sound) with dual meanings that are linked to parts of speech. Such homographs as *lead, record,* and *desert* often change from nouns or adjectives to verbs. The slight changes in pronunciation—usually a shift in stress—signal the change in meaning. Despite the difference in part of speech, the words remain very closely related in meaning. If you want to have a *record* of a meeting, someone must *record* the minutes. Other grammar rules can create additional functions for these words; for example, a noun can be used as a verb, which then turns into an adjective (participle). Also bedeviling are word pairs like *affect* and *effect,* which include a slight spelling change that is tied to part of speech. This is another way that versatility raises the bar on language proficiency.

Idioms

If I told you that "I'm not hanging noodles on your ears,"[16] you would probably be puzzled. But if repeated that expression in Russian to a Russian speaker, it would be easily understood. On the other hand, if I said in Russian, "I'm not pulling your leg," a Russian speaker would probably be baffled. These phrases, which defy literal translation, are examples of idioms. Incidentally, both expressions mean, "I'm not lying to you."

For English language learners, idioms are especially challenging. It is not that they do not know what idioms are. They do and could give examples in their own language. But they have a difficult time recognizing idioms in English, and when they do, they do not necessarily understand the meaning. The meanings of the individual words considered literally often seem far-fetched and even silly. Non-native speakers are likely to question their own comprehension before realizing they have hit upon an unfamiliar idiom such as *it's raining cats and dogs* or *does the cat have your tongue.*

Idioms are much less frequent in informational texts where language is more precise and less colloquial. But they are plentiful in stories, where figurative use of language is common. In fact, some idioms are literary in nature, for example, "sour grapes" or "crying over spilt milk." The origin of these expressions is fairly straightforward, at least to those of a certain age. Yet, the origins of most idioms are lost in the mists of time, and most people who repeat idioms would be hard pressed to explain them.

Idioms develop over time as a form of cultural shorthand. The word *idiom,* like the word *idiosyncratic,* shares the same Greek root "idio," which means "private, personal, or peculiar." The use of idioms in common speech and informal writing is ubiquitous and often automatic. Sometimes, however, idioms are deployed purposefully to declare membership in a culture or cultural subgroup. Adolescents is an example of a group that often acquires a wealth of slang filled with idioms to set themselves apart from children and adults. When adults adopt these expressions and they enter the general culture, the language loses its original cachet.

Many compound words are idiomatic as well. They use words in a figurative way to create new concepts. For example, *housebound* does not mean one is literally tied to a house nor does *tongue-tied* mean that one's tongue is physically knotted. Acronyms (e.g., *sonar,* created from **so**und **n**avigation **a**nd **r**anging), initialisms (e.g., CEO), portmanteaux (e.g., *blog*), and symbols (e.g., MHz for *Megahertz*), also fall into the category of idiomatic language because the way they are created is somewhat arbitrary, and the words enter the language by cultural consent. New words formed in these ways are entering the language at a rapid pace, partially as a result of new technologies: *The band's new CD was reviewed on my favorite music blog, and I've been listening to it 24/7 on my mp3 player.*

Helping students develop facility with the idiomatic expressions of language is a critical part of vocabulary development and instruction. Idioms cannot be taught in their entirety so the basic instructional procedure is to assist students in becoming aware of idiomatic language in English and to explore equivalents in their own native languages. However, idioms also present a challenge to native-speaking educators. This kind of language is so familiar that it becomes practically "invisible," and, therefore, it takes a bit of effort to avoid using it with beginning language learners or to call attention to it with more advanced language learners.

Cognates

It is interesting to point out that native Spanish speakers in our school systems are often able to make connections to vocabulary that are considered to be challenging by native English speakers.[17] For example, Spanish-speaking children understand the word *valor* long before most American children understand the concept of valor. Other examples of common words in Spanish that have English cognates, words of similar origin, include *facile* and *edifice* (*fácil* and *edificio* in Spanish). Cognates have similar meanings and spellings but are pronounced differently. Native Spanish speakers who cannot read Spanish (as is often the case with the children of immigrants) need to be supported in making these connections because the pronunciations of the words can differ greatly across the languages. Once English language learners learn to read, it is easier for them to see the connections across languages than it is to hear the connections. A list of Spanish cognates that are common words in Spanish but are typically in the academic vocabulary of English is provided in Table 9.2.

Table 9.2.   Twenty-five Spanish–English cognates: Words in literary/academic English

Latin root	Spanish common word	English literary/academic words	English common word
arbor (tree)	árbol	arbor, arborous, arboreal, Arbor Day, arboretum	tree
avis (bird)	ave	avian, aviary, aviation, aviator/aviatrix	bird
bonus (good)	bonitas	bonus, bonanza, bonny Phrases: bon voyage, bonafide: in good faith; bon vivant: person who enjoys good food/luxuries; bon mot: clever comment	beautiful
cavus (hollow)	cavar	cavern(ous), cave, cavity	dig
detinere (to keep back)	detenerse	detain, detention, détente	stop
frigus (coldness, frost)	frío (el)	frigid; Frigid Zones: South & North; Frigidaire (fridge); Freon: trademark for low-boiling refrigerants and solvents	cold
grandis (great)	grande	grand, grandiose, grandeur, grandiloquent, grandiflora, grandstand, grand tour Phrases: grande dame, grand monde	big
insectum	insecto	insect, insecticide, insectivore, insectile	bug
lavare (to wash)	lavar	lather, lathery, lavender (originally used as a bath perfume), lavatory, lavation, laver (large basin, also water plant), lavish	wash
liber (book)	libro	library, librarian, libretto	book
luna (the moon)	luna	lunar, Luna, lunacy, lunatic, lunation, lunarian; Phrases: lunar month, lunar year, lunatic fringe	moon
necessitas	necesitar	necessity, necessary, necessitate, necessarily	need
noctis (night)	noche	nocturnal, nocturne	night
observatio (attention)	observar	observe, observation, observance, obsequious	watch
primus (first)	primero	prime, primate, primal, primacy, primary, primarily, primer, primitive, primeval, primogeniture, primordial	first
re (back) spondere (pledge)	responder	response, respond, respondent, responder, responsibility, responsible	answer
regis (king)	rey/reina	regent, regal, regalia, reign; related words: regime, regimen, regiment, region, Rex; official title of a reigning king	king/queen

Latin root	Spanish common word	English literary/academic words	English common word
scribere (to write)	escribir	scribe, script, Scripture, scribbler, scribble	write
significans (meaning)	significar	significance, significant	mean
sol (the sun)	sol	solar, solstice, solarium	sun
sufficiere (to provide)	suficiente	sufficient, suffice, sufficiency	enough
terra (earth)	tierra	terrain, subterranean, terrace, terrestrial, terrene, terrarium Phrases: terra firma (solid ground), terra incognita (unexplored territory), terra cotta	ground
vacare (to be empty)	vacía	vacant, vacate, vacancy, vacation	empty
valere (to be strong)	valiente	valiant, valid, value, valorous, valor	brave
venus (sale)	vender	vender, vender, vend, venal (can be bribed, corrupted), vending machine	sell

From Hiebert, E.H. (2003). *25 Spanish-English cognates: Words in literary/academic English.* Santa Cruz, CA: TextProject, Inc.; reprinted by permission.

CONCLUSION

To sum up, English is an especially challenging language because it draws on two primary languages—Anglo-Saxon (which is a Germanic language) and French (which is a Romance language)—and, in content areas such as science and social studies, it draws on a third language—Greek. The systems of each of these languages differ, including differences in the ways that words are constructed. It also means that there are often several words in English that can be used to describe the same phenomenon, as is evident in the way we can describe a drop in temperature. We can say: *It is cold* (Anglo-Saxon). *It is frigid!* (Romance). Or we can say, *I am about to become an experiment in cryogenics* (Greek).

As these examples show, the three language sources permit nuances and elaboration. Therein lies the good news about English—its ability to communicate nuances and complexity. The focus is often on the challenges of English—that it has a puzzling letter–sound system (which also can be traced to its multilingual roots). Another part of the good news, resulting from studies of large databases of words, is we know which words are the most frequently used and, therefore, can focus on those of highest utility to students. Focusing on these frequently used words is important because they display quite a bit of versatility in the language when they take on multiple meanings, shift into different parts of speech, and are used in creative, idiomatic ways. Bearing all this in mind will help teachers guide students through the gauntlet of English vocabulary so that they can gain enough proficiency to partake in its many riches.

APPLICATION ASSIGNMENTS

In-Class Assignments

1. Write the following words on pieces of paper. Using a sticky board, sort the words into their probable origin: Anglo-Saxon/German, Greek, Latin, or French.

   Words to sort: decathlon, petrify, ambassador, pacifier, cohort, alphabet, microscopic, apple, pharmacology, haute couture, heart, life, liquid, meteorologist, grass, vice versa, charisma, food, filet.

2. Make a flip chart to help students practice learning the meanings of common prefixes and suffixes. Follow these steps:

   a. Select five common prefixes and five suffixes that your student may encounter (web site).

b. List which root words would make sense with a prefix, a suffix, or both a prefix and a suffix.

c. Take three pieces of paper. Align the papers on top of each other about 1 inch apart.

d. Fold the papers so that you have a series of small 1-inch portions.

e. Staple across the top.

f. Fold the papers into thirds and crease.

g. Cut along each crease, leaving about 3 inches on the top intact. Do not cut all the way to the top.

h. Now, you should have a flip chart.

i. On the top left third, write in green marker "prefix." Use green because green means go or start, reminding students that prefixes are at the start, or beginning, of the word.

j. On the middle top, write "root" in black, blue, or brown.

k. On the right side, write "suffix" in red. Red means stop or the end, reminding students that suffixes are at the end of the word.

l. Write your prefixes, in green, on the left side flaps.

m. Write your suffixes, in red, on the right side flaps.

n. Write the root words, not aligned with prefixes or suffixes that make sense, in the middle.

o. Flip the portions of the chart to create words. It is also fun to create made-up words and definitions (Just be sure your students, especially English language learners, know that the words are not real words!)

p. Define the words you create. To scaffold your new learning, write definitions or draw pictures on the back of each prefix, root word, and suffix.

q. Discuss how you could use this activity with your students and how you adapt it to meet the needs of each student.

Tutoring Assignments

Select two prefixes and teach them to your student. Prepare a set of cards including words that contain those prefixes and some that do not. Together, sort the words into those that contain the targeted prefixes and those that do not. Ask your student to determine the meaning of the word with and without the prefix.

1. Repeat the activity above, using suffixes.

2. Select five words from Greek (relating to science) or French (relating to food). Explain to your student the nature of words from Greek (scientific) and those from French (in this case, cuisine). Have the student read and then sort the words into Greek and French origin.

Homework Assignments

1. Read *How Spelling Supports Reading and Why It Is More Regular and Predictable Than You Think* by Louisa Moats, available to download at http://www.aft.org.

2. Write a paper synthesizing the new information you learned about the English language in both this chapter and in the Moats article.

ENDNOTES

1. Henry (2003).
2. McCrum, MacNeil, & Cran (2002).
3. Beowulf in Chickering & Howell (2006).
4. Tolkien (1954-1955/2005).
5. Claiborne (1983).
6. Zeno, Ivens, Millard, & Duvvuri (1995).
7. Zipf (1935).
8. Zeno et al. (1995).
9. Leech, Rayson, & Wilson (2001).
10. Nagy, Anderson, Schommer, Scott, & Stallman (1989).
11. Pirotta (2005).
12. Laufer (1990).
13. Bensoussan & Laufer (1984).
14. Parrish (2003).
15. Gwynne (1987).
16. Bhalla (2009).
17. Bravo, Hiebert, & Pearson (2007).

REFERENCES

Bensoussan, M., & Laufer, B. (1984). Lexical guessing in context in EFL reading comprehension. *Journal of Research in Reading, 7*(1), 15–32.

Bhalla, J. (2009). I'm not hanging noodles on your ears and other intriguing idioms from around the world. Washington, DC: National Geographic.

Bravo, M.A., Hiebert, E.H., & Pearson, P.D. (2007). Tapping the linguistic resources of Spanish/English bilinguals: The role of cognates in science. In R.K. Wagner, A. Muse, & K. Tannenbaum (Eds.), *Vocabulary development and its implications for reading comprehension* (pp. 140–156). New York: Guilford.

Calfee, R.C. (1981–1984). *The book: Components of reading instruction* (Unpublished manuscript). Palo Alto, CA: Stanford University.

Chickering, I., & Howell, D. (Eds.). (2006). *Beowulf: A dual-language edition.* New York: Anchor Books.

Claiborne, R. (1983). *Our marvelous native tongue. The life and times of the English language.* New York: New York Times Book Co.

Gwynne, F. (1987). *The sixteen hand horse.* New York: Simon & Schuster Books.

Henry, M.K. (2003). *Unlocking literacy: Effective decoding and spelling instruction.* Baltimore: Paul H. Brookes Publishing Co.

Hiebert, E.H. (2003). *25 Spanish-English Cognates: Words in Literary/Academic English.* Santa Cruz, CA: TextProject, Inc.

Laufer, B. (1990). Why are some words more difficult than others? Some intralexical factors that affect the learning of words. *International Review of Applied Linguistics in Language Teaching, 28*(4), 293–307.

Leech, G., Rayson, P., & Wilson, A. (2001). *Word frequencies in written and spoken English based on The British National Corpus.* London: Longman.

McCrum, R., MacNeil, R., & Cran, W. (2002). *The story of English* (3rd ed.). New York: Penguin.

Most Common Words in English (July 28, 2011). Retrieved August 9, 2011, from http://en.wikipedia.org/wiki/Most_common_words_in_English

Nagy, W.E., Anderson, R.C., Schommer, M., Scott, J.A., & Stallman, A.C. (1989). Morphological families in the internal lexicon. *Reading Research Quarterly, 24*(3), 262–282.

Parrish, P. (2003). *Good work, Amelia Bedelia.* New York: Greenwillow Books.

Pirotta, S. (2005). *Turtle Bay.* London, UK: Frances Lincoln Children's Books.

Tolkien, J.R.R. (1954–1955/2005). *The lord of the rings.* New York: Mariner Books.

Zeno, S.M., Ivens, S.H., Millard, R.T., & Duvvuri, R. (1995). *The educator's word frequency guide.* New York: Touchstone Applied Science Associates.

Zipf, G.K. (1935). *The psychobiology of language.* Boston: Houghton-Mifflin.

10

A Comprehensive, Interactive Approach to Vocabulary Development

by Martha C. Hougen
and Susan M. Ebbers

"In our classroom, we call new vocabulary words from the story we're reading 'Big Dog Words.' These words are placed on the wall with a photocopy of the front cover of the story. Students get to pick any of the words and use them as they act out a scene, whenever we have a spare minute. We call them Big Dog Words because you certainly must feed a big dog often, just like you must 'feed' your words, or use them often, to make them grow. I've done this for 2 years with the same group, because I taught third grade and then fourth grade the next year. The kids still remember the words from last year. This is not my idea, I picked it up at a conference—and I love it!"

WHAT IS EFFECTIVE VOCABULARY INSTRUCTION?
WHY TEACH VOCABULARY? WHAT DOES THE RESEARCH SAY?

For decades, it has been known that insufficient vocabulary and limited ease with language is one of the major reasons more than 30% of the students in grades 3 and beyond struggle with reading comprehension, experience the "fourth-grade slump" and eventually drop out of school.[1] As a teacher, you will address these concerns daily. This chapter provides the rationale for teaching vocabulary and presents effective and engaging ways to select, teach, and assess vocabulary as part of any lesson, infused into any subject area. This chapter also provides suggestions for increasing each student's "word consciousness" and "morphological awareness" (special kinds of linguistic insight). The objective is to teach vocabulary in ways that increase your students' reading comprehension and overall academic achievement and to motivate them to learn more new words and to read more.

Objectives: After studying this chapter, you will be able to do the following:

1. Explain the importance of teaching vocabulary.
2. Utilize a method for assessing vocabulary knowledge.
3. Choose the best words to teach to your students.
4. Implement effective strategies when teaching.
5. Model the use of semantic maps.
6. Explain how to foster word consciousness with students.
7. Define morphology and explain how it supports vocabulary growth.

It has been well-documented that vocabulary knowledge is related to reading comprehension, vital to success in school.[2] The National Research Council and the National Reading Panel determined that vocabulary development is essential for students in the early grades, yet little time is devoted to vocabulary instruction.[3] Teachers may assign a list of vocabulary words (which is not an effective practice if the teacher relies on students to learn the list independently), and teachers may administer spelling tests, but teachers rarely spend sufficient time on teaching vocabulary. This is problematic, because a student's vocabulary knowledge in first grade predicts his or her ability to read with comprehension 10 years later, in high school.[4] Students with a restricted vocabulary in primary grades typically show declining reading comprehension as they get older, unless teachers intervene early.

In an insightful study, researchers Betty Hart and Todd Risley visited young children of varied socioeconomic status at home, tape-recorded their interactions with their caregivers for one full hour each month for 2.5 years, and tallied how many words and what kind of words the children heard. They found that the children of poor or working class families, whose parents had little education beyond high school, heard significantly fewer words than the children of the more financially and educationally advantaged parents. The vocabulary differences were vast. By age 3, the recorded spoken vocabularies of the children from the professional families were larger than those of the *parents* in the financially disadvantaged families. This study clearly illuminated vocabulary inequalities that already exist in kindergarten—hence the title of Hart and Risley's book, *Meaningful Differences in the Everyday Experience of Young American Children.*[5]

There is another rationale for teaching vocabulary: The student who reads fluently and frequently will rapidly learn hundreds of new words, independently. An average student in middle school might learn several thousand new words each year, simply by reading at school and at home.[6] In contrast, the student who does not read often or cannot read well learns fewer words—unless you intervene with vocabulary instruction.

But, it might be said, for the good readers, let us just rely on independent reading and let them learn words from context clues. Indeed, many words are learned from context, so this is an important venue for vocabulary growth. However, useful and clear context clues are not always provided. In one investigation of varied school texts, context provided helpful clues for only 5%–15% of the unknown words encountered.[7]

Last, and yet perhaps first, vocabulary is taught to create a learning community that enjoys language and appreciates its power. During vocabulary lessons, and all day, students are taught to use words to help, not to hurt. Noted linguists Denning, Kessler, and Leben provided a good metaphor for this, in their text *English Vocabulary Elements*:

> Ultimately, an enhanced and enlarged vocabulary, like any part of the complex phenomenon called language, is a multipurpose tool. Like a hammer, it can be used either to build or to injure. The individual is responsible for the use to which it is put. (Denning, Kessler, & Leben, p. 182)[8]

WHAT WORD-LEARNING SKILLS SHOULD STUDENTS KNOW, PRE-K–6?

Teachers must consciously extend the vocabulary knowledge of their students by using rich vocabulary themselves and teaching new words, directly and indirectly. There is no limit to which words or the number of words students can learn, as long as the students have the conceptual knowledge to understand the meaning of the word. Recently, a toddler was explaining the difference between rudders on an airplane and the functions of the yaw! One kindergarten teacher worried that she used too many "big" words with her students. However, she continued to do so, and by the end of the year, her students were using words such as *graceful, admirable, doubtful, puzzling,* and *consequently.* Teachers must expect their students to understand and use myriad new words every day.

BOX 10.1. UNIVERSITY OF OREGON WEB ADDRESS

http://reading.uoregon.edu

Teaching vocabulary: http://reading.uoregon.edu/big_ideas/voc/index.php

The Center for Teaching & Learning at the University of Oregon provides suggestions about what students should learn about vocabulary in each grade (Box 10.1). The Big Ideas in Beginning Reading documents contain curriculum maps for grades K–3, outlining skills for each of those grade levels, including vocabulary instruction.[9]

The Common Core State Standards[10] describe what students are expected to learn at each grade level. The expectations for vocabulary acquisition and use can be found at http://www.corestandards.org/the-standards/english-language-arts-standards/language-standards-k-5/. For example, during kindergarten students learn new vocabulary words through listening, talking, and reading. Students learn to name pictures of common concepts, use words to describe location, size, color, and shape, sort pictures of words into basic categories, and learn new vocabulary through stories. Kindergartners must learn that words may have more than one meaning, as in *rose*, the flower, and *rose*, the verb. They are also expected to learn basic prefixes and suffixes.

By third grade, students increase vocabulary through independent reading, use a dictionary, and use knowledge of many prefixes and suffixes to help determine word meaning.

Beginning in fourth grade, students are expected to gradually become more independent word-learners. With repeated modeling by the teacher, they learn how to infer meaning by combining context clues with *morpheme* clues (prefixes, suffixes, and roots), using strategies described later in this chapter. As students advance, they gradually become more adept at using bound and digital reference tools, including a dictionary and a thesaurus.

HOW DO YOU ASSESS VOCABULARY GROWTH?

Researchers and teachers have struggled with the best ways to assess the effectiveness of vocabulary instruction. Students must be able to understand and use the words throughout their lives, not memorize definitions for a test and promptly forget them. So, how will vocabulary growth be assessed? You will use several different types of assessments, and you will detect partial knowledge.

A perceptive researcher, E. Dale, created one informal assessment many years ago. His tool still provides students and teachers with a measure of how well they know words.[11] Using a tool like the one shown in Figure 10.1, students evaluate their own understanding. Students rate words on a scale from 1 to 4 based on their knowledge of the word, from, "I have never heard of the word" to "I have a deep understanding of this word." Students who indicate the highest level of understanding are expected to explain what the word means and to use the word in a sentence. Dale's scale can be adapted and used to survey knowledge before and after vocabulary study. Students monitor their growth and are proud when they have increased their knowledge! By using Dale's scale, students and teachers are reminded that word learning is a growth construct, meaning we continue to "grow" our vocabulary, all our lives, through many encounters with the word in varied context. Learning vocabulary is not like learning the alphabet, which can be fully mastered in school. Understanding of vocabulary— even words and phrases already known—continues to become more multifaceted throughout our lives.[12] Partial knowledge of a word gradually becomes more complete. The detection of partial knowledge is important to assessing and learning vocabulary. As a pre-teaching tool,

1	2	3	⌐ 4 ⌐

Legend: 1) I have never heard this word before. 2) I've heard this word before, but I do not know what it means. 3) I know a little about what this word means, but I need more context (a sentence at least). 4) I could teach this word to someone else; I know its meaning and can pronounce it.

Figure 10.1. Vocabulary knowledge rating scale. (From Dale, E. [1965]. Vocabulary measurement: techniques and major findings. *Elementary English, 42,* 895–901.)

this type of self-assessment provides information useful for planning lessons, helping decide which words to focus on and how much time to spend on each word. If used before and after a unit, students see growth; success is highly motivating. This scale allows students to play a deeper role in their own learning.

Let us use Dale's scale now. As shown in Figure 10.1, fold your paper into four columns, labeled 1, 2, 3, and 4. Referring to the legend, insert the following words in the appropriate column: *myriad, hubris, sagacious,* and *morphology.* Do not say the words aloud. Warning: If a word is written in the fourth column, you may be asked to explain it!

Tally your assessment, giving yourself one point for each word in the far-left column, two points for each word in the second column, etc. Record your total. When you complete this chapter, you will have the opportunity to take this assessment again. Your knowledge will have progressed along Dale's scale.

Dale's scale is sound; however, a variety of assessments must be used. Here is how two researchers have successfully measured vocabulary learning[13]: Ask the class to write the taught word in a sentence, and score each response on a range from 0 to 2 points. Score 2 points if the word is used correctly, reflecting mastery (*The baby felt drowsy, so we put him to bed*). Score one point if the sentence demonstrates only partial understanding (*Drowsy is how you feel sometimes*). Score 0 points if the sentence reflects minimal or no understanding of the word (*I was drowsy, but you saved me*). You may also ask students to use two taught words in the same sentence (*The drowsy kitten went to sleep in the cottage*). By looking for partial knowledge instead of using a right–wrong scoring technique, you are more likely to find growth, which is motivating. Students note the growth and feel **sagacious**, insightful, and wise.

Students learn **myriad** words even in primary grades, so assessment starts early. Some words are fairly hefty! Consider the preschooler who can name several *dinosaurs,* state whether they are *carnivores* or *herbivores,* and describe their *ferocious, predatory* behaviors, demonstrating an immense capability to learn **myriad** new concepts. How to assess word learning in early childhood? Children can sort word or picture cards, create sketches, or act out phrases.

Also, children could respond to a spoken sentence. You say a word and a statement aloud, and the students listen. When asked if the sentence makes sense and sounds right, students write *Yes, No,* or *Partly,* as shown below (or use Pinch Papers, discussed later in the chapter). Repeat if needed. As with all new types of tests, model a few examples, thinking aloud to make your reasoning clear. Discuss the answers, and encourage students to explain their thinking, valuing their thought process.

drench	If something is *drenched*, it is very wet. (yes)
slumber	If I am *slumbering*, it means I am sleeping. (yes)
gloomy	If a room is *gloomy*, it seems very dark and very scary. (partly)
honest	A person who is *honest* likes to tell a lie. (no)

HOW DO YOU TEACH VOCABULARY EFFECTIVELY, EFFICIENTLY, AND IN A MANNER APPROPRIATE TO YOUR STUDENTS AGE/GRADE?

A Comprehensive Approach to Vocabulary Learning

After examining the available research, foremost vocabulary researcher Michael Graves concluded that four different but interconnected components are necessary to optimize vocabulary growth across the school year. Another researcher carried out his plan with fifth graders for nearly a full school year, resulting in better-than-expected vocabulary growth. The "Four-Part Vocabulary Plan" created by Dr. Graves is outlined below, written as "to do" statements for the teacher.[14]

1. Provide rich and varied language experiences: Create a language-rich, highly verbal learning atmosphere. Read aloud to the class, engage in poetry and drama, encourage elaborative discussions and debate, and plan for topic-pertinent peer conversations. Promote listening, speaking, reading, and writing. Encourage students to read daily, from fiction and nonfiction. Help students find reading materials that align with their interests.

2. Teach individual words: Select a few words to teach carefully, as time is limited. Teach the words with explicit and cognitively engaging methods. Provide students with two key essentials: a learner-friendly definition and context. Form word associations, creating networks of related words. Provide examples and nonexamples of the meaning, as in, "That music is *remarkable*, but this pencil is not *remarkable*." Revisit the words over time in differing context, providing multiple and varied exposures.

3. Teach word-learning strategies: Teach students how and when to use a dictionary and a thesaurus. Also, teach advancing readers how to infer the meaning of an unknown word, by examining context clues as well as word parts: prefixes, suffixes, and roots.

4. Foster word consciousness: Help students develop a love for language; kindle interest and engagement with words. Help them appreciate a word or phrase as uniquely useful, much as they might perceive the varied shades of blue in their large box of crayons. Help them recognize the power of words. Model curiosity with words, phrases, and word origins.

Because understanding the vocabulary of a given passage enhances comprehension of the passage, this chapter focuses primarily on the second component in Graves' comprehensive plan, describing several ways to teach new words. However, all four components are important; therefore, the chapter closes with suggestions relative to the other three components. As a teacher, you will incorporate each component on a regular basis.

Choosing Words to Teach: Teacher Discretion and Published Word Lists

There has not been definitive research about which specific words students should know at each grade, although some researchers have attempted to create lists to help guide teachers. Three lists are mentioned in this section. Researchers created word lists to optimize learning and teaching. It would be a misuse of research to distribute excerpts from a word list for weekly rote memorization. Effective, memorable vocabulary instruction includes context, a student-friendly definition, and engaging discussion.

Because time is limited, you must be judicious in selecting words to teach. Isabel Beck and her colleagues have developed a system to help teachers choose words to teach directly.[15] They organize words into three somewhat flexible levels or tiers.

Tier One words are words that most children know already, so you should not have to spend time teaching them, unless you are teaching English language learners. Examples of Tier One words for a student in first grade might include *baby, run, clock, happy.*

Tier Two words are the words that students will see repeatedly and in nearly every subject area. Some examples include *final, former, exhausted, demonstrate, analyze, distribute, emphasize, complete, generate,* and *frequently.* These are academic words, scholastic words. In many cases, there is a simple Tier One word for a more academic Tier Two word. For example, typically *get* is learned before *obtain.* An applied linguist, Averil Coxhead, listed the most common academic words for older students (grades 6–college), including English language learners. Her *New Academic Word List*[16] is available online and is discussed on the web site *Vocabulogic. Vocabulogic* is written for teachers by researers, to bridge the gap between research and practice, and to bridge the verbal divide among students.[17]

Tier Three words are specific words related to a particular subject area or unit of study, such as *integer, tundra, hieroglyphics,* and *photosynthesis.* This type of word is not used broadly, across varied types of content. Students need to have an in-depth understanding of these words only if it is necessary for understanding the unit or the passage. Otherwise, a quick explanation is sufficient. For example, if the word *epidermis* appears in the text and your instructional objective is *not* deep understanding of the cellular components or kinetics of the epidermis, you could easily provide a quick explanation, "The epidermis is the outer layer of skin" and move on.

Another rationale for word selection is based in morphology. If a word has a root that is shared by several morphologically related words, it might be worth teaching, along with its relatives. For example, it makes sense to teach the word *form* and to show how it is morphologically related to *formation, reform, reformation, formulate, formulaic,* etc.

It may seem obvious, but words to teach are also selected based on student knowledge. If there is a word or phrase that only a few students in the class do NOT know, it is time for differentiated instruction. Andrew Biemiller has shown that elementary school children learn words in a fairly typical order, and that they move along from partial knowledge to a more complete knowledge of the same word (see his list in *Words Worth Teaching*).[18] At the web site *The First 4,000 Words.com,* Michael Graves has listed words that are most frequently used in primary grades—a good place to start.

Effective Vocabulary Strategies

Think for a moment about how you learned vocabulary. Most of you would report that you were given a list of words, typically not related to anything you were reading or studying at the time, and were asked to copy the word, copy the definition from the dictionary, and use the word in a sentence. Now, consider how many words that you "learned" this way that you remember and use today. How much interest did that exercise promote? Teaching vocabulary primarily—or only—through dictionary or glossary study is not effective, especially for students with learning difficulties, at-risk readers, and English language learners. Likewise, assigning a list of words to be studied and memorized each week, with minimal use in speaking or writing and with minimal instruction, is not likely to significantly and positively effect vocabulary growth and will probably diminish motivation.[19] Logically, it follows that copying

BOX 10.2. VOCABULOGIC: Bridging the Verbal Divide

http://vocablog-plc.blogspot.com/

words repeatedly and alphabetizing words should not be expected to promote vocabulary breadth or depth. Neither should we hope to see expressive or even receptive vocabulary expand as a result of completing word-search worksheets.

THREE OVERARCHING QUALITIES OF EFFECTIVE VOCABULARY INSTRUCTION

How then, should vocabulary be taught? Bill Nagy describes three qualities of effective vocabulary instruction: integration, repetition, and meaningful use.[20] As you read through the models and activities provided in this section, note which qualities of effective vocabulary instruction are applied with each activity.

1. Integration: Link the new learning with something already known, so it has a cognitive hook—a place to hang its hat! Mix together and combine new concepts with old. Integrate *famished*, for example, with the known synonym *starving*. Contrast *famished* against antonyms, too. Connect it with concepts, like *famine* and *drought*. Build networks of related concepts.

2. Repetition: Provide multiple and varied exposures to the word in differing contexts so the student does not have to think about it anymore. The word must become an automatically recognized concept, freeing the mind for higher-level thinking. Depending on the learner and on the word, more than 20 exposures may be required before the word is remembered.[21] If you want students to freely say the word aloud, without fear of mispronunciation, teach them how to pronounce it. Have them say it aloud several times. That is another form of repetition.

3. Meaningful use: Use the word in varied applications, or context. Draw associations, make connections, contrast and compare words and concepts, etc. The more one thinks about something, the more likely it will be understood and remembered. If one thinks about something in myriad ways, there are **myriad** ways to remember it!

Anita Archer, a prominent educator, uses a mnemonic to help teachers remember these three principles. The photographs illustrate the hand motions for her mnemonic. Try it! The three principles of effective vocabulary instruction are 1) multiple exposures, 2) with deep understanding, 3) connected to what they know.[22]

Explicit Methods for Teaching Words

In addition to the three general qualities described above, there are several specific elements that are often included in a lesson. When you teach vocabulary, include the following two elements, as applied in student-friendly language to the word *drenched*.

1. Context, including spoken and printed context
2. A student-friendly definition (not taken from an academic dictionary)
   - Example: The word *drenched* means very, very wet. Dripping wet! Little Bear got drenched in our story, didn't he?

The two elements described above have been found to be essential aspects of memorable vocabulary instruction. However, you can do even better, especially for your at-risk readers. What else could be added to our lesson? Learners need details; they need to think and make decisions; they need multiple and varied exposures to the word.

(The *drenched* lesson continues):

- Provide examples and nonexamples, so students can tighten their understanding:
  - An example of *drenched* is how wet I am if I am stuck in a downpour for 10 minutes without an umbrella.
  - A nonexample of *drenched* is how wet I am if I run out to the mailbox for a moment when it is sprinkling.
- Built-in or embedded quiz, often in spoken or oral language: If I say something that describes *drenched*, say, "You got so drenched!"
  - I fell into the pool, with my clothes on.
    - o Students: "You got so drenched!"
  - I quickly ran through the sprinkler, but only once.
    - o Students: "You did not get drenched."
- Student-generated context
  - Tell your neighbor a very short story about a time you were *drenched*. Use the word *drenched* in your story. Listen to your neighbor's story, too.
- Fold old words into new words/concepts:
  - Last week, we learned *spunky,* and this week we learned *drenched*. Think of a way to use both words in the same sentence.
  - What are some synonyms that mean nearly the same thing as *drenched*?
  - What are some antonyms that mean nearly the opposite of *drenched*?
- Distributed practice:
  - Review vocabulary words in varied spoken and/or printed context over time.
  - Use taught words when speaking to the class, whenever appropriate ("Put up your hood everybody, or you will get *drenched*!").
  - Gradually, lengthen the time interval between word rehearsals.

TEACH WORD-LEARNING STRATEGIES

This is the third component in Michael Graves' four-part framework. The first component is creating a language-rich learning environment, including a lot of reading and discussion. The second component involves directly teaching the meaning of carefully selected words. If a teacher's goal is to teach the meanings of a group of words necessary to comprehend a given text, it is best to teach the meanings directly. However, it is impossible to directly teach all the words in a text, so you must teach older students how to "figure out" what an unknown word might mean when reading independently. Thus, Graves' third component involves teaching students how to become independent and life-long word learners. Depending on the grade level, teach students to use a dictionary, a thesaurus, context clues, and morphological clues. Morphology, followed by morphemic analysis in context, is described here.

Morphology. Morphology, or structural analysis, refers to the study of word formation. It involves learning about word structure, including the study of morphemes, such as prefixes, suffixes, and roots. Morphemes are indivisible units of meaning and the building blocks for words. Morphologically complex words contain more than one morpheme, but simple words contain only one: The simple word *cat* is one morpheme, but *cats* contains two morphemes, *cat* and the suffix *–s*. *Unbreakable* is complex because it has three morphemes: *un–, break, –able*. Through brief **morphology** lessons, students are taught to look within words, seeking out recognizable morphemes to better read, spell, understand, and remember words. Students work with morphological families—words that share the same root and are semantically similar, such as *act, action, active, react, enact*. According to Nagy and Anderson, school texts contain more than 88,500 morphological families.[23] Students are taught to look across families of morphologically related words, finding similarities and differences. For example, in fifth grade, it might be asked, "What is similar about *secret* and *secretary*? How are they different?" In second grade, it might be asked, "What is similar and different about *cartoon, cartoonish,* and *cartoonist*?" Students are taught the most common base words and roots, those that form the largest morphological families. For example, from the base word *sun* comes many words: *sunny, sunnier, sunniest, sunshine, suntan, sunscreen, sunning*, etc. Likewise, from the Latin root *port*, meaning "to carry," one can derive *import, export, deport, transport, support, report, porter, portable, portability*, etc. As teachers, you will help students learn to see words as part of a network of related concepts. As your students develop this type of linguistic insight, called *morphological awareness*, their vocabulary will grow. Vocabulary and comprehension are linked to **morphological** awareness.[24]

By age 10, morphological awareness appears to be a better predictor of reading skill than phonological awareness.[25] As children learn to read, it is important for them to eventually examine both the phonology of a word, looking at the sound–letter relationships, as well as the morphology of a word, looking for units of meaning. For example, you might teach first or second graders to decode *teacher, preacher, painter,* and *singer,* and at about the same time you would teach them that the letters that represent the sound /er/ also represent meaning: In the aforementioned words the suffix *–er* denotes "one who." It is helpful to point out to students how morphemes and phonology overlap and that morphemes differ from syllables. Morphemes are units of meaning, but syllables are units of sound/spelling. *Purple, magenta,* and *giraffe* have multiple syllables but only one morpheme.

Prefixes and suffixes are morphemes. There are two types of suffixes, inflectional and derivational. Inflectional suffixes include *–s, –ed, –ing, –er, –est*. When added to a base word, an inflectional suffix can change the form of the word, but they typically do not change the part of speech, nor do they create a new and different word. For example, *horse* and *horses* are both nouns, despite the addition of the suffix *–s*, and they are the same word, just in different form.

In contrast, derivational suffixes have the potential to change the part of speech of the word. When a derivational suffix is added, a new word is created, not just a form of the old word. For example, the verb *type* is changed to a noun when the derivational suffix *–ist* is added: A *typist* is "one who types." Some suffixes can serve as either inflectional or derivational. Consider the suffix *–er*: In transforming the adjective *cold* to the comparative adjective *colder,* this suffix is inflectional, but when added to *heat* to create *heater,* it is derivational, creating a new word and transforming a verb to a noun. It is context that helps us put the entire package together. Context is part of the study of morphology.

The structure of compound words also needs to be understood. A compound is created by joining two or more words to create a new concept. Connected compounds include *songbook, blueberry,* and *placemat*. Compounds can also be disconnected, with a space between the words, as in *redwing blackbird, polar bear,* and *greenhouse gasses*. Finally, some compounds are hyphenated, as with *self-esteem, jack-in-the-box,* and *son-in-law*.

By second grade, average readers typically understand, subconsciously and intuitively, that for many compounds, the final word—the right-most word of the compound—indicates the category. So, a *doghouse* is not a type of dog, but a type of *house,* as with *birdhouse* and *dollhouse*. However, a *housedog,* ending with *dog,* is a type of dog, as is a *bulldog*. There are some compounds that simply must be memorized, because the right-most word does not describe the category: A *pickpocket* is not a type of pocket. To understand *pickpocket*, context needs to be examined, or dictionary should be used. If children do not understand how compound words work, teach them, by discussing the meaning of a variety of compounds.

The Outside-In Strategy: Inferring Word Meaning Independently

By explicitly teaching students a new word teachers "give them a fish," but they must also be taught "how to fish" for a lifetime. Beginning in grade 4, teach students how to infer word meaning from context clues and from morphological clues, via the *outside-in strategy*. Researchers have shown that, by sixth grade, just more than half of the unknown words students encounter in school texts can be resolved—to some extent—by merging contextual and morphemic information.[26] This objective is worthwhile, but not easily or quickly achieved.[27] An important aspect of learning to independently infer word meaning is self-confidence. Students must be encouraged to look for clues and then "go with the gut" or "take a shot at it" until they begin to believe in themselves. As students experience success, they will enjoy a rising sense of self-efficacy, which is highly motivating.[28]

The Outside-In Strategy

1. First, look <u>outside</u> the word, at context clues in the neighboring words and sentences.
2. Then, look <u>inside</u> the word, at the word parts (prefix, root, suffix).
3. Next, re-read the entire context, keeping the meaningful word parts in mind. Make an inference: What do you think the word might mean?

You might model this strategy with a "think-aloud." Reveal your reasoning by speaking your thoughts aloud to the class. Use a short text excerpt to model the strategy. Select a word that has common affixes or roots. Also, show cases where this strategy will not work. Learning when to apply a strategy is important.

Fostering Word Consciousness

Development of word consciousness is the fourth component in Michael Graves' four-part framework. Word consciousness refers to an awareness and appreciation of the power of language, especially of words and phrases, as they are situated in context. Students who are word conscious notice whether a word or phrase is new or unknown, majestic, scientific, old-fashioned and archaic, idiomatic, figurative, whimsical, silly, very long, very short, etc. Also, word consciousness includes an awareness of *connotations*, the emotions a word prompts. Words can incite positive, negative, or neutral feelings. Many words and phrases are neutral, but some connote judgment, for example. Would you rather be described as *relaxed, inactive,* or *lazy*? Which word has a more positive connotation? An important aspect of word consciousness is understanding the pragmatics of language, or the language that is appropriate to use in varying social circumstances, such as while playing with their friends versus talking with the principal.

Teachers need to help students become aware of words, turned on to language and tuned in to words; help them become word-savvy, understanding the difference between an academic word like *demonstrate* and an everyday word like *show*; teach them to understand when the use of formal language is appropriate and when slang is more suitable. Use poetry to help students become picky about words—to value each word for its uniqueness and nuance. Use meaningful prose to foster an interest in words and an awareness of their utility and power. For field-tested suggestions for developing word consciousness, refer to *The Word Conscious Classroom* by Scott et al.[29]

Teaching English Language Learners

"I have a kindergarten student in my class where the primary language spoken at home is Korean. The mother expressed a concern that when she reads aloud to him she is not able to explain the English vocabulary from some books and she would like to know how she could help him improve his vocabulary. We do a lot with vocabulary at school through our reading program, but I did not know quite how to respond."

This email illustrates the challenge for English language learners, a challenge that teachers, parents, and students experience daily—a challenge that you will likely have to address, too. This teacher was able to send home the "story summaries" provided by the reading curriculum publisher in several languages, including Korean. Most reading programs also include translations for key vocabulary, certainly in Spanish, and perhaps in other languages. This teacher was also able to use free online language translation tools to help the parent and child learn together at home.

What can teachers do to help each English language learner master English during the school day? First, allocate extra TIME for vocabulary instruction, especially for oral language development—time for teacher-guided speaking and listening. Researchers have timed how long teachers spend directly teaching vocabulary using oral language, not copying from a dictionary or completing worksheets. Sadly, the average amount of time spent on verbalized and vocalized vocabulary instruction was only 6.7% of the class period in classrooms with no English language development block and only 2.6% in classrooms with such a block.[30] This is insufficient for English learners to gain competence and confidence with academic language.

In addition to allocating extra time and using publisher-created story summaries and/or translations with parents and students, use the following practices to help English language learners develop vocabulary. These suggestions vary by the student's degree of fluency with the English language. Researchers[31] have found that the following practices benefit English language learners:

- Teach words that are conceptually linked. For example, help learners develop a conceptual framework or schema for *transportation, car, truck, train, vehicle, locomotive, travel, route, map* and *delivery*. This includes focusing on synonyms and antonyms, providing examples and nonexamples. Avoid disconnected word lists.

- Prompt instructional conversations as two or three peers focus on a text or picture. Provide a semiscript, sentence starter, or framed sentence to enable conversations.

- Use pictures to teach word meaning, but link the pictures to speech and print.

- Role-play or enact the meanings of words, phrases, idiomatic expressions, etc.

- Model how to pronounce the word and listen to students pronounce it, providing them with explicit feedback (e.g., "Say the second syllable the loudest, in *assume*.").

- Link speaking, reading, and writing together, especially for academic words, making the learning more concrete. For example, for the academic words *approach, assume,* and *in addition*, have students say the word, learn the meaning, and then write them in sentences or a brief essay.

- Teach the conventions of English grammar and punctuation.

- Teach the most common prefixes and suffixes; develop morphological awareness.

- Teach older students to recognize *cognates*. Cognates are words from different languages that flow from the same root, usually Latin or Greek. Cognates share similarities in spelling and meaning. For example, the Spanish word *insecto* is a cognate for the English word *insect*. Cognates are more readily recognized in printed form, because speech moves too quickly. One web site that lists numerous Spanish–English cognate pairs is Latin America Links: http://www.latinamericalinks.com/spanish_cognates.htm

Finally, everything you have learned about teaching vocabulary concepts to native English speakers also applies to English language learners, but to greater extent. Review words, and review again in differing context—even more frequently and more deliberately. Provide even more practice opportunities, beginning with listening comprehension. Expect the transition from receptive language to expressive, productive speech, and writing to take longer than it might for native speakers of English. If you accept this challenge, and devote yourself to the goal, there is every reason to expect your language learners will make good progress, fairly comparable to your native speakers.

Activities and Strategies for Teaching Vocabulary

Let us look at some actual strategies and tools for teaching vocabulary. These activities provide students with many opportunities to hear, read, and use words in different contexts (multiple exposures). As you consider the following suggestions, keep in mind Bill Nagy's overarching principles of integration, repetition, and meaningful use and Anita Archer's three principles of multiple exposures, with deep understanding, connected to what they know.

There are myriad books available about how to teach vocabulary. One that is referenced often in this chapter and offers numerous ideas about how to teach vocabulary in meaningful and engaging ways is *Bringing Words to Life: Robust Vocabulary Instruction*, by Isabel Beck and colleagues.[32] Another book with excellent strategies is *Vocabulary Development* by Stephen Stahl.[33] These resources, as well as others listed in Appendix C, provide specific illustrations of how to teach vocabulary to diverse learners.

Reading Aloud to the Class

One of the best ways to expose students to new words is by reading books aloud to them. Teachers are encouraged to read to students in every grade level, but "read-alouds" are essential to primary grades. Even if you only read a book one time to young children, your effort is not wasted. According to a rather promising bit of research, children can learn a new word through only one exposure to it, as a process called "fast mapping" takes place.[34] Children mentally map the new word to a superficial and story-specific meaning—it is not deep understanding, but learning does occur.

Paraphrasing: If needed, when reading aloud at any grade level, teachers may embed a simple translation to ensure the students understand the book. This differs from directly teaching new words in-depth. Paraphrasing can occur as you read aloud. For example, "Once upon a time, a *maiden* [a young girl] lived in a tiny *village* [a very small town]." If you want to focus on directly teaching a new word, first, read the whole story without stopping. This provides context. After reading the story, teach the in-depth word, then re-read the story, asking students to listen for their new word.

Pre-teaching: For some books, you will need to pre-teach one or two key words. Often, an understanding of a specific concept is required so the reader can understand the text. For example, for the story *Elmer* by David McKee, the word *herd* is a key concept.[35] So, you will first show your students the picture of a herd of elephants and say, "This is a herd of elephants—a group of elephants that live together." Then read the story without stopping. After reading the story, or the next day, you can teach the word *herd* more fully; the students will have a better idea of what it means because you read the book to them. Pre-teaching key vocabulary becomes more essential as texts become more academic and challenging, but it is a practice that applies to every grade level and every subject area.

Extending: For children in preschool through first or second grade, experts suggest that you read the story once without stopping, then read the story again the next day, and then again a third day, to provide the repetition needed at that phase of development.[36] Each day, you teach a few more words from the story. On the fourth day, you review all the taught words.

On the fifth day, assess. Do not expect total recall after just a week of exposure. Do expect—and look for—partial mastery. Review words in the weeks to come.

Dialogic reading: As the name suggests, this involves having a dialogue with a small group of very young children while reading aloud to them. This method was designed especially for children of limited verbal skills who do not engage in rich discussions in the home. The dialogues are brief. For example, if reading *Green Eggs and Ham* by Dr. Seuss,[37] stop and point to a picture, saying, "Look! His arms are folded. Why do you think he is standing that way, with his arms crossed? What is he thinking and feeling?" Encourage children to respond, and insert the word *stubborn* into the dialogue. "He is feeling very stubborn!"

There are a number of activities that encourage vocabulary growth. Many of these activities are described and used in the teacher's guide for your comprehensive reading and language arts programs. Effective activities are listed below.

SEMANTIC MAPS

There are numerous kinds of semantic maps, or word maps. Semantic maps call for students to draw on their background knowledge and deepen their word knowledge. When using semantic maps, encourage students to work with a peer, discussing their thinking. Encourage them to refer to an applicable section of the text. Below, we describe several maps found to be effective tools for a range of students, including English language learners.[38]

Concept map: Let us use the word *scaffold* as our focus word (Figure 10.2). Write *scaffold* in the center box. Write a student-friendly definition under the word, such as "short-term, temporary support." Do not have your students guess what the word might mean. Guessing incorrectly confuses many students and takes up too much valuable class time. On the right side, ask your students to provide concrete examples of *scaffolds*, such as training wheels on a bicycle, crutches for someone with a broken leg, or a wooden structure to support painters working on a high story building. On the left side, give examples of what scaffold does not mean (for example, a permanent concrete wall, an office building, or a basketball). In the three boxes at the bottom of the concept map, ask students to provide examples of *scaffold*, as used in the context of the text they are reading. Because you are reading a book about teaching, brainstorm examples of scaffolds you might use to provide temporary support to students, such as modeling, breaking the task into small chunks, providing pictures, and providing additional opportunities for practice.

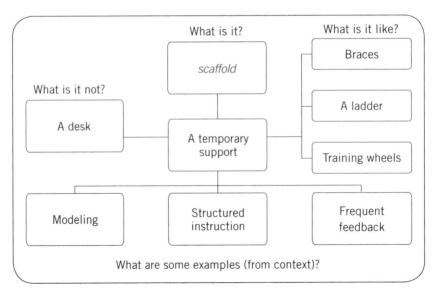

Figure 10.2. A word map. (From Schwartz, R.M., & Raphael, T.E. [1985]. Concept of definition: A key to improving students' vocabulary. *The Reading Teacher*, *39*, 198–203; adapted by permission.)

Table 10.1. Semantic feature analysis for animal classification

	Fur	Feathers	Scales	Forest	Ocean	Desert	Plains
hare	+	–	–	+	–	+	+
snake	–	–	+	?	–	+	?
vulture							
coyote							
owl							
deer							
lizard							

From Heimlich, J.E. & Pittelman, S.D. (1986). *Semantic mapping: Classroom applications*. Newark, DE: International Reading Association; adapted by permission.

Semantic Feature Analysis[39]: This type of mapping should involve partner discussion and debate, as peers use their background knowledge and a textbook to analyze features and consider attributes. Have students place a plus sign (+) for a match, a minus sign (–) for a negative example, and a question mark (?) if there may be a match in special circumstances, which must then be described. An example of a completed map is shown in Table 10.1.

Four Square: The four square model (Figure 10.3) was developed by Frayer[40] and is easy and explicit. This tool prompts visual and verbal word associations. Have students create a four square grid. Write the targeted vocabulary word in the upper left box, the definition in the left bottom box, a personal association in the upper right box, and a nonexample in the lower right box. Encourage students to use the four square as a scaffold for spoken language.

Try making a four square diagram using one of the words targeted in this chapter: **hubris, sagacious, myriad,** or **morphology**. An example using the word **morphology** is shown in Table 10.2.

Word Associations

Another way to increase vocabulary knowledge is to guide students to form associations among words and ask the students to explain the association. One such teaching routine is called VOCAB, developed by Gail Cheever.[41] Note each letter of VOCAB is linked to the steps of the routine.

VOCAB: A Routine for Vocabulary Development

Verify key vocabulary to be learned; put on individual pieces of paper/cards/sticky notes (see Figure 10.4) *(teachers should visually present the words and pronounce them)*.

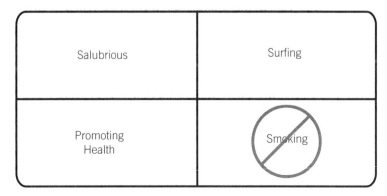

Figure 10.3. Frayer diagram. (From Frayer, D., Frederick, W.C., & Klausmeier, H.J. [1969]. *A Schema for testing the level of cognitive mastery*. Madison, WI: Wisconsin Center for Education.)

Table 10.2. Morphology

Word: Morphology	Examples:
	Prefixes, suffixes, roots, and other meaningful word parts
	Un+break+able ⇒ unbreakable (3 morphemes)
	cat =1 morpheme
Definition: Study of word formation	Nonexample: Phonemes
	Individual sounds in words
	cat = 3 phonemes/k/ /a/ /t/

Organize the words into a diagram that shows the relationship of the words to each other as you understand them (cue students to work independently using their own thinking to create their diagrams; sharing will come next).

Communicate your reasoning and share your diagram with a partner or two; listen while they share theirs. (Tell students that they may adjust/change their diagrams at any time during the activity.)

Assess the diagrams; discuss sameness and differences; share point of view; adjust your diagram.

Build your understanding with self-testing; Expand your diagram with new/related words.

Students organize word cards into a diagram that shows the relationships of the words to each other, as they understand them. They explain their reasoning to others, showing their diagram. Provide students multiple opportunities to share their diagrams and reasoning. This will allow them to develop verbal confidence and will greatly improve the likelihood that they will participate in large group discussions.

For example, pretend you have taught a lesson about health and wellness. You selected the following words as important for your students to learn well: wellness, mental health, environment, self-esteem, nutrition, physical fitness, relationships, and disease. The students tear a piece of paper into 10 small pieces and write each word on a small piece of paper (two pieces will be left to be used later).

The students arrange these words on their desk, in any configuration that makes sense to them. After a few minutes, the students share with a partner and explain why they arranged

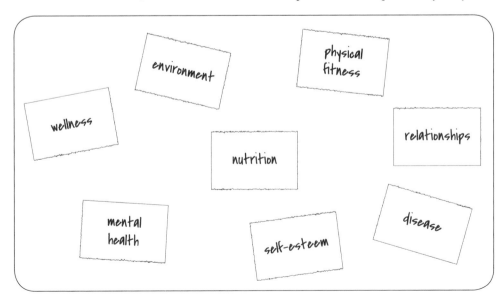

Figure 10.4. Vocabulary words scattered. (From Cheever, G. [2011]. VOCAB. personal communication; adapted by permission.)

the words as they did. Students are free to diagram the words in any way they choose, as long as they can explain their reasoning. What you will observe is that students will create many different diagrams, but it is their explanations that will give you insight into their thinking. For example, some students may put *environment* on top while others may organize around another word. It is important that students compare diagrams, share their thinking, and consider the different points of view rather than focusing on the "right answer" (see Figure 10.5).

Once students have created their initial diagrams, they are ready to build and expand upon them. One option is to give them another word(s) that they must incorporate into their diagrams. For example, ask them to write the word, *stress,* on one of the extra pieces of paper. The students add *stress* to their diagrams, rearranging if necessary to accommodate the new word. Ask them to assess the diagram once again. Did the diagram change? Why? Again, have the students share with a peer, telling why they arranged the words as they did. Next, tell students to form a small group to discuss which word they feel should be written on the last piece of paper and added to the diagram. They may go back to the chapter on health and wellness and reread it to determine one more important concept about that topic they feel they should remember. The group must reach consensus, so encourage discussion and debate. Some examples of words students may want to add include *choices, spirituality, balance,* or *diet.* As long as the students can justify why they think that word is important, their selected word is accepted. The students add their new word to their diagram. Each group shares with the class their chosen word, rationale for selecting that word, and how their diagram changed when the new word was added.

> Manipulation + Meaning = Memory

Providing students opportunities to manipulate material in meaningful ways increases their memory of the new material. To help teachers remember this concept, Don Deshler formulated the 3M Principle: Manipulation + Meaning = Memory.[42] When you provide students with multiple opportunities to manipulate (hear, use, and think about) new vocabulary words that are meaningful to them, the students are more likely to remember the meaning of the new words.

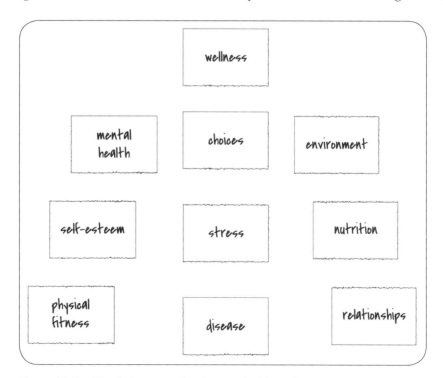

Figure 10.5. Vocabulary completed example. (From Cheever, G. [2011]. VOCAB. personal communication; adapted by permission.)

Word Line

Students are expected to learn that words can express degrees or shades of meaning. Often, students are confused by the slight nuanced differences in word meanings. For example, what is the difference between *slender* and *thin*? Which has a more positive connotation? What about *emaciated, skinny,* and *gaunt*? To actively involve students in pondering these differences, have them create a word line.[42] This activity could be done several ways. In the first example, the teacher provides a scaffold by providing a list of words and having the students place the words on the word line. Let us use the following words as an example: *walk, crawl, run, sprint, stroll,* and *jog.* Ask the students to place the words on the number line with the slowest type of movement on the left and the fastest on the right. One way to scaffold this task is to place the word in the middle of the number line, i.e., *walk.* The students complete the word line by placing the "slow" words to the left of *walk* and the "faster" words to the right of *walk.* (see Figure 10.6).

Pinch Papers with Examples and Nonexamples

Use pinch papers to make responses observable and interactive. Pinch papers are a form of response that involves the whole group and allows the teacher to quickly gauge understanding. For example, you might use pinch papers along with examples and nonexamples. Pretend you are helping students think deeply about the learned word *hubris,* using pinch papers: First, ask students to fold a piece of paper in two, vertically. Have students print "1" in large block letters on top of the column and "2" on the bottom of the column (see Figure 10.7). Proceed to read two sentences aloud, asking the students to pinch the number of the sentence in which the word *hubris* is used correctly.

Say: Which is correct? 1) Some politicians have so much *hubris* they think they can change the world alone or 2) The kind nun's *hubris* kept her from helping the poor.

Note which students correctly selected #1, which ones hesitated, and which ones had no clue. Gradually make the sample sentences more difficult. For example:

Say: Which is correct? 1) Students competing in spelling bees are often very nervous; their *hubris* can interfere with their thinking, or 2) The *hubris* of the owners of the Titanic was a major reason the ship sank. The owners were convinced they had built an unsinkable ship. (The correct answer is #2. Notice the importance of background knowledge.)

POST-ASSESSMENT

Refer to the assessment that was completed at the beginning of this chapter. Think about the four target words: *myriad, hubris, sagacious,* and *morphology.* Write them again on the Dale's scale, in the column that you now feel is appropriate. Did any of the words move up to column 4? Score the number of points earned. Four new vocabulary words were learned, easily, without using boring worksheets, just by reading this chapter! Care has been taken to provide explicit context clues, embedded definitions, and multiple exposures of each word.

Figure 10.6.   Word line.

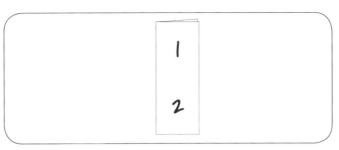

Figure 10.7. Pinch paper 1 & 2.

APPLICATION ASSIGNMENTS

In-Class Assignments

1. Retrieve the curriculum maps from the University of Oregon IDEA (http://reading. uoregon.edu/). With a partner, create a graphic organizer illustrating what vocabulary skills should be taught when.

2. With a partner, consider why teachers still use the vocabulary list/copy definition/use word in a sentence vocabulary routine. What alternative assignments would you suggest to a colleague who relies on this activity to teach new vocabulary to students?

3. Discuss when you would teach students the meanings of individual words and when you would teach word-learning strategies. Consider whether your objective is to improve immediate reading comprehension of a passage, to teach students to generate new words, or to transfer their knowledge of words to learn new words and skills. Provide examples from a text you plan to use with your student.

Tutoring Assignments

1. Select a book your student is reading or would be interested in reading. Select which words you should pre-teach, which words your student should be able to figure out using context, and which words you would teach in-depth after reading. Design a lesson plan to implement strategies from this chapter to teach the words you selected.

2. From the list of prefixes and suffixes you selected for the homework assignment, plan a lesson to teach 2–3 new vocabulary words to your student. If appropriate, include teaching the meaning of the prefix or suffix, how it changes the meaning of the word, and other words that fit that pattern.

3. Plan a lesson to teach students about morphemic analysis. Explain the definition of a morpheme and how being able to identify morphemes will help the student discern the meaning of unfamiliar vocabulary words. Teach the lesson. Afterward, reflect upon how you might have taught the lesson differently to scaffold for struggling students, accelerate for advanced students, or support English language learners.

Homework Assignments

1. Explore the following web sites and report to a partner how each may be useful to you as a teacher.

   a. http://www.textproject.org

      Explore the Summer Reads, free books for students, grades 4–6, to read over the summer. What vocabulary strategies would help students prepare to read those books?

   b. http://www.fcrr.org

      Go to Instructional Materials for Teachers, student center activities and pick a grade level, then select vocabulary activities. Review an activity and prepare to share it with a peer.

    c. http://vocablog-plc.blogspot.com

        Read an entry of interest to you concerning vocabulary. Be prepared to synthesize the information to share with a peer.

2. Using Internet resources, a textbook, or a core reading program, obtain a list of the 50 most common prefixes and the 50 most common suffixes. Which five would you teach first? Why?

3. Pick a children's book, fiction or expository, that you could use as a read aloud. Decide which are Tier One words that do not need direct instruction; which are Tier Three words that may need a quick explanation but do not need to be known in-depth, and pick 3–5 Tier Two words, words you should directly teach, the words for life. Be prepared to justify your selections with a peer.

4. Select two vocabulary words appropriate for students in K–2 and prepare two activities to teach those words with deep understanding.

5. Select two vocabulary words appropriate for students in grades 3–6 and prepare two activities to teach those words with deep understanding.

6. Select a text from a grade level you plan to teach. Find examples of difficult vocabulary words and misleading, misdirective context as well as explicit, helpful context.

ENDNOTES

1. Chall & Jacobs (2003).
2. Anderson & Nagy (1991); Becker (1977); Lehr, Osborn, & Hiebert (2004).
3. Biemiller (2001); Foorman, Schatschneider, Eakin, Fletcher, Moats, & Francis (2006).
4. Cunningham & Stanovich (1997).
5. Hart & Risley (1995).
6. Nagy, Anderson, & Herman (1987).
7. Ibid. (1987).
8. Denning, Kessler, & Leben (2007).
9. University of Oregon Center on Teaching and Learning, http://reading.uoregon.edu/
10. The Common Core Standards, http://www.corestandards.org
11. Dale (1965).
12. Stahl (2004).
13. Curtis & Longo (1999).
14. Graves (2006).
15. Beck, McKeown, & Kucan (2002); Beck, McKeown, & Kucan (2008).
16. Coxhead (2000). The Academic Word List. Retrieved April 19, 2011 from http://www.victoria.ac.nz/lals/resources/academicwordlist/information.aspx
17. Vocabulogic, http://vocablog-plc.blogspot.com.
18. Biemiller (2009).
19. Bryant, Goodwin, Bryant, & Higgins (2003); Nagy & Scott (2000).
20. Nagy (2004).
21. Beck et al. (2002).
22. Archer (2004); Archer & Hughes, (2011).
23. Nagy & Anderson (1984).
24. Nagy, Berninger, & Abbott (2006).
25. Singson, Mahony, & Mann (2000).
26. Nagy & Anderson (1984).
27. Baumann et al. (2003); Baumann et al. (2002); Baumann, Ware, & Edwards (2007).
28. Bandura (1997).
29. Scott, Skobel, & Wells (2008).
30. Saunders, Foorman, & Carlson (2006).
31. Carlo, et al. (2004); Gersten, Baker, Haager, & Graves (2005).
32. Beck et al. (2002).
33. Stahl (1999).
34. Carey & Bartlett (1978).
35. McKee (1968).
36. Biemiller & Boote (2006).
37. Geisel (1960).
38. Stahl (1999).
39. Heimlich & Pittelman (1986).
40. Frayer, Frederick, & Klausmeier (1969).
41. Cheever (2011).
42. Deshler (2009).

REFERENCES

Anderson, R.C., & Nagy, W.E. (1991). Word meanings. In R. Barr, M.L. Kamil, P. Mosenthal, & P.D. Pearson (Eds.), Handbook of reading research, Vol. II (pp. 690–724). Longman, NY: Routledge.

Archer, A. (2004). Personal communication.

Archer, A., & Hughes, C. (2011). Explicit instruction: Effective and efficient teaching. (What works for special-needs learners). New York: Guilford Press.

Bandura, A. (1997). Self-efficacy: The exercise of control. New York: Freeman.

Baumann, J.F., Edwards, E.C., Boland, E., Olejnik, S., & Kame'enui, E.J. (2003). Vocabulary tricks: Effects of instruction in morphology and context on fifth-grade students' ability to derive and infer word meaning. American Educational Research Journal, 40, 447–494.

Baumann, J.F., Edwards, E., Font, G., Tereshinski, C.A., Kame'enui, E.J., & Olejnik, S. (2002). Teaching morphemic and contextual analysis to fifth-grade students. Reading Research Quarterly, 37(2), 150–176.

Baumann, J.F., Ware, D., & Edwards, E.C. (2007). Bumping into spicy, tasty words that catch your tongue: A formative experiment on vocabulary instruction. *The Reading Teacher, 61*(2), 108–122.

Beck, I., McKeown, M., & Kucan, L. (2002). *Bringing words to life: Robust vocabulary instruction.* New York: Guilford Press.

Beck, I., McKeown, M., & Kucan, L. (2008). *Creating robust vocabulary: Frequently asked questions and extended examples (Solving problems in the teaching of literacy).* New York: Guildford Press.

Becker, W.C. (1977). Teaching reading and language to the disadvantaged—What we have learned from field research. *Harvard Educational Review, 47,* 518–543.

Biemiller, A. (2001). Teaching vocabulary: Early, direct, and sequential. *American Educator, 25,* 24–28.

Biemiller, A. (2009). *Words worth teaching: Closing the vocabulary gap.* Columbus, OH: SRA/McGraw-Hill.

Biemiller, A., & Boote, C. (2006). An effective method for building meaning vocabulary in primary grades. *Journal of Educational Psychology, 98,* 44–62.

Bryant, D.P., Goodwin, M., Bryant, B.R., & Higgins, K. (2003). Vocabulary instruction for students with learning disabilities: A review of the research. *Learning Disability Quarterly, 26,* 117–128.

Carey, S., & Bartlett, E. (1978). Acquiring a single new word. Proceedings of the Stanford Child Language Conference, 15, 17–29. (Republished in *Papers and Reports on Child Language Development 15,* 17–29.)

Carlo, M.S., August, D., McLaughlin, B., Snow, C.E., Dressler, C., Lippman, D., et al. (2004). Closing the gap: Addressing the vocabulary needs of English language learners in bilingual and mainstream classrooms. *Reading Research Quarterly, 39,* 188–215.

Center on Teaching & Learning. *Big ideas in beginning reading.* University of Oregon, College of Education. Retrieved April 9, 2011 from http://reading.uoregon.edu/

Chall, J.S., & Jacobs, V.A. (2003, Spring). Poor children's fourth-grade slump. *American Educator, 27*(1), 14–15, 44.

Cheever, G. (2011). VOCAB. Personal communication.

Coxhead, A. (2000). A new academic word list. *TESOL Quarterly, 34*(2), 213–238.

Cunningham, A.E., & Stanovich, K.E. (1997). Early reading acquisition and its relation to reading experience and ability 10 years later. *Developmental Psychology, 33,* 934–945.

Curtis, M.E., & Longo, A.M. (1999). When adolescents can't read: Methods and materials that work. Cambridge, MA: Brookline.

Dale, E. (1965). Vocabulary measurement: techniques and major findings. *Elementary English, 42,* 895–90l.

Denning, K., Kessler, B., & Leben, W. (2007). *English vocabulary elements, second edition.* Bethesda, MD: Oxford University Press.

Deshler, D.D. (2009). *Moving the needle on adolescent literacy.* Alameda, CA: Alameda Unified School District. Retrieved August 19, 2011 from http://www.mikemcmahon.info/Deschler09AUSD.ppt

Foorman, B., Schatschneider, C., Eakin, M., Fletcher, J., Moats, L., & Francis, D. (2006). The impact of instructional practices in grades 1 and 2 on reading and spelling achievement in high poverty schools. *Contemporary Educational Psychology, 31*(1), 1–29.

Frayer, D., Frederick, W.C., & Klausmeier, H.J. (1969). *A schema for testing the level of cognitive mastery.* Madison, WI: Wisconsin Center for Education.

Geisel, T.S. (Dr. Seuss). (1960). *Green eggs and ham.* New York: Random House Books for Young Readers.

Gersten, R., Baker, S., Haager, D., & Graves, A. (2005). Exploring the role of teacher quality in predicting reading outcomes for first grade English learners: An observational study. *Remedial and Special Education, 26,* 197–206.

Graves, M.F. (2006). *The vocabulary book: Learning and instruction.* New York: Teachers College Press.

Hart, B., & Risley, T.R. (1995). *Meaningful differences in the everyday experience of young American children* (pp. 70–71). Baltimore: Paul H. Brookes Publishing Co.

Heimlich, J.E. & Pittelman, S.D. (1986). *Semantic mapping: Classroom applications.* Newark, DE: International Reading Association.

Lehr, F., Osborn, J., & Hiebert, E.H. (2004). *A focus on vocabulary.* Pacific Resources for Education and Learning (PREL). Retrieved on May 30, 2011 from http://www.prel.org/products/reading-and-literacy/focus-on-vocabulary,-a-.aspx

McKee, D. (1968). *Elmer.* New York: Lothrop, Lee and Shepard Books.

Nagy, W. (2004). *Teaching vocabulary to improve reading comprehension.* Newark, DE: International Reading Association.

Nagy, W., Berninger, V., & Abbott, R. (2006). Contributions of morphology beyond phonology to literacy outcomes of upper elementary and middle school students. *Journal of Educational Psychology, 98*(1), 134–147.

Nagy, W.E., & Anderson, R.C. (1984). How many words are there in printed school English? *Reading Research Quarterly, 19,* 304–330.

Nagy, W.E., Anderson, R.C., & Herman, P.A. (1987). Learning word meanings from context during normal reading. *American Educational Research Journal, 24*(2), 237–270.

Nagy, W.E., & Scott, J.A. (2000). Vocabulary processes. In M.L. Kamil, P.B. Mosenthal, & P.D. Pearson (Eds.), *Handbook of reading research: Volume III* (pp. 269–284). Mahwah, NJ: Erlbaum.

National Governors Association Center for Best Practices and Council of Chief State School Officers. (2010). *Common Core State Standards.* Retrieved on May 31, 2011 from http://www.corestandards.org

Saunders, W.M., Foorman, B.R., & Carlson, C.D. (2006). Is a separate block of time for oral English language development in programs for English learners needed? *The Elementary School Journal, 107*(2), 181–198.

Schwartz, R.M. & Raphael, T. (1985). Concept of definition: A key to improving students' vocabulary. *The Reading Teacher, 39,* 198–203.

Scott, J., Skobel, B., & Wells, J. (2008). *The word-conscious classroom: Building the vocabulary readers and writers need.* New York: Scholastic.

Singson, M., Mahony, D., & Mann V. (2000). The relation between reading ability and morphological skills: Evidence from derivational suffixes. *Reading and Writing: An Interdisciplinary Journal, 12,* 219–252.

Stahl, S.A. (1999). *Vocabulary development.* Newton Upper Falls, MA: Brookline Books.

Stahl, S.A. (2004, winter). Scaly? Audacious? Debris? Salubrious? Vocabulary learning and the child with learning disabilities. *Perspectives on Language and Literacy, 30*(1), 5–12.

11

Comprehension, Grades K–3

by Darcy Dycha

"It was routine in our household. We'd done it for years. Each night before bedtime, we'd cuddle together to read. We'd stop to talk and share our thinking and our questions. We'd giggle at the funny parts and cry at the sad parts. This was how it always was. But this night was different. At a confusing point in the story, I stopped and asked my 7-year-old if she was wondering anything, like we'd done countless times before while we were reading. Her reply to me was startling, 'Oh no, Mommy, I know that the questions come at the end. I shouldn't interrupt during the story. You can ask me the questions when you are done reading.' Her words hit me so hard that I'm certain I gasped out loud. It was in that instant I realized, my child no longer viewed reading as an enjoyable, active, thinking activity. Instead, somehow outside of our reading experience together, she had concluded that reading occurred simply for the purpose of answering questions at the end of the story. I was mortified."

Parker and Hurry[1] report that teachers lack awareness that children need to be active participants in the comprehension process. Instead, teachers rely on direct oral questioning as the primary strategy for teaching reading comprehension. With this type of instruction, not only do students play a passive role in comprehending text, but also the teacher is largely using instructional time to assess comprehension rather than teaching students how to comprehend.

This chapter addresses the most effective ways to assess and teach comprehension to younger students. The goal is to help build your knowledge and understanding of the importance of comprehension instruction and how to teach students to comprehend in an explicit and supportive manner.

Objectives: After studying this chapter, you will be able to do the following:

1. Articulate the importance of comprehension instruction in grades K–3.
2. Identify key comprehension strategies that should be taught to students in grades K–3.
3. Understand the importance of an explicit routine for comprehension instruction.
4. Identify the eight steps of the comprehension instruction routine and understand how each step supports student learning.
5. Confidently plan comprehension instruction for any grade, K–3, using the comprehension instruction routine.

WHAT IS IT? WHY IS IT IMPORTANT? WHAT DOES THE RESEARCH SAY ABOUT IT?

"Reading is essential to success in our society. The ability to read is highly valued and important for social and economic advancement."[2]

Before beginning to think about comprehension instruction, it is necessary to clarify that comprehension is the purpose for reading. If one can read the words but does not understand what the text is conveying, then reading is not successful.[3-5] This point is significant for all students. Most of the school curriculum requires students to understand what they are reading. Failure to teach students to comprehend in the early school years excludes them from critical learning.[6] Teachers who have made comprehension instruction a priority for students at an early age help students to "gain access to a broader range of texts, knowledge, and educational opportunities."[7]

Thus, it is clear that a focus on explicit comprehension instruction must be a priority for you when teaching students to read. When establishing this priority, you will realize that this is not an easy task. Comprehension does not just happen. For comprehension to occur successfully, readers must purposefully and actively construct meaning as they navigate their way through the text. They do this by relying on their background knowledge, while considering the meanings of words and how the text is organized. They also make inferences, determine what information is most important in the text, and create mental images of the text.[8]

You might wonder: Can children just entering their elementary years learn to do this? The answer is a resounding yes. A large volume of work indicates that one can help students acquire the strategies and processes used by good readers—and that this improves their overall comprehension of text.[9] Comprehension instruction must occur at the onset of reading instruction and occur over years.[10] The general rule is, teach children many strategies, teach them early, reteach them often, and connect assessment with reteaching.[11]

WHAT SHOULD STUDENTS KNOW AND BE ABLE TO DO AT SPECIFIC GRADE LEVELS, PRE-K–3?

Fortunately, we know where to begin. Comprehension instruction begins through direct instruction in listening comprehension, which occurs when you read aloud to your class. Young students who have been read to frequently, who have been exposed to explicit comprehension instruction, and who have had many opportunities to share and talk about text should be able to communicate their understanding of text. You will likely read aloud to your students multiple times throughout the day in all subject areas. Even if your lesson objective is to teach a science concept, you can still model and reinforce reading strategically for comprehension.

The literacy experiences children are exposed to in pre-K form the foundation for early reading skills (see Chapter 3). As the student's language abilities improve, you should expect pre-K students to demonstrate a greater understanding of what has been read to them. Students should be able to reenact a story using puppets or through dramatic play, or provide a simple oral retelling of the story. Students should be able to identify their favorite part of the story and should also be able to ask and answer questions about the text.[12]

In kindergarten, students can be expected to be able to make logical predictions and to retell stories including information from the beginning, middle, and end of the text. Students should be able to identify the main character and setting and retell the main event. At this age, students begin to make inferences and create mental images to support their listening comprehension.

As students enter grades 1 and 2, one should expect to see growth based on the foundational skills identified in pre-K and kindergarten. Students in these grades should be able to make inferences and provide evidence from the text to support their thinking. Retellings should be sequenced appropriately and should include the problem and solution of a story or topic of nonfiction text.

By third grade, students are seen to monitor and adjust the use of strategies to improve their comprehension of more complex text. Students begin to summarize the plot's main events and can describe characters, their relationships, and changes they undergo. Third-grade students are able to explain cause-and-effect relationships and can identify details that support the main idea in nonfiction texts.[13]

HOW DO YOU ASSESS WHAT STUDENTS KNOW AND HOW MUCH THEY ARE LEARNING?

"The main reason for assessing strategies is to find clues about what the student is not doing or what is being done incorrectly so that teachers can reteach better strategies."[14]

There are various ways to assess comprehension. It is important for you to keep in mind that each type of assessment will provide you with only a piece of a student's comprehension ability. It is through putting these "pieces" together that you will begin to understand students' strengths and weaknesses in comprehension.

Benchmark assessments such as the Texas Primary Reading Inventory (TPRI) or Developmental Reading Assessment (DRA) are typically given to students two or three times a year.[15,16] These types of assessments require students to read a short text and then answer questions. Sometimes, retellings are included and a rubric is used to score student responses. Benchmark assessments provide information to help you see if students have weaknesses in answering certain types of questions. For example, a student might answer all of the text-explicit questions correctly, but miss all of the inferential questions. This information is useful in helping you to see general weaknesses in reading comprehension and to help you know where to focus your instruction.

Informal assessments are used more frequently, as this type of assessment is typically embedded within reading instruction.[17] For example, you might encourage students to retell part of the text or engage in dialogue about the text with a small group of students. You might also include thoughtful, planned prompts or questions before, during, and after reading. This type of questioning will help you to dig into student understanding and will also give you insight into how students use specific strategies. Providing students with think-time and talk-time is essential if you are to gather accurate information about student understanding. As students discuss aspects of text with you or others, it is important to ask them to explain their thinking. Not only does this help students to become better learners,[18] but it also will help you to draw accurate conclusions about student understanding. For example, imagine a student who answers an inferential question incorrectly or shares a misunderstanding with a classmate during discussion time. As the student explains why she thinks what she does, you might discover that her misunderstanding is not because she is unable to make inferences, but rather, she does not have the background knowledge to make a correct inference. The student's explanation has helped you to avoid making an inaccurate assumption about her comprehension ability.

Other types of assessment include basal quizzes, teacher-made assessments, and occasionally practice worksheets. Most of these forms of assessment are paper-and-pencil in nature and require students to answer either multiple-choice questions or in short-answer form. These assessments are only helpful in guiding your instruction if you take the time to follow up with each student to find out why he or she has answered a question incorrectly.

HOW DO YOU USE ASSESSMENTS TO PLAN INSTRUCTION?

As we reflect on all of the "pieces" of our assessment puzzle, keep in mind that comprehension instruction is not a set of linear skills that can be mastered in a sequence of lessons. Reading comprehension is a developmental process and increases with complexity as texts become more difficult. Good readers are always improving in their use of comprehension strategies because each reading situation is unique.

You can use your assessment data to help you target areas that appear to be weak, but you will also often cycle back to skills and strategies that have been previously taught. Instruction will need to be adjusted and differentiated to meet the needs of your students. The goal is to help students employ multiple strategies automatically as required for understanding. You need to help students know what to do, when to do it, and when it works. "Successful teachers of reading comprehension must respond flexibly and opportunistically to students' needs for instructive feedback as they read."[19] Having a targeted plan for your instruction is important, but you will also need to respond to students as they navigate through the text.

HOW DO YOU TEACH COMPREHENSION SKILLS EFFECTIVELY, EFFICIENTLY, AND APPROPRIATELY?

Comprehension strategies may be taught individually or in concert with other strategies. With young students, you will often begin instruction by focusing on one strategy at a time simply to clarify what it is you are talking about. Instruction of a single strategy typically occurs over a period of a few weeks. This allows for teacher modeling and guided practice before focusing on a new strategy. Recall the "I do, we do, you do" model discussed earlier in this text. As students learn a new strategy, you should encourage them to use previously learned strategies as well.[20] If you are teaching strategies one at a time, it is important for students to realize that good readers use comprehension strategies in combination.

Instruction should focus on the strategies that research has identified as the most important for reading comprehension in the primary grades (Table 11.1). Reading experts have identified a number of strategies to aid effective reading comprehension.[21-23] When beginning strategy instruction, it is important you select texts that obviously require the reader to use the focus strategy. You will also want to reinforce that good readers use the same comprehension strategies to understand both fiction and nonfiction texts.

Now that which strategies to teach have been identified, we need to address how to teach these strategies effectively.

Comprehension Instruction Routine

When you are beginning instruction in comprehension, it is helpful to have a set routine for how to teach the strategies to students. A routine, developed from a series of steps, will help you to be consistent in your instruction and will also help you to ensure that your lessons are direct and explicit.[24] The routine suggested here includes a gradual release of responsibility model that scaffolds learning so that all students in the classroom experience success (Figure 11.1).[25,26]

This comprehension instruction routine is drawn from the work completed at the University of Texas Health Science Center at Houston, the Texas Education Agency, and the University of Texas System.[27]

This straightforward routine includes the following eight steps:

1. **Anchor Experience.** The comprehension instruction routine begins by introducing students to the strategy your reading lessons will focus on over the next few weeks. For many students, these strategies are ambiguous, so it is important that you help them understand what it is you are talking about before asking them to apply the strategy to text. An anchor lesson occurs only once and typically will take 20–30 minutes to complete.

   To clarify, an anchor lesson does not include text. Your goal is to help students see how they use the strategy in their everyday lives so that they can use that knowledge when comprehending text. Plan an activity you think will actively involve students and one that they will *all* be able to relate to. You want the activity to be clear and memorable so that you can use it to "anchor" student understanding and you can refer to the activity each time you teach the strategy.

   The following is an example of an anchor lesson for the questioning strategy:

   "Friends, I notice that you are all very good at asking me questions. Yesterday, some of you asked me when the 100th day of school would be, and somebody else asked me what my favorite color was. We ask questions when we want to find out about something. Today, I want to share something with you. This [the teacher shows the artifact] is very special to me. I want you to think for a moment. Do you have any questions you would like to ask me about my special thing? [The teacher provides think-time.] Turn and share your questions with your partner." After partner talk, the teacher uses popsicle sticks with names printed

Table 11.1. Strategies to aid effective reading comprehension in grades K–3

Strategy	Description	Tips for selecting books
Activating background knowledge/ making connections	Before reading, you can activate students' background knowledge by briefly discussing what the text will be about. This helps students to think about their background knowledge and use it during reading. If students lack background knowledge about the topic you will be reading about, you may need to build background knowledge. You will need to spend a few minutes each day for a week or two before reading to build student background knowledge of important concepts included in the text. When reading, good readers make connections from the text to their background knowledge to help them comprehend.	Include narrative and expository texts in your instruction Select texts with common themes or topics that most students will be able to connect to. Begin strategy instruction with fiction. Select stories that include themes students can relate to; for example, being scared, going to school for the first time, friendship, etc. Kevin Henkes books are good for teaching making connections. Include examples of how good readers make connections while reading nonfiction. Select texts that contain topics that most students will be able to connect to. For example, information books about dogs, school, family, etc. Begin with simple texts that are written clearly and are easy for students to understand.
Creating mental images	Good readers create a mental movie of the text as they are reading. This movie constantly changes as the reader continues to read. Mental images include smells, tastes, sounds, sights, and how something feels to touch. Most mental images are formed by relying on background knowledge.	Choose short pieces of descriptive text that students can connect to. For example, if most students have never seen a barn before, do not begin teaching mental imagery with a description of a barn. Gradually move to more abstract concepts after students have experienced success in using the strategy. Use a balance of fiction and nonfiction when teaching this strategy.
Making inferences	Authors do not directly provide all of the information to the reader. If authors had to explicitly tell the reader everything, books would be too big to lift. Good readers use their background knowledge along with clues in the text to make inferences. The inferences readers make fill in information not directly stated by the author.	Begin instruction with simple fictional texts that have a balance of information that is directly told to the reader and information that must be inferred by the reader. The *Frog and Toad* series by Arnold Lobel is a great place to start. Nonfiction text that is written in a narrative form often lends itself well to teaching this strategy. For example, *The Emperor's Egg* by Martin Jenkins.
Questioning	Good readers are active readers. One way to stay engaged in the text is to be aware of the questions that come to mind while reading. Questions help provide a purpose for reading and also help the reader to remember the text better. Questions often begin with who, what, when, where, why, and how.	Begin strategy instruction with nonfiction texts you know your students will be interested in, for example, a brief article about octopuses or skateboarding. *Time for Kids* has good articles for various grade levels in both English and Spanish (http://www.timeforkids.com/TFK/). Introduce fiction by finding a story you think will evoke students to ask questions.
Retelling/ summarizing	Good readers are able to identify information that is most important in the text, and they are able to pull together the key information and explain it in their own words. In fiction, readers retell key events from the beginning, middle, and end of the story in the correct sequence. They identify the main character, setting, problem, and solution. These story elements are critical for helping students to comprehend. With nonfiction, readers identify the topic and main ideas of the text by differentiating between what is important and what is interesting. Good readers understand that nonfiction text is organized in many different ways, for example, cause and effect versus a descriptive informational piece.	Teach this strategy by focusing on either fiction or nonfiction for a period of time before teaching the other genre. For fiction, select texts that have few characters with a clear and direct plot. For nonfiction, begin with simple straightforward informational texts. Headings and subheadings support students to identify the topic and main ideas of the selection.
Monitoring, clarifying, and fixing up	Good readers know when their understanding breaks down, and then they do something to repair their misunderstanding. Good readers reread the text and apply other strategies to "fix-up" their confusion.	Look for a variety of texts where you have seen students experience misunderstandings and confusions.

1. Anchor experience
2. Explicit explanation of the strategy
3. Touchstones and anchors
4. Planned thoughtful teacher questions before, during, and after reading
5. Teacher modeling through think-aloud
6. Whole group guided practice
7. Small group instruction and guided practice
8. Independent use of the strategy with accountability

High level of teacher support

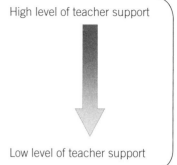

Low level of teacher support

Figure 11.1. Comprehension instruction routine. (From The University of Texas Health Science Center at Houston/Texas Education Agency/The University of Texas System [2008]. *Elements of understanding: Deeper instruction of reading and listening comprehension, cognitive strategy routine.* Houston, TX: Author; adapted by permission.)

on them to randomly select students to share their questions with the whole group. As they do, the teacher charts their questions, taking time to validate their importance.

2. **Explicit Explanation.** The phrase "explicit instruction" means that you clearly explain to students in language they understand, what it is you are going to do and why you are going to do it. "The explicitness with which teachers teach comprehension strategies makes a difference in learner outcomes, especially for low-achieving students."[28] In fact, researchers who study students with learning disabilities explain that students who do not receive explicit instruction of comprehension strategies often "fail" to discover strategies on their own[29] and that highly structured and explicit instruction in comprehension is appropriate for early elementary school students.[30]

Explicit instruction is most helpful if it is applied routinely across all grade levels. This also includes using consistent language on a campus.[31] For example, the kindergarten teacher on your campus might refer to creating mental images as "making movies in your head," and the second grade teacher might call it "imaging." If you are the first-grade teacher and decide to call the strategy, "creating mental images," you are not setting students up for success. Instead, your students are left to figure out that their teachers from year to year are all talking about the same thing. This might cause confusion or a delay in your strategy instruction. It is wise for teachers on a campus to decide what each comprehension strategy will be called. Your reading curriculum might also help with these decisions. Often, schools have adopted a reading curriculum that is used at all grade levels. If this is the case, teachers may agree to refer to the strategies the way the curriculum suggests.

The following is an example of an explicit explanation for the questioning strategy: "Today, we are going to learn a reading strategy called questioning. Questions often begin with who, what, when, where, why, or how. You ask great questions in class all of the time. Yesterday, you asked me lots of great questions about the special artifact I brought to school. Today, however, we are going to learn how great questions can help us when we read or listen to a story. When I am reading, the questions that come into my mind help me pay attention to what the author is saying, and my questions also help me to remember the important parts."

This example of an explicit strategy explanation is one that will need to be repeated multiple times for students. You can not just explain the strategy like this once and assume that students are going to understand. Instead, before the start of each lesson that focuses on questioning, you will need to repeat a similar explanation. Using consistent language every time you talk about the strategy helps students to understand why and when they can use the strategy to support their comprehension.

3. **Touchstones and Anchors.** For young children especially, having touchstones to remind them of the strategy is most helpful. Touchstones can come in many forms. A visual

representation of the strategy might come in the form of a strategy poster. A kinesthetic reminder of the strategy might come in the form of a hand signal or gesture.[32] When selecting a hand gesture to represent a strategy, you may wish to consider creating a signal that can be performed with one hand. One-handed signals or gestures work well for teacher modeling. It allows the teacher to hold a book with one hand while gesturing with the other. Your anchor lesson may also act as a touchstone. Every time you refer to that initial lesson, students should immediately connect the experience to the strategy. If they do not, then you may wish to reconsider your anchor lesson, because the lesson failed to "anchor" the concept of the strategy in their understanding. Teachers might also create charts recording student use of the strategy while reading. Expert teacher Debbie Miller refers to these anchor charts as a way of making thinking permanent and public.[33] Anchor charts also validate for students the importance of strategy use during reading.

When you are developing touchstones for strategies, remember that consistency is important. If you choose a hand signal or visual icon to represent the strategy in kindergarten, then use the same ones at each grade level on your campus.

The following is an example of the teacher introducing the touchstones for the questioning strategy: "When I am reading, you will know when a question pops into my head. I'll show you by making this hand signal. I'll place my fingers underneath my chin and look up a little bit. That's how I usually look when I'm thinking of a question. Can you do the hand signal with me? Oh, good for you! I can see that you all will be able to show me when you are thinking of a question during reading time."

"I also have this big poster to remind us to think of our own questions when we read. It has a big question mark on it as well as some question words: who, what, when, where, why, and how. These words will remind us how questions often begin."

4. **Planned Thoughtful Teacher Questions Before, During, and After Reading.** Teacher questions have played a major role in the history of comprehension. In her landmark study of comprehension instruction, Deloris Durkin[34] found that teachers dedicated less than 1% of the reading block to comprehension instruction. Instead, teachers she observed tended to spend the majority of instructional time on asking students low-level questions. Recent research confirms that in today's classrooms, teacher questioning is still the predominant way that teachers address reading comprehension with students.[35,36] This is not to say that questions should not be used along with explicit instruction of comprehension skills and strategies, but rather questions should be used to support instruction by guiding students to think more deeply about text.

There are three places that thoughtful teacher questioning can be brought into the reading lesson. Posing questions before, during, and after reading requires students to be active thinkers throughout the reading process.[37] Teachers plan higher-order questions to prompt students to think more deeply about the reading and to engage students in high-quality discussion.[38]

BOX 11.1. Afflerbach states, "How we think about reading, the purposes of reading instruction, and the development of the students we teach should influence the nature of the questions we ask."[39]

A single guiding question can be introduced to students *before* reading. This type of question supports students who struggle in setting their own purpose for reading and helps them to focus on why they are reading a particular text. This helps them to read more efficiently and helps them to understand key elements of the text.[40] Planning this type of guiding question effectively requires thinking about the objective of your lesson. It also requires that you read the text from start to finish and think about the message the author is trying to convey. A guiding question should support students' comprehension and should apply to the whole reading selection.

If you will be reading a text multiple times with the class, you might consider a more general question for the first reading, For example,

What do we learn about (the main character)?

What happens to (the main character)?

When you read the story for a second or third time, the guiding question can facilitate deeper understanding of the text. For example,

Why does …

How does …

Thoughtful teacher questions can also be included *during* the reading. Students are more responsive and performance is enhanced when text-based discussion takes place during the reading.[41–43] These types of discussions have been found to improve students' vocabulary and comprehension.[44] Like guiding questions, during-reading questions must be thoughtful and planned in advance of the lesson. Consider stopping to ask students to think and discuss at a point in the text where a critical event occurs, the problem is identified or solved, important information is conveyed, or you think a specific part of the text is confusing or complex. You might also stop to have students think about the guiding question at a point in the text that seems logical.

After reading, it is imperative to discuss the guiding question. If you have selected a good question, then there should be lots to discuss. Ensure that the students are doing the majority of the talking, and keep in mind that your role is to facilitate and extend their discussion by following-up with, "What makes you think that?" type questions. You may also wish to include other questions at the end of the reading to help students to clarify understanding or to assess comprehension of the text.

> **BOX 11.2.**
>
> You think aloud for students because you cannot make assumptions that students understand what you mean when you simply tell them to do something.

The following is an example of the teacher introducing the guiding question: "When we read the story, *Chester's Big Day*, I want you to think about this question: Why is it Chester's big day? Ready to listen? Why is it Chester's big day?"

5. **Teacher Modeling Through Think-Aloud.** An important step in strategy instruction includes teacher modeling. This is an opportunity for you to think out loud for students, sharing what is happening inside your head as you make sense of the text you are reading. This is sometimes referred to as making the invisible visible for students.[45]

You think aloud for students because you cannot make assumptions that students understand what you mean when you simply tell them to do something. Instead, you must take the time to show them. For example, you can tell students to create mental images while reading. You might explicitly explain the strategy and tell how it helps with reading, but if you do not show them how you create mental images while reading, they might not successfully apply the strategy. Some think-aloud teacher tips are listed in Table 11.2 below.

Table 11.2. Think-aloud teacher tips

Strategy	Teaching tips	Example of how it might sound in the classroom
Activating background knowledge/making connections	Keep your think-aloud authentic. Really connect the text to something in your life. Keep your explanation brief so that you do not take away from the text. For expository text, model how you can use your background knowledge to understand a new or unfamiliar concept. When thinking aloud, use the stem, "This part in the story reminds me of ...." Follow up with, "My connection helps me to understand ...."	"Jason is sad that his mom and dad are leaving. That reminds me of a time when my parents left me with a babysitter for a few days. My tummy felt all funny, and I couldn't stop crying. I really didn't want my parents to leave me. My connection helps me to understand how Jason is feeling right now. He's really upset that his parents are leaving."
Creating mental images	Think aloud for students how you use all five senses to create mental images of the text. Make your thinking specific and descriptive. Help students to clearly understand the images that are in your head. Reinforce that good readers also use the pictures provided in the text to help them create mental images. When thinking aloud, explain to students how your mental images help you to understand the text.	"Wow, I can clearly picture in my head the storm the author is describing. I can see the bright light flash across the dark sky, and I can hear the loud crrraaaack when the lightning hit the tree. I can imagine the burnt smell from the top of the tree wafting down to the kids huddled below and what it must have felt like to have the leaves of the broken branch scratch against their arms. My mental image helps me to understand how scary it must have been to be under that tree during the storm!"
Making inferences	Think aloud for students demonstrating the difference between information that is directly stated in the text and information that must be inferred. Plan in advance how you will share the inferences you make while reading. You will want to identify the clues in the text as well as the background knowledge you used to make the inference.	"I know that Rosa is sad because the author told us. The author wrote, 'Rosa is sad.' I didn't have to make an inference." "I'm inferring that Rosa is feeling happy now. The author didn't say that Rosa is happy, but the author told us that Rosa smiled a big smile and clapped her hands together when she saw the surprise. I know from my background knowledge that people smile when they are happy and that they usually feel happy when they get a surprise."
Questioning	Post question stems (e.g., who, what) in the classroom to help prompt students to be aware of the questions that come to mind while reading. During your think-aloud, model referring to the posted question stems. In your think-aloud, model how you continue to reflect on your questions as you read looking for answers to your questions. You can expand your think-aloud by noting where you find answers to your questions. Often, answers to questions can be found right in the text because the author tells them to you directly, or questions can sometimes be answered by making an inference. Model that occasionally good questions go unanswered, and that's okay, too. When thinking aloud, use the stem, "This part in the text makes me wonder...." Follow-up with, "My questions help keep me interested in the text and I remember better too."	"Hmm. I'm wondering something. Why do octopuses need three hearts? Can they still live if something happens to one of their hearts? Let me read on to see if I can find the answers to my questions." "Here is the answer to my first question right here in the text. The three hearts each do a different job."

(continued)

Retelling/ summarizing	For both fiction and nonfiction text, graphic organizers are helpful in teaching this strategy. Be consistent in the type of organizer you use for instruction.	"This story is mostly about Bear so far. I think that he is the main character."
	For fiction, ensure that the story elements you wish to teach are included on the organizer. For young students, organizers may include a place to record character, setting, beginning, middle, and end. As students get comfortable with these concepts, introduce problem, solution, events, and eventually theme. Teaching story elements explicitly is crucial for comprehension.	"The problem is that Bear won't share his toys with anyone so he doesn't have any friends. I'm inferring that's why he feels lonely."
		"Bear has figured out the solution to his problem. He knows now that if he shares with others, they will want to play with him. Now he is having fun with the other animals in the forest."
	For nonfiction text, you need to help students to distinguish between essential and nonessential information. Use stems such as, "This is mostly about …" to help identify the main idea.	
Monitoring, clarifying, and fixing up	Plan in advance how you will model a lack of understanding while reading. Then, ensure that you think out loud what your confusion is and what your plan is for "fixing" it.	"I'm confused by this part. It says that Sherri slipped on her shirt and quickly went out the door. But if she slipped on her shirt, doesn't that mean that she fell down? Let me reread this part again and I'll try to create a mental image of what she is doing."
		"Now I understand. I inferred that the word slipped meant that she fell down. But in this case, the word slipped means that she quickly put her shirt on and then went out the door. Now, I can create a mental image of Sherri getting dressed quickly so that she wouldn't be late for school."

A think-aloud should be authentic, a reflection of what is actually going on inside your head as you read. It should also be planned in advance so that how you explain what you are doing is clear and concise.

6. **Whole Group Guided Practice.** "Reading instruction can follow a regular cycle of modeling, explaining, and guiding (all features of learning strategies) that leads to independent practice and fluency. If practice does not lead to fluency, then more diagnostic and strategic teaching is warranted."[46]

In step 6 of the strategy instruction routine, you model for students how you use the strategy(ies) to help you comprehend. This step is critical, but providing multiple opportunities for students to practice applying the strategy to text is also critical. Throughout the text you use for your instruction, look for opportunities to stop and prompt students to apply the strategy. In the first week you are teaching the strategy, you might use short pieces of text and prompt the students to apply the strategy using very specific prompts that relate to the text.

For example, if you were teaching the strategy making connections to first grade students, your prompting for students to apply the strategy might be as shown in Table 11.3.

Remember to follow up student sharing with, "Why do you think that?" to get a clear picture of their strategy use and understanding of the text.

If students struggle to apply the strategy, then it is important to offer support. Corrective feedback must be timely. Also, ensure that you hold every student in the classroom accountable for applying the strategy, not just the vocal students who always like to share. You might achieve whole-class accountability by implementing ways to randomly select students to answer and by implementing instructional routines for sharing thinking such as Think, Pair, Share.[47]

Table 11.3. Example cycle of whole group guided practice

Week 1	Week 2	Week 3	Week 4
Anchor lesson Teacher think-aloud Teacher think-aloud and specific prompting on small chunks of text (e.g., "Have you ever felt scared before?").	Teacher think-aloud 2–3 times in each lesson. Prompting for student application of the strategy is specific but may gradually become more general (e.g., "Can you make a connection to how Josh is feeling?).	Teacher think-aloud 1–2 times in each lesson. Prompting for student application of the strategy might be more general (e.g., "Are you making any connections?").	Prompting for student application of the strategy might be general (e.g., "What are you thinking right now?"). Encourage students to use previously taught strategies as well

7. **Small Group Instruction and Guided Practice.** As you may have concluded, Steps 2–6 occur over a period of weeks and take place with the whole class. Steps 2–5 can and should be replicated in your small group regular classroom instruction as well as in your intervention instruction. In fact, it is important that instruction be consistent, especially for those students who struggle.

   Time spent in small group reading instruction can greatly influence student achievement.[48] Students placed in a small group usually have similar needs and abilities (homogeneous grouping). You can rely on all forms of your assessments to help you group students. During your small group time, you can target instruction to student needs by reteaching strategies and scaffolding for student success. You also can provide more opportunities for student practice as you are able to attend to their individual needs more readily.

   With small groups, you can introduce "tools" to facilitate strategy use. For example, you might provide first graders with an index card containing three colored sticky flags. You can explain to students that they can place a sticky flag right on the spot where a question comes into mind while they are reading. Not only will this encourage students to use the strategy, but it also provides you with a visual cue as to who is using the strategy. At the end of the reading, you can ask students to share where they put their flag and to tell what their question was and why they wondered what they did. Strategy book marks, sticky notes, and flags are just some of the examples of comprehension "tools" you might wish to bring into your small group instruction.

8. **Independent Use of the Strategy with Accountability.** As students begin to use the strategy successfully, you will want to provide opportunities for them to use the strategy during independent reading time. It is important that you include some sort of accountability measure to ensure that students are using their independent reading time effectively. Even young kindergarten students can be expected to record something to reflect their time spent browsing through books. A "Literacy Log" or "Reading Reflection Journal" accomplishes this task well. Set an appropriate amount of time for reading, and then follow up the reading time with a brief reflection time. Students can record in their journals something that relates to the strategy you are focusing on. For example, younger students might draw a picture of something they made a connection to, while older students might create a T-chart in their journal by recording an excerpt of text on the left and their connection to the text on the right.

   This type of accountability helps students stay on task and also helps you to see who is using the strategy effectively. One first-grade teacher ends her independent reading time by randomly selecting two students to share their reflection with the class. This helped to ensure that all students in the class had a reflection completed and also gave students an opportunity to be the "star" as she had them read their entry over the class microphone.

HOW DO YOU DEVELOP INSTRUCTIONAL PLANS THAT INCORPORATE STANDARD AND EVIDENCE-BASED STRATEGIES?

You can ensure that your instructional plans are strong by selecting to teach the key strategies research has identified as important. You can also ensure that your instruction will be explicit by following the eight steps of the comprehension instruction routine. Remember to keep your instruction and vocabulary consistent. This will be most beneficial in helping your students to comprehend successfully.

CONCLUSION

At the beginning of this chapter, you read about an experience a parent had with her 7-year-old daughter. After reading this chapter, you should agree that comprehension instruction must include more than simply asking students to answer your questions. Instead, you should now have a good understanding of the most effective ways to assess and teach comprehension to younger students. An easy way to tell if your instruction is successful is to take a step back and listen to your students. If they are doing the majority of thinking and talking about texts in the classroom, then likely your instruction is successful.

APPLICATION ASSIGNMENTS

In-Class Assignments

When beginning strategy instruction, it is always helpful to think about yourself as a reader. This helps you to be more aware of how comprehension strategies work, and it also helps you to understand how you really do use them to comprehend.

1. Select a fictional piece of text at an adult reading level. You will need to read at least 10 pages of text for this exercise.
2. Along with the text, you will need small sticky notes and a pencil to record your thinking as you read.
3. Have the following information nearby to refer to as you are reading:

   - Making connections (MC)—The text reminds you of something you have experienced, seen, heard, or read about before. You might think, "This reminds me of…."
   - Creating mental images (CMI)—When reading the text, you use any of the five senses to create a "movie" in your head.
   - Making inferences (MI)—The author does not tell you the information directly, but you are able to fill in the missing information to have complete understanding. You might think, "I think…."
   - Questioning (Q)—As you are reading, you wonder something. Your question might be answered in the text, you might infer the answer to your question, or your question might not be answered at all. You might think, "I wonder …."
   - Retelling/summarizing (R/S)—As you are reading, are you aware of the characters, the events, the problem, or the solution? Are you aware of how the main character's actions affect other characters? You might think, "Now I understand why …." or, "This is important because …."
   - Monitoring, clarifying and fixing-up (M)—When you are reading, is there a time when you lose your train of thought or something does not quite make sense? Be aware of these times. What do you do when this happens? Hopefully, you will go back and re-read and use the strategies listed above to help you comprehend. You might think, "That part didn't make sense…."

4. As you read, stop after every paragraph or two. Reflect on your thinking. What did you do to make sense of the text you just read? Record on sticky notes the abbreviation of the strategy you used along with any information that will help you to remember what you were thinking as you were reading. Place the sticky note in the text.

5. When you finish reading the selection, reflect on your sticky notes. Which strategies did you tend to rely on most? Which strategy did you use the least?

6. Consider the following questions:
   a) What did you learn about yourself as a reader?
   b) What did you learn about comprehension from completing this exercise?
   c) How might your strategy use impact your teaching in the classroom?
   d) How might this exercise affect your personal reading in the future?

Tutoring Assignments

Complete one of the following to demonstrate your learning:

1. Select a grade-appropriate text for the student you will be teaching. Read the text and plan a guiding question you will pose before reading. Plan two or three questions you will stop to ask during the reading. Make sure to follow student answers up by asking, "What makes you think that?" After teaching the lesson, reflect on the effectiveness of your questions by asking yourself what you learned about the student's comprehension when he or she answered your questions. Plan how you will use this information to guide what you will teach in the next lesson.

2. Choose one of the comprehension strategies listed in the chapter. Select an age-appropriate text, and plan how you will teach the strategy to the student using the first five steps of the comprehension instruction routine. Teach the lesson you planned, and reflect on how you could improve it the next time you teach it.

Homework Assignments

Complete one of the following activities to demonstrate your learning of this chapter:

1. Draw a comic strip depicting good strategy instruction.
2. Create a poster to help you and others remember what to include in effective strategy instruction.
3. Create a T chart containing the following information:

Quote from the chapter	My thinking

4. Create a PowerPoint presentation highlighting the key understandings from this chapter. Include a section at the end explaining how you will use the information from this chapter in your teaching.

HELPFUL RESOURCES FOR EFFECTIVE COMPREHENSION INSTRUCTION

Books

- Harvey, S., & Goudvis, A. (2007). *Strategies that work: Teaching comprehension to enhance understanding (2nd ed.).* Portland, ME: Stenhouse Publishers.
- Miller, D. (2002). *Reading with meaning: Teaching comprehension in the primary grades.* Portland, ME: Stenhouse Publishers.
- Routman, R. (2003). *Reading essentials.* Portsmouth, NH: Heinemann.
- Zimmermann, S., & Hutchins, C. (2003). *7 keys to comprehension: How to help your kids read it and get it!* New York: Three River Press.

Video Series

- Harvey, S., & Goudvis, A. (2006). *Strategy instruction in action.* Portland, ME: Stenhouse Publishers.
- Miller, D. (2006). *Happy reading!* Portland, ME: Stenhouse Publishers.

ENDNOTES

1. Parker & Hurry (2007).
2. Snow, Burns, & Griffin (1998, p. 1).
3. Coyne, Chard, Zipoli, & Ruby (2007).
4. National Reading Panel (2000).
5. RAND Reading Study Group (2002).
6. Docknell & McShane (1993) cited in McGee & Johnson (2003).
7. Shanahan, Callison, Carriere, Duke, Pearson, Schatschneider, et al. (2010).
8. Coyne, Zipoli, Chard, Fagella-Luby, Ruby, Santoro, et al. (2009).
9. Duke & Pearson (2002).
10. Pressley (2001).
11. Afflerbach, Pearson, & Paris (2008, p. 371).
12. The University of Texas System and Texas Education Agency (2008).
13. Texas Education Agency (2009).
14. Afflerbach, Pearson, & Paris (2008).
15. Texas Education Agency and The University of Texas System (2010–2014).
16. Beaver (2006).
17. Afflerbach, Pearson, & Paris (2008).
18. Wilde (1998).
19. RAND Reading Study Group (2002, p. 34).
20. Shanahan, Callison, Carriere, Duke, Pearson, Schatschneider, et al. (2010).
21. Coyne, Chard, Zipoli, & Ruby (2007).
22. Duke & Pearson (2002).
23. Shanahan, Callison, Carriere, Duke, Pearson, Schatschneider, et al. (2010).
24. Coyne, Chard, Zipoli, & Ruby (2007).
25. Duke & Pearson (2002).
26. Shanahan, Callison, Carriere, Duke, Pearson, Schatschneider, et al. (2010).
27. The University of Texas Health Science Center at Houston/Texas Education Agency/The University of Texas System (2008).
28. RAND Reading Study Group (2002, p. 33).
29. Gersten, Fuchs, Williams, & Baker (2001).
30. Williams (2005).
31. Coyne, Chard, Zipoli, & Ruby (2007).
32. Block, Parris, & Whiteley (2008).
33. Miller (2002).
34. Durkin (1978–1979).
35. Parker & Hurry (2007).
36. RAND Reading Study Group (2002).
37. Coyne, Chard, Zipoli, & Ruby (2007).
38. Shanahan, Callison, Carriere, Duke, Pearson, Schatschneider, et al. (2010).
39. Afflerbach (2007, p. 51).
40. Klingner, Vaughn, & Boardman (2007).
41. Denton, Solari, Ciancio, Hecht, & Swank (2010).
42. McGee & Schickedanz (2007).
43. Santoro, Chard, Howard, & Baker (2008).
44. Beck & McKeown (2001).
45. Coyne, Chard, Zipoli, & Ruby (2007).
46. Afflerbach, Pearson, & Paris (2008).
47. Lyman (1981).
48. Taylor, Pearson, Clark, & Walpole (2000).

REFERENCES

Afflerbach, P. (2007). *Understanding and using reading assessment, K–12.* Newark, DE: International Reading Association.

Afflerbach, P., Pearson, P.D., & Paris, S.G. (2008). Clarifying differences between reading skills and reading strategies. *The Reading Teacher, 61*(5), 364–373.

Beaver, J.M., (2006). *Developmental reading assessment: Teacher's guide (DRA 2, K–3).* Upper Saddle River, N J: Pearson Education, Inc./Celebration Press.

Beck, I., & McKeown, M. (2001). Text talk: Capturing the benefits of read-aloud experiences for young children. *The Reading Teacher, 61*(1), 10–20.

Block, C., Parris, S., & Whiteley, C. (2008). CMPs: A kinesthetic comprehension strategy. *The Reading Teacher, 61*(6), 460–470.

Coyne, M., Chard, D., Zipoli, R., & Ruby, M. (2007). Effective strategies for teaching comprehension. In M. Coyne, E. Kame'enui, D. Carnine (Eds.), *Effective teaching strategies that accommodate diverse learners* (pp. 80–109). Upper Saddle River, NJ: Pearson Education, Inc.

Coyne, M.D., Zipoli, R.P., Chard, D.J., Faggella-Luby, M., Ruby, M., Santoro, L.E., et al. (2009). Direct instruction of comprehension: Instructional examples from intervention research on listening and reading comprehension. *Reading Research Quarterly, 25,* 221–245.

Denton, C., Solari, E., Ciancio, D., Hecht, S., & Swank, P. (2010). A pilot study of a kindergarten summer school reading program in high-poverty urban schools. *The Elementary School Journal, 110*(4), 423–439.

Duke, N., & Pearson, P.D. (2002). Effective practices for developing reading comprehension. In A. Farstrup & J. Samuels (Eds.), *What research has to say about reading instruction* (pp. 205–242). Newark, DE: International Reading Association.

Durkin, D. (1978–1979). What classroom observations reveal about reading comprehension instruction. *Reading Research Quarterly, 14,* 481–533.

Gersten, R., Fuchs, L., Williams, J., & Baker, S. (2001). Teaching reading comprehension strategies to students with learning disabilities: A review of research. *Review of Educational Research, 71*(2), 279–320.

Klingner, J.K., Vaughn, S., & Boardman, A. (2007). *Teaching reading comprehension to students with learning difficulties.* New York: The Guilford Press.

Lyman, F. (1981). The responsive classroom discussion: The inclusion of all students. In A. Anderson (Ed.), *Mainstreaming digest* (pp. 109–113). College Park, MD: University of Maryland Press.

McGee, A., & Johnson, H. (2003). The effect of inference training on skilled and less skilled comprehenders. *Educational Psychology, 23*(1), 49–59.

McGee, L., & Schickedanz, J. (2007). Repeated interactive read-alouds in preschool and kindergarten. *The Reading Teacher, 60,* 742–751.

Miller, D. (2002). *Reading with meaning: Teaching comprehension in the primary grades.* Portland, ME: Stenhouse Publishers.

National Reading Panel. (2000, April). *Report of the National Reading Panel: Teaching children to read.* Washington, DC: National Institute of Child Health and Human Development, National Institutes of Health, U.S. Department of Health and Human Services.

Parker, M., & Hurry, J. (2007). Teacher's use of questioning and modeling comprehension skills in primary classrooms. *Educational Review, 59*(3), 299–314.

Pressley, M. (2001, September). Comprehension instruction: What makes sense now, what might make sense soon. *Reading Online, 5*(2). Available: literacyworldwide.org

RAND Reading Study Group. (2002). *Reading for understanding: Toward a R&D program in reading comprehension.* Santa Monica, CA: RAND.

Santoro, L., Chard, D., Howard, L., & Baker, S. (2008). Making the very most of classroom read-alouds to promote comprehension and vocabulary. *The Reading Teacher, 61*(5), 396–408.

Shanahan, T., Callison, K., Carriere, C., Duke, N.K., Pearson, P.D., Schatschneider, C., et al. (2010). *Improving reading comprehension in kindergarten through 3rd grade: A practice guide* (NCEE 210-4038). Washington, DC: National Center for Education Evaluation and Regional Assistance, Institute of Education Sciences, U.S. Department of Education. Retrieved from what works.ed.gov/publications/practice guides.

Snow, C., Burns, S., & Griffin, P. (1998). *Preventing reading difficulties in young children.* Washington, DC: National Academy Press.

Taylor, B.M., Pearson, P.D., Clark, K., & Walpole, S. (2000). Effective schools and accomplished teachers: Lessons about primary grade reading instruction in low-income schools. *Elementary School Journal, 101,* 121–166.

Texas Education Agency & the University of Texas System. (2010–2014). *TPRI.* Austin, TX: Author.

Texas Education Agency. (2009). *Chapter 110. Texas Essential Knowledge and Skills for English Language Arts and Reading Subchapter A.* Elementary. Retrieved 1/17/2011 from http://ritter.tea.state.tx.us/rules/tac/chapter110/

The University of Texas Health Science Center at Houston/Texas Education Agency/The University of Texas System (2008). *Elements of understanding: Deeper instruction of reading and listening comprehension, cognitive strategy routine.* Houston, TX: Author.

The University of Texas System and Texas Education Agency. (2008). *Texas prekindergarten guidelines.* Austin, TX: Author.

Wilde, J. (1998). Theory of mind goes to school. *Educational Leadership, 56*(3), 46–48.

Williams, J. (2005). Instruction in reading comprehension for primary-grade students: a focus on text structure. *The Journal of Special Education, 39*(1), 6–2.

12

Comprehension, Grades 4–6

by Stephen Ciullo
and Colleen Klein Reutebuch

Mr. Hudson's sixth-grade class is studying a process called photosynthesis. He introduces some key terms including carbon dioxide, light, chlorophyll, glucose, and oxygen before directing students to read a chapter in their textbooks on plants so they can respond to the following questions independently in their spiral notebooks:

1. *What is photosynthesis?*
2. *How do plants make food?*
3. *What ingredients do plants use to make food?*
4. *Why is photosynthesis important to life on Earth?*
5. *How is photosynthesis similar to cellular respiration? How is it different?*

Some students turn to the beginning of the chapter and start to read and seem to be paying attention to headings, captions, illustrations, and using self-questioning strategies (i.e., Does that makes sense to me? What is the most important thing about what I just read?) to navigate through the assigned text. Several other students begin flipping to the book's glossary and copying down the definition of photosynthesis before returning to the chapter and scanning the text haphazardly in order to answer the remaining questions. A quick check for understanding by the teacher reveals that although most students read the chapter, they were not strategic about reading for meaning.

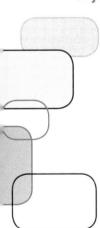

Objectives: After studying this chapter you will be able to do the following:

1. Describe reading comprehension.
2. Explain the importance of reading comprehension for narrative and informational text.
3. Explain what the research says about effective comprehension instruction.
4. Identify scientifically based or evidence-based research, and explain its significance to practice.
5. Identify and design effective comprehension instruction for students in grades 4–6.
6. Identify the challenges encountered by upper elementary students in effectively comprehending text.
7. Understand the importance of strategic reading for meaning.
8. Explain what students should be able to perform in grades 4–6 to demonstrate ability to read for understanding.
9. Apply reading assessment knowledge to evaluate what students know.
10. Analyze assessment data and use it to plan comprehension instruction.

Posted in Mr. Hudson's classroom are his rules of reading:

1. *Understand what you read.*
2. *Read to understand.*

Although the above rules seem simple, the process of comprehending, that is, understanding or making sense of text, is not. Think of a time when you mindlessly read through a book chapter or magazine article. You were probably able to read all the words, but when you got to the end, you could not recall what you just read. Unfortunately, this is the consequence of reading without purpose or engagement. Reading comprehension should be an active process used to gain meaning from text. This process does not just happen for most readers, but must be developed through explicit, direct, and high-quality comprehension instruction that is grounded in scientific reading research. Teaching practices and interventions are scientifically based if the practice has undergone rigorous research trials and replication by different researchers. When researchers identify instructional practices as being evidence based, research findings are typically published in peer-reviewed professional journals or approved by a panel of independent experts.[1]

Continuing with the theme of Chapter 11, comprehension instruction is more than just asking questions after reading. Good teachers teach students to be strategic before, during, and after reading.

During the upper elementary grades, students shift from "learning to read" to "reading to learn." This transition can present challenges for readers. It is during this time that readers need to become more strategic or purposeful due to increased difficulty of the subject matter, exposure to different types of text (narrative and expository or informational, explained below), and challenging vocabulary. This chapter describes how to effectively teach and assess reading comprehension in grades 4–6.[2] Research indicates that even students who have reading difficulties do benefit from comprehension instruction.[3] Teachers should not wait until foundation or basic reading skills are mastered to provide instruction in comprehension, though the amount, intensity, and duration of instruction may need to differ for struggling readers.[4] The critical elements to prepare you to deliver comprehension strategy instruction are addressed, because comprehension can be improved if you teach students to be strategic.[5] You are encouraged to teach thoughtfully selected, scientifically based reading comprehension strategies to enable your students to understand and remember what they read across various types of texts and reading demands, thus becoming independent readers.

Types of Texts: There are different types of texts, or print material, that students should read. Often, teachers in elementary school rely on narratives, but students need to read expository texts also.

- Narrative text portrays a story or sequence of events involving individuals or fictional characters.
- Expository or informational text is nonfiction and conveys information about the natural or social world. The structure varies widely and can include descriptions, sequences of events, problem/solution, cause/effect, and compare/contrast.

WHAT IS READING COMPREHENSION? WHY IS IT IMPORTANT? WHAT DOES THE RESEARCH SAY ABOUT IT?

Reading comprehension is a multicomponent, highly complex process that involves many interactions between readers and what they bring to the text (previous knowledge, strategy use) as well as variables related to the text itself (interest in text, understanding text types).[6]

The ultimate goal of reading is to understand what you read. More than 30 years of reading research confirms that good readers are strategic. They use strategies to uncover meaning and gain new or deeper knowledge. A strategy is a plan knowingly selected by the reader to reach a desired goal or to complete a task.[7] What is known about good readers is that they do the following:[8]

1. Set a *purpose* for reading, *preview* the text before reading to make connections with what they already know, and predict what they will learn or find out.

2. *Monitor* and *adjust* while reading when understanding breaks down.[9] This means that good readers know why they are reading a text, and they remain conscious of their understanding while reading. They maintain their focus on the text by questioning, associating ideas in text to earlier knowledge, revising their earlier knowledge when new ideas conflict with previous ones, and figuring out unknown words using content clues. They also use word knowledge and reference materials, or ask for help if they get stuck, make note of important points, re-read if necessary, and interpret the text and its quality.

3. *Reflect* on important points at the conclusion of reading and *think* about how ideas in the text might be applied in the future.

That is quite an amazing list! Most mature readers never stop to think what goes into the process of comprehending text.

In order to become strategic about reading, it is necessary for students to be provided with the support they need to develop their skills while reading, writing, and thinking.[10] These skills do not come naturally for many at-risk or struggling readers. The main purpose for teaching reading comprehension strategies is to teach your students how to think while reading. Comprehension strategies can help readers enhance their thinking and improve their understanding, overcome barriers to comprehending text, and compensate for limited knowledge related to the text.[11] For some teachers, like Mr. Hudson, comprehension instruction is little more than asking students to answer questions at the end of a reading assignment. However, a much more effective way to guarantee comprehension is to directly and explicitly model using comprehension strategies and teach your students how to use comprehension strategies with the goal to gradually release your students to read and understand independently, as well as enjoy and learn from text. If students learn that strategies are tools to help them understand ideas in texts, then the strategies become purposeful and fundamental. The National Reading Panel[12] acknowledged the effectiveness of various strategies, some taught as single strategies, others combined into multiple strategy instruction for building comprehension: summarizing, self-questioning, story structure instruction (including story maps), graphic and semantic organizers, and comprehension monitoring (see Table 12.1). Instruction with a single strategy introduces each strategy individually and includes practice for a given period, usually a few weeks, before another strategy is introduced. Over time, the expectation is that students will master a collection of strategies. With multiple-strategy instruction, several strategies are introduced simultaneously and are practiced in combination so that students learn to use them together. Your comfort level with the strategies, your students' needs and capabilities, and the reading purposes and type of text should be taken into consideration when deciding which strategies to teach and when to introduce them to your students).[13]

WHAT READING COMPREHENSION SKILLS SHOULD STUDENTS KNOW AND BE ABLE TO DO IN GRADES 4–6?

Reading to Learn

Fourth, fifth, and sixth graders are at a critical stage of their educational development in terms of reading comprehension. In the primary grades (K–3), the educational journey for students in English Language Arts classes emphasizes learning to read, with a heavy emphasis on word study, phonics, and developing fluency. In fourth grade, the focus of reading changes from *learning to read* to *reading to learn*![14] Students begin reading more complex text

Table 12.1.   Effective scientifically based strategies

	Strategy	Description	Examples of classroom strategy practice
Single strategy instruction	Summarizing	Students describe, in writing or verbally, the main points of what they read.	Students identify *who* or *what* they just read about and tell *what is the most important thing or idea about the who or what* after a sentence, a section of text, or a chapter in the book.
	Questioning	Students create their own questions about the important ideas in the text while reading and answer them using the text to confirm their responses.	Students ask questions using *who, what, where, why,* and *how* as they read (e.g., *How* are mammals and amphibians alike? *How* are they different?). The key is that students refer back to the text to confirm answers. Teachers need to promote critical thinking by having students answer and develop higher-order questions.
	Story structure instruction for narrative text	Students grasp how stories are organized in order to distinguish between major and minor events and details.	Students recognize beginning, middle, and end of story and can identify story elements including characters, setting, problem or conflict, plot, resolution, and theme.
	Graphic and semantic organizers	Students use visual representations (e.g., maps, diagrams, tables, charts) to display and/or organize knowledge, concepts, thoughts, or ideas about a topic.	Students work collaboratively to complete a graphic organizer to show a process, e.g., the metamorphosis of a butterfly: 1. Egg 2. Larva 3. Pupa (chrysalis) 4. Butterfly
	Comprehension monitoring	Students self-assess their understanding and if they encounter a barrier to understanding, they clarify their understanding by using "fix-up" strategies to regain a sense of meaning.	As difficulties occur, students stop and use a variety of techniques to clarify meaning. They may re-read a sentence or section of a passage, use a reference tool to look something up, ask others for assistance, and/or think about what they already know (e.g., I know a horned toad is a reptile, not an amphibian, so I think I am going to learn about a type of lizard).
Multiple strategy instruction	Reciprocal teaching[15]	A dialogue between teachers and students regarding segments of text is structured by the use of four strategies: summarizing, question generating, clarifying, and predicting. The teacher and students take turns assuming the role of teacher in leading this dialogue.	When generating questions about the text, students are to test themselves, and they must provide both a question and the answer. Clarifying is meant to assist the readers in stopping and applying fix-up strategies if difficulties in understanding arise. A student might re-read or ask for help. When predicting, a student is meant to link the new knowledge he or she will encounter in the text with the knowledge he or she already possesses (e.g., I know siege means to block something off or surround it, so I think I am going to learn about how the Mexican army's *siege* led to their victory at the Alamo). Students may summarize at the sentence, paragraph, or whole passage level in order to sum up what they just read about (e.g., After reading a paragraph about *The Helpful Arachnids,* a student sums up the main idea of the passage with, "Most spiders, classified as arachnids, are harmless and help control insects.").
	Transactional strategies instruction[16]	Students are taught a variety of strategies over time, which are meant for flexible use depending on the aim, including predicting, asking questions, activating background knowledge, visualizing, summarizing, using "fix-up" strategies, and/or using knowledge of text structure.	In small groups, students may share what they know about the topic of informational text to be read, then they visualize what they will learn about after reading, and then they turn to a neighbor before sharing their visualization. After reading, students verify if they learned what they thought they were going to in their initial predictions.

in fourth grade, including narrative stories and informational text (including content-area reading such as science and history). Making inferences, reflecting on material that was previously read, and evaluating what was read are essential comprehension skills at this level.[17]

What should students be able to do in grades 4–6? Many states are now turning to the Common Core State Standards for English Language Arts for those answers.[18] One integral skill that students should be able to accomplish before leaving sixth grade when reading narrative text is comparing and contrasting stories of different genres based on their approaches to a similar theme or topic (e.g., comparing a Sherlock Holmes novel to the main idea of a historical novel about a famous police officer). Additionally, teachers should get into the habit of *requiring* students to cite text evidence and quotes to support their inferences and summary statements. For example, "Michael, thank you for sharing that you think the summary of the paragraph is that the main character, Lisa, was scared to enter the old, dark mansion. Please show me where in the story you were able to find information supporting your idea." By requiring students to use text to support their discussion and answers, students will get into the habit of reading carefully and purposefully.

High standards for reading comprehension must also be adhered to for nonfiction text (informational texts such as social studies and science textbooks).[19] According to the Common Core State Standards, before leaving sixth grade, students are expected to perform the following major skills: 1) refer to quotes in the text when drawing inferences, 2) compare and contrast one author's version of events to another's, 3) integrate information and facts from several sources in order to write or speak effectively about an issue or event, and 4) read fifth-grade–level texts independently and answer comprehension questions.

Using details in the text to support a classroom discussion or a writing assignment can also help students' ability to read for understanding with informational texts. A sample prompt you could use in social studies after students silently read is, "From what you just read, tell me why the Industrial Revolution changed people's lives. Find a sentence on the page describing an invention that helped make our lives easier."

State standards are also of great importance to educators. Teachers are encouraged to consult their state and district curriculum guidelines.

Independent Reading

How should your students read for understanding in grades 4–6? Whenever possible, students should be reading silently and independently. All too often, teachers are engaging students in "round robin" reading. "Round robin" means having an entire class read together, with students taking turns and having each student read a paragraph or two while others follow along. There is no research to support the use of "round robin" or "popcorn" reading for enhancing comprehension development. There are two main concerns with the round robin reading approach. The first problem is that some students do not enjoy reading orally in front of a group of peers. This could lead to anxiety or even a negative attitude toward reading. Another reason this technique is not effective is because only *one* student is practicing reading, while other students are less engaged, often not even following along. More effective reading methods include individual silent reading (when the text is at the student's instructional level), partner reading with corrective feedback, and silent reading followed by a teacher re-reading of the text (see Table 12.2 for reading strategies that support comprehension).

HOW DO YOU ASSESS WHAT STUDENTS KNOW AND HOW MUCH THEY ARE LEARNING?

Using assessment data to ask questions and obtain insight about student progress is a logical way to monitor improvement and tailor instruction to each student's needs.[20]

Table 12.2. Reading techniques for upper elementary school

Reading technique	Procedures	Benefits
Individual silent reading	Teachers provide independent-level (90%–95% word reading accuracy) or instructional-level (85%–90%) passages. Procedures: Provide background information and review vocabulary before reading. Provide a purpose for reading ("Read to find out how the Louisiana Purchase made the U.S. a powerful country").	Builds reading stamina High level of engagement Student accountability for acquiring information and reading for understanding
Partner reading	Procedures: Teachers select partners with similar reading fluency (assessment-based) or one student with high fluency and one low. Provide the following instructions (have students demonstrate procedures to provide a strong example): 1. Take turns reading orally every two paragraphs. 2. The "listening" partner provides corrective feedback on word errors ("That word was _____"). 3. Students cooperatively state the main idea at each stopping point OR complete a graphic organizer, chart, or comprehension questions. 4. Teacher circulates to monitor groups.	High level of student engagement with text Provides students frequent speaking opportunities during main idea summary statements (excellent for English language learners!) Shared accountability for oral reading and comprehension
Student silent reading followed by oral teacher read-aloud (This can be used effectively for informational/content-area texts like science or social studies)	Procedures: Preview by providing background information and preview vocabulary (including proper nouns). Provide a purpose ("Read to find out what a Biome is and what Biome we live in"). Students read the page or short passage silently. Teacher re-reads the entire passage to the students to ensure that all students have access to the material.	Meets the needs of a wide range of reading abilities Students with advanced skills practice at an independent or instructional level Students of lower ability practice with the assurance that they will have access to the text twice Teacher re-read models oral reading fluency and an additional opportunity for an exposure to content

Other strategies based on research	Collaborative strategic reading (CSR)
	A more detailed explanation of CSR found in the "How to teach?" section
	Peer-assisted learning strategies (PALS)
	A more detailed explanation of PALS found in the "How to teach?" section
		CSR benefits
		  Shared student accountability
		  An excellent intervention for English language learners—CSR couples reading practice with oral language skills
		PALS benefits
		  Shared accountability
		  Helps meet a wide range of student ability needs
		  High level of student engagement in the reading process

There is no one assessment that provides all the information you will need to make decisions about your students' comprehension abilities and needs. Presently, widely used standardized comprehension measures are focused on tasks such as basic recall and reading to

Table 12.3. Various reading comprehension assessments

Type	Description	Purposes
Formal tests	Given according to a standard set of circumstances/directions	Provides information on students' reading strengths and weaknesses, reading level, or how well students do in comparison to pre-determined criterion
Curriculum-based assessment	Tests or measures student progress with what is taught in the curriculum	Indicates a student's progress towards mastery of the curriculum and/or how effective the instruction being provided is in moving students toward desired learning outcomes
Progress monitoring	A frequent measurement of student performance (with class, small group, or individual) of academic tasks (i.e., teacher-made quizzes, end-of-chapter or unit checks in textbooks, or curriculum-based measures)	Determines whether students are profiting appropriately from instruction, including the curriculum; used to develop more effective programs for students not progressing or progressing at an appropriate rate for the task or grade-level; and to estimate rates of student improvement
Interviews and questionnaires	A series of questions asked individually or group administered to explore students' thinking processing and various strategies applied	Uncovers students' understanding of the reading process and their knowledge of reading strategies and which ones they use, overly rely on, and/or misuse
Observation	Recording of student reading behaviors using anecdotal records, a checklist, or note taking	Yields information about what students do during reading tasks
Reading inventory	Students read narrative and/or expository texts aloud and/or silently and are asked to respond to comprehension questions and/or retell about what they read	Captures information about a student's reading level, word analysis skills, and comprehension abilities; may also gauge interest or attitude toward reading

identify the main idea and/or word meaning. These measures tell us how students are performing, but do not provide insight into what kinds of comprehension instruction are needed.[21] As mentioned in the previous chapter, benchmark assessments offer check-ups, usually during three different points in the year (beginning, middle, and end), on student progress and provide data for teachers to adjust their instruction to target student weaknesses. Formal tests, including norm- and criterion-referenced tests, and curriculum-based assessments, along with more informal assessments such as student interviews and questionnaires, observations, and reading inventories, can all contribute to identifying students' strengths and areas of difficulty (see Table 12.3).

Indeed, all interactions with your students provide an opportunity for informal, authentic assessments of reading skills. This can include asking students to summarize or retell important details and asking them to respond to the text by writing in a journal, log, blog, or to open-ended questions. You can also observe student contributions to discussions about the text or ask them to tell you about the processes they used to respond to a question, to infer meaning, to draw a conclusion, or to develop a question requiring critical thinking. The RAND Research Group[22] emphasized that, because knowledge, application, and engagement are the critical aspects of reading comprehension, assessments that reflect all three are needed.

Both formal and more informal assessments enlighten teachers about whether or not students comprehend adequately and indicate red flags when students may be in need of more intensive assistance. However, nothing is more relevant for making discoveries about levels of comprehension than careful observation of students engaged in reading and discussions with them about the processes they use to gain meaning. Prompting students to tell about their own understanding or the methods they used to determine meaning from text help you learn about students' strategic processes (Tell me how you decided that was an important detail?

BOX 12.1. FORMAL TESTS

- Norm-referenced test (NRT)—compares a person's score against the scores of a group of people who have already taken the same exam, called the "norming group."
- Criterion-referenced test (CRT)—intended to measure how well a person has learned a specific body of knowledge and skills.
- Curriculum-based assessment (CBM)—a method of monitoring student educational progress through direct assessment of academic skills. CBMs usually consist of short tests, called probes, to ascertain student achievement on basic skills in reading, math, writing, and/or spelling.

What strategy did you use to figure out that word or concept?). Conducting observations, on the other hand, provides insight into what reading behaviors students actually utilize (stop and reread, use fix-up strategies, preview text before reading, self-question, etc.).

Regardless of assessment methods used, you should keep in mind what your purpose is for assessing a student[23,24]: screening for difficulties, progress monitoring, assessing reading level, or assessing a student's competence in comparison to peers or other established criteria. Ask yourself, "What is it that I want to know, and how will this knowledge help me target my instruction?" A norm-referenced test cannot tell you about a student's attitude toward reading, and an informal reading inventory does not identify a student's progress toward meeting curriculum-based learning outcomes (e.g., Does the student understand why the belief in manifest destiny led the United States to expand in the West?). Each assessment method has its own purpose.

Important Tips

When you are assessing for comprehension, the materials students are asked to read should be at his or her instructional level, meaning the student should be able to read 95% of the words accurately.

A chart can be a helpful tool for identifying main ideas and important details. Ask students to identify the topic, main idea, and key details after reading using simple tables or charts to help frame their thoughts and organize information (see Figure 12.1).

It is important for you to check the accuracy of the main ideas and key details identified by students. To do so, ask yourself the following questions:

1. Does the main ideas statement include significant details from the text?
2. Are the details accurate and directly related to the main idea?

HOW DO YOU USE ASSESSMENTS TO PLAN INSTRUCTION?

In reality, it is through classroom assessment that attitudes, skill, knowledge, and thinking are fostered, nurtured, and accelerated—or stifled.[25]

Teachers use a variety of assessment tools to help plan reading comprehension instruction to meet the needs of students during various grouping arrangements (whole class, small groups, or individuals). In addition to measuring learning outcomes, assessments should also promote

BOX 12.2.

Encouraging higher-order thinking through higher-order questioning.

Monitoring learning: Checking in to ensure students do not check out.

You can quickly and effectively gather information to help you check for students' understanding. During "Quick Writes," a literacy strategy designed to provide opportunities to reflect on learning[26] and understanding, students respond to a question or prompt related to the text by writing down whatever comes to mind. Quick Writes can be used as a reading assessment activity to help you take your students' pulse to inform how much support and guidance you should provide.

Before reading

Ask students to quickly preview the text and do a Quick Write about

- Something they already know about the text or topic
- Something they think they are going to learn after reading

Have students share their completed Quick Writes in small groups or with partners while you monitor, then pull the whole class together, making sure to validate when students are on the right track and to redirect students who need it. Quick Writes can reveal areas requiring you to provide or build upon students' background knowledge or vocabulary weaknesses that can be enhanced by teaching to small groups or individuals as needed.

During reading

Decide on a predetermined stopping point during reading, and ask students to do a Quick Write about what they have read so far. These can be compared with partners or in small groups. For example, ask students to write and share about

- What they have learned so far
- Problems they have encountered
- What they like or do not like
- How well they understand the concept, problem, or issue

After reading

Hold students accountable for what they read by having them do a Quick Write. Some things you can ask them to do:

- Summarize what they learned.
- Explain a given concept or vocabulary term
- Pose questions to others that can be responded to in small groups, or have students complete written responses that you can use as a guide to provide a quick review or to revisit learning or unanswered questions from the previous day's lesson.

Whereas lower-level questioning (i.e., who, what, where, when, why, how) relies on simple recall, and identification, responding to higher-order questions is more cognitively demanding and requires thinking beyond what is presented in the text.

(continued)

BOX 12.2. *(continued)*

The basic question types include

1. Right There: Answers are found by locating and copying down information in the text (What is the definition of an arachnid?).

   Student is expected to locate: *Who, what, where, when, why, how many, list, what kind, name.*

2. Think and Search: Answer is in the reading, but in one or more sentences or paragraphs requiring that information be combined in a meaningful way (Why do people fear spiders?).

   Student is expected to process information by describing, summarizing, comparing, explaining, reporting, citing examples, and organizing.

3. The Author and You: The answer is not in the reading. Readers use what they know and clues from the author. Sometimes more research is necessary. (What is the difference between a spider and an insect?)

   Student is expected to contrast, analyze, examine, differentiate, demonstrate, illustrate, infer, solve, and compose.

4. On Your Own: The answers are not in the book at all. The questions require that readers use background knowledge to support their opinions (What do you think might happen if spiders did not exist?).

   Student is expected to judge, evaluate, rate, defend, and justify.

To help develop your students' abilities as critical thinkers, it is essential that you build into your assessments various types of questions that demand students read and apply, analyze, evaluate, and synthesize information rather than just remember it. You want to widen students' abilities so that you eventually release them to create their own higher-order questions to answer themselves and to share with others.

Sample question stems to assess student's knowledge acquisition:

- Why do you think _____?
- How are ___ and ____ alike?
- How are ___ and ____different?
- What do you think would happen if ____?
- What caused ____ to happen?
- What other solution can you think of?
- What might have prevented____?
- What are the strengths (or weaknesses) of ____?

learning by students and their teachers. Students tend to be more actively involved in their learning and willing to strive for continued improvement of comprehension skills when they receive ongoing feedback about how they are doing, what they are doing well, in addition to what they need to focus on to become better readers.[27] Motivation to read text can be

Topic	Main idea (what text was mostly about)	Key details
		1. 2. 3. 4.

Figure 12.1. Sample main idea chart.

heightened when students are encouraged to be critical thinkers about what they are reading. For you, the teacher, this means previewing text before designing your lessons and developing higher-level questions to engage students on a deeper level than required by identification or recall of information. It also means building students' skills so that eventually they will be able to independently develop higher-order questions and activities (Table 12.4).

Assessment data can help students to self-analyze and reflect on their strategy use and knowledge acquisition. Students should be guided to ask themselves the following questions and then discuss their responses during a teacher/student conference:

- Am I improving in my reading comprehension skills?
- Do I know how to succeed with this reading activity or assignment?
- What are my strengths and weaknesses when reading for understanding?
- What areas do I need help with?

When thinking about making adjustments to instruction, teachers should look at assessment data (quiz and test scores, completed assignments including writing samples, and graphic organizers, along with interview, questionnaire, or observation information). With these queries in mind, it is time to plan accordingly:

- What do these students need?
- What do I need to do differently for these students or this student?
- What strengths can I build upon?
- How should I group students?
- Am I moving too fast and for which students?
- Am I moving too slowly and for which students?
- Is there a problem with my instruction?
- Where did learning break down?

Use your assessment data to confirm whether or not reading comprehension has taken place, but more importantly to inform your planning and providing of additional learning opportunities for students to improve their reading comprehension skills. An analysis of what you taught and to what extent students mastered your learning objectives may indicate that it is necessary for you to do the following:

- Designate time to preteach, provide more guided practice, or reteach.
- Schedule more instructional time for certain topics that students have difficulty with, or for struggling readers who need more practice and feedback.

Table 12.4. Questions/tasks to develop and assess critical thinking

Skills required	Question/task
Recall	Who, what, when, where, how?
	List or name….
Identify: attributes/parts	What are the characteristics/parts of _____?
Identify: relationships/patterns	Develop an outline/diagram/web of….
Compare	How is/similar to/different from_____?
Classify	How might you organize these?
Order	Arrange in sequence according to….
Represent	In what ways might you show/illustrate….
Infer	What might you infer from _____?
	What conclusions might you draw?
Predict	What might happen if _____?
Elaborate	What ideas/details can you add to _____?
	I wonder if _____?
Summarize	I learned, realized, discovered, that….
Verify	What evidence supports _____?
	How might you prove/confirm _____?
Analyze	Contrast _____ and _____.
Evaluate	I think/believe/understand that….
	It seems to me that….

- Build or strengthen foundational skills for students who are deficient (listening comprehension, fluency, word learning strategies, or vocabulary).
- Group or regroup students to target specific skills (e.g., making inferences, identifying main idea, summarizing, questioning).
- Implement more modeling and guided practice for students who do not demonstrate knowledge of or sufficient use of strategies.

Assessing for instructional purposes provides teachers with reason to gather and interpret useful information both about how effective instruction is and how well students are comprehending. In addition to outcome measures (scores, ranks, number correct or incorrect), assessment results reveal insight into your students' earlier knowledge, attitudes toward reading, and ability to learn from and think about texts, all of which should drive your instructional planning in order to maximize student success as readers.

HOW DO YOU TEACH READING COMPREHENSION STRATEGIES EFFECTIVELY AND EFFICIENTLY?

So far, this chapter has discussed skills that students should possess in grades 4–6 that enable them to read for understanding. You have learned some of the best ways for students to engage in reading, and how assessments can drive instructional planning. Now you may be asking yourself, "How do I teach comprehension strategies? What strategies and interventions are based on research?" This section will answer those questions by providing the following information:

1. A description of what you can do before, during, and after reading to enhance reading comprehension for your students.
2. A brief summary of several research-based programs with a record of positively impacting the reading comprehension of general education students and students with learning disabilities. The strategies presented here can be used immediately, and references are included for more detailed information for each technique.

Before, During, and After Reading

Reading comprehension instruction begins before students begin reading an assigned chapter. Before reading new material, teachers must provide a preview of what the passage will be about and link the new information to the student's background or culture whenever possible. Next, preteaching essential vocabulary words and reviewing important proper nouns for informational text like science and social studies readings is a must.[28] Students are also encouraged to write down their predictions about the story / reading and refer back to the predictions later to confirm or explain what happened.

Modeling how students can monitor their comprehension should be done whenever possible during reading. Teachers can apply two useful strategies when reading aloud to demonstrate what students should do: 1) the "think-aloud" strategy and 2) effectively using "stopping points," or places in the text where the teacher stops to check for understanding by clarifying, summarizing what has been read, posing a question, or having students generate questions. The "think-aloud" strategy means encouraging students to verbalize their thoughts during reading in order to make text connections and encourage active thinking and questioning.[29] Teachers model the think-aloud strategy all year whenever they read to students. Teachers stop and make connections to their lives, to other books, and to the world (like a news story). An example of this while reading about sharks would be, "Sharks are fascinating! This page about the hunting habits of sharks reminds me of a show I saw on the Discovery Channel about tiger sharks. I think I am going to Google 'tiger sharks' tonight to learn about their lifespan and diets."

Efficient use of "stopping points" is another opportunity to instill comprehension skills. You must always preview a text and select stopping points before students read, anticipating the places in text where comprehension may break down without your guidance. During stopping points, teachers model how to summarize the main idea of the preceding section, ask literal and inferential questions to students, and complete a graphic organizer or take notes (if applicable, such as when reading a history textbook). For example, "That page was mostly about how steam engines helped make people's lives easier during the Industrial Revolution. On my chart I am going to write about how steam engines made it cheaper and faster to trade." After modeling this type of thought process and helping students practice on their own, teachers gradually turn this responsibility completely over to students when they seem ready to summarize and cite evidence independently.

After the text is read, students extend their comprehension through discussion or writing. Students can turn to a partner and explain the summary of what was just read. In addition, the teacher can put a question on the board such as, "Do you agree with Tom's decision to leave his family and go to work in New York City? What was the economic and emotional impact on his family in Pennsylvania after he left?" Students turn to a partner and discuss this prompt, or it can be used as a writing topic. There is evidence to support that working on post-reading assignments in pairs is associated with improved comprehension compared to working alone,[30] and these academic speaking opportunities are beneficial for students who are English language learners.[31] Other post-reading activities include completing and studying from graphic organizers for content-area text[32] or engaging the class in a structured academic discussion.[33]

Collaborative Strategic Reading

Collaborative strategic reading (CSR) is made up of four strategies designed to help students better understand narrative or expository text. It is based on years of research that boasts a record of success for students with a wide range of ability levels, including English language learners and students with learning disabilities. CSR combines specific reading comprehension strategies with structured cooperative learning for students in upper-elementary and middle school.[34]

CSR is a collection of four strategies that must be followed with integrity to achieve positive results. The following summary explains CSR:

CSR Preview

- Teacher engages students in a preview including looking at pictures and headings, brainstorming what is known about the topic, and writing down a prediction.
- Brief video clips or images with background or supporting information about a topic can be shown to stimulate interest and activate earlier knowledge.

CSR During Reading: "Click & Clunk" and "Get the Gist"

- Students work in groups of four to six and read a short passage independently (or orally with the group depending on ability level).
- "Clicking" refers to smooth and easy reading when a student has no difficulty with vocabulary or understanding of the passage.
- "Clunks" refer to difficult words or phrases that students circle as they read. Students learn to use four "fix-up strategies" to comprehend clunks. These are re-reading and looking for context clues; re-reading the sentence before and after the sentence with the clunk; using the prefix, suffix, root word or a smaller word within the word that make sense; and finally, identify cognates (recognizing cognates can be helpful for students speaking languages that share cognates with the English language).
- At the end of each paragraph or section, students write a "gist" statement on their learning log. The gist is a brief sentence stating the main idea of that section in 10 words or less. To identify the "gist," or main idea, students complete the following three steps: First, students identify the most important *who* or *what* in a paragraph or section. Next, students identify what is most important about the *who* or *what*. Finally, students write a sentence about the main idea in 10 words or fewer, typically beginning with the who or what.
- For group work, there are student roles for CSR. There is a leader, a clunk expert, gist expert, and a question expert.
- Students share their gists and clunks with the students in the group to promote interaction and language skills.

CSR After Reading (Wrap Up)

- Students generate three questions about what they read. The first question type that students create is a *Right There* question. For example, "In what year was the first model car invented?" The second type is called *Think and Search*, which asks the students to locate information in different parts of a text. An example is, "How did the Erie Canal impact both businesses and common people?" Finally, students generate an *Author and You* question, which requires synthesizing and inferences. For example, "What could NASA build in the future that could assist hurricane prediction on earth?"
- Finally, students write one or two sentences summarizing the entire passage.

Graphic Organizers

Graphic organizers (GOs) can be used for narrative (fiction) text or with informational and expository texts. GOs are linked to improving reading outcomes for students in general education, English language learners, and those with disabilities. GOs include the following terms: cognitive maps, semantic maps, story maps, Venn diagrams, framed outlines, or advanced organizers.[35] GOs offer a "visual-spatial display of information extracted from text passages."[36] GOs are used for the following: 1) to teach the major parts of fiction stories (e.g., characters, plot, setting); 2) to provide access to complex information in content-

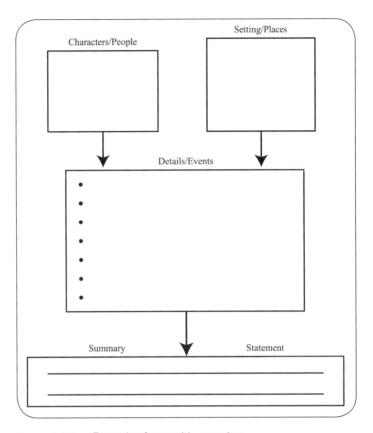

Figure 12.2.   Example of a graphic organizer.

area classes; 3) as a study guide; and 4) to develop students' comprehension skills by having students select the most meaningful and important details from text to display in visual form (Figure 12.2).

The following lesson plan procedures have demonstrated success in research studies.[37]

1. Introduce the GO before reading as a tool to enable students to capture main ideas and details.

2. Teach vocabulary before reading. For informational or expository text, review proper nouns that are integral to understanding the chapter.[38]

3. Read and stop periodically to identify ideas, concepts, and main ideas. Teachers must model the main idea and summary first, and then after several weeks of practice, students assume responsibility to complete the GO independently or with a partner.

4. When students complete GOs independently or with a partner, ask students to justify their selection of details and ideas on the GO by showing where in the text they found that information. Provide feedback and support for inaccurate responses.

5. For social studies and science, the GO can be used as a study guide to study key concepts and vocabulary for later application in discussion, writing, or for a quiz or test.[39]

Teaching Tip: For students with learning disabilities, struggling readers, or English language learners, teachers should review each cell or box in the graphic organizer after it has been filled out. The teacher should lead the class in chorally stating (student and teacher read together in unison) each idea or concept on the GO. Explicit instruction using a GO has demonstrated positive outcomes for students with learning disabilities in social studies.[40]

Peer-Assisted Learning Strategies (PALS)

A peer-assisted learning strategy, or PALS, is a program that boasts a record of promising results. The goal of PALS is to address the needs of all students in the class and provide differentiation of instruction.[41] A brief summary of PALS is provided below[42]:

Grouping:

- Students work in groups of two.
- Teachers pair students by ranking them based on reading performance and then splitting the list in half. The top-scoring reader in the upper-half is paired with the top-scoring reader in the lower half. This process continues until all students have a partner.
- The assigned groups should remain constant for 4 weeks at a time.

PALS procedure for reading and retelling:

- Student pairs read passages that are at the instructional-reading level of the weaker reader.
- The stronger partner (the tutor) reads orally for 5 minutes. Next, the second student reads the *same* passage again. During reading, the tutor provides immediate corrective feedback on word errors.

- After reading, the second student orally retells what he or she read. The tutor prompts the retell by asking, "What did you learn first?" and "What happened next?" For concepts that the second student does not remember accurately, the tutor provides the information.

PALS procedure for summary:

- Students take turns reading aloud one paragraph at a time. After reading, the student states the subject and main idea of the paragraph. Index cards serve as prompts with the questions: "What was that paragraph about?" and "What was the most important thing you read?"
- For incorrect responses, the listening partner asks the reader to go back to the paragraph to re-read it silently and then try again.

Reciprocal Teaching

In 2000, the National Reading Panel cited the Reciprocal Teaching strategy as an evidence-based framework for improving reading comprehension. This reading comprehension strategy instruction has been effective for students in general education and for students who speak English as a second language.[43] In reciprocal teaching, the adult and students take turns serving as the teacher. This model teaches students to apply four reading strategies: prediction, summarization, question generation, and clarification. A summary of the procedures is listed below.

Predictions:

- The students and teacher share predictions about the coming story based on previous knowledge and a brief preview of the text and pictures.
- The student assigned to serve as the "teacher" begins the discussion with a prompt that is written on prepared cue cards such as, "What does our previous knowledge of mystery stories tell us might happen here?" While other students share predictions, the classroom teacher serves as facilitator.[44]

Question generation:

- Students generate their own questions before reading, and the questions are answered during or after reading. This increases motivation and engagement because students are answering their own questions. The teacher should preview questions and provide assistance during the process to ensure students are on target!

Summarizing:

- The students discuss as a group what was the most important part of the section they read (stop students every 2–3 paragraphs to summarize). One student who is assigned as the leader that day can start by saying, "for that section, my summary is…." Other students will then add to this summary or offer an original one. The teacher serves as the facilitator to monitor accuracy.

Clarifying:

- The teacher initially models for students how to "clarify." This is a process where, eventually, the students learn to clarify and ask questions to their peers about words and phrases that were difficult to understand. This is comprehension monitoring, where students acquire an awareness of their cognition and learning during reading.

Note: The procedure for reciprocal teaching must be taught and modeled for students for 2–4 weeks before students assume responsibility. The above description of reciprocal teaching is a brief summary.[45]

PUTTING IT ALL TOGETHER: DEVELOPING LESSON PLANS THAT INCORPORATE STANDARDS AND EVIDENCE-BASED STRATEGIES

The scenario presented at the opening of this chapter presents a very basic and realistic depiction of instruction that many students in our nation's schools encounter. Although this chapter could not provide you with everything you need to know about teaching reading comprehension to students in grades 4–6, the strategies and ideas presented in this text are grounded in research and provide you with an excellent starting point in your educational journey.

The list of strategies to effectively teach reading comprehension could not be covered in a single chapter. However, the strategies presented here have a record of success! You are encouraged to find out more about each, while continuing to pursue additional teaching methods and interventions that will help your students succeed!

What Do I Now Know about Reading Comprehension Instruction for Students in Grades 4–6?

Our parting advice is for you to remember two key points as you embark on your career as a teacher of students in grades 4–6:

1. The ultimate goal of teaching students to read is for them to have the necessary skills and the motivation to read for understanding! The ability to read with comprehension ensures that students will be able to succeed in academic subjects requiring literacy, read for enjoyment on their own, and use their literacy skills to accomplish their dreams and contribute to society.
2. Never stop learning! The field of educational research is emerging. As a teacher, seek out professional development opportunities and read professional, peer-reviewed journals to stay up to date on the most current research-based practices.

APPLICATION ASSIGNMENTS

In-Class Assignments

1. With a partner, refer back to Mr. Hudson's reading comprehension assignment for his sixth-grade class. He started off by preteaching some important vocabulary to assist students in their reading about the process of photosynthesis, and he did provide a purpose for reading (assigned questions to be answered).

   - In what areas could he improve comprehension instruction?
   - Design a script for Mr. Hudson to follow that includes explicit directives for students to guide their use of reading comprehension strategies before, during, and after reading the chapter about the process of photosynthesis.

2. Work with a partner for 5 minutes. Think of a book that you have read recently, and create three examples of "think aloud" connections that you would use if you were reading to your class. Create think-aloud examples of the following types of connections: text to self-connection, a connection to another book or text, and one text to the world connection!

Tutoring Assignments

1. Implement PALS for several tutoring sessions using the procedures outlined in this chapter. Write a one-page paper describing your experiences and how this strategy was beneficial for you student(s).

2. Select one of the strategies that comprise CSR that your student needs most. Teach the strategy to your student, and provide several opportunities for the student to practice the strategy.

Homework Assignments

1. Write a paper addressing the following statements:

   - A description of what reading comprehension is, why it is important, and what the research says about effective teaching
   - An explanation of what students should be able to perform in grades 4–6 to demonstrate an ability to read for understanding
   - Explain how to select and use assessments to measure reading comprehension.
   - Explain how to use assessment data to target students' needs in reading comprehension

2. Locate a one-page reading passage. Select a page from an expository text, such as a science or social studies text or from this text. Read through the passage completing the CSR steps as previously explained. Read the passage, circle clunks and use "fix-up strategies," write gist statements, generate the three types of questions, and write a summary statement at the end. This may seem like an easy task, but practicing CSR is the BEST way to learn it, and will make it easier to introduce to your students!

ENDNOTES

1. Stanovich & Stanovich, (2006).
2. Teaching struggling readers, including second language learners: This chapter emphasizes the importance of comprehension instruction for students in grades 4–6, but readers who are struggling or learning English as a second language will still need instruction in foundational reading skills such as phonics, word recognition, and fluency. Research indicates that even students who have reading difficulties do benefit from comprehension instruction.
3. Wanzek, Wexler, Vaughn, & Ciullo (2010).
4. Shanahan, Callison, Carriere, Duke, Pearson, Schatschneider, et al. (2010).
5. National Reading Panel (2000).

6. Klingner, Vaughn, & Boardman (2007, p. 8).
7. Paris, Lipson, & Wixson (1983); Paris, Wasik, & Turner (1991).
8. Baker & Brown (1984); Pressley (2001).
9. Baker & Brown (1984).
10. Wells (1990).
11. Shanahan, Callison, Carriere, Duke, Pearson, Schatschneider, et al. (2010).
12. National Reading Panel (2000).
13. Shanahan, Callison, Carriere, Duke, Pearson, Schatschneider, et al. (2010).
14. Gajria, Jitendra, Sood, & Sacks (2007).
15. Palinscar & Brown (1984)
16. Pressley (2001)
17. DiCecco & Gleason (2002).
18. See http://www.corestandards.org/the-standards/english-language-arts-standards
19. When teaching, check with your district for the official determination for what state and district curriculum map and standards you are to follow.
20. Hamilton, Halverson, Jackson, Mandinach, Supovitz, & Wayman (2009).
21. Klingner, Vaughn, & Boardman (2007); Klingner & Vaughn (1999); Klingner, Vaughn & Schumm (1998).
22. RAND Reading Study Group (2002).
23. Evaluating background and vocabulary knowledge of students: Before assigning reading material and a comprehension task, you should evaluate whether students possess the necessary background and vocabulary knowledge in order to be successful with the activity. These areas can easily be addressed before reading in a mini-lesson where you provide background information and preteach vocabulary or concepts essential to understanding the text.
24. Assessing using different types of text: When assessing a student's comprehension abilities, make sure to provide students with both narrative and informational text. Narrative and informational texts are structured differently, and students should employ different reading strategies when attempting to read them for meaning. Usually, narrative text is more predictable (beginning, middle, end) and easier to read. Structure contributes to students' comprehension of the text, and students may need more instruction and practice applying strategies with informational texts.
25. Hynes (2003, p. 24).
26. Green, Smith, & Brown (2007); Mason, Benedek-Wood, Valasa (2009).
27. Hamilton, Halverson, Jackson, Mandinach, Supovitz, & Wayman (2009, p. 5).
28. Simmons, Hairrell, Edmonds, Vaughn, Larsen, Willson, et al. (2010).
29. Oster (2001).
30. Gersten, Baker, Smith-Johnson, Dimino, & Peterson (2006).
31. Echevaria, Vogt, & Short (2010).
32. DiCecco & Gleason (2002).
33. Zwiers (2008).
34. Vaughn, Dimino, Schumm, & Bryant (2001).
35. Kim, Vaughn, Wanzek, & Wei (2004).
36. Griffin, Simmons, & Kame'enui (1991).
37. DiCecco & Gleason (2002); Gardill & Jitendra (1999); Gersten, Baker, Smith-Johnson, Dimino, & Peterson (2006).
38. Simmons, Hairrell, Edmonds, Vaughn, Larsen, Willson, et al. (2010).
39. Darch & Carnine (1986); DiCecco & Gleason (2002).
40. DiCecco & Gleason (2002).
41. Fuchs, Fuchs, Mathes, & Simmons (1997).
42. Fuchs et al. (1997).
43. Klingner & Vaughn (1996); Palinscar & Brown (1986).
44. Palinscar & Brown (1986); Oczkus (2010).
45. Palinscar & Brown (1984).

REFERENCES

Baker, L., & Brown, A.L. (1984). Metacognitive skills and reading. In P.D. Pearson, R. Barr, M.L. Kamil, & P. Mosenthal (Eds.), *Handbook of reading research* (pp. 353–394). White Plains, NY: Longman.

The Common Core State Standards Initiative. (2010). Retrieved August 31, 2011 from http://www.corestandards.org

Darch, C., & Carnine, D. (1986). Teaching content area material to learning disabled students. *Exceptional Children, 53,* 240–246.

DiCecco, V., & Gleason, M.M. (2002). Using graphic organizers to attain relational knowledge from expository text. *Journal of Learning Disabilities, 35*(4), 306–320.

Echevaria, J., Vogt, M.E., & Short, D. (2010). *Making content comprehensible for secondary English learners: The SIOP model.* Boston: Allyn & Bacon.

Fuchs, D., Fuchs, L.S., Mathes, P.G., & Simmons, D.C. (1997). Peer-assisted learning strategies: Making classrooms more responsive to diversity. *American Educational Research Journal, 34*(1), 174–205.

Gardill, M.C., & Jitendra, A.K. (1999). Advanced story map instruction: Effects on their reading comprehension of students with learning disabilities. *The Journal of Special Education, 33,* 2–17.

Gersten, R., Baker, S.K., Smith-Johnson, J., Dimino, J., & Peterson A. (2006). Eyes on the prize: Teaching complex historical content to middle-school students with learning disabilities. *Exceptional Children, 72,* 264–280.

Green, S.K., Smith, J. III, & Brown, K.E. (2007). Using quick writes as classroom assessment tools: Prospects and problems. *Journal of Educational Research, 7*(2), 38–52.

Griffin, C.C., Simmons, D.C., & Kame'enui, E.J. (1991). Investigating the effectiveness of graphic organizer instruction on the comprehension and recall of science content by students with learning disabilities. *Reading, Writing, and Learning Disabilities, 7,* 355–376.

Hamilton, L., Halverson, R., Jackson, S., Mandinach, E., Supovitz, J., & Wayman, J. (2009). Using student achievement data to support instructional decision making (NCEE 2009-4067), Washington, DC: National Center for Educational Evaluation and Regional Assistance, Institute of Education Sciences, U.S. Department of Education. Retrieved from http://ies.ed.gov/ncee/wwc/publications/practiceguides/

Hynes, W. As cited In Earl, L.M. (Ed.), (2003). *Assessment as learning: Using classroom achievement to maximize student learning. Experts in Assessment Series.* Thousand Oaks, CA: Corwin Press, Inc.

Kim, A., Vaughn, S., Wanzek, J., & Wei, S. (2004). Graphic organizers and their effects on the reading comprehension of students with LD: A synthesis of research. *Journal of Learning Disabilities, 37*, 105–118.

Klingner, J.K., & Vaughn, S. (1996). Reciprocal teaching of reading comprehension strategies for students with learning disabilities who use English as a second language. *The Elementary School Journal, 96*(3), 275–293.

Klingner, J.K., & Vaughn, S. (1999). Promoting reading comprehension, content learning, and English acquisition through collaborative strategic reading (CSR). *The Reading Teacher, 52*(7), 738–747.

Klingner, J.K., Vaughn, S., & Boardman, A. (2007). *Teaching reading comprehension to students with learning difficulties.* New York: The Guilford Press.

Klingner, J.K., Vaughn, S., & Schumm, J.S. (1998). Collaborative strategic reading during social studies in heterogeneous fourth-grade classrooms. *The Elementary School Journal, 99*(1), 3–22.

Mason, L.H., Benedek-Wood, E., & Valasa, L. (2009). Teaching low-achieving students to self-regulate persuasive quick-write responses. *Journal of Adolescent & Adult Literacy, 53*(4), 303–312.

National Reading Panel. (2000, April). *Report of the National Reading Panel: Teaching children to read.* Washington, DC: National Institute of Child Health and Human Development, National Institutes of Health, U.S. Department of Health and Human Services.

No Child Left Behind, 42 U.S.C. 9401 (2001).

Oczkus, L.D. (2010). *Reciprocal teaching at work: Powerful strategies and lessons for improving reading comprehension* (2nd ed.). Newark, DE: International Reading Association.

Oster, L. (2001). Using the think-aloud for reading instruction. *The Reading Teacher, 55*(1), 64–69.

Palinscar, A.S., & Brown, A.L. (1984). Reciprocal teaching of comprehension fostering and comprehension monitoring activities. *Cognition and Instruction, 1*(2), 117–175.

Palinscar, A.S., & Brown, A.L. (1986). Interactive teaching to promote independent learning from text. *The Reading Teacher, 39*(8), 771–777.

Paris, S.G., Lipson, M.Y., & Wixson, K.K. (1983). Becoming a strategic reader. *Contemporary Educational Psychology, 8*(3), 293–316.

Paris, S.G., Wasik, B.A., & Turner, J.C. (1991). The development of strategic readers. In R. Barr, M.L. Kamil, P.B. Mosenthal, & P.D. Pearson (Eds.), *Handbook of reading research* (Vol. 2, pp. 609–640). New York: Longman.

Pressley, M. (2001, September). Comprehension instruction: What makes sense now, what might make sense soon. *Reading Online, 5*(2). Available: http://www.readingonline.org/articles/art_index.asp?HREF=/articles/handbook/pressley/index.html

RAND Reading Study Group. (2002). *Reading for understanding: Toward a R&D program in reading comprehension.* Santa Monica, CA: RAND.

Shanahan, T., Callison, K., Carriere, C., Duke, N.K., Pearson, P.D., Schatschneider, C., et al. (2010). *Improving reading comprehension in kindergarten through 3rd grade: A practice guide* (NCEE 210-4038). Washington, DC: National Center for Education Evaluation and Regional Assistance, Institute of Education Sciences, U.S. Department of Education. Retrieved from whatworks.ed.gov/publications/practiceguides

Simmons, D., Hairrell, A., Edmonds, M., Vaughn, S., Larsen, R., Willson, V., et al. (2010). A comparison of multiple-strategy methods: Effects on fourth-grade students' general and content specific reading comprehension and vocabulary development. *Journal of Research on Educational Effectiveness, 3*, 121–156.

Stanovich, P.J., & Stanovich, K.E. (2006). *Using research and reason in education: How teachers can use scientifically based research to make curricular and instructional decisions* (No. ED-OOCO-0093). Portsmouth, NH: The National Institute of Literacy, The Partnership for Reading.

Vaughn, S., Dimino, J., Schumm, J.S., & Bryant, D.P. (2001). *Collaborative strategic reading: From click to clunk.* Longmont, CO: Sopris West.

Wanzek, J., Wexler, J., Vaughn, S., & Ciullo, S. (2010). Reading interventions for struggling readers in the upper elementary grades. A synthesis of 20 years of research. *Reading and Writing, 23*(8), 889–912.

Wells, G. (1990). Creating the conditions to encourage literate thinking. *Educational Leadership, 47*(6), 13–17.

Zwiers, J. (2008). *Building academic language: Essential practices for content classrooms, grades 5–12.* Newark, DE: International Reading Association.

Strategic, Meaningful, and Effective Writing Instruction for Elementary Students

by Natalie G. Olinghouse
and Joshua Wilson

A classroom full of students is engaged in their daily writing, absorbed in their learning. Students are located around the room: some in their desks working independently; some in pairs working collaboratively, sharing and exchanging ideas and suggestions; and some in a teacher-guided small group. The students are self-directed and confident, enjoying the power and possibility of writing, the excitement of being able to write words on a page that elicit laughter, sadness, or a thoughtful response from their audience. The students know that, through writing, they have a voice. They have an outlet for their natural desire to communicate, to share and to describe, to inform and to persuade. With guidance from their teacher, these students have come to see and feel the power of writing.

Like speaking, writing is a form of communication, a way to share ideas and experiences. However, unlike speaking, most students do not learn to write simply by being immersed in a writing environment. All of us were taught how to write, beginning with the basics of handwriting and spelling and progressing to the complexities of composing longer pieces of writing. Knowing that writing requires instruction, an inevitable question is how to best teach writing.

This is where you come in.

The vision of writing instruction described above is one that sees writing as a powerful tool for communication and expression. It is also a vision that sees students as self-directed, confident, and engaged writers. The teacher in the opening scenario provided strategic and meaningful writing instruction, and her students thrived. The goal of this chapter is to show you how to do this, too.

Objectives: After studying this chapter you will be able to do the following:

1. Name and describe the key subcomponents of writing instruction.
2. Understand reasons why writing instruction is important for students.
3. Understand how to apply different forms of writing assessment to plan and evaluate instruction.
4. Explain the benefits and limitations of a writing process approach, and understand how to embed evidence-based practices within this instructional approach.
5. Name and describe the six stages of self-regulated strategy development (SRSD) and understand how to apply this method to writing instruction.

WHAT IS WRITING? WHY IS WRITING IMPORTANT? WHAT DOES THE RESEARCH SAY?

Writing is used to communicate, but it is also important because it helps support critical thinking. In their influential report, *How Writing Shapes Thinking*, Judith Langer and Arthur Applebee[1] demonstrated that different types of writing develop different critical thinking skills, such as questioning, recalling, reflecting, planning, analyzing, or synthesizing. Their findings helped researchers and educators think about ways that writing could reinforce other cognitive and academic skills, such as reading ability.

Writing instruction is also important for achievement in college and the workplace. Writing is used in almost every college class and in almost every kind of job. In addition, writing is used more and more in our community to start and maintain relationships—from e-mails to text messages, from blogs to social community networks

Unfortunately, many students do not adequately develop the basic writing skills to communicate their ideas and support critical thinking development. Results from the National Assessment of Educational Progress (NAEP) found that less than one third of fourth-, eighth-, and twelfth-grade students demonstrated grade-level writing proficiency scores.[2] The problem carries over into postsecondary environments as well. In a series of annual reports, the National Commission on Writing[3] found that fewer than half of incoming freshmen met college writing expectations and that businesses and state governments spend more than $3 billion annually to improve the writing skills of their employees.

The Need for Strategic and Meaningful Instruction

Because many students struggle with developing effective writing skills, teachers need to design and deliver strategic, meaningful, and effective writing instruction in the classroom. Writing instruction needs to be strategic because writing is complex; it involves many skills. Think about all the skills that you employ when you write. You generate ideas in your mind, put those ideas on paper by handwriting or keyboarding, spell your words correctly, organize your ideas into sentences and paragraphs, correctly punctuate your sentences, create some form of organization, and include content that you wish to communicate.

When a task is complex, it is helpful to have a method for completing it. In education, having a careful and efficient method for completing a task and evaluating the results is known as having a strategy. Writing instruction needs to be strategic because there are many different aspects of writing to juggle while composing. When students use writing strategies, they approach the complexities of writing equipped with a method for success. It is this type of instruction that allowed the students in the opening scenario to be self-directed and confident writers.

Writing also is a meaningful and powerful activity. It has many purposes. Think of all the ways you rely on writing in your life. Certainly, you rely on writing for academic purposes, but what about in your daily life? You use writing for organizing and planning (to-do lists, shopping or grocery lists, trip itineraries), for socializing (texts, e-mails, social networking), for persuasion (job or college applications), or for personal reflection (journal or diary entries). You write for real purposes that are meaningful to you. The teacher in the scenario created opportunities for engaging in meaningful and authentic communication through writing, which helped her students to understand that writing is powerful because it has actual purposes in their lives.

Learning how to write can and should be both strategic and meaningful. So should learning how to teach writing! In the following pages, you will be given the tools to make a complex task—writing instruction—easier, strategic, meaningful, and effective.

WHAT SHOULD STUDENTS KNOW AND BE ABLE TO DO AT SPECIFIC GRADE LEVELS, PRE-K–6?

Before embarking down the road of strategic and meaningful writing, it is important for a teacher to understand what writing is and how it develops. This helps a teacher know what aspects of writing should be taught and what students can be expected to do at different grade levels. Table 13.1 provides an overview of the different components of writing and why each is important to writing development. Take time to read through each element and think about how it relates to your own writing and the writing of children you know.

Researchers have studied the growth of different subcomponents of writing, such as handwriting, vocabulary, and genre-knowledge; however, we still do not have a complete understanding of how writing develops from grade to grade. Because writing is composed of so

Table 13.1. Elements of an effective writing instruction program

Instructional element	Definition	Purpose
Transcription skills	Transcription skills refer to handwriting and spelling, skills needed to convert ideas into written letters and words. Handwriting is the ability to legibly and quickly reproduce letters and words from sight and memory. Spelling ability encompasses knowledge of phonemes, graphemes, and morphemes.	When handwriting and spelling are fluent, mental energy is freed up to focus on expressing ideas. Fluent writers often produce texts of higher quality than dysfluent writers.
Word choice	Word choice refers to the development of a wide range of vocabulary needed to express ideas (content-vocabulary, descriptive words, figurative language), or create mature and coherent texts (transition words, academic vocabulary, genre-specific vocabulary).	When students have a robust vocabulary they can 1) express their ideas with greater ease and clarity, 2) produce rich texts that interest a reader, and 3) select words for different genres, tasks, and purposes.
Sentence conventions	Sentence conventions refer to those skills needed to produce coherent sentences of varying length and complexity. Such skills include punctuation, capitalization, and sentence construction skills.	When students master a range of sentence structures, they express their ideas with greater clarity and maturity. Embedding instruction in these skills in authentic writing tasks is more powerful than "drill-and-kill" grammar exercises, which have a negative effect on writing performance.[4]
Paragraph construction skills	Paragraph construction skills refer to students' ability to create meaningfully related, logically organized, and appropriately formatted paragraphs, both for narrative and expository text.	When students are able to write meaningful, coherent, and well-organized paragraphs, they are poised to create texts of greater length, maturity, and complexity. Their writing is better organized and coherent.
Genre and text structure skills	Genre and text structure skills refer to students' ability to recognize and reproduce the key elements of different genres such as narrative, persuasive, or informational text.	When students are taught to recognize the key elements of different genres and text structures, they not only write texts that include those elements, but their ability to read and comprehend those genres improves as well.
Writing process strategies	Writing process strategies are explicitly taught procedures used to create a written text. These procedures are designed to help students approach the task of writing strategically. Students should be competent with strategies for pre-writing (planning), drafting, and post-writing (editing and revising).	When students do not approach the task of writing systematically and strategically, they are often overwhelmed by the task, and their writing suffers. Explicit strategy instruction is the single most effective way to improve students' writing.
Self-regulation skills	Self-regulation skills are explicitly taught skills that help students persevere, problem-solve, and self-evaluate as they compose.	When students approach writing with confidence and self-awareness, they are better able to guide and manage the complexities of writing. Self-regulated writers are effective writers.

many different skills, each takes time to develop and master. This is why it is difficult to fully determine how writing develops. Two things can, however, be concluded from the research:

1. Writing development is growth in the breadth and depth of students' abilities in each of the subcomponents of writing.
2. Writing development requires instruction that targets each of these subcomponents simultaneously rather than sequentially.

As an example of the first point, consider two subcomponents of effective writing instruction: transcription skills (handwriting and spelling) and word choice. Over the course of several years, students' transcription skills develop as handwriting becomes more fluent and spelling becomes increasingly automatic. During this same time, students' vocabulary grows through instruction and through exposure to words in text. As a result of growth in these areas, students gradually become more selective and purposeful in their choice of words as they write. Thus, over time, students acquire more skills (breadth) and develop greater facility in those skills (depth).

Like reading, writing development is best supported by focusing on multiple skills simultaneously within the context of strategic and meaningful instruction. For example, students should not be expected to master spelling before writing sentences, nor should they be expected to master sentence conventions before writing paragraphs. Students gain greater breadth and depth of skills through simultaneous instruction in multiple subcomponents of writing.

The timeline for developing mastery varies among individuals and groups of students. Students with learning disabilities, even those in middle or high school, may have difficulties with writing subcomponents such as transcription skills, word-choice, and sentence construction skills.[5] Similar deficits have been found with students with language impairments.[6] As a result, establishing an exact timeline that functions for all students is quite difficult.

USING STANDARDS TO UNDERSTAND WRITING DEVELOPMENT AND PLAN INSTRUCTION

The difficulty in determining an exact developmental timeline for writing means that your state's standards will be a great help in deciding what to teach and when to teach it. For example, your state's writing or English language arts (ELA) standards provide a set of student outcomes for each grade level. The new Common Core State Standards[7] is another resource for examining a sequence of writing skills: http://www.corestandards.org/assets/CCSSI_ELA%20 Standards.pdf, and many states have adopted these standards to guide English language arts and math instruction. The sequence of the Common Core standards demonstrates the principles of writing development referred to earlier: 1) increasing the breadth and depth of students' writing skills over time and 2) instructing multiple skills simultaneously instead of sequentially.

Accordingly, you should become familiar with the Common Core Writing Standards or your state's ELA standards. Activity 1 of the In-Class Application Assignment will help you do so. Once you better understand the writing standards that will guide your instruction, you are ready to begin thinking about what to teach!

The Common Core Writing Standards address specific areas of writing to be taught from kindergarten to 12th grade. Although a few standards only apply to specific grades, most standards start introducing simple writing concepts very early and then help students develop more complex skills over the course of time. If your state has not adopted Common Core State Standards, your state standards probably address similar concepts even though they may be structured differently. For example, Texas has adopted The College and Career Readiness Standards that specifically address expectations for student writing.[8]

Common Core Writing Standards emphasize key aspects of writing development: 1) students develop writing skills in different text types, writing processes, and writing for different purposes and audiences; 2) students use technology to plan, draft, and publish their writing; 3) students learn to respond to literature and other kinds of text and conduct short and longer research projects to demonstrate their learning and convey information; and, finally, 4) students use evidence in their writing from traditional print resources as well as digital sources.[9] You may have noticed that some aspects of writing are missing from these standards, such as spelling, handwriting, and sentence construction! Common Core has another set of standards called Language Standards that address these key areas.

Text-Types, Purposes, and Audiences

Composing different types of writing for multiple purposes and audiences is an important part of becoming an accomplished writer. Skilled writers deliberately select a type of writing based on their purpose and their audience; as such, there is a strong connection between text types, purposes, and audiences. To illustrate the connection, consider this: what form does your writing take when you compose a grocery list? You probably do not write a narrative for your shopping list, with well-elaborated characters and setting, with rising action, and the climax of going to the check-out counter and bagging your groceries. Your decision to compose a list instead of a story was not random. Your decision was perfectly aligned with your purpose for writing (to make sure you get everything you need) and your audience (you!). Whether consciously or not, you understand that your purpose and audience for writing expresses itself in the form your writing takes. Effective writing instruction helps students understand these connections, too.

In elementary school, students develop their understanding of how literacy and communication are connected. They learn that different types of text are used for different purposes of communication. Explicitly teaching students about common text-types is an evidence-based practice that promotes reading comprehension and writing ability,[10] and you will learn more about how to do so later in the chapter.

HOW DO YOU ASSESS WRITING?

Some of you may already be cringing at the thought of writing assessment, recalling papers slaved and toiled over, mercilessly returned, bleeding with red ink. Or some of you may recall another form of assessment injustice: the completely unmarked paper, stamped with a grade, as if the heavens above have deemed the paper worthy or unworthy.

For students, receiving feedback is an essential aspect of learning to write. How else will students learn that writing is a form of communication unless there are opportunities for others to respond to writing? Writing assessment can, and should, be a strategic and meaningful part of your instruction, but clearly the bleeding paper and the grade-stamp methods do not provide useful feedback to students.

The first thing to remember is that effective assessment differs from grading, which is only one aspect of assessment. Assessment is a strategic process of formulating questions and obtaining information for the purpose of making educational decisions. The kind of questions you wish to answer guide the assessment process. As teachers of writing, you may ask some of the following questions:

- Which students are at risk of becoming struggling writers?
- What writing skills do my students need to learn?
- How are my students responding to writing instruction and/or intervention?
- Are my students on track to master my state's writing standards?
- Have my students mastered the writing skills that I have taught them?

These questions, and other iterations of them, represent four different purposes for assessment: screening, diagnostic, progress monitoring, and summative assessment. The purpose of screening is to quickly determine which students are struggling with writing. Screening assessments are administered three or four times a year. These assessments tend to be quick to administer and score and provide an overall snapshot of a student's skills. The purpose of diagnostic assessments is to obtain an in-depth profile of a student's skills and needs to inform instructional planning. Assessments used to diagnose what a student needs take longer to administer and score but provide detailed information that is used for planning targeted instruction or intervention. The purpose of progress monitoring is to determine how a student(s) is responding to instruction and whether he or she is making adequate progress toward specific curricular goals. Progress monitoring assessments are general indicators of a student's overall writing ability. They are not meant to diagnose how or why a student is succeeding/struggling, but to simply provide an indication of how that student is progressing. The purpose of summative assessment, or outcome assessment, is to evaluate student learning after instruction has already occurred. These four purposes of assessment—screening, diagnostic, progress monitoring, and summative assessment—categorize the vast majority of questions you will ask as teachers to inform planning of instruction.

Different types of writing assessment have been developed to address these four assessment purposes; however, the most prevalent is rubric-based assessment. In the next section, you will learn more about different kinds of rubric-based assessments, as well as other kinds of writing assessment. Pay attention to the kinds of questions these tools can answer as well as the specific assessment purposes they address. Rest assured—none of them require you to use a red pen!

Rubric-Based Assessment

A rubric is a scoring tool that defines "the criteria for a piece of work...and articulates gradations of quality for each criterion, from excellent to poor."[11] Rubrics are useful for students and teachers alike because they specify what elements of a text to examine and the criteria for assessing the quality of those elements. The three main types of writing rubrics are holistic, analytic, and primary trait.

Holistic rubrics. Holistic rubrics establish a range of performance levels that are used to rank a student's writing from low to high, generally on a 0–6 scale, according to pre-established expectations for each level. In holistic scoring, a rater gives his or her overall impression of the writing compared with other samples in the group. Because only one score is used to represent multiple aspects of writing, holistic scoring does not provide enough information to be useful for instructional decision-making, nor is it sufficiently sensitive for the purpose of progress monitoring. Holistic rubrics are most often used for the purposes of screening and summative assessment, addressing such questions as: Who of my students is at risk for experiencing difficulties with writing? What is the overall writing ability of my students? Has my students' writing improved since the beginning of the year? To see an example of the NAEP fourth-grade holistic rubric for narrative writing go to[12] http://nces.ed.gov/pubs2000/2000495.PDF.

Analytic rubrics. In contrast to holistic rubrics, which assign a single score, analytic rubrics assign multiple scores, one for each aspect of the text that is analyzed, such as ideas, organization, word choice, sentence fluency, and conventions. Analytic rubrics require more time to score than holistic rubrics, but they are intended to provide more information about a student's writing skills. Analytic rubrics are frequently used for the purpose of instructional planning, though they can also be used for the purposes of screening and summative assessment as well. Analytic rubrics are not useful for progress monitoring because they are less sensitive to small changes in a student's skills, especially over short time frames. Analytic rubrics can address the questions: What do my students currently do well/struggle with? What writing skills should I focus instruction on? To see an example of a commonly used analytic rubric, the 6+1 Trait Writing Rubric,[13] visit http://educationnorthwest.org/webfm_send/773.

Primary trait rubrics. Like analytic rubrics, primary trait rubrics provide information on multiple aspects of a student's writing; however, primary trait rubrics are developed for the specific purposes of each writing assignment. This is quite different from analytic rubrics, which are developed to be used across multiple writing assignments and emphasize broad categories of writing ability such as ideas or organization. In contrast, primary trait rubrics are able to assess finer categories of writing ability, including specific lesson objectives and/or specific genre requirements. As an example, a primary trait rubric for story writing may address character and setting development, plot elements, and use of dialogue. A primary trait rubric for an opinion essay may address an introduction, a thesis statement, reasons to support the thesis, details to support each reason, and a strong conclusion. For this reason, primary trait rubrics can provide you with detailed information about a student's skills relative to a specific assignment, or specific standards and instructional goals. When you develop primary trait rubrics before instruction, you can use them for instructional planning. Used after instruction, they serve the purpose of summative assessment. They may also be used for the purpose of progress monitoring, because they are sensitive to small changes in a student's skills. However, due to the time required to develop these rubrics, they are not recommended for the purpose of screening. Figure 13.1 illustrates the type of rubric, purposes, and questions answered.

Other Types of Writing Assessment

Other types of writing assessment include curriculum-based measurement for writing (W-CBM) and component skills assessment. W-CBM consists of short, simple measures, called probes, which assess different writing skills. Depending on the grade and ability level of the student, CBM writing probes may consist of a sentence copying task, picture prompt, or written prompt that assesses the skills students are expected to master during one school year. W-CBM yield objective measures of writing such as the number of words written, number or percentage of words spelled correctly, and number or percentage of correct word sequences—the number of neighboring words that have correct spelling, grammar, and semantic usage. These objective measures address several essential aspects of written communication such as transcription skills, word choice, and sentence conventions.

Component-skills testing incorporates a number of assessments that provide information about the subcomponents of writing. Specific assessments have been developed for each of these aspects of a student's writing profile, such as sentence construction skills, spelling, or handwriting. You may find it useful to incorporate such assessments in addition to rubric-based assessment because a student's overall writing ability may be impacted by

Purpose	Questions answered	Type of rubric
Screening	Who of my students is at risk for experiencing difficulties with writing?	Holistic Analytic
Diagnostic	What skills do my students presently demonstrate/lack? What writing skills should I focus instruction on?	Analytic Primary trait
Progress monitoring	Are my students progressing at a sufficient rate to achieve grade-level goals? Is this intervention working?	Primary trait
Summative	What is the overall writing ability of my students? Has my students' writing improved since the beginning of the year? Have my students demonstrated growth in their writing skills during this unit?	Holistic Analytic Primary trait

Figure 13.1. Matching types of rubrics with the different purposes for assessment.

deficits in these subcomponents. To learn more about component-skills testing see Olinghouse and Santangelo, 2010.[14]

Assessing writing in a purposeful, strategic way is quite different from grading and using that infamous red pen. Rubric-based assessment is excellent for the purposes of screening, diagnosing, progress monitoring, and summative assessment and to guide your instruction. Rubrics can address many purposes and questions you will have as a teacher of writing. You may also wish to incorporate W-CBM or component skills testing for the purposes of progress-monitoring and instructional planning. Effective teachers use assessments before, during, and after instruction to strategically and meaningfully improve their instruction and student learning. However, just using these assessments will not magically make your students better writers. The "magic" is in the ability of good assessment practices to foster strategic instruction. The "magic" is in you. When you are making strategic decisions and providing strategic instruction, your students will learn.

HOW DO YOU TEACH WRITING EFFECTIVELY, EFFICIENTLY, AND IN A MANNER APPROPRIATE TO THE STUDENTS' ABILITY LEVEL?

As discussed earlier, writing is both a complex task and a vibrant form of communication. Teaching writing effectively, efficiently, and appropriately means addressing both the complexities and the vibrancy of writing. Writing instruction that simplifies the complexities of the writing process is strategic instruction. Writing instruction that shows students the communicative power of writing is meaningful instruction. When you provide writing instruction that is both strategic and meaningful, your students will succeed.

Entire books can be written about illustrating and describing how to teach writing. In fact, when you look at the number of techniques designed to make you an effective writing teacher, it can feel overwhelming at times. The thing to remember is that the magic is not in the techniques, just as the magic is not in specific assessments. The "magic" comes from adopting an instructional framework that is strategic and meaningful. With this framework, you can provide effective writing instruction. Without a framework, your instruction, like a text without organization, would be disjointed, confusing, and ineffective. The goal of the following section is for you to learn how to create a strategic and meaningful framework for writing instruction. First, you will learn about four key areas to think about while planning your writing instruction. Then, you will learn about evidence-based practices to incorporate into your instruction that will be most effective in helping students learn to write.

Planning Before Teaching: Standards, Assessment, Purposes, and Publishing

Before you teach, you first need to make sure that what you are teaching and asking students to compose is meaningful and appropriate. There are four areas to consider in order to maximize your instruction (Figure 13.2).

Standards. One source to consider when deciding what to teach is your state's standards. Look at what has been taught in previous grades: What is new to your grade? Look at what students are expected to learn during the school year: What will require a lot of instruction and practice? For each grade level, writing standards 1–3 of the Common Core addresses opinion writing, informative/explanatory writing, and narrative writing. If you are teaching a unit on travel brochures, a type of informational text, you could address standard 2 (writing informational text). You could also address standard 5, which relates to the writing process, and standard 4, which relates to producing clear, coherent writing appropriate to task, purpose, and audience.

The framework of strategic and meaningful writing instruction outlined in this chapter can be easily aligned with standards; however, it is not necessary to address each standard within every unit. Writing skills develop slowly and with continued practice. It is not recom-

Consideration	Rationale
Standards	Effective instruction is aligned with standards and builds the depth and breadth of students' writing skills across grade levels. Examine your state's standards or the Common Core State Standards to determine what skills should be mastered in your grade level. Look also at skills introduced in previous grades, as these provide a scaffold for developing new skills.
Assessment	Effective writing instruction is targeted instruction. Targeted instruction can only occur when you know which specific skills your students possess. Information from previous assessments is essential for targeting instruction to student needs.
Writing activities	Effective instruction is meaningful instruction. Choose writing activities that simultaneously allow for skill development and meaningful communication. This ensures that students experience writing as a purposeful and motivating activity. Move beyond prompt writing and select creative activities like brochures, posters, e-mails, reflections, movie reviews, or research projects.
Publishing	Effective instruction is aligned with the authentic uses of writing in real-life. In conjunction with selecting meaningful writing activities, also think of how your students can share their writing in authentic ways.

Figure 13.2.   Key considerations in writing instruction.

mended that you address all the standards related to a particular text type or particular stage of the writing process at one time. For example, your first writing unit should not address every standard related to the writing process, nor should your first unit on opinion writing address every standard related to persuasive text. Be confident that your instructional framework enables you to address every standard, each in its own time, strategically and meaningfully in a way that gradually develops the breadth and depth of your students' writing skills.

Assessment. Assessment helps you before teaching because it determines which areas to target for instruction. For example, in the previous writing unit, maybe you learned that many of your students demonstrate grade-level abilities in developing characters in their realistic fiction writing; however, they still struggle with sequencing plot elements in their stories. In your next writing unit on mystery writing, you would then choose to focus a lot of instruction on developing and sequencing the story's plot. Rather than guessing at what your students need to learn and practice, good assessment will tell you the specific needs of your students!

Writing activities. Another area to consider is the purpose for writing and the specific kind of writing students will compose. Table 13.2 lists examples of different purposes and kinds of writing students can complete for each text type in the Common Core State Standards.

Although this step may seem obvious, many students feel like most writing tasks are simply exercises to teach writing as an academic skill and are not related to any kind of authentic communicative purpose. As teachers of writing, you are encouraged to think carefully about the purpose of the writing activities you select for your students. You are encouraged to select those activities that provide opportunities for expressing ideas, concerns, and topics of interest and sharing published text with real audiences. Writing tasks that accomplish these goals are referred to as authentic writing tasks. Authentic writing tasks make writing a meaningful activity and may be a factor in increasing writing motivation, particularly for struggling writers.[15]

Publishing. The final area to think about is creating opportunities for your students to publish their writing. Meaningful publishing is related to the purpose and specific kind of writing they compose. Far too often, students compose texts for teachers only and do not

Table 13.2.   Text-types and communicating for a purpose

Text-type	Purpose	Specific examples
Opinion	To persuade To advocate To recommend To argue	Opinion letter Persuasive essay Advertisement Movie or book review Speech Blog
Informative/explanatory	To explain To inform To instruct To analyze To evaluate	Feature article Report Character analysis Book report Autobiography Experiment
Narrative	To tell To recount To describe To express To entertain	Fable Memoir Fairy tale Character study Realistic fiction Fantasy

experience writing for authentic purposes and audiences. Along with carefully developed authentic writing tasks, you are encouraged to think of meaningful ways to publish and share student writing with a variety of audiences. For each writing task you assign, ask yourself, "How can students share this writing with a real audience?" To help answer that question, think about for which audiences your students would find it meaningful to write. Do your students value sharing their writing with their family? Do they wish to share their writing with their peers, or younger or older students? Or, perhaps, your students would value sharing their writing through an electronic medium such as a web page, blog, podcast, or video. Being creative and responsive to your students' interests will help your students see the expressive power of writing.

Evidence-Based Writing Practices

There are a lot of different ways to teach writing—and teachers are often overwhelmed when deciding how to teach writing! Fortunately, educational research can help you decide how to teach. In this section, you will learn about different research-based methods that will be most effective in developing your students' writing abilities. While writing instruction should focus on all subcomponents of writing, focus should more broadly be on the text as a whole rather than on smaller aspects of the text. Chapter 6 provides more in-depth information about the letter and word level subcomponents, such as handwriting, spelling, and early composition skills.

The writing process. Most skilled writers engage in cycles of planning, drafting, revising, and editing before finally publishing. Writing instruction that provides instruction and opportunities for engaging in each of these stages is known as a writing process approach.[16] To learn more about the writing process, see Table 13.3.

A writing process approach is the foundation for strategic and meaningful writing instruction. It is the framework around which to build. As a foundation, it has many desirable traits, including students repeatedly practicing composing a single text; students learning that writing is a cyclical process; and students having opportunities to work collaboratively and share their writing.

Table 13.3. Stages of the writing process

Stage	Definition	Example activities
Planning	The activities done before, and in preparation for, drafting.	• Brainstorming ideas • Using a graphic organizer • Drawing pictures • Using a story planner • Writing an outline • Researching • Summarizing notes • Organizing notes
Drafting	The actual writing of the text. This stage can itself have multiple stages: e.g., rough, first, and final.	• Working from an outline to begin a rough draft • Trying different styles of introductions • Beginning a word processing file • Creating a "sloppy copy"
Revising	Re-reading and evaluating the text to see if "big changes" need to be made. Big changes relate to the structure, organization, and content of the text, and evaluating whether the text achieves its purpose.	• Restructuring or reorganizing the text, or sections of the text • Adding additional information or details • Removing redundant information • Evaluating the tone
Editing	Re-reading and evaluating the text to see if "little changes" need to be made. Little changes do not alter the meaning or content of the text, but help improve its readability and appearance.	• Editing for correct sentence conventions (capitalization, punctuation, grammar) and correct spelling • Adding interesting words • Using synonyms for frequently used words
Publishing	Producing a final copy for display, sharing, or submission for assessment.	• Creating a title page • Creating a class poetry book • Producing a script and acting it out • Hosting a book club where students read each other's writing

Applying the writing process approach instructionally. Remember the four key areas to consider while planning your writing instruction? Now, you apply those to the writing process. After you have chosen your standards to address and have defined the specific writing task and audience, you next need to decide two things: 1) how much time will be devoted to composing this task (e.g., 2, 3, or 5 weeks) and 2) what skills, knowledge, or strategies will your students need to successfully compose the text? The results of previous assessments and new formative assessments will help with instructional planning. You will likely teach both generalized writing skills and genre-specific writing skills. Generalized writing skills are those skills that are needed in every writing situation (e.g., sentence construction skills, organization, and idea development). Genre-specific writing skills are those skills that are needed to compose a specific writing task, such as knowing how travel brochures are organized.

Once you have specified the task, established the duration of your unit, assessed students' writing skills, and selected the generalized and genre-specific writing skills to teach, sequence those skills based on each stage of the writing process. For example, if the task is composing a travel brochure to a student's favorite place, instruction during the planning stage could focus on learning important features of travel brochures and on developing an outline before drafting. During the drafting stage, you might teach students how to write a captivating introduction or how to use descriptive vocabulary to evoke imagery of the location. During the revi-

Feature	Purpose
Interesting title	States the destination and includes a descriptive phrase to immediately interest readers.
Destination facts	Informs the reader about the unique features of the destination.
Things to do section	Describes exciting things to do at the destination that appeal to the reader's interests.
Exciting pictures	Pictures help the reader imagine the fun they could have at the destination. The pictures often feature images of elements from the Things to do section.
Descriptive vocabulary	Travel brochures include descriptive words and words designed to "paint a picture" of the destination.
Traveler's comments	Comments from travelers who have gone to the destination help convince readers to travel to the destination, too.

Figure 13.3.   Revision checklist for a travel brochure.

sion stage, students evaluate their text to make "big changes." Big changes refer to changing the content, organization, or structure of a text. Using the example of a travel brochure, students could evaluate their text to determine if their travel brochure includes all the important features that the class discussed during the planning stage. You might teach students different ways of answering the questions: "Is this travel brochure saying what I want it to say? If I read this travel brochure, would I want to go to this place?" (Figure 13.3), In addition, the revision stage is an ideal time to embed instruction in sentence conventions (Figure 13.4). It is also

---

Teaching sentence conventions strategically and meaningfully

By the end of elementary school, students should be familiar with the conventions for each of the four types of sentences: simple, compound, complex, and compound–complex. For more information about these sentence types visit http://www.towson.edu/ows/sentences.htm

Step 1—Develop background knowledge

- Introduce convention (skill).
- Explain and define key terms.
- Explain when and why the convention is used.
- Emphasize how this skill helps authors effectively convey their message.

Step 2—Model the skill (oral language)

- Write examples on the board and have students practice orally.
- Practicing orally helps teach the skill without the constraints of handwriting or spelling.

Step 3—Guided practice (moving from oral to written practice)

- Teacher models the skill, eliciting student help in composing the sentences.
- Teacher uses questioning to build metacognitive awareness.
  - "Why do you think this is a good example of [convention concept]?"
- Teacher provides error correction.
  - "How can we revise this sentence so that it demonstrates [the convention concept]?"
- Students then practice the skill by writing sentences with peers.

Step 4—Independent practice

- Students are encouraged to embed the skill in their writing during the stages of drafting and/or revision.

Figure 13.4.   Teaching sentence conventions.

Did I include a title that is capitalized and underlined?	Yes	No
Did I capitalize the first letter of each new sentence?	Yes	No
Did I capitalize all proper nouns?	Yes	No
Did I include the proper end-punctuation at the end of each sentence (.?!)?	Yes	No
Did I use a comma between items in a list?	Yes	No
Did I indent the first line of each new paragraph?	Yes	No
Did I spell all high-frequency words correctly?	Yes	No
Did I use quotation marks correctly for all dialogue?	Yes	No

Figure 13.5.   Sample editing checklist for elementary students.

an excellent opportunity for students to work collaboratively to evaluate each other's drafts using rubrics.

The final two stages of the writing process, editing and publishing, are stages for polishing a text. During the editing stage, students evaluate their text to make "little changes." Little changes do not alter the meaning, organization, tone, or content of the text, but address things including spelling, grammar, sentence structure, and word choice. Editing improves the clarity and readability of a text. While students are editing, rather than emphasizing that good writing follows rigid grammatical rules, emphasize the purpose of those rules: that writing is meant to be read, that readers enjoy and learn more from writing that is easy to read, and that clear writing allows an author to better communicate his or her message. This makes editing a meaningful activity rather than a laborious procedure of applying strict grammatical rules. To help students learn to edit their work, teach students how to use an editing checklist to examine their writing for specific writing features. You can initiate this activity by developing the editing checklist as a class, using a discussion-based approach to build students' awareness of the features of polished writing. After developing a list of ideas, consolidate them into an editing checklist for students to use for self- and peer-editing (Figure 13.5).

The publishing stage is a chance for students to share their writing with a real audience. Hosting a "Writing Celebration Day" is an excellent way to promote these publishing activities and to increase student motivation around the writing process. You might host a Travel Agent Convention where students share their brochures as if they were travel agents advertising an exciting destination. The publishing stage is an opportunity for students to experience writing as a purposeful form of communication that connects with real audiences.

Embedding other evidence-based practices within a writing process approach. As the foundation for your writing instruction framework, the writing process approach is an effective way to structure your teaching. However, this approach is not without its limitations. Some research has found that this approach is insufficient to meet the needs of students with disabilities and other struggling writers, such as English language learners.[17] For these students, simply engaging in the writing process is insufficient for developing competent self-directed writing skills. This is why it is suggested that you adopt the process writing approach as the foundation of your instructional framework, rather than the entire structure. By embedding additional strategic instruction within this meaningful framework, your instruction will be effective for a greater number of students. The following evidence-based practices are examples of such strategic supports.

Explicitly teach general and genre-specific writing strategies. Explicit strategy instruction has proven to be one of the most powerful evidence-based methods for improving students' writing abilities.[18] Such instruction involves explicitly teaching the thought processes and skills needed to simplify and execute the complex task of writing. Strategies are often given acronyms that serve as mnemonics to help students recall and independently apply the strategies. One example is the strategy WRITE,[19] which stands for Work from your plan to develop your thesis statement; Remember your goals; Include transition words for each paragraph; Try to use different kinds of sentences; and use Exciting, interesting, $100,000 words. There are many strategies for each stage of the writing process, and students should learn strategies for each. An excellent online resource listing effective writing strategies is hosted by University of Nebraska, Lincoln (http://www.unl.edu/csi/writing.shtml). There, you will find a number of strategies for teaching each stage of the writing process. Embedding explicit strategy instruction for each stage of the writing process will ensure that your students acquire the necessary skills to become independent and effective writers.

Teaching strategically: The SRSD approach. Many methods of strategy instruction have been developed; however, one method, developed by Steve Graham and Karen Harris, called Self-Regulated Strategy Development (SRSD), has proven to be among the most effective.[20] Their method relies on explicit instruction, teacher modeling, guided practice, and independent practice. Consequently, more than 25 years of research and more than 40 published studies have shown SRSD to improve the writing of typically developing writers, struggling writers, and students with disabilities.

The goals of SRSD are 1) to help students learn and independently apply the kinds of strategies that effective writers use, 2) to help students learn self-regulation procedures to manage the decisions and the difficulties that arise during writing, 3) to help students acquire greater writing knowledge and skill, and 4) to increase students' motivation toward writing, as well as their attitude, self-efficacy, and effort. These goals are achieved through the six-stage instructional method listed below and described in detail in Table 13.4.

1. Develop background knowledge
2. Discuss it
3. Model it
4. Memorize it
5. Support it
6. Independent performance

In SRSD, teachers guide their students through each of these six stages according to a student's individual rate of progress. This makes SRSD an ideal method for instructing diverse learners. SRSD instruction does not follow a pre-established timetable and allows teachers to flexibly combine whole-group, small-group, and individualized instruction to ensure that each student successfully progresses to subsequent stages. Students and teachers can go back and revisit stages if needed, and more capable students can skip stages if not needed. The important part of SRSD is that it is based on mastery of learning rather than moving from stage to stage without ensuring that learning has happened.

Graham, Harris, and colleagues have developed numerous genre-specific strategies using the principles of SRSD.[21] The following strategy, C-SPACE, is only one example.[22] Though the strategy itself is important, the power of SRSD is the instructional method for teaching the strategy. The same method and teacher language illustrated here for C-SPACE can be applied to any writing strategy, either researcher-developed or teacher-developed. In the future, you may decide to use a different strategy or to develop your own strategy for your writing class. If you teach strategies using the SRSD method, you will capitalize upon one of the most effective, research-based practices for teaching writing skills.

C-SPACE is an acronym, used as a mnemonic to help students remember the main elements of narrative text. What follows is a brief overview for how you would teach C-SPACE using the six stages of SRSD.

C = Characters
S = Setting
P = Purpose
A = Action
C = Conclusion
E = Emotions

Table 13.4. The six stages of self-regulated strategy development (SRSD) instruction

SRSD stage	Purpose	Example activities[23]
Develop background knowledge	Ensure that students understand all foundational concepts and are prepared to learn the specific writing strategy and self-regulation procedures.	Assess students' existing knowledge of the genre or the strategy. Define key terms related to the genre or the strategy. Introduce the steps of the strategy.
Discuss it	Teacher and students discuss the benefits of the strategy so that students understand its purpose. Students make a commitment to learning the strategy.	Students examine their current writing in light of the targeted writing skill. Students chart/graph current performance to establish baseline performance. Teachers and students discuss how the writing strategy will improve their writing, and students commit to make a real effort to learn and apply the strategy.
Model it	The teacher models the use of the strategy and the self-regulation procedures using a think-aloud procedure.	Teachers model the strategy while creating a new composition. Teacher models any self-regulation statements that have been introduced.
Memorize it	Students participate in fun and engaging activities to memorize the strategy and their self-regulation statements.	Students quiz each other on the steps of the strategy. Students struggling to memorize the mnemonic develop flashcards.
Support it	Guided practice is used to help students gradually assume responsibility for using the writing strategy and the self-regulation statements.	Students and teachers use the writing strategy and self-regulation statements collaboratively to create a composition. Teachers and peers provide prompts and guidance. Chart continued progress.
Independent performance	Students independently use the writing strategy and self-regulation statements.	Students independently compose a text using the strategy. Develop plans for maintenance and generalization.

Source: Harris, Graham, Mason, & Friedlander (2008).

Stage 1—Develop background knowledge: During this stage, build students' background knowledge by defining a narrative and its key elements. Read model narrative texts as a class, and analyze the key elements of a narrative. Once your discussion has concluded, create a list of these main elements.

Next, introduce the strategy C-SPACE, paying careful attention to define each of the elements in the strategy. Make sure to link the elements of the strategy to the list of genre elements that you developed as a class. C-SPACE is a strategy for helping students remember to include all the main elements of narrative text when they write a narrative.

During this stage, it is also important to discuss the role of self-regulation in writing. Self-regulation skills help students persevere, problem-solve, and self-evaluate as they compose.

Stage 2—Discuss it: During this stage, students learn about the benefits of using C-SPACE, and they make a commitment to learning and using it. Then, students should assess their own previously written stories to see how many elements of C-SPACE they have included. Students can then set personal goals for future story writing.

Stage 3—Model it: The goal of this stage is to explicitly model the strategy. As the teacher, you should begin by assessing a story you have written or another example story. Then, set a goal for improving your writing based on the results. Model the use of the strategy as you compose a new story and achieve your writing goal. It is important to think aloud as you model. Share your thoughts about writing ideas, difficulties and struggles, ways of overcoming challenges, and how you rely on C-SPACE to write your story.

Stage 4—Memorize it: Memorizing the steps in the strategy will help your students become independent writers. Have students quiz each other on what C-SPACE stands for. Students who have a difficult time memorizing the strategy may benefit from having flashcards. It is important to convey that this stage is not merely a memorization task. It is a meaningful step in developing writing skills.

Stage 5—Support it: Through a series of activities, students assume greater responsibility for using their strategy. Lead a guided practice activity in which you and your class collaborate to create a narrative using C-SPACE. Continue to use a think-aloud procedure to problem-solve and narrate your inner dialogue; however, transfer the responsibility of solving those problems to your students.

Stage 6—Independent performance: Students who are prepared to move to this stage have the goal of independently using their strategy, C-SPACE, and their self-regulation skills to compose a narrative. Stress the significance of this stage: when students can use their strategy independently, they have the ability to write a story anytime they want.

C-SPACE, used to teach narrative text, is an example of how SRSD can be applied in the classroom. SRSD is far different from teaching an acronym and expecting students to apply a strategy independently. Each of the six stages is essential and combines to comprise a truly effective method for improving writing skills.

It is important to remember that these strategies should become lasting tools for your students. Instead of teaching a strategy once and moving on, provide opportunities for students to maintain their writing strategies by returning to previously instructed genres and cueing students to use their strategies. Another way to promote maintenance and generalization is to extend strategy use beyond the walls of your classroom. With your grade-level team, brainstorm ideas for using these strategies in other disciplines including math, science, social studies, or even art and music. For example, if you teach a strategy for composing informational text, discuss with the social studies teacher ways of incorporating that strategy into their assignments. Working with other members of your team will help your students maintain and generalize their writing skills.

Explicitly teach strategies for summarizing text. Many struggling writers and students with disabilities face difficulties with topic selection and content knowledge. This poses a challenge because writing is never devoid of content: whenever you write, you always write about a topic. Because these students may lack content knowledge, they tend to gravitate toward the same topic for every writing assignment. It is essential for students to learn how to gain topic knowledge by gathering and organizing relevant information.

Explicitly teaching summarization will not only support improved writing performance but reading comprehension as well. A recent report titled *Writing to Read: Evidence for How Writing Can Improve Reading*[24] finds that teaching summarization also improves reading comprehension skills. One strategy for teaching summarization involves directly teaching four "summarization operations,"[25] consisting of

1. Identifying and selecting the main information from a text
2. Deleting trivial information
3. Deleting redundant information
4. Organizing and writing a summary of the main and supporting information

Instruction begins with explicitly defining what a summary is, how it is helpful, and how to follow these four steps to construct a summary. Using a think-aloud procedure, teachers model the strategy by constructing a summary of a short text. After several examples, students help the teacher construct a summary during a guided-practice stage. Then, students work in pairs and finally independently to produce their own summaries. The authors recommend that students begin creating a summary for each paragraph in a text and then create a summary of those summaries. This allows students to practice using the strategy on smaller units of text before applying it to longer, more challenging text. Ultimately, students are expected to produce a summary without the scaffold of intermediary summaries. When students can apply this strategy independently, they will have gained an effective technique for gathering and organizing information for use in their writing.

Model texts. Using model texts is an evidence-based practice for improving writing ability. It consists of providing students with example texts that demonstrate particular features of writing to emulate. Model texts can be published, teacher-created, or student-created texts. Students analyze and evaluate the models to construct their own understanding of salient writing features. Then, students are encouraged to apply these features in their own writing. Model texts are particularly useful during the planning stage of the writing process to help students build background knowledge, and they can be used during the "develop background knowledge" stage in SRSD. Using the example of a travel brochure, students would analyze and evaluate model travel brochures to construct an understanding of their main purposes (to persuade people to go to their vacation resort), features (scuba diving, swimming pools, great food), and formats (lots of pictures, comments from enthusiastic travelers). This understanding would then assist students in picking a topic, gathering content, and creating an organizational structure for their brochure. Model texts also are useful to support revision. For example, during the revision stage, students can examine model travel brochures for word choice and then evaluate their own travel brochures to determine if they include similar language.

Text structures. Students need to learn the different kinds of text types that occur in writing. The three main text types taught in the elementary grades in Common Core are opinion, informative/explanatory, and narrative (Table 13.2). Within opinion and informative/explanatory texts, there are four common text structures (Table 13.5), or common ways of organizing information within a text type.

Teaching your students strategies for 1) understanding and 2) composing these different text structures will help your students improve their writing as well as reading comprehension. As they gain understanding and command over different text structures, students are able to compose texts that better fulfill the purposes of each of those genres. Teachers can easily pair using model texts with teaching different text structures.

Collaborative writing. During collaborative writing, students work in pairs or small groups to plan, compose, revise, and edit their text. Students may work collaboratively during one or all stages of the writing process. This technique emphasizes the communicative aspects

Table 13.5.   Four common text structures of opinion or informative/explanatory writing[26]

Text structure	Definition	Example
Description/collection	The most basic structure of expository text, which is organized by making a statement about a topic and then elaborating on it. When a number of descriptions are organized together, the resulting structure is known as a collection.	A text that describes and elaborates upon three features of cloud formation.
Cause and effect	A more advanced form of description/collection in which the content is organized so that the results and causes of an event are presented. This is done by organizing content sequentially and using "if–then" reasoning.	A text that explains the causes and effects of Columbus' voyage to America.
Compare and contrast	A more advanced form of description/collection in which two or more things are described in terms of their similarities and differences.	A text that compares and contrasts the features of reptiles and mammals.
Order/sequence	A structure organized by explaining the steps in a process or a sequence of events. These texts are also known as procedural texts.	A text that explains the life cycle of a star, describing its birth, life, and death.

Source: Meyer (1979).

of writing as students grapple with conveying meaning to an audience. The ability to work in collaborative groups is an expectation of several sets of standards.[27]

One common application of collaborative writing in the elementary grades is peer revision.[28] Students should be explicitly taught procedures for conducting peer revision. Common steps for teaching these procedures are

1. Establish classroom norms related to discussing and sharing writing.

   It is important to create a safe and positive climate for students to share their work.

2. Model how to provide feedback. Give examples and nonexamples of helpful comments. It may be useful to adopt a form of the golden rule: "Give the type of comments that you yourself would like to receive if your writing was being reviewed." Make sure students know to comment on both what the writer does well and what the writer could improve on.

3. Define the purpose for peer revision. Explicitly tell students what features of their partner's writing to pay attention to. The purpose of peer revision may change with different assignments or at different stages of an assignment.

4. Provide students with a rubric or checklist of the items you defined in Step 3. Ideally, this should be the same rubric that you will use to assess students' writing. Rubric-based assessment is a successful form of self- and peer-assessment,[29] helping students 1) familiarize themselves with the features of writing that they will be assessed on and 2) identify areas for improving a text.

5. Monitor students as they conduct peer revision. Walking around the classroom and observing your students will give you the chance to reinforce the norms and procedures your class has developed. Use specific praise statements such as, "I like the way this group is using their rubric to discuss ideas for organizing their writing."

6. Provide students a chance to reflect on the peer-revision process. This will help refine class norms, highlight strengths and weaknesses, and ensure that peer-revision activities continue to be successful.

CONCLUSION

Writing is a very important skill, affecting students' ability to comprehend text, form new understandings, communicate effectively, and succeed in school and beyond. By embedding strategic instruction and evidence-based practices within a meaningful writing-process framework, you will help students achieve each of these outcomes. By adopting a framework for writing instruction that is strategic and meaningful, you will be well on your way to realizing the vision of writing instruction that was introduced in this chapter.

The writing process approach is an excellent foundation for writing instruction. It has many benefits, particularly with regard to offering meaningful and authentic opportunities to write. By embedding evidence-based strategic supports into this approach, you expand your framework for writing instruction, making it more effective for diverse learners.

As you embark on your new career as a teacher, remember that writing can be strategic and meaningful to teach and learn. As a final note to end this chapter, it is important for teachers to provide a lot of time for students to write. After all, writing is just like any other skill—without ample time to practice, it is impossible to get better!

APPLICATION ASSIGNMENTS

In-class Assignments

Compare and contrast the writing instruction you received when you learned to write with the framework for writing instruction described in this chapter. What are the points of similarity and difference? How have your own attitudes toward writing and writing instruction been shaped by those experiences?

Homework Assignments

1. Compare and contrast the Common Core Writing Standards (W.1–W.10) for grades K–6. Note which subcomponents are taught at each grade level and how each subcomponent is sequenced throughout the grades. Briefly look at the standards for grades 7–12 and note which subcomponents are emphasized and how writing becomes more complex. How do these standards reflect the principles of writing development discussed in the chapter?

2. Log on to the IRIS center home page and complete the online module titled Improving Writing Performance: A Strategy for Writing Expository Essays. Answer the questions on the "assessment" page of the module (http://iris.peabody.vanderbilt.edu/pow/chalcycle.htm).

Tutoring Assignments

1. Obtain a narrative writing sample from a student in grades 3–6 (either one that was previously written or ask a student to complete one). Go to the links referenced earlier in the chapter, and print out the NAEP narrative rubric and the 6+1 Trait Writing Rubric. Assess the writing using a holistic rubric and then an analytic rubric. What type of information do you gain from each? What are the benefits and limitations of these methods of assessment? Using what you learned about the student's writing ability, identify what you will focus on in the next writing unit for this student.

ENDNOTES

1. Langer & Applebee (1987).
2. Persky, Daane, & Santangelo (2003); Salahu-Din, Persky, & Miller. (2008).
3. National Commission on Writing in America's Schools and Colleges (2003); National Commission on Writing in America's Schools and Colleges (2004); National Commission on Writing in America's Schools and Colleges (2005).
4. Graham & Perin (2007).
5. Newcomer, Barenbaum, & Nodine (1988).
6. Nelson, Roth, & Van Meter (2009).
7. National Governors Association & Council of Chief State School Officers (2010).
8. Texas Higher Education Coordinating Board (2008).
9. Common Core State Standards Initiative (2010).
10. Graham & Hebert (2010).
11. Andrade (2005).
12. National Center for Education Statistics (2000) holistic rubric.
13. 2010, Education Northwest.
14. Olinghouse & Santangelo (2010).
15. Pressley, Gaskins, Solic, & Gollins. (2006).
16. Graves (1983); Murray (1973).
17. Sandmel & Graham (2009); Troia, Lin, Monroe, & Cohen (2009).
18. Graham & Perin (2007).
19. De la Paz & Graham (2002).
20. Graham & Perin (2007).
21. Harris, Graham, Mason, & Friedlander (2008).
22. Harris, Graham, Mason, & Friedlander (2008).
23. Harris, Graham, Mason, & Friedlander (2008).
24. Graham & Hebert (2010).
25. Rinehardt, Stahl, & Erickson (1986).
26. Meyer (1979).
27. Texas CCRS.
28. MacArthur, Swartz, & Graham (1991).
29. Andrade & Boulay (2003).

REFERENCES

Andrade, H.A. (2005). Teaching with rubrics: The good, the bad, and the ugly. *College Teaching, 53*(1), 27–31.

Andrade, H.A., & Boulay, B.A. (2003). Role of rubric-referenced self-assessment in learning to write. *The Journal of Educational Research, 97*(1), 21–34.

Common Core State Standards Initiative. (2010). Common core state standards for English language arts & literacy in history/social studies, science, and technical subjects. Retrieved from http://www.corestandards.org/assets/CCSSI_ELA%20Standards.pdf

De la Paz, S., & Graham, S. (2002). Explicitly teaching strategies, skills, and knowledge: Writing instruction in middle school classrooms. *Journal of Educational Psychology, 94*(4), 687–698.

Graham, S., & Hebert, M. (2010). *Writing to read: Evidence for how writing can improve reading.* A Carnegie Corporation Time to Act Report. Washington, DC: Alliance for Excellent Education.

Graham, S., & Perin, D. (2007). *Writing next: Effective strategies to improve writing of adolescents in middle and high* schools—A report to Carnegie Corporation of New York. *Washington, DC: Alliance for Excellent Education.*

Graves, D.H. (1983). *Writing: Teachers and children at work.* Portsmouth, NH: Heinemann.

Harris, K.R., Graham, S., Mason, L.M., & Friedlander, B. (2008). *Powerful writing strategies for all students.* Baltimore: Paul H. Brookes Publishing Company.

Langer, J.A., & Applebee, A.N. (1987). *How writing shapes thinking: A study of teaching and learning.* NCTE Research Report No. 22.

MacArthur, C., Schwartz, S., & Graham, S. (1991). Effects of a reciprocal peer revision strategy in special education classrooms. *Learning Disability Research and Practice, 6,* 201–210.

Meyer, B.J.F. (1979). Organizational patterns in prose and their use in reading. In M.L. Kamil & A.J. Moe (Eds.), *Reading research: Studies and applications.* Clemson, S.C.: National Reading Conference, Inc.

Murray, D.M. (1973). Why teach writing—And how? *The Engish Journal, 62*(9), 1234-1237.

National Center for Education Statistics. (2000). NAEP scoring of Fourth-Grade Narrative Writing (NCES 2000–495). *NAEP Facts, 5*(1), 1–5.

National Commission on Writing in America's Schools and Colleges. (2003). *The neglected "R": The need for a writing Revolution.* College Board.

National Commission on Writing in America's Schools and Colleges. (2004). *Writing: Ticket to work…or a ticket out: A survey of business leaders.* College Board.

National Commission on Writing in America's Schools and Colleges. (2005). *Writing: A powerful message from state government.* College Board.

Nelson, N.W., Roth, F.P., & Van Meter, A.M. (2009). Written composition instruction and intervention for students with language impairment. In G.A. Troia (Ed.), *Instruction and assessment for struggling writers: Evidence-based practices* (pp. 187–212). New York: Guilford.

Newcomer, P.L., Barenbaum, E.M., & Nodine, B.F. (1988). Comparison of the story production of LD, normal-achieving, and low-achieving children under two modes of production. *Learning Disability Quarterly, 11*(2), 82–96.

Northwest Regional Educational Laboratory. (2004). *An introduction to the 6+1 trait writing assessment model.* Portland, OR: Author.

Olinghouse, N.G., & Santangelo, T. (2010). Assessing the writing of struggling learners. *Focus on Exceptional Children, 43*(4), 1–27.

Persky, H.R., Daane, M.C., & Jin, Y. (2003). *The nation's report card: Writing 2002.* U. S. Department of Education, Institute of Education Sciences. Washington, DC: National Center for Education Statistics.

Pressley, M., Gaskins, I.W., Solic, K., & Gollins, S. (2006). A portrait of Benchmark School: How a school produces high achievement in students who previously failed. *Journal of Educational Psychology, 98,* 282–306.

Rinehardt, S.D., Stahl, S.A., & Erickson, L.G. (1986). Some effects of summarization training on reading and studying. *Reading Research Quarterly, 21*(4), 422–438.

Salahu-Din, D., Persky, H., & Miller, J. (2008). *The Nation's Report Card: Writing 2007* (NCES 2008–468). National Center for Education Statistics, Institute of Education Sciences, U.S. Department of Education Sciences, U.S. Department of Education, Washington, D.C.

Sandmel, K., & Graham, S. (2009, February). *A meta-analysis of the effects of process writing instruction.* Poster presented at Pacific Coast Research Conference, Coronado, CA.

Texas Higher Education Coordinating Board. (2008). *Texas college and career readiness standards.* Austin, TX: Author.

Troia, G.A., Lin, S.C, Monroe, B.W., & Cohen, S. (2009). The effects of Writing Workshop instruction on the performance and motivation of good and poor writers. In G.A. Troia (Ed.), *Instruction and assessment for struggling writers: Evidence-based practices* (pp. 77–112). New York, NY: Guilford Press.

14

Disciplinary Literacy

by Kristie Hotchkiss
and Susan M. Smartt

"My teachers keep telling me I'm a good reader, but when I read my social studies or science book, I fall asleep. I don't remember anything. Yes, I can 'read' all the words, but somehow I don't know what's important, all the dates and details confuse me, and I give up. I heard it only gets worse in high school and forget college!"

Although not many students could articulate their frustrations reading in their content area texts as well as this one did, many experience these same feelings. Why is it so difficult to read in the disciplines?

Objectives: After studying this chapter you will be able to do the following:

1. Comprehend the importance of embedding literacy instruction into discipline content.
2. Identify the unique skills that are essential for reading in English language arts, social studies, science, and math.
3. Use discipline-specific instructional strategies.
4. Adapt generic literacy strategies to teach discipline-specific skills.
5. Build critical thinking skills.

WHAT IS DISCIPLINARY LITERACY? WHY IS IT IMPORTANT? WHAT DOES THE RESEARCH SAY?

Think of a time when you acquired a new gadget: a flat-screen television perhaps or a new piece of personal technology (i.e., a cell phone or electronic reader). The moment you want to use this exciting new purchase, you are faced with a pragmatic, yet deceivingly complex task: you must read the instruction booklet and follow the directions for its proper assembly and use. In other words, you must use your powers of reading and thinking to comprehend the material that is presented. This is one critical aspect of the skill of literacy, the ability to make sense of textual content, regardless of genre or discipline.

But, suppose when you open the box, grab the instruction book, and begin reading, you find that the technological format and language presupposes a level of knowledge that you simply do not have. The charts and labeled diagrams are indecipherable because you just do not know how to read them. This is where instruction in literacy strategies specific to disciplines would have come in handy. In this case, knowledge about scientific and mathematical graphic representations and data systems used to convey information would be useful.

Disciplinary literacy is "the ability to use reading and writing for the acquisition of new content in a given discipline."[1] It differs from content area literacy instruction in that disciplinary literacy recognizes the specialized skills needed to read and comprehend in each discipline. For example, how does a historian read a historical text or a mathematician approach a mathematics chapter? This is not simply a movement to change the name from content area literacy to disciplinary literacy. These are two distinctly different terms with different meanings. This chapter will present the thinking behind disciplinary literacy, the research that supports specific disciplinary literacy strategies, the connections between the Common Core State Literacy Standards, and effective strategies for teaching disciplinary literacy. (The reader is referred to Chapter 12 for reading-comprehension strategies that are more generic yet still applicable to content area reading.)

Researchers such as Elizabeth Moje and Dolores Perin are proponents of including explicit literacy instruction in content areas traditionally lacking such efforts.[2] Disciplinary literacy, says Moje,[3] "is giving children access to content and to the processes." Simply put, students need to learn different ways of doing things in each different content class. If a science class is investigating photosynthesis and its effects on human life, there is bound to be a graph involved at some point. And the extent to which students will be able to make sense of the information presented in graphical form, according to current research on the topic, would be positively affected by guidance and practice in how to read and interpret information presented in graphical form. It makes sense, then, to include explicit instruction in reading charts and graphs and to provide students with authentic practice using those required tools in content-specific text (e.g., social studies, science, mathematics) in order to build disciplinary-specific literacy.

"Disciplinary literacy is the specialized ways of knowing and communicating in the different disciplines."[4]

When one thinks of content-area reading strategies, one usually thinks of more generalized reading comprehension strategies, not necessarily content-or discipline-specific. For example, graphic organizers can enhance comprehension and learning in many different disciplines. Content area reading strategies may in fact be more helpful in the lower grades and for remediation, whereas disciplinary literacy strategies come into play more vividly as students move into upper elementary, middle, and high school.

It is known that reading skills taught in the early grades do not automatically transfer to the complex, discipline-specific texts used in the middle and upper grades. Therefore, it is important to explicitly teach the literacy skills that are going to be needed for reading beyond fourth grade. Students need to learn the specialized language conventions, sophisticated genres, and higher-level interpretive processes to be successful in the secondary setting.[5] Teaching students discipline literacy strategies to use while reading content texts should be part of your daily routine.

As a teacher of content, it is critical to pass on your knowledge of how you, as the content expert, approach reading and writing so that students can understand the content language and logic. You need to model the dynamic relationship between the demands of the text and your students' previous knowledge and goals for reading.[6]

WHAT DISCIPLINARY LITERACY SKILLS SHOULD STUDENTS KNOW AND BE ABLE TO DO IN GRADES 4–6?

Increasing Specialization of Literacy Development

As you learned in the chapters addressing comprehension instruction, during the upper elementary grades, students shift from "learning to read" to "reading to learn." The basic reading skills that were taught in the early grades are just that, basic. As students enter upper elementary grades, they encounter increasingly complex texts with challenging vocabulary. To comprehend the texts, they need to build their literacy skill repertoire beyond that of decoding, understanding basic text, recognition of high-frequency words, and basic fluency.

Shanahan and Shanahan explain this as the "increasing specialization of literacy development" (Figure 14.1).[7]

The foundation in the pyramid is basic literacy, which includes the basic skills of decoding, understanding high-frequency words, and basic punctuation. As students pass into

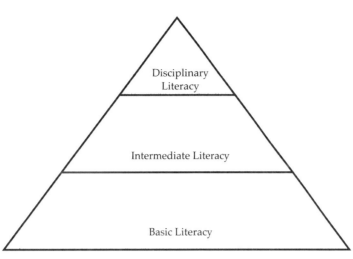

Figure 14.1. Increasing specialty of literacy. (From Shanahan, T., & Shanahan, C. [2008]. Teaching disciplinary literacy to adolescents: Rethinking content-area literacy. *Harvard Educational Review, 78*[1], 40–61; reprinted by permission. Copyright © the President and Fellows of Harvard College. All rights reserved. For more information, please visit harvardeducationalreview.org)

the upper elementary grades, the skills at the intermediate literacy level include knowledge to tackle more demanding content materials by decoding multisyllabic words, learning specialized vocabulary, understanding more complex text structure, and sustaining or even increasing their reading time. As students move into disciplinary literacy, the skills required for success are more complex and demanding. For instance, in history, students need to learn how to think about the author's perspective while reading a primary document. In mathematics, close, attentive reading and re-reading is critical for understanding. It is important for students to have explicit instruction so they know how to apply these advanced skills to demanding and complex texts.

Torgesen et al. define academic literacy as, "the ability to make inferences from text, to learn new vocabulary from context, to link ideas across texts, and to identify and summarize the most important ideas or content with a text."[8]

What does this mean for you as a content teacher? You must teach students the skills that are required in your discipline. Each discipline has unique properties that are essential for comprehending the text. You can not read a novel the same way you read a science book. You can not read a primary document the same way you read a mathematical problem.

You must teach all those skills and a vast amount of content. And, you may not be a reading teacher! The purpose of this chapter is to provide you with the knowledge to teach the skills of reading while teaching your content material. The fact is, without the necessary skills to tackle the assigned reading and writing, student achievement is undermined, and success in content areas may be limited.

Explicit instruction, modeling, and guided practice teaching students specific reading strategies have been shown to improve performance in the content areas.[9] Let us review some of the skills specific to each discipline.

BOX 14.1. As students begin reading these more complex discipline-specific texts, they need to be taught what to expect in the reading, how to approach the reading, how to monitor their comprehension, and how to extend their cognitive endurance.

In science, visual literacy is important. Students need to understand how diagrams, drawings, and photographs convey meaning and support the text. Students also need to be able to understand technical vocabulary and the unique syntax used in science texts. It is not uncommon to find embedded clauses, where one clause is included in a sentence (i.e., "in the deciduous forest, that is, a forest biome with trees that lose their leaves in autumn") or nominal appositions, phrases placed next to each other (i.e., "when the air is saturated, cannot hold any more water, it rains"), to define vocabulary.[10] Therefore, it is important to teach students how to use context clues to find word meanings and to be on the lookout for a variety of syntax possibilities throughout the text. In addition, if students understand the text structure of typical science books, (e.g., problem–solution or cause and effect), they can better anticipate how the material will be presented, thereby increasing their comprehension.

In social studies, students need to have strategies for reading primary documents.[11] They need to be able to identify the context of the source and the author's point of view to assist them in determining any bias in the text. For example, if the text they are reading was written during or about the Civil War, it is imperative the students know something about the political and social climate during that period of history. In addition, students need to know how to compare multiple documents to deepen their understanding of historical events. Synthesizing this information also assists critical analysis.[12] Your students, however, may need specific guidelines and support for learning how to synthesize.

In language arts classes at the fourth-, fifth-, and sixth-grade levels, students will begin to read literature that requires them to have an understanding of rhetorical tools employed in fiction and nonfiction. Knowing how to identify the themes, character development, allusions to other works, and the difference between literal and implied meaning is necessary as they are presented with more challenging fictional works. Students will be expected to understand genres in fiction (drama, fable, historical fiction, mythology, short story, nonfiction biography, narrative nonfiction, and speech).

Reading mathematics is a unique challenge. The National Council of Teachers of Mathematics (NCTM) defines mathematics as a language and a form of communication.[13] To succeed in mathematics, students need to interpret graphic information, comprehend technical language, and understand how common words like "the" and "a" have specific mathematical meaning.[14] Students need to understand the importance of close reading and re-reading to construct meaning. They also need to understand the logic of words to better understand their functionality.

HOW DO YOU ASSESS WHAT STUDENTS KNOW AND HOW MUCH THEY ARE LEARNING?

As you have learned, disciplinary literacy is made up of many components. Students first are expected to already have the basic reading skills mastered: decoding, understanding basic text, recognition of high-frequency words, and basic fluency. Disciplinary literacy also requires students' awareness of text structure and variability, adequate and specific background knowledge, and the practice of setting goals for reading. It requires self-monitoring and the ability to initiate fix-up strategies when comprehension breaks down.

When students are not successful in reading and interpreting disciplinary texts, teachers must assume a detective role and discern which pieces of the puzzle are missing. The easiest way to get started is by giving the student a quick R-CBM[15] (Reading-Curriculum-Based Measure) passage to determine whether or not he or she has basic reading skills in place (see Chapter 8 for directions on administering and interpreting a reading CBM). If the students' performance on the R-CBM is consistent with their grade level and compatible expectations, you can generally assume they have acquired basic reading skills and the problem does not lie in that area. Next, ask pointed questions that will yield more diagnostic information about the reading process. For example, is the student using conventional content reading strategies such as previewing, predicting, self-questioning or self-monitoring, and summarizing as tools to get the gist or meaning of the text? What about background knowledge? Question the student to determine what framework or knowledge base he or she brings to the text.

Finally, think about the specific disciplinary knowledge that is required (this knowledge will be different across the various disciplines), and query the student to determine if this is the missing link. As you can see, there is no exact science for evaluating disciplinary; however, a R-CBM can be helpful to rule out the lack of basic reading skills, and questioning and process-of-elimination logic may help to identify the specific skills challenging your students. (The reader is referred to Chapter 12, which provides a set of questions used to identify more specific areas of potential weakness.)

HOW DO YOU USE ASSESSMENTS TO PLAN INSTRUCTION?

At this time, informal assessments are the most useful for classroom teachers to determine how well students comprehend complex expository text. Observe your students as they apply the skills of disciplinary literacy to classroom assignments. Examples of application assignments include requiring the students to synthesize the main ideas from multiple documents, solve problems using data, and think critically about the text, author's purpose, and historical context. By observing how your students perform on these and other tasks, you can identify and design targeted instruction to enhance their ability to comprehend disciplinary texts.

HOW DO YOU TEACH DISCIPLINARY LITERACY EFFECTIVELY, EFFICIENTLY, AND IN A MANNER APPROPRIATE TO THE AGE/GRADE OF YOUR STUDENTS?

Now that you know the skills that are essential for success in the disciplines, how do you develop lessons that teach students the content that is required and at the same time give them tools they need to be successful reading and writing in the discipline? The first thing you need to do is think about the materials you will be using and ask yourself some questions like

- What kind of pre-existing knowledge might my students possess on this topic?
- How might I connect the new concepts with concepts previously learned?
- What materials are most suited to this topic: the textbook? primary documents? charts and graphs? periodicals? fiction or nonfiction texts?

In all disciplines, you must anticipate the challenges your students are going to encounter with the reading. Tailor your instruction to address before, during, and after reading activities. Many generic literacy strategies, such as those discussed in Chapter 12, are effective if they are redesigned for the specific content being taught.

First, let us look at the generic strategy of previewing the text. Before reading literature, you might ask: What is the significance of the title? What is the genre and who is the author? In history, you want to ask: Who is the author? When was it written? What is the topic? For previewing in science, you might ask: What is the problem/phenomenon? What do I know about this topic? What do I predict about this problem/phenomenon? In mathematics, you want to get the big picture first, so it is important to get an overview by skimming the chapter then reading the chapter introduction, the section titles, and section summaries.[16]

Second, tapping a students' previously gained knowledge has been shown to predict improved comprehension.[17] A strategy you might choose to use is KWL[18] (What do we know? What do we want to find out? What did we learn?) or KWHL (What do we know? What do we want to find out? How can we find out what we want to learn? What did we learn?). However, without some advance thought and planning, this strategy could fall flat if you do not ask the right questions. For instance, in science if you ask, "What do you know about relative density?" the students are likely to say "Nothing!" If you ask, "What do you want to know about relative density?" Same response: "Nothing!" But, if you show students a steel block and an igneous rock and ask, "Which one do you think is more buoyant?" your students have something to respond to because they have some pre-existing knowledge about the weights of these items.

Shanahan, Moje, and Lee have identified generic reading strategies that can be adapted for all disciplines.[19] These strategies include before-reading activities such as pre-reading to both activate previous knowledge and build upon previous knowledge. It is important to learn critical vocabulary before reading commences, so your students are better equipped to comprehend the text (see Chapters 9 and 10 for suggestions regarding explicit vocabulary instruction). The discipline-specific vocabulary requires explicit instruction. Another challenge for students reading complex text is to understand the unique arrangement of words in a sentence (syntax), as well as the way in which the text is organized, or the text structure. Helping students understand the unique text patterns will improve comprehension. For example, narrative text is usually written around a story structure framework that includes setting, characters, goal, problem, plot or action, resolution, and theme, and students get accustomed to this specific framework in lower elementary grades.[20] Expository or informational texts, on the other hand, have a totally different design format. It is important to note, however, that a predictable framework assists readers in comprehending text. Characteristics of expository or information text include description, sequence, problem and solution, cause and effect, and compare and contrast.

Strategies during reading include questioning, visualizing, and monitoring learning. To promote active reading, you can teach students to question while they are reading. Teach them to interact with the text by asking questions like, What does the author mean when he or she says this? and What is this about?[21] For example, in a literature unit on character development, you could model questioning the author to identify character traits like, "How have things changed for the character now?" and "How did this description show a change in the character?" Now that they have seen your thinking and the questions you asked, they are ready to try it themselves. Provide students with open-ended questions to answer as they read the text. As they locate the answer, ask them to write the answer on a sticky note in the text. Once everyone has had an opportunity to read, have the students get into small groups to share what they have found. The teacher monitors the discussions and provides feedback in each of the groups.

Visualizing is another strategy that brings the text alive by helping students see a visual image of the text they are reading. However, content teachers need to help students learn this strategy by supporting the text with visual images and modeling the strategy.[22] A think-aloud would be a great way to show how you visualize text. While reading out loud, stop when a passage "paints a picture" for you showing your students how you visualize while reading. The following example illustrates this skill.

"The tattered rim of the mystery man's cap dripped grey water down the slope of his crooked nose. We would have run if our feet weren't frozen stiff. But as he approached, he tilted his head just slightly as if to greet us. And turning toward us, as he brushed past, flashed a smile before disappearing into the cloak of night."

Teacher: "As I was reading this, my mind immediately saw a dark and rainy night with a scary old man dressed in rags walking towards a couple of petrified kids.. But then, as he draws closer to the kids he flashes a smile. My image of him changed as I realized he was harmless."

Being an active reader also means that students are monitoring their learning as they read. For example, do they understand when they have a problem or when things do not make sense? Can they identify what it is they do not understand? Can they determine what they can do to fix the problem? Possible solutions might include re-reading the text, looking ahead to see if there might be some clarifying information, or restating the text into their own words.

After-reading strategies include summarizing and synthesizing. The goal is to teach students the processes necessary to tackle the challenging texts. With any strategy, it is important to remember that each strategy needs to be explicitly taught and modeled, and multiple opportunities for guided practice must be provided.

PUTTING IT ALL TOGETHER: DEVELOPING LESSON PLANS THAT INCORPORATE STANDARDS AND EVIDENCE-BASED INSTRUCTION

Discipline-Specific Instruction in English Language Arts

Now let us look at discipline-specific instruction. In English language arts, the Common Core State Standards expect students to read widely and deeply from among a broad range of high-quality, increasingly challenging literary and informational texts. Through extensive reading of stories, dramas, poems, and myths from diverse cultures and different time periods, students gain literary and cultural knowledge as well as familiarity with various text structures and elements.[23] You can teach students the various genres and categories of literature by using author studies (see later in this section) to evaluate the author's themes, character development, point of view, and writing style. For example, in an author study, students can study the life of the author to analyze how life experiences have influenced the writing. As students read, they would identify sections of the text where this is evident. The study could be expanded to read several works by a specific author to compare and contrast the author's themes, setting, characters, and genre. As they read, students can gather information in their journals to note similarities and differences. The culminating activity could be a written analysis showing how life events influenced sections of the works supported by specific examples.[24] The author's study addresses the English Language Arts Reading Standard for Literature K–5: #3 Compare and contrast two or more characters, settings, or events in a story or drama, drawing on specific details in the text (e.g., how characters interact).[25]

To read literature critically, it is important to analyze and understand literary elements. Teaching students how to identify mood helps them to better comprehend the feeling the author is portraying. The mood is established through setting, characters, and actions. You can teach mood by explaining to your students that mood is the overall feeling the author creates through careful word choice and phrasing. Model for your students by using a think-aloud, showing your students how you determine the mood by identifying critical text or pieces of evidence that support your opinion. For example, using this passage from Mark Twain's, *The Adventures of Huckleberry Finn*,[26] you can feel how lonely and anxious Huck is as he describes sitting in his room:

Then I set down in a chair by the window and tried to think of something cheerful, but it warn't no use. I felt so lonesome I most wished I was dead. The stars were shining, and the leaves rustled in the woods ever so mournful; and I heard an owl, away off, who-whooing about somebody that was dead, and a whippowill and a dog crying about somebody that was going to die; and the wind was trying to whisper something to me, and I couldn't make out what it was, and so it made the cold shivers run over me. Then away out in the woods I heard that kind of a sound that a ghost makes when it wants to tell about something that's on its mind and can't make itself understood and so can't rest easy in its grave, and has to go about that way every night grieving. I got so downhearted and scared I did wish I had some company.

To illustrate to your students how you can identify tone, mark the text with a light colored highlighter identifying all the words and phrases that give the reader a feeling of loneliness. With a dark colored highlighter, mark the words and phrases that give the feeling of anxiety.

> Then I set down in a chair by the window and tried to think of something cheerful, but it warn't no use. I felt so lonesome I most wished I was dead. The stars were shining, and the leaves rustled in the woods ever so mournful; and I heard an owl, away off, who-whooing about somebody that was dead, and a whippowill and a dog crying about somebody that was going to die; and the wind was trying to whisper something to me, and I couldn't make out what it was, and so it made the cold shivers run over me. Then away out in the woods I heard that kind of a sound that a ghost makes when it wants to tell about something that's on its mind and can't make itself understood and so can't rest easy in its grave, and has to go about that way every night grieving. I got so downhearted and scared I did wish I had some company.

After modeling the reading and marking of the passage, ask your students to explain how you determined the mood, making sure they understand that you were paying close attention to words and phrases that identified the mood. For guided practice, pair the students, give them a passage and highlighters, and ask them to read the passage out loud to each other. After reading, determine what the mood is, and highlight the words and phrases that support that mood. This instructional strategy is one that helps students analyze prose for deeper meaning.

Students often struggle with identifying the theme in a literary work. It is typically difficult for students to differentiate between the plot and the theme, and they struggle with recognizing key details. Tim Shanahan created a Character Change Chart[27] to teach students how to identify theme in a story. Shanahan's chart helps students become aware of details that contribute to theme identification. Using this chart, students observe characteristics of the main character at the beginning of the story and then note changes over the course of the story. Students now have this critical information about the character that can be used to help them figure out the theme (Figure 14.2).

Using the character chart to explicitly teach students how to identify the theme in a work addresses the Common Core State Reading Standard for Literature: Grade 5 #2: Determine a theme of a story, drama, or poem from details in the text, including how characters in a story or drama respond to challenges or how the speaker in a poem reflects upon a topic.[28]

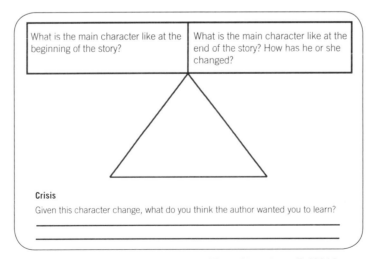

Figure 14.2. Character change chart. (From Shanahan, T. [2010, July 11]. *Content area versus disciplinary literacy.* Retrieved from http://www.shanahanonliteracy.com/2010/07/content-area-reading-versus.html; reprinted by permission.)

DISCIPLINE-SPECIFIC INSTRUCTION IN SOCIAL STUDIES

In social studies, historians like to read several documents on a similar event to better understand the occurrence. In addition to reading the textbook, students can also read documents from a variety of sources to get a more complete picture. A strategy that is effective in teaching students how to assimilate numerous readings and synthesize the information is called the Multiple Gist strategy.[29] After reading one text, students are asked to write the gist, or summary, of the text using a set number of words. Students then read a second text and incorporate the gist of the second text into the original summary. This process is repeated for each text selection. The summary length is established, so each additional reading requires the student to synthesize the textual information to identify the gist before incorporating the new material into the original summary.

Understanding text structure is critical in content area reading, especially in expository text. Primary documents often are written to show cause and effect, sequence, problem solution, comparison, and description. You can teach your students the logic of writing with a particular style of text to help them see the organizational pattern and anticipate what is coming next.[30] The cause–effect strategy is particularly effective because of the nature of text in social studies.[31] In the first step, the teacher uses explicit instruction to introduce the students to cause and effect by defining the words "cause" and "effect" and giving examples. The second step is to teach cause–effect clue words: as a result of, because, since, therefore, consequently, in order that, then, if…then, thus, due to. In step three, students complete a graphic organizer with the cause–effect sentences (Figure 14.3).

To practice this strategy, you can give the students a paragraph and ask them to read it aloud to a partner. Following the reading, the pair reviews the paragraph, circles the signal words, underlines the cause or effect that follows the signal word, and completes the cause and effect chart. To assess how well the students understand the text structure, the teacher can check their understanding by asking specific cause and effect questions to reinforce the importance of analyzing text structure.

This, like many strategies, can be time consuming. Therefore, it is important that you identify the kind of reading that will be common in your discipline. If your history students often read text that is cause and effect, it is worth the time to make sure they can use a specific process, like the one described above, to better comprehend complex text.

Another strategy that works well with history is called problematic perspectives.[32] Before assigning a reading, you present a problem to the class and ask a variety of thought-provoking questions. While discussing these questions, students will try to seek possible solutions by tapping their earlier knowledge. This discussion sets the stage for the upcoming reading by raising student interest and presenting a situation that needs to be addressed. You then assign

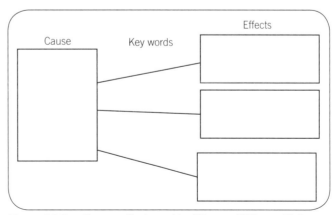

Figure 14.3. Cause–effect graphic. (*Source*: Williams, Hall, Lauer, Stafford, DeSisto, & De Cani, 2005.)

a role to the students, to give them a unique perspective and a purpose for reading the text. For example, before reading about the Battle of the Alamo, read William Travis' *Letter from the Alamo* and Santa Anna's terms for surrender out loud to the class. Put the students in groups and ask them to brainstorm answers to the following questions:

- Why did the Texians (what the people who lived in Texas were called) who were fighting under the command of William Travis, refuse to surrender?
- Why was Santa Anna unwilling to amend his terms for surrender?
- Why were both commanders, Santa Anna and Travis, willing to lose so many lives at the Alamo?

After the discussion, assign half the class to assume the role of William Travis and the other half the role of Santa Anna. As the students read, they will be thinking critically about the text through the eyes of the commanders. Following the reading, ask the students to respond to the questions from their unique perspective. By putting themselves into a different role, they will actively focus on the important details as they read.[33]

Discipline-Specific Instruction in Science

Science presents students with text that is dense and contains technical vocabulary that requires deep understanding for absorbing the concepts.[34] Science also provides opportunities for interesting and exciting activities! Anticipatory sets are an excellent way to prepare your students for reading like a scientist. Anticipatory sets are used at the beginning of a lesson to pique the students' interest, to tap background knowledge, and/or to provide a transition from one lesson to the next. Let us say you are about to begin a unit on elements and compounds. Doing a simple experiment like pouring hot water into liquid nitrogen to create a cloud can be a great way to stimulate your students to reflect upon what happened, ask questions, offer ideas, tap background knowledge, and reveal to you any misconceptions they might have. Simple experiments, mini–field trips around the school, and YouTube videos are examples of anticipatory sets that can be used to set the stage by raising the level of interest before reading.

Another pre-reading strategy that is particularly useful in science is the list-group-label strategy.[35] First, you identify a concept or topic from the reading using one or two words. For example, in a chapter on earthquakes and volcanoes, the concept might be "the Earth's changing crust." Next, you introduce and model the list-group-label strategy:

List: Identify the topic/concept, generate words or phrases related to the topic.
Group: Organize the words into clusters of ideas.
Label: Label each of the clusters.
After you have modeled each part of this strategy, have the students do the following:

List: In small groups or pairs, generate a list of words based on the topic.
Group: Read the lists out loud, and define any unknown words. (Words can be written on small pieces of paper for ease in grouping.) Ask the students to group the items into categories of their choice.
Label: Following the categorization, ask the students to label the groups. When they have finished labeling, ask them to explain how and why they arrived at the group labels (Figure 14.4).

An instructional strategy that improves comprehension and vocabulary by examining features that are similar and different is called feature analysis.[36] Appropriate to all disciplines, feature analysis is especially useful in clarifying difficult scientific concepts. Typically, it is used following the reading of the text. First, identify the concept for instruction. Then, create a chart with examples in the first column and the features in the column headings (Table 14.1). The features are items that the examples may or may not possess. As a class activity, you

Figure 14.4. Photograph of example list (part 1 and part 2).

will ask students to place a plus or minus in the appropriate column to indicate whether or not the example possesses the characteristic. It is important that you model aloud your thinking process for the first few items so the students can see how you process the information. For instance, "In the chart below, you see the first example is the planet Mercury. Is there a gravitational force on Mercury? Does Mercury have water? Are there moons surrounding Mercury?"

After you have modeled the first example, you can either continue as a whole class activity or put students in groups or pairs to continue working on the chart. As you move around the room, answer questions, clarify points, and ask students to show you in the text where they got their answer. This discussion not only helps your students see similarities and differences, but they are also manipulating the text by identifying textual characteristics and putting it into a graphic format. This activity allows for good discussion and referencing the text.

Discipline-Specific Instruction in Mathematics

A strategy that is particularly effective in mathematics is the use of webbing as a pre-reading strategy. This exercise helps to tap students' existing knowledge and gives you an opportunity to see what your students know about a concept. You also get insights into any misconceptions they might have. Begin by writing a concept on the board, and ask students for terms, ideas, or examples they might have. Through this discussion, the teacher constructs a web illustrating

Table 14.1. Features analysis chart

Solar system facts: Place a + in the column if the feature applies to the planet								
Moons	Water	Dwarf planet	Terrestrial planet	Gas giant	Icy surface	Volcanoes	Rings surround planet	Gravitational force
Mercury	–	–	+	–	+	+	–	+
Venus								
Earth								
Mars								
Jupiter								
Saturn								
Uranus								
Neptune								
Pluto								

From Anders, P.L., & Bos, C.S. (1986). Semantic feature analysis: An interactive strategy for vocabulary development and text comprehension. *Journal of Reading, 29(7)*, 610–616; reprinted by permission.

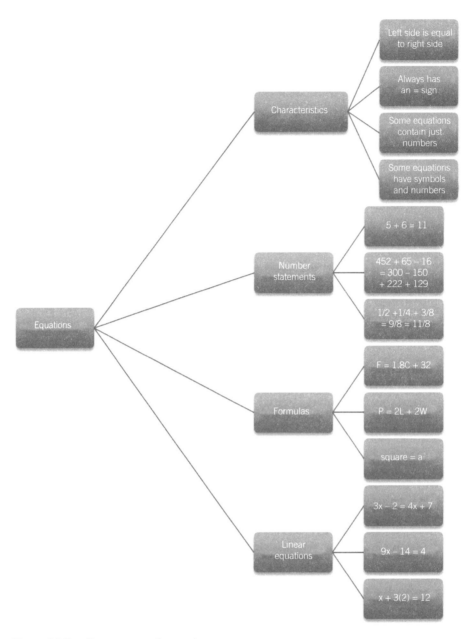

Figure 14.5. Features equations web.

how the students' ideas can be organized and adds critical information to the discussion. Refer to the example in Figure 14.5, illustrating the concept of equations.

After the web is constructed, the students can use it as a reference tool that will give them a way to make connections as they begin reading the chapter.[37] Be sure to model or demonstrate how you use the web to help you understand the information in the chapter.

Another approach that is effective for math is the mathematics-structured note-taking strategy[38] that is completed during reading. Instruct your students to divide their notepaper (or journal) into three columns. Identify the concept or "big idea," and ask them to write it in the first column. In the second column, have the students write an explanation of this "big idea." In the third column, the students would decide how they would illustrate the concept. They could create a chart, make a graph, craft a formula, or anything that would show how to apply the concept. It is important that you monitor their explanations and illustrations to make sure that the precise mathematical language is being used properly (Table 14.2).

Table 14.2. Big idea chart

Big idea	Explanation	Graphic representation
Temperature conversion: Celsius to Fahrenheit	Temperature is measured using two different systems.	$20° × 9/5=180/5=36$
	The metric system uses the Celsius scale and the U.S. uses the Fahrenheit scale.	$36 + 32°=68°F$
	To convert from Celsius to Fahrenheit you need to multiply the Celsius temperature by 9/5 and add 32° to that number.	$20°C=68°F$

Example of a mathematics-structured note-taking activity.

Understanding mathematics-specific vocabulary is critical for comprehension. Many words have different meanings when used in mathematics. Take, for instance, the word *prime*. The definition outside of mathematics is first in importance, most suitable, or earliest. In mathematics, prime means that it is not divisible without a remainder. To help students conceptually understand the mathematics-specific vocabulary, you can use the vocabulary reinforcer, which is a modification of the list-group-label exercise described earlier (Figure 14.6).[39] When students have a solid understanding of the terms, they can better perform the exercises and comprehend the concepts.

In this strategy, the students must do two things: Students are given grouped lists of three to five words. First, they must study the lists to find the one word that does not belong. Next, they must come up with a label for the lists. You can scaffold this activity by having words for them to pick from. This activity helps students see how words can be organized (the label) while helping them to make connections between words (the lists).

CLOSING THOUGHTS

Preparing the students with 21st century skills is critical. It is essential that teachers give their students the necessary tools to excel in all disciplines in school, in college, and in the workplace, beginning in the elementary grades.

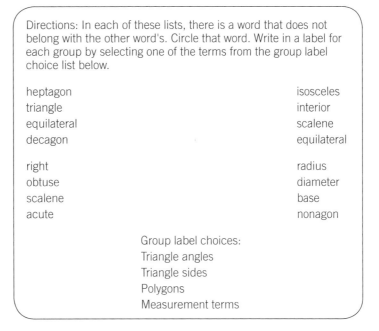

Directions: In each of these lists, there is a word that does not belong with the other word's. Circle that word. Write in a label for each group by selecting one of the terms from the group label choice list below.

heptagon	isosceles
triangle	interior
equilateral	scalene
decagon	equilateral
right	radius
obtuse	diameter
scalene	base
acute	nonagon

Group label choices:
Triangle angles
Triangle sides
Polygons
Measurement terms

Figure 14.6. Vocabulary reinforcer.

It is clear from the research that discipline learning improves when students are explicitly taught how to approach the reading, how to analyze the information, and how to critically think about the content. Educators can no longer expect that their students can "figure out" complex text and high-level metacognitive tasks without explicit instruction. It is the educator's job to identify and teach discipline-specific skills, to create routines that help students become active readers and critical thinkers. In so doing, they will raise the reading achievement for all students in all disciplines.

APPLICATION ASSIGNMENTS

In-Class Assignments

1. Choose one of the content areas you will be teaching as an elementary teacher: English/language arts, mathematics, science, or social studies. Partner with someone who selected the same content area. Complete the following:

   a. Summarize what makes literacy in this content (discipline) unique from the others.

   b. List and briefly describe strategies from this text that you could use while teaching your content.

2. Prepare a mini-lesson using one of the strategies to share with the class.

Tutoring Assignments

1. Consider the disciplines that most challenge your student. Analyze the specific areas of difficulty, and plan a lesson to address those difficulties. Specifically address how you would increase critical thinking skills.

2. Teach the lesson, and evaluate the effectiveness of the lesson. Did your student learn and apply the strategy? Did your student's ability to think critically about the reading improve? How do you know? How could you modify the lesson to better meet the needs of your student?

Homework Assignments

1. Select one of the discipline-specific strategies discussed in this text, and apply it while reading this text or a text of your choice or while working on a writing assignment. Reflect upon how the strategy supported your learning.

2. Use a generic reading strategy, such as KWL, and apply it while reading this text or a text of your choice. Reflect upon the usefulness of the generic strategy. Should the strategy be modified? If so, how?

3. Write a one-page paper comparing and contrasting your experiences using the two types of strategies. Include thoughts about how you might adapt generic strategies to be used effectively with specific disciplines.

ENDNOTES

1. McKenna & Robinson (2009, p. 6).
2. Perin (2010).
3. Moje (2010, p. 69).
4. Shanahan (2010, p. 41).
5. Shanahan & Shanahan (2008).
6. Lee & Spratley (2010).
7. Shanahan & Shanahan (2008, p. 138).
8. Torgesen, Houston, Rissman, Decker, Roberts, Vaughn, et al. (2007, p. 3).
9. Kamil (2003).
10. Wignell (1998).
11. Donovan & Bransford (2005).
12. Hynd (1999).
13. Lee (2010).
14. Shanahan & Shanahan (2008).
15. Graves, Plasencia-Peinando, Deno, & Johnson (2005); Hasbrouck & Tindal (2005).
16. Nolting (1997).

17. Dole, Valencia, Greer, & Wardrop (1991).
18. Ogle (1986).
19. Shanahan & Shanahan (1997); Lee (2010); Moje (2010).
20. Williams, Hall, Lauer, Stafford, DeSisto, & De Cani (2005).
21. Beck & McKeown (2006).
22. Moje (2010).
23. National Governors Association Center for Best Practices and Council of Chief State School Officers (2010).
24. Fox (2006).
25. National Governors Association Center for Best Practices and Council of Chief State School Officers (2010).
26. Twain (1947, p. 20).
27. Shanahan & Shanahan (1997).
28. National Governors Association Center for Best Practices and Council of Chief State School Officers (2010).
29. Shanahan & Shanahan (2008).
30. Williams, Nubla-Kung, Pollini, Stafford, Garcia, & Snyder (2007).
31. Ciardiello (2002).
32. Vacca, Vacca, & Mraz (2011).
33. Pichert & Anderson (1977).
34. Hunter (1982).
35. Perin (2010).
36. Anders & Bos (1986).
37. Barton & Heidema (2002).
38. Shanahan & Shanahan (2008).
39. Alvermann, Phelps, & Gilis (2010).

REFERENCES

Anders, P.L., & Bos, C.S. (1986). Semantic feature analysis: An interactive strategy for vocabulary development and text comprehension. *Journal of Reading, 29(7)*, 610–616.

Alvermann, D.E., Phelps, S.F., & Gilis, V.R. (2010). *Content area reading and literacy.* Boston: Allyn & Bacon.

Barton, M.L., & Heidema, C. (2002). *Teaching reading in mathematics* (2nd ed.). Aurora, CO: Mid-continent Research for Education and Learning.

Beck, I.L., & McKeown, M.G. (2006). *Improving comprehension with questioning the author: A fresh and expanded view of a powerful approach.* New York: Scholastic.

Ciardiello, A.V. (2002). Helping adolescents understand cause/effect text structure in social studies. *Social Studies, 93(1)*, 31–36.

Dole, J.A., Valencia, S.W., Greer, E.A., & Wardrop, J.L. (1991). Effects of tow types of prereading instruction on the comprehension of narrative and expository text. *Reading Research Quarterly, 26(2)*, 142–159.

Donovan, M.S., & Bransford, J. (Eds.). (2005). *How students learn: History, mathematics, and science in the classroom.* Washington, DC: National Academies Press.

Fox, K.R. (2006). Using author studies in children's literature to explore social justice issues. *Social Studies, 97(6)*, 251–256.

Graves, A.W., Plasencia-Peinando, J., Deno, S.L., & Johnson, J.R. (2005). *Formatively evaluating the reading progress of first-grade English learners in multiple-langauge classrooms.* Remedial and Special Education, 26, 215-225.

Hasbrouck, J., & Tindal, G. (2005). *Oral reading fluency: 90 years of measurement (Tech. Rep. NO. 33).* Eugene: University of Oregon, College of Education, Behavioral Research and Teaching.

Hunter, M. (1982). *Mastery teaching: increasing instructional effectiveness in secondary schools, colleges, and universities.* El Segundo, CA: TIP Publications.

Hynd, C.R. (1999). Teaching students to think critically using multiple texts in history. *Journal of Adolescent and Adult Literacy, 42*, 428–436.

Kamil, M.L. (2003). *Adolescents and literacy: Reading for the 21st century.* Washington, DC: Alliance for Excellent Education.

Lee, C. (2010). *Text types, strategies and disciplinary tasks: Fundamentals of teaching reading comprehension in the content areas.* In A. Rivet, A. Marri, & Y. Lyons (Eds.). Proceedings of the Content Area Literacy Conference 2010 (p. 138); July 7–8; New York: Teachers College Columbia University.

Lee, C., & Spratley, A. (2010). *Reading in the disciplines: The challenges of adolescent literacy. A report to Carnegie Corporation of New York.* Washington, DC: Alliance for Excellent Education. NAEP statistics.

McKenna, M., & Robinson, R. (2009). *Teaching through text: Reading and writing in the content areas.* Boston: Allyn and Bacon.

Moje, E. (2010). *But my English teacher said…: Supporting students in how to read and write in the natural and social sciences.* In A. Rivet, A. Marri, & Y. Lyons (Eds.), Proceedings of the Content Area Literacy Conference 2010 (p. 138); July 7–8; New York, NY: Teachers College Columbia University.

National Governors Association Center for Best Practices & Council of Chief State School Officers. (2010). *Common core state standards initiative: Preparing America's students for college and career.* Retrieved from http://www.corestandards.org/the-standards

Nolting, P.D. (1997). *Winning at math: Your guide to learning mathematics through successful study skills.* Bradenton, FL: Academic Success Press, Inc.

Ogle, D. (1986). KWL in action: Secondary teachers find applications that work. In E.K. Dishner, T.W. Bean, J.E. Readence, & D.W. Moore (Eds.), *Reading in the content areas: Improving classroom instruction* (3rd ed., pp. 270–281). Dubuque, IA: Kendall-Hunt.

Perin, D. (2010). *Literacy concepts and strategies for embedding in content instruction.* From College and Career Readiness Initiative: ELA Faculty Collaborative on *Promoting content learning through embedding literacy strategies;* May 17; Dallas, TX: Meadows Center for Preventing Educational Risk, College of Education, The University of Texas at Austin.

Pichert, J.W., & Anderson, R.C. (1977). Taking different perspectives on a story. *Journal of Educational Psychology, 69(4)*, 309–315.

Shanahan, T. (2010). *Content area versus disciplinary literacy.* Retrieved from http://www.shanahanonliteracy.com/2010/07/content-area-reading-versus.html

Shanahan, T., & Shanahan, S. (1997). Character perspective charting: Helping children to develop a more complete conception of story. *The Reading Teacher, 50*, 668–677.

Shanahan, T., & Shanahan, C. (2008). Teaching disciplinary literacy to adolescents: Rethinking content-area literacy. *Harvard Educational Review, 78(1)*, 40–61.

The Common Core State Standards Initiative. (2010). Retrieved August 31, 2011 from http://www.corestandards.org

Torgesen, J.K., Houston, D.D., Rissman, L.M., Decker, S.M., Roberts, G., Vaughn, S., et al. (2007). *Academic literacy instruction for adolescents: A guidance document from the Center on Instruction.* Portsmouth, NH: RMC Research Corporation, Center on Instruction.

Twain, Mark. (1947). *The Adventures of Huckleberry Finn.* Cleveland, OH: The World Publishing Company.

Vacca, R.T., Vacca, J.L., & Mraz, M. (2011). *Content area reading: Literacy and learning across the curriculum.* Boston: Pearson.

Wignell, P. (1998). Technicality and abstraction in social science. In J.R. Martin & R. Veel (Eds.), *Reading science: Critical and functional perspectives on discourse of science* (pp. 297–326). New York: Routledge.

Williams, J.P., Hall, K.M., Lauer, K.D., Stafford, K.B., DeSisto, L.A., & De Cani, J.S. (2005). Expository text comprehension in the primary grade classroom. *Journal of Educational Psychology, 97,* 235–248.

Williams, J.P., Nubla-Kung, A.M., Pollini, S., Stafford, K.B., Garcia, A., & Snyder, A.E. (2007). Teaching cause-effect text structure through social studies content to at-risk second graders. *Journal of Learning Disabilities, 40*(2), 111–120.

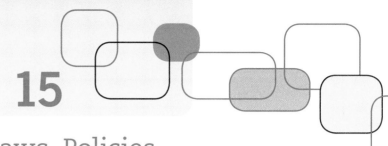

15

Current Laws, Policies, Initiatives, Common Core State Standards, and Response to Intervention

by Susan M. Smartt

Nothing ever stays the same, and that is especially true in the education arena. The United States provides a free education for all students and has led the world in ensuring universal education, including students who come to school not speaking English, who have disabilities, who have few school readiness skills, and who come from abject poverty. Educating all children to a high level is a challenge, and educators are always trying to improve the way they educate their students. A current effort at improving educational outcomes for students is the renewed focus to increase the number of students who leave high school with a diploma and are prepared to be successful in college and careers. Improving education is a priority of almost every parent, educator, and politician. Democracy has been called a messy business, and this is true for educational policy decision-making procedures, also. Consequently, as a teacher, you will experience frequent alterations in educational policy that will affect your life and that of your students. This chapter provides a concise overview of some of the most important policies, standards, and initiatives that influence your profession.

Objectives: After studying this chapter you will be able to do the following:

1. Describe the role federal laws and policies play in what you must teach your students.
2. Explain the background leading to the No Child Left Behind (NCLB/ESEA) legislation.
3. List four goals of NCLB.
4. Describe the Common Core State Standards (CCSS) in English Language Arts and how these standards will affect your teaching.[1]
5. Explain the rationale behind the initiative to provide students with multi-tiered systems for support, including Response to Intervention (RTI), and how this initiative will impact your teaching.
6. Explain the use of standards, what standards you must implement, and other standards that are available to support your instruction.

The purpose of this chapter is to increase your awareness of the role federal policy plays in your decisions about what and how to teach literacy and to provide you with important background knowledge that will help you become a more effective teacher. The history of the current law, No Child Left Behind of 2001 (NCLB), also known as the ESEA (Elementary and Secondary Education Act, 2001), will be examined.[2] This law is important because it dictates much of the instructional focus for schools throughout the United States.

In addition, we will study in-depth the Common Core State Standards (CCSS) and response to intervention (RTI), a multitier system of support, and how these initiatives affect classroom instruction.

A BRIEF HISTORY OF FEDERAL GOVERNMENT INVOLVEMENT IN PUBLIC EDUCATION

Lyndon Baines Johnson, our 36th president, is credited for initiating the legislation known as the Elementary and Secondary Education Act (ESEA, 1965). Having been a classroom teacher himself, President Johnson believed strongly that legislation was needed to provide a more level playing field for all students. The Civil Rights Act of 1964 opened the door, revealing great inequality in education.[3] As part of his "War on Poverty," President Johnson believed the federal government should play a significant role in providing educational funding to local and state governments.[4] Several sections (Titles) were included in the Johnson legislation (ESEA-PL 89-10); but the Title you may be most familiar with is Title I. Title I provides funding and guidelines for educating educationally disadvantaged children. At that time, Congress budgeted more than 80% of the monies appropriated for ESEA to Title I programs.[5]

In 1975 Congress enacted the Education for All Children Act (PL 94-142). The purpose of this law was to protect the rights of all handicapped children by meeting their individual learning needs. Prior to the passage of this law, over one million children with disabilities were denied access to the public education system for appropriate instruction (http://www2.ed.gov/policy/speced/leg/idea/history.html).

The original law was amended in 1997 and today is known as the Individuals with Disabilities Education Act (IDEA). As a result of IDEA, progress has been made over the last three decades in developing and implementing services for early intervention and special education. PL 94-142 guarantees a free, appropriate public education for all children with a disability such as learning disabilities, emotional disturbance, speech and language impaired, blind, deaf and so on.

The presidents who followed President Johnson continued to support education. Initiatives funding Head Start early childhood programs and programs supporting reading excellence were enacted. Major legislation was passed in 2001–2002, including a reauthorization of ESEA in January 2002.

> The quality of our public schools affects us all—as parents, as students, and as citizens. Yet too many children in America are segregated by low expectations, illiteracy, and self-doubt. In a constantly changing world that is demanding increasingly complex skills from its workforce, children are literally being left behind (Forward to NCLB legislation, George W. Bush, 2001).[6]

With these words, President George W. Bush introduced the sweeping, bipartisan legislation known as No Child Left Behind (NCLB, 2001).[7] NCLB was basically a reauthorization of President Johnson's earlier 1965 ESEA law and President Clinton's Reading Excellence Initiative.[8] By passing NCLB, Congress set the expectations that by 2014 all students would be reading on grade level by the end of third grade and that they would remain on grade level. Sweeping changes have been made in all U.S. public schools as a result of NCLB. As you read, you will begin to appreciate the many positive reforms brought about as a result of this law, especially for economically disadvantaged and low performing students.

The blueprint of the NCLB legislation was designed to address four areas:

1. Increasing accountability for student performance, including subgroups such as students from poverty, students with disabilities, and ethnic subgroups.
2. Focusing on what works, including research-based reading programs and instruction.
3. Reducing bureaucracy and increasing flexibility.
4. Empowering parents.

Through this vision, NCLB formally linked federal dollars to specific school and student performance goals to ensure improved results. Key components of the legislation included closing the achievement gap, improving literacy by putting reading first, and expanding flexibility, reducing bureaucracy.[9] For the first time, teachers and school administrators began to look at the school performance (e.g., achievement test data) by individual demographic groups such as White, Asian, Hispanic, and Black; students from poverty; students with disabilities; and students at risk. Requirements for academic achievement were constant and consistent across all demographic groups. By forcing the breakout of individual demographic populations' achievement test scores, the country could now recognize what many in the classroom already knew—highly disparate learning was taking place across the country. The achievement gap between middle class and students from poverty, and between White, Black, and Hispanic students, was alarming.

In order to "close the achievement gap," specific features were included in NCLB:

1.   Accountability and high standards for all populations
2.   Annual academic assessments
3.   Consequences for schools that failed to educate disadvantaged students

Although earlier legislation had sought to remove the inequality in public education, NCLB was the first time the federal government had taken such a strong stand on trying to ensure all students had a quality education by imposing sanctions on schools that failed to make adequate yearly progress (AYP).[10]

In an effort to ensure that all students learned to read, President Bush's NCLB legislation provided a focus on reading in early grades and early reading instruction.[11] Most low-performing schools with a high population of economically disadvantaged students were eligible to participate in the Reading First and Early Reading First initiatives.

Cornerstones of these two reading initiatives were the requirements to screen all students for reading difficulties, progress monitor student achievement, implement research-based core reading programs, and provide a 90-minute block of uninterrupted reading instruction. Data-based decision making, using screening and progress monitoring data to plan instruction, was required in schools receiving Reading First funding.

In 2004, the Individuals with Disabilities Education Improvement Act (IDEA) was reauthorized and reinforced the mandate to provide all students with scientific, research-based instruction. Teachers were required to use scientific, research-based instruction *before* referring students for an assessment to confirm or rule out the presence of a specific learning disability. If students responded to the intervention and learned to read, most likely they did not have a specific learning disability. However, if students did not improve in reading, despite scientifically based instruction implemented with fidelity, the student could be referred for an evaluation to determine if they did, indeed, have a disability and required specialized instruction.

With these specific stipulations, what is now known as RTI was born and introduced as an early identification and intervention model. School districts had the option to continue using the traditional discrepancy model for determining eligibility for specific learning disabilities or implementing RTI. Whichever route schools decided to choose they still had to document that students were receiving scientific, evidence-based instruction and that students were not failing to learn or falling behind due to lack of appropriately designed instruction.

CURRENT LAWS AND POLICIES THAT IMPACT CLASSROOM INSTRUCTION

As this text goes to press, there is strong bipartisan effort to revise NCLB. This effort is referred to as the Reauthorization of ESEA. President Obama has put forth a blueprint for changing the Bush version of ESEA (NCLB).

The current blueprint for ESEA reauthorization asserts that all students can learn and are worth our investment.[12] There are harsh repercussions for schools that have low student achievement and high dropout rates, for example. The most recent ESEA blueprint differs from the 2001 version in that it supports a less punitive and more supportive response to failing schools.

The proposed new law recognizes the importance of teachers and mandates that they are included in the decision-making process about what might work with low-performing students in their own classroom and school settings.

The curriculum focus in the new ESEA blueprint shifts from primarily a reading and math agenda to include accountability in art, history, and other disciplines that have been slighted in the past few years.[13]

The newest version of the blueprint for the ESEA reauthorization continues to place heavy emphasis on school accountability, requiring the use of evidence-based practices and data-driven instruction.[14] Data will not be used exclusively for showing achievement, but for demonstrating growth as well. Finally, the new ESEA, as reflected in the blueprint document, introduces rewards and incentives for students and teachers when goals are achieved.

There is discussion about including a specific literacy section in the legislation, similar to Reading First, and yet with a much broader scope. The current proposal is known as the LEARN Act and targets students birth to 12th grade. Rather than focusing on improving reading only, the act expands to include all skills needed to be literate (e.g., writing, speaking, listening, and using language effectively).

As of the publication of this text, the ESEA had not been reauthorized by Congress though many states requested guidelines and waivers to relieve them from key provisions of NCLB. To respond to the concerns of the states, the U.S. Department of Education announced in August 2011 that states may apply for waivers in exchange for reforms. Those reforms include raising standards for student achievement, implementing school improvement plans, and creating new teacher evaluation systems. During this time of uncertainty, however, states will remain accountable to the original NCLB guidelines currently in place.

The Common Core State Standards

In an effort to unify and improve achievement across the nation and to ensure that all students are college and career ready no later than high school, the National Governors Association (NGA) and the Council of Chief State School Officers (CCSSO) collaborated in 2010 to develop the Common Core State Standards (CCSS).[15] The official title related to literacy achievement is Common Core State Standards for English Language Arts and Literacy in History/Social Science and Technical Subjects. Most states have adopted the standards with only a few states opting to maintain their own state literacy standards.[16] The CCSS represent a synthesis of the most effective elements of the standards-related work from states as well as other contributors.[17]

The CCSS are designed to reflect current research evidence, and are aligned with college and work expectations, rigorous expectations of students, and efforts to improve the status of American students on international benchmarks.

What the Common Core State Standards Include

The Common Core State Standards for literacy include 10 Grade K–12 Anchor Standards in each of the following domains: reading, writing, speaking, listening, and language. In addition, there are grade-specific expectations in grades K–8. The grade-specific standards are written for both literature and informational text (K–5) and are designed around the K–12 Anchor Standards. The grade specific expectations, on the other hand, are meant to provide examples

College and Career Readiness Anchor Standards for Reading

Key Ideas and Details

1. Read closely to determine what the text says explicitly and to make logical inferences from it; cite specific textual evidence when writing or speaking to support conclusions drawn from the text.
2. Determine central ideas or themes of a text and analyze their development; summarize the key supporting details and ideas.
3. Analyze how and why individuals, events, and ideas develop and interact over the course of a text.

Craft and Structure

4. Interpret words and phrases as they are used in a text, including determining technical, connotative, and figurative meanings, and analyze how specific word choices shape meaning or tone.
5. Analyze the structure of texts, including how specific sentences, paragraphs, and larger portions of the text (e.g., a section, chapter, scene, or stanza) relate to each other and the whole.
6. Assess how point of view or purpose shapes the content and style of a text.

Integration of Knowledge and Ideas

7. Integrate and evaluate content presented in diverse media and formats, including visually and quantitatively, as well as in words.
8. Delineate and evaluate the argument and specific claims in a text, including the validity of the reasoning as well as the relevance and sufficiency of the evidence.
9. Analyze how two or more texts address similar themes or topics in order to build knowledge or to compare the approaches the authors take.

Range of Reading and Level of Text Complexity

10. Read and comprehend complex literary and informational text independently and proficiently.

Figure 15.1. Common Core State Standards. (Reprinted from http://www.corestandards.org. Copyright © 2010. National Governors Association Center for Best Practices and Council of Chief State School Officers. All rights reserved.)

of grade-level specific work to support students' mastery of various forms of literature, such as narrative, drama, poetry, and historical fiction. The grade-specific expectations based on informational texts are designed to assist students as they develop academic literacy, or disciplinary literacy, and become competent in learning from informational texts such as textbooks, reports, journals, newspapers, and other non-narrative texts.

The 10 Grade K–12 Anchor Standards for reading are presented in Figure 15.1.[18]

The CCSS establish requirements not only for English Language Arts (ELA), but also for literacy in history/social studies, science, and technical subjects. Think of the CCSS as a body of work that lays out the vision of what it means to be a literate individual in the 21st century.

There is an interdisciplinary approach implicit in the CCSS. Traditionally, it has been considered the work of the ELA teachers to ensure K–5 students are competent in reading, writing, speaking, listening, and language. But the new CCSS expect *all* of these five language-based functions to be integrated across other subjects or disciplines. In other words, students must be encouraged to practice reading, writing, speaking, listening, and using effective language in content subjects including social studies, science, and mathematics. Teachers will need to provide direct, systematic instruction and practice opportunities for the language-based functions in informative and expository texts, across the disciplines, to ensure young readers are moving toward the goal of college and career readiness.

The grade 6–12 standards are divided into two sections: one for ELA and the other for history/social studies, science, and technical subjects. By dividing the standards, there is a clear message that other teachers, in addition to ELA teachers, play a major role in developing

Note: In kindergarten, children are expected to demonstrate increasing awareness and competence in the areas that follow.

Print Concepts

1. Demonstrate understanding of the organization and basic features of print.
   a. Follow words from left or right.
   b. Recognize that spoken words are represented in written language by specific sequences of letters.
   c. Understand that words are separated by spaces in print.
   d. Recognize and name all upper- and lowercase letters of the alphabet.

Phonological Awareness

2. Demonstrate understanding of spoken words, syllables, and sounds (phonemes).
   a. Recognize and produce rhyming words.
   b. Count, pronounce, blend, and segment syllables in spoken words.
   c. Blend and segment onsets and rimes of single-syllable spoken words.
   d. Isolate and pronounce the initial, medial vowel, and final sounds (phonemes) in three-phoneme (consonant–vowel–consonant) or CVC words. (This does not include CVCs ending with /l/, /r/, or /x/.)
   e. Add or substitute individual sounds (phonemes) in simple one-syllable words to make new words.

Phonics and Word Recognition

3. Know and apply grade-level phonics and word analysis skills in decoding words.
   a. Demonstrate basic knowledge of one-to-one letter–sound correspondences by producing the primary or many of the most frequent sounds for each consonant.
   b. Associate the long and short sounds with common spellings (graphemes) for the five major vowels.
   c. Read common high-frequency words by sight (e.g., the, of, to, you, she, my, is, are, do, does).
   d. Distinguish between similarly spelled words by identifying the sounds of the letters that differ.

Fluency

4. Read emergent-reader texts with purpose and understanding.

Figure 15.2. Reading standards: foundational skills (K–5). (Reprinted from http://www.corestandards.org. Copyright © 2010. National Governors Association Center for Best Practices and Council of Chief State School Officers. All rights reserved.)

literacy and language skills. This interdisciplinary approach to literacy development encouraged by the standards is supported by specific research that indicates mature readers are those who are proficient in reading complex informational text independently in a variety of disciplines (or subjects).

In addition to the global anchors and grade-specific standards, there are also foundational skills standards. Foundational skills standards are designed to support students' understanding and knowledge of concepts of print, the alphabetic principle, and other basic conventions of the English writing system.[19]

See Figure 15.2 for a sample of the Kindergarten Foundation Skills Standards. The entire CCSS document can be obtained at http://www.corestandards.com.

Additional Standards

Your State Standards

There are other sets of instructional standards that outline what and how students are to be taught literacy skills in the United States. The most important for you and your students are the standards your state expects you to address. Obtain those standards, and study them carefully. Typically, they will inform you what to teach; how you teach is up to you and hopefully will be based on what you learn in this text about effective instructional practices. Please note that you are legally responsible for teaching the standards developed by your state.

There are additional sets of standards that may help you formulate your instructional plans. Several are highlighted below.

Texas College & Career Readiness Standards: In 2008, the Higher Education Coordinating Board in Texas published the Texas College & Career Readiness Standards. The Coordinating Board worked closely with P–16 professionals, including P–12 and university faculty members to identify gaps in student knowledge. These standards outline expectations in science, social studies, mathematics, English/language arts, and cross-disciplinary skills.[20] High school students are tested on these standards, and, if they pass the test, they are deemed ready to enroll in credit-bearing university courses and prepared to be successful in college and a career. The standards are available at http://www.txfacultycollaboratives.org/images/documents/CCRS.pdf.

Interstate Teacher Assessment and Support Consortium (InTASC): InTASC recently revised and published standards for teacher education.[21] InTASC is a consortium of state education agencies and national educational organizations dedicated to the reform of the preparation, licensing, and professional development of teachers. It provides guidance to state education agencies in teacher licensing, program approval, and professional development. Their web site states: "An effective teacher must be able to integrate content knowledge with the specific strengths and needs of students to assure that all students learn and perform at high levels."[22] You may review these standards, released in April 2011, at http://www.ccsso.org/resources/programs/interstate_teacher_assessment_consortium_(intasc).html.

The Knowledge and Practice Standards for Teachers of Reading: In 2010, The International Dyslexia Association published the *Knowledge and Practice Standards for Teachers of Reading.* This document is designed to guide the reading instruction of all students, supporting teachers in their efforts to know what to teach and how to conduct both effective initial and preventive instruction in the general education classroom. A section of the standards is designed to be used by those engaged in training reading specialists. The intent is to ensure reading specialists are prepared to teach students with reading disabilities, such as dyslexia, and to provide students with specialized intervention instruction when needed.[23]

This text is aligned with the content of the *Knowledge and Practice Standards for Teachers of Reading.*[24] For example, the *Knowledge and Practice Standards* stress the importance that teachers have a strong literacy knowledge base built upon current research, including how students learn to read, what it takes to become an effective reading teacher, and how to be successful in enhancing the literacy potential for ALL students. The *Knowledge and Practice Standards* emphasize the importance of teachers providing instruction that is explicit, systematic, cumulative, and multisensory and integrating listening, speaking, reading, and writing throughout their instructional practices. Examples of the specific content from the *Knowledge and Practice Standards* that constitutes effective reading instruction include knowledge of the:

- Structure of language including the speech sound system (phonology)
- Writing system (orthography)
- Structure of sentences (syntax)
- Meaningful parts of words (morphology)
- Meaning relationships among words and their referents (semantics)
- Organization of spoken and written discourse[25]

In addition, these standards emphasize the importance of utilizing strategies that teach planning, organization, attention to task, critical thinking, and self-management. As you can see, these elements are important for the instruction of all students in order to foster successful reading achievement, and the elements are critical for those students with dyslexia.

At this time, the *Knowledge and Practice Standards for Teachers of Reading* provide detailed and explicit support to teachers and specific guidance on how to teach not only students who are on grade level and above, but also those who are struggling and at risk for reading failure.[26] To review the *Knowledge and Practice Standards for Teachers of Reading*, go to http://www.interdys.org.

The International Reading Association and the **Council for Exceptional Children** have also published standards for instruction, although they are not as specific as the ones discussed above. However, it would behoove you to examine these standards as well.[27]

RESPONSE TO INTERVENTION, A MULTI-TIER SYSTEM OF SUPPORT

The reauthorization of IDEA in 2004 includes provisions for schools to provide instructional interventions when students are not progressing in any subject. Such interventions should be implemented for a period of time before students can be referred for an evaluation to determine eligibility for special education services. The majority of recent research has concentrated on implementing RTI to address the needs of students who have difficulties in reading, mathematics, and behavior.

There are two major purposes of RTI:

1. Prevent educational failure by intervening early, as soon as students experience difficulties learning.
2. Consider how students respond to interventions when referring them for special education services.

RTI integrates assessment and intervention within a school-wide, multitiered instructional system to maximize student achievement and reduce behavior problems. RTI suggests that schools identify students at risk for poor learning outcomes, monitor student progress, provide evidence-based interventions, and adjust the intensity and nature of those interventions depending on a student's responsiveness. RTI may be used as part of the determination process for specific learning disabilities as outlined by the National Center on Response to Intervention.[28] In other words, RTI is a multitier instructional framework that offers a system for early detection and prevention of academic failure and behavioral difficulties.

RTI: A Preventive Framework

Historically, schools have waited until around third grade to evaluate, diagnose, and begin remedial instruction with struggling learners. When a RTI model is implemented, teachers are expected to immediately identify students who are struggling to learn and need intervention instruction. Teachers also decide which specific types of intervention or remediation should be used. Rather than waiting until students begin to experience failure, RTI ensures that schools catch students before they start to fall behind. The RTI process typically begins in kindergarten as soon as students enter school.

The Essential Components of RTI

RTI consists of the following components:

1. A school-wide, multilevel instructional system for preventing school failure that includes the following elements or levels of instruction or support. Most people refer to these levels as tiers:

   • Primary (Tier 1): The general education classroom implementing the core instructional program.

> ## BOX 15.1.
>
> RTI is a multilevel instructional framework aimed at improving outcomes for *all* students.
>
> RTI is preventive and provides immediate support to students who are at risk for poor learning outcomes.
>
> RTI begins in the general education classroom with excellent core instruction.
>
> RTI may be a component of a comprehensive evaluation for students with learning disabilities.

- Secondary (Tier 2): Small group interventions, usually provided by the general classroom teacher in the classroom
- Tertiary (Tier 3): Small group interventions, usually provided by a specialist

2. Universal screening: All students are assessed two or three times a year.
3. Progress monitoring: The progress of all students is monitored several times a year; the progress of those at risk is monitored more frequently.
4. Instruction: Evidence-based instruction is required.
5. Movement within the multilevel system: The goal is to ensure all students are successful in the general education curriculum; students may move between tiered levels of instruction as their progress indicates.
6. Disability identification (in accordance with state law): Schools have the option of using data about how students respond to instruction as part of the special education referral and assessment process.

MULTILEVEL SYSTEM FOR PREVENTION

Figure 15.3 demonstrates the progression of support across the multilevel prevention system. The image of this triangle is what most people envision when they think of RTI. It represents the instructional levels or tiers available to students, which is only one component or aspect of RTI.

There is a second graphic used by the National Response to Intervention Center (Figure 15.4).[29] This graphic incorporates all of the essential components of RTI and is helpful in understanding the "big picture."

The first or primary level (Tier 1) is typically designed around a 90-minute reading block. The instruction for the grades K–3 is systematic and explicit in the essential elements of reading that are identified in the National Reading Panel Report (2000): phonological awareness, phonics, vocabulary, fluency, and comprehension strategy instruction.[30]

The instructional focus for the grades 4–5 of first-level prevention, Tier 1 (Figure 15.5), is an expansion of the core instruction from the earlier grades and includes reading instruction in the content areas and disciplinary literacy.[31]

As discussed in this text, it is important to provide differentiated instruction based on assessment data during Tier 1 core instruction so that all students master the core reading skills. Teachers provide effective differentiated instruction in Tier 1 by using various grouping formats, including whole class, independent study, and small group instruction with high levels of student engagement throughout the reading block (the uninterrupted time allotted for reading).

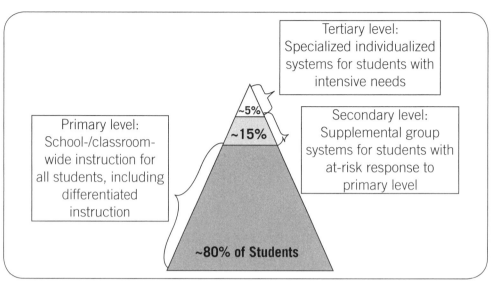

Figure 15.3. Multilevel prevention system. (From National Center on Response to Intervention. [2010]. *What is RTI? [PPT]*. Washington, DC: U.S. Department of Education, Office of Special Education Programs, National Center on Response to Intervention.)

Universal screening is conducted with all students typically two or three times per year, fall and winter, and sometimes in the spring. Some districts call these periodic assessments "benchmark assessments." It is important to screen not just the at-risk students but all students to ensure that they are progressing as expected to prevent learning difficulties. Results of the screening measures indicate which students are at risk for reading difficulties and also provide a baseline from which instructional recommendations can be made.

Common screening measures include DIBELS NEXT, AIMSWeb, and TPRI.[32]

Progress monitoring assessments are also a critical component of the RTI or a multitier system of support. Students in Tier 2 and Tier 3 may have their progress monitored every week or two. For Tier 1 students, progress monitoring may take place one time per month. The purpose of progress monitoring is to help you know if what you are teaching and the way you

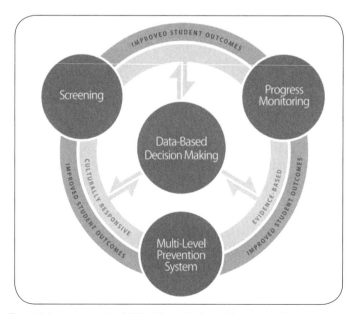

Figure 15.4. Essential components of RTI. (From National Center on Response to Intervention. [2010]. *What is RTI?* [PPT]. Washington, DC: U.S. Department of Education, Office of Special Education Programs, National Center on Response to Intervention.)

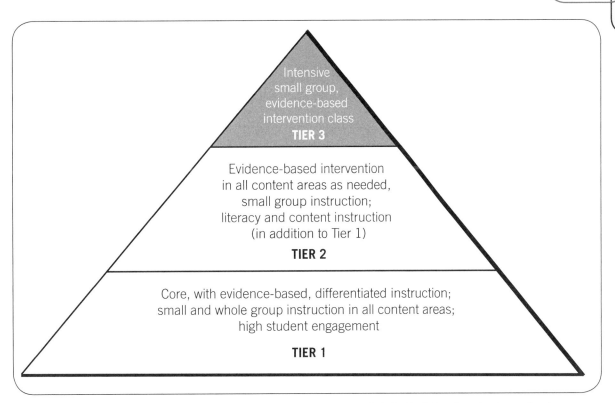

Intensive
small group,
evidence-based
intervention class
TIER 3

Evidence-based intervention
in all content areas as needed,
small group instruction;
literacy and content instruction
(in addition to Tier 1)
TIER 2

Core, with evidence-based, differentiated instruction;
small and whole group instruction in all content areas;
high student engagement
TIER 1

Figure 15.5. Tiered instruction and intervention for Grade 4–5. (From ***"RTI for Early Readers: Implementing Common Core Standards in Your K-5 RTI"*** Copyright 2011 by LRP Publications, P.O. Box 24668, West Palm Beach, FL 33416-4668. All rights reserved. For more information on this or other products published by LRP Publications, please call 1-800-341-7874 or visit our website at: www.shoplrp.com; reprinted by permission.)

are teaching is effective. If your students are not making the expected progress, that is, they are not progressing toward their target goal, you must change or alter your teaching approach.

The next level, Tier 2 or secondary level (see Figure 15.5), is supplemental to the primary level. This means that the secondary level does not replace the primary level; rather, it is in addition to the core instruction. The secondary level (Tier 2) is provided only for those students who are not making expected progress in Tier 1.

In general, approximately 10%–15% of students may need supplemental, small group intervention instruction. Ten percent to 15% is a global estimate; in your school, the numbers may be higher or lower. The number of students needing Tier 2 instruction will depend on the overall level of need in your school. Factors such as economic disadvantage, ethnic representation, number of English language learners, and students with disabilities contribute to the percentages expected in each level of intervention. However, the most important determinant of the number of students who may need intervention instruction is the quality of the core instructional program in the general education class (Tier 1). If your school has more than 15% of students who are not progressing and need Tier 2 or Tier 3 support, your core instruction should be examined and strengthened.

Intervention programs for students in Tier 2 are selected based on individual student need. There are two models to determine the type of instruction provided: The Problem Solving Model and the Standard Treatment Protocol Model.

The Problem Solving Model considers the needs of an individual student and plans instruction based on those needs. The Standard Treatment Protocol Model utilizes a research-based published program that is selected by the school to address specific skills needed by most students with reading difficulties.

Instruction for students in Tier 2 is typically provided by the general education classroom teacher and takes place in the classroom. Tier 2 instruction is provided in a small group (three to six students) for 20–30 minutes 4 or 5 days a week.

BOX 15.2. CHARACTERISTICS OF RTI LEVELS

PRIMARY LEVEL: Tier 1

Who: All students

Instructional content: District curriculum and instructional practices that are evidence-based; aligned with state, district, or national standards; incorporate differentiated instruction

Setting: General education classroom

Assessments: Screening, continuous progress monitoring, and outcome measures

The core curriculum is

- Evidence-based
- Aligned with state and national standards
- Well articulated both across grades levels (vertical) and within grade levels (horizontal)
- Differentiated to address the varied needs of students
- Supported by school-based professional development

SECONDARY LEVEL: Tier 2

Who: Students identified through screening as at risk for poor learning outcomes

Instructional content: Targeted, supplemental instruction delivered to small groups, in addition to Tier I core instruction

Setting: General education classroom or other general education location within the school

Assessments: Progress monitoring, diagnostic

Interventions are

- Evidence-based, supported by research for the target population
- Well-defined
- Aligned with the core curriculum
- Implemented using standard protocol procedures
- Provided in teacher-led small groups
- In addition to the core curriculum

TERTIARY LEVEL: Tier 3

Who: Students who have not responded to primary or secondary level prevention

Instructional content: Intensive, supplemental instruction delivered to small groups or individually

Setting: General education classroom or other general education location within the school (some districts may consider pull out)

Assessments: Progress monitoring, diagnostic

Interventions are

- Evidence-based, supported by research for the target population
- Implemented using standard protocol
- More intense than secondary and continuously individualized based on student needs
- Monitored regularly based on established learning trajectories
- In addition to the core curriculum

Supplemental reading intervention programs are frequently used in both Tier 2 and Tier 3 intervention. Although many core reading programs purport to provide an additional focus for Tier 2 intervention, this intervention support is typically insufficient for many Tier 2 students. Teachers often seek outside resources to provide the level of intensive, systematic instruction and repeated practice required by students in both Tiers 2 and 3. You may review evaluations of several supplemental programs at http://www.fcrr.org/FCRRReports/CReportsCS.aspx?rep=supp, http://ies.ed.gov/ncee/wwc/reports/Topic.aspx?tid=01, and http://ies.ed.gov/ncee/wwc/reports/topic.aspx?tid=15

For grades 4–5, Tier 2 intervention should focus on both literacy and content instruction. This intervention should be incorporated into each content class or period throughout the day. Gibbs suggests that as students are working in their collaborative groups, teachers can use the results of data to pull homogeneous or heterogeneous groups for focused small-group Tier 2 instruction.[33] In homogeneous groups, teachers work to strengthen the common foundation skills the students lack and to provide scaffolding for content literacy and background knowledge.

You may select a heterogeneous grouping format, matching a stronger reader with one who is not as strong, to engage in peer-assisted learning activities (PALS).[34] Gibbs suggests that teachers use this format (i.e., collaborative and small-group learning groups with both heterogeneous and homogeneous grouping) throughout the day in grades 4–5 so that Tier 2 students will receive the literacy and academic support they need in all content areas.[35]

The top level of the triangle (pyramid), or the Tertiary Level (Tier 3), is also considered supplemental instruction to primary instruction (see Figure 15.5). It includes specialized, individualized systems for students with intensive needs. Tier 3 typically involves small-group instruction of one to three students who are significantly behind their peers, 5 days a week. The format is the same for grades K–5. As with the other levels, the intervention program must be research-based and must be presented in the exact way the publisher intended. Any deviation from the publishers' directions will result in the program potentially being unsuccessful with your students. When teachers follow the directives of the program with precision, we call this fidelity or integrity of implementation. Integrity of implementation is critical for your students' success when you are using a research-based program for intervention.

It is especially critical for Tier 3 students that their individual learning strengths and weaknesses be identified and targeted. For example, some students will need intervention focused at the word level while others may have word level skills in place and need focused instruction in vocabulary and comprehension. Although some of this information may be obtained through screening assessments, it is more likely that a diagnostic measure will need to be given to clarify the precise area of need (see Gibbs, 2011, for a list of diagnostic measures appropriate for each of the five elements of reading).[36]

WHAT TEACHERS NEED TO KNOW ABOUT DATA-BASED INSTRUCTION

Data, from screening and progress monitoring measures and other classroom assessment results, guide decisions about the level of instructional support needed for students to be successful. Remember, changing the intensity is a two-way street. In cases where students are responding well, teams may consider decreasing the instructional intensity. In cases where students are not responding or are not making adequate progress toward their goal, the team may consider increasing the intensity of the instruction. Sometimes, a different intervention may be needed, but that is not always the answer. If student data indicate a student is making some progress but not necessarily adequate progress, the data-based decision-making team may decide to change the intensity of support by manipulating one or more factors of the intervention, including the amount of time, the size of the group, and the explicitness of the instruction.

METHODS TO INCREASE THE INTENSITY OF INSTRUCTION

When your students are not making the expected rate of growth and are at risk for failing to reach their targeted goal or benchmark, you may need to increase the intensity of instruction. You can increase intensity of instruction in four ways.

1. **Duration:** The intensity can be increased by changing how long the student is receiving the intervention each time. For example, the intervention may be increased from 20 minutes a day to 40 minutes a day.
2. **Frequency:** The intensity may be strengthened by increasing the number of times a student participates in the intervention. For example, the delivery of the intervention may increase from three to five times a week or increase the number of times per day, from one to two times per day.
3. **Interventionist:** In some cases, the intensity may be increased by changing the interventionist. For example, some schools use para-educators to deliver supplemental interventions. The intensity of the intervention may be changed by using a content specialist, a teacher trained as reading specialist.
4. **Group size:** Consider decreasing the number of students participating in the intervention group. For example, the instructional team may decide to reduce the group size from five to two students in order to provide the students more direct instruction and opportunities to respond.

In cases where the current intervention is believed to be ineffective for the student, the team may consider selecting a different intervention program.[37]

THE TEACHER'S ROLE IN RTI

The teacher is the most important member of the instructional team. It is up to the teacher to notice which students are not progressing as expected, to conduct the initial screening assessments, and to provide the initial instruction. Specifically, the teacher is responsible for the following:

- Delivering the core instructional program with fidelity and integrity
- Ensuring that cultural, linguistic, and socioeconomic factors are considered and that cultural diversity is respected when selecting instructional materials
- Selecting and implementing evidence-based interventions with fidelity and integrity[38]
- Collaborating with the instructional leadership team to regularly review progress monitoring data and to make decisions about any modifications that have to be made to ensure all students are progressing

SUMMARY

As this chapter demonstrates, there are numerous federal and state policies, standards, and initiatives that influence what happens in schools. Here are a few suggestions to help you synthesize this information.

- Pay attention to the legislation reauthorizing ESEA; there will be opportunities for you to learn more about it.
- Be aware of standards for teaching. They are developed by experts in the field to help teachers plan and deliver instruction so that students are successful. You must address the standards of your state; other sets of standards will support your instruction.
- Collaborate with your colleagues and administrators to ensure you make wise decisions about providing appropriate and timely interventions to students at risk for academic difficulties.
- RTI is the responsibility of everyone in the school.
- Refer to the additional resources in Appendix C.

ENDNOTES

1. Common Core State Standards, English Language Arts Standards and Literacy in History/Social Studies, Science, and Technical Subjects. Reprinted from http://www.corestandards.org © Copyright 2010. National Governors Association Center for Best Practices and Council of Chief State School Officers. All rights reserved.

2. No Child Left Behind Act of 2001, PL 107-110, 115 Stat. 1425, 20 U.S.C. §6301 *et seq.*

3. Civil Rights Act of 1964, PL 88-352, 78 Stat. 241. 42 U.S.C., Ch. 21.

4. President Lyndon Johnson's State of the Union Address, Proposing the Great Society, the War on Poverty, January, 4, 1965. http://www.infoplease.com/ipa/A0900149.html

5. Title I, http://www2.ed.gov/legislation/ESEA02/pg1.html

6. NCLB quote. (2001), http://georgewbush.whitehouse.archives.gov/news/releases/2002/0120020108-1.html

7. NCLB Creation, No Child Left Behind Act of 2001, PL 107-110, 115 Stat. 1425, 20 U.S.C. §§ 6301 et seq.

8. Reading Excellence Act, Reading Excellence Initiative Reading Excellence Act, PL 105-277, 112 Stat. 2681-337, 2681-393, 20 U. S. C. §§ 6661a *et seq.*

9. No Child Left Behind Act of 2001, PL 107-110, 115 Stat. 1425, 20 U.S.C. §§ 6301 *et seq.*

10. AYP, Annual Yearly Progress. Term came from The No Child Left Behind Act of 2001, Sec. 1111 (b) (F), requires that "each state shall establish a timeline for adequate yearly progress."

11. No Child Left Behind Act of 2001, PL 107-110, 115 Stat. 1425, 20 U.S.C. §§ 6301 et seq.

12. New ESEA, ESEA Elementary and Secondary Education Act of 1965, PL 89-10, 20 U.S.C. §§ 241 et seq.

13. ESEA blueprint, http://www2.ed.gov/policy/elsec/leg/blueprint/blueprint.pdf

14. ESEA Accountability, ESEA blueprint, http://www2.ed.gov/policy/elsec/leg/blueprint/blueprint.pdf

15. Common Core State Standards, English Language Arts Standards and Literacy in History/Social Studies, Science, and Technical Subjects, "Reprinted from http://www.corestandards.org. © Copyright 2010. National Governors Association Center for Best Practices and Council of Chief State School Officers.

16. Six states have not adopted CCSS as of September 3, 2011: Alaska, Nebraska, Minnesota, Montana, Texas, and Virginia.

17 Common Core State Standards, English Language Arts Standards and Literacy in History/Social Studies, Science, and Technical Subjects, "Reprinted from http://www.corestandards.org. © Copyright 2010. National Governors Association Center for Best Practices and Council of Chief State School Officers.

18. Common Core State Standards, English Language Art Standards, Anchor Standards, College and Career Readiness Anchor Standards for Reading; http://www.corestandards.org/the-standards/english-language-arts-standards/anchor-standards/college-and-career-readiness-anchor-standards-for-reading/ © Copyright 2010. National Governors Association Center for Best Practices and Council of Chief State School Officers. All rights reserved.

19. Common Core State Standards, English Language Arts Standards, Reading: Foundational Skills, Introduction: http://www.corestandards.org/the-standards/english-language-arts-standards/reading-foundational-skills/introduction/ © Copyright 2010. National Governors Association Center for Best Practices and Council of Chief State School Officers.

20. The Texas College & Career Readiness Standards, Texas CCRS Texas Higher Education Coordinating Board (2008). Available at http://www.thecb.state.tx.us/collegereadiness/crs.pdf

21. Interstate Teacher Assessment and Support Consortium (InTASC) Model Core Teacher Standards. Retrieved on May 1, 2011 from http://www.ccsso.org/resources/programs/interstate_teacher_assessment_consortium_(intasc).html

22. Common Core State Standards, English Language Arts Standards, Reading: Foundational Skills, Introduction: http://www.corestandards.org/the-standards/english-language-arts-standards/reading-foundational-skills/introduction/ © Copyright 2010. National Governors Association Center for Best Practices and Council of Chief State School Officers. Retrieved on May 1, 2011.

23. The Internaltional Dyslexia Association (2010). Knoweldge and practic standards for teachers of reading, Baltimore: The International Dyslexia Association. Available from http://www.interdys.org/Standards.htm

24. Internaltional Dyslexia Association (2010). Knowledge and practic standards for teachers of reading, Baltimore: The International Dyslexia Association. Availabe from http://www.interdys.org/Standards.htm

25. The Internaltional Dyslexia Association (2010). Knoweldge and practic standards for teachers of reading, Baltimore: The International Dyslexia Association. Availabe from http://www.interdys.org/Standards.htm, p.2.

26. Perspectives on Langue and Literacy, Fall, 2010. The International Dyslexia Association, http://www.onlinedigeditions.com/publication/?i=48994

27. Standards for Reading Professionals - Revised 2010. International Reading Association Standards available for download at http://www.reading.org/General/CurrentResearch/Standards/ProfessionalStandards2010.aspx
IDA Standards, The International Dyslexia Association (2010). Knowledge and practice standards for teachers of reading. Baltimore, MD: The International Dyslexia Association. Standards available for download from http://www.interdys.org/Standards.htm
The Council for Exceptional Children, (2009). What every special educator must know: Ethics, standards, and guidelines (6th Ed.) Arlington, VA: Author. Standards available for download at http://www.cec.sped.org/Content/NavigationMenu/ProfessionalDevelopment/ProfessionalStandards/TeacherPrepStandards/default.htm

28. National Center on RTI.

29. National center for response to intervention graphic.

30. NRP, National Reading Panel, (2000).

31. Gibbs (2011).

32. AIMSweb, http://www.aimsweb.com/; http://DIBELS.uoregon.edu/; http://TPRI www.tpri.com

33. Gibbs (2011).

34. PALS, Peer Assisted Learning Strategies (2007), http://kc.vanderbilt.edu/pals

35. Gibbs (2011).
36. Gibbs (2011).
37. Florida Center for Reading Research, http://www.fcrr.org/fcrrreports/guides/CCRP.pdf University of Oregon, http://oregonreadingfirst.uoregon.edu/inst_curr_review_core.html

38. International Reading Association: hpp://www.reading.org/General/Publications/Books/Supplemental Content/BK707_SUPPLEMENT.aspx

REFERENCES

AIMSweb, http://www.aimsweb.com/

AYP—Annual Yearly Progress, http://www2.ed.gov/nclb/accountability/ayp/edpicks.jhtml

Civil Rights Act of 1964, PL 88-352, 78 Stat. 241, 42 U.S.C. ch 21. http://finduslaw.com/civil_rights_act_of_1964_cra_title_vii_equal_employment_opportunities _42_us_code_chapter_21

The Common Core State Standards Initiative. (2010). http://www.corestandards.org/ National Governors Center for Best Practices and Council of Chief State School Officers.

The Council for Exceptional Children, (2009). What every special educator must know: Ethics, standards, and guidelines (6th Ed.) Arlington, VA: Author. Standards can be downloaded at http://www.cec.sped.org/Content/NavigationMenu/ProfessionalDevelopment/ProfessionalStandards/TeacherPrepStandards/default.htm

Dewitz, P., Leahy, S.B., Jones, J. & Sullivan P. M. (2010). *The essential guide to selecting and using core reading programs*, The International Reading Association, Newark: NJ.

Dynamic Measurement Group. (2010). DIBELS Next (7th ed.). Eugene, OR: Author. http://dibels.uoregon.edu/

Elementary and Secondary Education Act of 1965, PL 89-10, 20 U.S.C. §§ 241 *et seq.*

ESEA blueprint, http://www2.ed.gov/policy/elsec/leg/blueprint/blueprint.pdf

Florida Center for Reading Research, http://www.fcrr.org/FCRR?CReportsCS.aspx?

Gibbs, D.P. (2011). RTI for early readers: Implementing Common Core Standards in your K–5 RTI Model. Horsham, PA: LRP Publications.

IES What Works Clearinghouse, U.S. Department of Education Institute of Education Sciences, http://ies.ed.gov/ncee/wwc/reports/Topics.aspx?tid=01

IES What Works Clearinghouse, U.S. Department of Education Institute of Education Sciences http://ies.ed.gov/ncee/wwc/reports/Topics.aspx?tid=15

IES What Works Clearinghouse, U.S. Department of Education Institute of Education Sciences, http://ies.ed.gov/ncee/wwc/publications_reviews.aspx

Individuals with Disabilities Education Improvement Act (IDEA) of 2004, PL 108-446, 20 U.S.C. §§ 1400 *et seq.*

Interstate Teacher Assessment and Support Consortium (InTASC). Model Core Teacher Standards, INTASC standards. Retrieved on May 1, 2011 from http://www.ccsso.org/resources/programs/interstate_teacher_assessment_consortium_(intasc).html

National Center on Response to Intervention, http://www.rti4 success.org/

National Reading Panel. (2000, April). *Report of the National Reading Panel: Teaching children to read*. Washington, DC: National Institute of Child Health and Human Development, National Institute of Health, U.S. Department of Health and Human Services (NIH Publication No. 00-4769). Washington, DC: U.S. Government Printing Office. http://www.nationalreadingpanel.org/

NCLB legislation, Bush quote. (2001). http://georgewbush.whitehouse.archives.gov/news/releases/2002/01/20020108-1.html

No Child Left Behind Act of 2001, PL 107-110, 115 Stat. 1425, 20 U.S.C. §§ 6301 *et seq.*

Peer Assisted Learning Strategies (PALS). (2007). http://kc.vanderbilt.edu/pals/

Reading Excellence Initiative Reading Excellence Act, PL 105-277, 112 Stat. 2681-337, 2681-393, 20 U. S. C. §§ 6661a *et seq.*

Standards for Reading Professionals - Revised 2010. International Reading Association Standards available for download at http://www.reading.org/General/CurrentResearch/Standards/ProfessionalStandards2010. aspx

The International Dyslexia Association. (2010). Knowledge and practice standards for teachers of reading. Baltimore: The International Dyslexia Association. Available from http://www.interdys.org/Standards.htm

Title 1, http:// www2.ed.gov/legislation/ESEA02/pg1.html

Texas Higher Education Coordinating Board (2008). The Texas College & Career Readiness Standards. Available at http://www.thecb.state.tx.us/collegereadiness/crs.pdf

Texas Primary Reading Inventory, http://www.tpri.org/ (and the Tejas LEE at http://www.tejaslee.org/).

War on Poverty, Lyndon Johnson's State of the Union Address, Proposing the "Great Society" Program, January 4, 1965, http://www.infoplease.com/ipa/A0900149.html

16

Putting It All Together: Becoming an Effective Literacy Teacher

by Heather A. Haynes

By now, you have had many opportunities to apply the research and lessons from the previous chapters. You have utilized resources, web sites, and readings suggested in this book. You have examined oral language, writing, spelling, and each of the five critical components of reading. You have explored opportunities to administer assessments. You have planned instruction addressing each of the critical components of reading instruction, applied your learning through tutoring, and created a tool kit of effective instructional strategies and materials. All in all, after working your way through this book, you have read and applied knowledge in meaningful, content-related chunks. Now what? It is time to put it *all* together!

This chapter provides an opportunity for you to reflect, synthesize your learning, and plan for classroom instruction and management. You will incorporate your knowledge of effective assessment and instruction of reading for a diverse group of students in Pre-K–6 classrooms by engaging in thoughtful reading of and reflection upon a realistic instructional case study.

As a preservice educator, you most likely have concerns about planning and implementing the 90-minute reading block providing core reading instruction for all students. You may be asking yourself a number of questions including:

1. How can I fit instruction in *all* of the components of reading and writing instruction into 90 minutes or 120 minutes when writing instruction is included?
2. How can I best address *each* of my students' needs and differentiate my instruction?
3. What tools exist to support me in planning for universal, whole class, core instruction, and targeted, small-group literacy instruction?
4. How do I provide intervention instruction for those who need additional scaffolding, including those who are learning English and those who have reading difficulties?
5. How do I accelerate instruction for advanced learners?

Objectives: After studying this chapter you will be able to do the following:

1. Complete activities reflecting on the case study, the instruction provided, and other facets of literacy instruction illustrated.
2. Critique and improve the instructional examples provided in the case study.
3. Make connections to the content of previous chapters.
4. Formulate a system to provide explicit, systematic instruction, provide opportunities for practice, and regularly monitor the progress of your students.
5. Plan a system to manage your classroom in a safe, organized, efficient, and positive manner.

To address these questions, a first-grade classroom case study is utilized. The students in this classroom case study reflect a wide range of skills and abilities. Using a case study is a method for illustrating how a representative teacher incorporates the critical components of reading and writing in a real classroom (The case study is fictional and created for this text).

This chapter provides opportunities for reflection on three practices crucial for effective and efficient instruction: 1) use of effective instructional strategies, validated by evidence-based research; 2) differentiation of instruction for students who need intensive scaffolding, are English language learners, or who are accelerated; and 3) implementation of the features of effective instruction.

PUTTING IT ALL TOGETHER

Louisa Moats reminds us that teaching reading really is like rocket science.[1] Educators have to be thoughtful about myriad factors to help students acquire the skills and knowledge to become successful, life-long readers and learners. You may recall the figure from Chapter 2 illustrating all of the skills captured and woven together to create a successful reader. In her illustration, Hollis Scarborough depicts the elements of reading, woven like strands into a rope, that produce skilled reading (Figure 16.1).[2]

On the left side of the illustration, the individual rope strands represent the discrete skills required for reading and are loosely woven together. As the skills develop, the strands become more tightly woven together. This indicates that the mature reader's skills and understanding of the critical components are integrated, becoming increasingly automatic and more strategic. The end result is fluent comprehension of text. This graphic illustrates the complexity involved in becoming a skilled reader. For a teacher to address the discrete skills and weave them together for students necessitates strategic planning. Planning ensures that instruction in all critical components is addressed and that opportunities for differentiated and targeted instruction are provided.

As you read the case study, notice how the features of effective instruction and the critical components of reading are interrelated. The following practices are also illustrated, to varying degrees, in this case study:

1. Differentiation, adaptations, and modifications of instruction for a diverse group of students with a range of skill levels

2. Multiple opportunities for students to practice their new learning

3. Effective techniques for managing the classroom, including descriptions of what students are doing while the teacher works with small groups

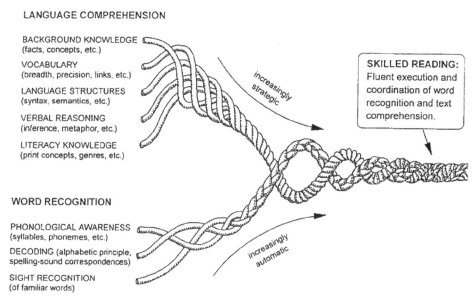

Figure 16.1. Scarborough's rope. (Republished by permission of Guilford Press, from Scarborough, H. [2001]. Connecting early language and literacy to later reading disabilities: Evidence, theory, and practice. In S.B. Neiman & D.K. Dickinson [Eds.], *Handbook of early literacy research* [pp. 97–110]; permission conveyed through Copyright Clearance Center, Inc.)

CASE STUDY—FIRST-GRADE CLASSROOM

Ms. Jenkins' first-grade class has 20 students. It is January, and Ms. Jenkins has just completed the middle-of-the year assessments. The results are presented in Table 16.1. The descriptive information and data to create such a table are available from a variety of sources including screening and diagnostic assessments, standardized test information from the previous year, teacher-created assessments, curriculum-based measures, and other formal and informal professional observations and assessments. The specific assessments reflected in this case study are provided in Table 16.2.

If a student is still developing in a skill area Ms. Jenkins indicates "IN" for instruction needed. If the student is meeting benchmarks and goals in an area, she indicates "B" for benchmark. (It is important to note Ms. Jenkins will also compile a similar chart around the end of the school year using updated data.) She continually updates the information in Table 16.1 throughout the spring using progress monitoring and formal and informal assessment data. (Note that each assessment system uses its own coding system.)

Ms. Jenkins realizes she must provide scaffolded instruction throughout the semester. She is aware of the needs of students who are acquiring English as a second language, students who need accelerated instruction, and students who are at risk or have qualified for special education support. She is part of a multidisciplinary team and shares and seeks information in collaborative planning meetings with other educators to coordinate and plan supports and instruction for her students. Currently in her class there is one student who is an English language learner, one student who will benefit from accelerated instruction, and one student receiving special education support and services (specific learning disability). It is important to note that the student in Ms. Jenkins class who qualifies for special education support and services receives all instruction in the general education classroom.

Table 16.1.   Ms. Jenkins' student assessment data

Ms. Jenkins' class: middle of the year

Student	Phonemic awareness	Phonics	Fluency (WCPM goal: 40)	Comprehension	Vocabulary	Oral language	Written expression
A.P.	IN	IN	17	B	IN	B	IN
A.V.	B	B	60	B	B	B	B
B.F.	B	B	65	IN	IN	B	IN
B.K.	B	B	67	B	B	B	B
C.S.	B	IN	37	B	B	B	IN
D.I.	B	IN	34	IN	B	B	IN
F.C.	B	B	105	B	B	B	B
H.S.	IN	IN	27	B	B	B	B
J.K.	B	B	75	B	B	B	B
K.H.	B	B	70	B	B	B	B
K.J.	B	B	40	B	B	B	IN
M.C.	B	B	42	IN	B	B	B
M.K.	B	B	38	B	IN	B	B
M.V.	B	B	51	B	B	B	B
P.H.	B	IN	37	B	B	B	B
R.G.	B	B	18	IN	IN	B	IN
R.R.	B	B	43	B	B	B	B
S.A.	B	B	49	B	B	B	B
S.V.	IN	IN	22	IN	IN	IN	IN
T.S.	B	IN	12	IN	IN	IN	IN

Note: The codes "IN" and "B" are used for this case study. Most assessments have their own codes.
Key: WCPM, words correct per minute; IN, instruction needed; B, benchmark.

Table 16.2.   Assessments used in case study

PA	AIMSweb, Test of Early Literacy: Phonemic Segmentation
	AIMSweb, Test of Early Literacy: Letter Sound Fluency
	Dynamic Indicators of Basic Early Literacy Skills (DIBELS): Initial Sound Fluency
Phonics	Quick Phonics Screener
	Dynamic Indicators of Basic Early Literacy Skills (DIBELS): Nonsense Word Fluency
Fluency	Curriculum Based Measurement in Reading (CBM-R): Passage Reading Fluency
Comprehension	Curriculum Based Measurement in Reading: (CBM-R): Maze Fluency
	Oral and Written Language Scales (OWLS): Listening Comprehension
Vocabulary	Informal assessment by teacher
Oral language and written expression	Informal assessment by teacher
	Oral and Written Language Scales (OWLS): Oral Expression
	Oral and Written Language Scales (OWLS): Written Expression

Key: PA, phonemic awareness.

The assessments Ms. Jenkins uses with her students are listed in Table 16.2. Note that there are several excellent assessments from which teachers and schools can select.

Ms. Jenkins uses data and professional judgment to determine a student's level of knowledge or skill mastery. She does not want to let any student fall through the cracks. Before the second semester of school begins, Ms. Jenkins formulates her literacy instructional plans using her core reading program. The school has a 90-minute block for literacy instruction with an additional 30 minutes for writing instruction. This time is uninterrupted, and all 20 students are present for this comprehensive reading block. Ms. Jenkins begins by completing a daily schedule with designated times for each critical component of reading. Process writing instruction occurs later in the day. Table 16.3 displays the general weekly lesson plan she completed.

In completing her general plan, Ms. Jenkins has a basic idea of what she will be teaching based on the scope and sequence provided by her district or as part of a comprehensive core literacy program adopted by her school. She purposefully utilizes a variety of flexible grouping formats, using student assessment data to target her instruction. All of the critical reading components are addressed in the general plan, and she plans a timeframe for the instruction. The time allotments may change, depending on the daily lesson and content.

Once her general plan is determined, Ms. Jenkins creates daily lesson plans. The plans incorporate specific instructional decisions based on the needs of the students in her class. Ms. Jenkins again refers to the data in Table 16.1. She determines the instructional focus and the routines for each day and for each component. For many teachers, Monday is often a full day of instruction as new concepts, skills, and strategies are introduced. As a result, the time for small group instruction is often shortened on Mondays. Table 16.4 illustrates Ms. Jenkins' daily lesson plan on Monday.

Note that Ms. Jenkins allots 5–10 minutes for instruction in phonemic awareness. However, she does not necessarily teach it all at the same time. The instruction in phonemic awareness can be distributed throughout the day.

Ms. Jenkins allots 15–20 minutes for instruction in phonics daily. Phonics instruction represents a large part of the appropriate developmental instruction in the first grade. By allotting this time daily, she ensures that she provides enough time to review letters, connect them with sounds, and put them together to build, read, spell, and write words.

The next 40 minutes in Ms. Jenkins' daily schedule is allotted to introducing a story using read-alouds and think-alouds. She has thoughtfully selected a book that reinforces concepts and skills the students are learning. The first 20 minutes addresses explicit vocabulary instruction, and the remaining 20 minutes focuses on comprehension. Instruction in both vocabulary

Table 16.3.   First grade weekly lesson plan

	Monday	Tuesday	Wednesday	Thursday	Friday
10–20 minutes	• Explicit instruction in phonological awareness and phonics • Introduction of spelling patterns using explicit spelling routine	• Explicit instruction in phonological awareness and phonics • Spelling patterns using explicit spelling routine	• Explicit instruction in phonological awareness and phonics • Teaching of spelling patterns using explicit spelling routine	• Explicit instruction in phonological awareness and phonics • Teaching of spelling patterns using explicit spelling routine	• Explicit instruction in phonological awareness and phonics
20–25 minutes	• Introduction of story and vocabulary words from story	• Review vocabulary words from story	• Introduce new vocabulary words or review vocabulary words from story	• Review vocabulary words from story	• Assess vocabulary knowledge
20 minutes	• Read-alouds and think-alouds • Comprehension focus: making connections	• Read-alouds and think-alouds • Comprehension focus: making connections	• Read-alouds and think-alouds • Comprehension focus: making connections	• Read-alouds and think-alouds • Comprehension focus: making connections	• Read-alouds and think-alouds • Comprehension focus: making connections
45 minutes	• Small-group instruction and literacy workstations running concurrently • Progress monitoring of four students daily	• Small-group instruction and literacy workstations running concurrently • Progress monitoring of four students daily	• Small-group instruction and literacy workstations running concurrently • Progress monitoring of four students daily	• Small-group instruction and literacy workstations running concurrently • Progress monitoring of four students daily	• Small-group instruction and literacy workstations running concurrently • Progress monitoring of four students daily

From Vaughn Gross Center at The University of Texas at Austin. (2009). Module 13: Putting it all together. In *Foundations of reading instruction presentations and print files*. Austin, TX: Author; reprinted by permission.

and comprehension are connected to the context of the story. In addition, Ms. Jenkins points out sounds, letters, and words presented in the phonics lesson.

For 45 minutes daily, students rotate from centers to small-group instruction with the teacher. Ms. Jenkins has established and explicitly taught routines for the students rotating through workstations and small-group instruction.

Using positive behavior interventions and supports,[3] Ms. Jenkins directly teaches behavior and social skills. Both the explicit routines and a positive approach to behavior management impact student engagement, learning, and management. Poor classroom management can lead to student misbehavior and can interfere with your ability to provide effective and efficient instruction in reading.[4]

You may be wondering how Ms. Jenkins is able to conduct small-group reading lessons without being interrupted. How do her students know where to go and what to do as they move through the various literacy stations? Ms. Jenkins learned the hard way that students do not "just know" how to do workstations. She learned the value of having a set of specific routines, procedures, and expectations for the class. Before beginning workstations, Ms. Jenkins determined the answers to these critical questions:

1. What kind of rotation chart or system do I want to use?
2. How do I need to organize my classroom to include small group instruction and work-stations?
3. Which centers and workstations do I need to use or create?

Table 16.4.   First grade daily lesson plan, Monday

	Components of reading	
	Description	Instructional routine
5–10 minutes: Phonological awareness	**Objective (what):** Given words with three or four phonemes, students will blend and segment four out of five words independently. **How:** Students will use the kinesthetic scaffold of arm tapping to deepen understanding of the concept. **Accountability:** The teacher will monitor students' progress by observing as they practice the skill to decide who needs additional instruction. **Intervention:** In small groups, students will blend and segment words at the onset and time level, using the palm-up kinesthetic scaffold until they have achieved mastery. Then, the teacher will reteach phoneme blending and segmenting.	1. **Set an instructional focus:** blending and segmenting sounds in words. 2. Model, using a kinesthetic activity. 3. Have students do guided practice. 4. Have students practice independently while you check for understanding.
20 minutes: Phonics	**Objective:** After being introduced to the *ut* and *ug* phonograms, students will sort four words with the *ut* phonogram and four with the *ug* phonogram. **How:** Using an instructional routine, the teacher will introduce the new phonogram. **Accountability:** The teacher will monitor progress by having the students read and sort the words by the phonogram to decide who needs additional instructions. **Intervention:** In a small-group, the teacher will reteach the phonograms and model making words on a pocket chart as the students do it with magnetic letters and boards.	1. **Set an instructional focus:** learning about the word families *ut* and *ug*. 2. Introduce the new phonograms. 3. Make words with the new phonograms and previously learned letters, using magnetic letters and magnetic boards. 4. Do a word sort with students, using the newly introduced phonograms.
10 minutes: Fluency	**Objective:** After practicing the poem, the students will read aloud grade-appropriate text with appropriate phrasing. **How:** Using a grade-appropriate poem, the teacher will introduce the poem by modeling fluent and nonfluent reading, focusing on appropriate phrasing. **Accountability:** During small-group instruction, the teacher will listen to each student read the weekly poem, listening for appropriate phrasing. **Intervention:** During small-group instruction, the teacher will model fluent reading, using phrases written on sentence strips, so that all students can follow along. The teacher will model the finger-sweeping scaffold as he or she reads each phrase. The students will have an opportunity to practice the scaffold using the sentence strips.	1. **State your instructional focus:** "Today we'll be working on fluent reading. That means we are going to try to read like we talk." 2. Model fluent and nonfluent reading. 3. Read poem by echo reading with teacher guidance. 4. Read poem three times. 5. Poem goes into student's poetry folder. 6. Large poem will be placed in a literacy workstation toward the end of the week.
20–25 minutes: Vocabulary	**Objective:** Given three Tier 2 vocabulary words from the book *Chrysanthemum* by Kevin Henkes, students will give examples and nonexamples of the meaning of the words by using them in a sentence. **How:** The teacher will choose vocabulary words from *Chrysanthemum* to teach explicitly, using an instructional routine. **Accountability:** In a literacy workstation, students will write a sentence for each vocabulary word using one of the following sentence starters: • I was envious when… • I found it fascinating when… • The _____ was absolutely _____ because _____. **Intervention:** In a small group, the teacher will reteach the vocabulary words, using pictures and concrete examples that build on the students' background knowledge. Then, the teacher and students will write sentences together, using the same sentence starters.	1. **State your instructional focus:** "Today I will introduce several vocabulary words from the book *Chrysanthemum*." 2. Introduce the words. 3. Present student-friendly definitions. 4. Illustrate words with examples and nonexamples. 5. Check for understanding. 6. Review words.

(continued)

Components of reading

	Description	Instructional routine
20–25 minutes: Compre-hension	**Objective:** Students will discuss their personal connections to the main character of the book, *Chrysanthemum*, with a partner. **How:** The teacher will introduce the comprehension strategy of making connections through a read-aloud and think-aloud with the story *Chrysanthemum* by Kevin Henkes. **Accountability:** The teacher will incorporate think, turn, talk opportunities to listen to 10 students and determine whether they are making personal connections, based on their background knowledge. **Intervention:** In a small group, the teacher will model making connections between the story and the students' background knowledge by using concrete examples, for example: "Have you ever been at school and wanted to go home because other kids were not being nice to you?'	1. **State your instructional focus:** "While I am reading our story, I will think about my personal connections to the character. I will give you an opportunity to think, turn, and talk to share your personal connections to the characters in the story." 2. Define the strategy, how and when it is used, and how it helps with reading. 3. Use real-world examples. 4. Give students a touchstone, such as a hand gesture or visual representation, to help them remember the strategy. 5. Think aloud, using the strategy in a variety of contexts. 6. Provide meaningful opportunities during the reading for students to share their thinking. 7. Practice shared application with planned discussion prompts. 8. Scaffold practice, providing opportunities for students to use the strategy while reading with your support and monitoring. 9. Provide accountability measures for students when using the strategy independently.

From Vaughn Gross Center at The University of Texas at Austin. (2009). Module 13: Putting it all together. In *Foundations of reading instruction presentations and print files*. Austin, TX: Author; reprinted by permission.

4. How will students know when to move or rotate from a center or workstation?

5. What kind of signal or procedure do I want to use for students to indicate they need help or materials when they are in a workstation and I am teaching a small group?

6. How would I prefer students to clean and leave their center or workstation at the end of a session?

In addition to determining how she wanted to manage workstations, Ms. Jenkins had to explicitly teach and model these routines. It took Ms. Jenkins several weeks to teach her students how to work in small groups or independently. To teach them these skills, Ms. Jenkins follows the routine outlined in Figure 16.2.[5] She incorporated four phases of guided practice and modeling for learning and rotating through small-group instruction and workstations in her class

BOX 16.1.

Visit http://www.pbis.org to access information on how to establish positive expectations and support for academic and behavioral development and how to implement positive behavioral interventions and supports.

Phase 1—Teacher monitors

Whole group completes one activity.

Phase 2—Teacher monitors

Whole group is introduced to a basic menu of activities. The students are assigned two "must do" activities, and emphasis is placed on students working independently and learning to transition from whole group to independent work.

Phase 3—Teacher pulls one group

Whole group is provided two or more "must do" activities and are introduced to "may do" activities. During this phase, the teacher also pulls a small group.

Phase 4—Teacher pulls multiple groups

Whole group is provided two or more "must do" activities and one or more "may do" activities. During this phase, the teacher also pulls multiple small groups while students are in workstations or working independently.

Figure 16.2.   Four phases of introducing small-group instruction and workstations. (From Children's Learning Institute at The University of Texas Health Science Center at Houston. [2008]. *Small group instruction: Your first 21 days.* Austin, TX: University of Texas System and Texas Education Agency; adapted by permission.)

(see Figure 16.2). Each of the phases is important and should not be overlooked when initially starting small-group instruction and workstations. Also, anytime Ms. Jenkins makes significant changes to the routines or expectations, she returns to this process to ensure that her students know the revised routines and expectations. This is the best way to ensure that students are successful and engaged in independent workstations while she is providing targeted instruction in small groups.

Look back to Table 16.4. Each lesson has an objective and provides details about how that objective will be taught and assessed. Ms. Jenkins also notes possibilities for providing intervention instruction for her students who need more scaffolding. Ms. Jenkins has placed sticky

notes with the initials of targeted students in her planning documents. The student initials remind Ms. Jenkins which students need additional support or instruction in specific skills and/or strategies.

Ms. Jenkins utilizes a variety of grouping formats throughout the 90-minute reading time. Typically, she provides initial instruction for the whole group. With a perky pace, she reviews what was learned the previous week and teaches new skills. Many opportunities are provided for students to ask questions, practice, and apply new learning. Ms. Jenkins has established student partners and often directs them to "Think, Turn, and Talk"[6] about their new learning. She clearly explains each concept, models the appropriate skills, and is clear about what she expects the students to learn and to do. Students take turns reading to their partners, positively supporting one another with the expectations Ms. Jenkins provided. Ms. Jenkins monitors the classroom and partner work. She provides immediate, corrective feedback when appropriate.

Ms. Jenkins designs instructional activities in which her students can experience success and have multiple opportunities to practice a new skill by responding frequently. She is confident that her students' skills in phonemic awareness, phonics, oral language, comprehension skills, fluency, sight word recognition, vocabulary, spelling, and writing are progressing. Informal progress monitoring is ongoing and daily, and on Fridays Ms. Jenkins formally collects, reflects, and records the data on her instructional planning sheet shown in Table 16.1. This

Table 16.5. First-grade daily lesson plan small groups and workstations

	Day: Monday	
	Activities	Grouping
45–60 minutes: Teacher-led small-group instruction	Lesson plans for each group are differentiated, based on student need: • Groups A and B: phonological awareness instruction in blending and segmenting phonemes; phonics instruction in the short-*u* sound, spelled *u* • Group C: phonics instruction in *ug* and *ut* phonograms • Group D: phonics instruction in *ug* and *ut* phonograms • Group E: phonics instruction in blends (*sl, st, sm*) in initial position, using instructional-level text.	Groups are differentiated, based on student data.
45–60 minutes: Literacy workstations (concurrent with small-group instruction)	1. Making words center (phonics) 2. Independent reading (fluency; some students will read sight words or phrases independently) 3. Four-square vocabulary map center (vocabulary): use words from explicit vocabulary lesson to create a map 4. Partner reading with reading response (comprehension) 5. Poetry center (phonics and fluency)	Groups are heterogeneous, or comprise students of various needs and ability level, and activities are differentiated within workstations.

From Vaughn Gross Center at The University of Texas at Austin. (2009). Module 13: Putting it all together. In *Foundations of reading instruction presentations and print files*. Austin, TX: Author; reprinted by permission.

week, she collects data based on the phonemes listed in her daily lesson plans, phonograms *ut* and *ug*, and a 1-minute oral reading fluency passage. The skills Ms. Jenkins monitors vary from week to week and are selected based on her curriculum scope and sequence and the instructional needs of her students.

Ms. Jenkins incorporates flexible partner grouping during independent writing activities completed in small groups or in workstations outside the 90-minute reading block. This week, she is not introducing a new writing skill. Her students are continuing to practice a skill that was introduced last week. Her general schedule integrates instruction in writing into the first 10–20 minutes of class each day and the last 45 minutes of the day. Ms. Jenkins chooses to incorporate much of the guided and independent practice in writing into small group work and workstations. Oral language development continues to be purposefully integrated into her daily instruction. Table 16.5 provides details of how Ms. Jenkins further extends and integrates learning and practice of the critical components of reading throughout the day, based on student data.

Students work in workstations while Ms. Jenkins is instructing a small group of students at the "teacher's table." Ms. Jenkins plans this instruction and activities beforehand, using student data to ensure the activities planned target the needs of her students. In addition, she plans and prepares the necessary materials: Ms. Jenkins knows she must not waste even a minute of instructional time, so advanced planning is critical. Using her student data from Table 16.1, she is able to implement the grouping strategies she has selected. Ms. Jenkins uses a variety of grouping strategies and is purposeful in selecting students to work together in workstations.

We have now completed the case study of Ms. Jenkins and learned how she "puts it all together."

CASE STUDY REFLECTION AND ACTIVITIES

Reflect on the case study of Ms. Jenkins and her first-grade class using the chart in Figure 16.3. Consider this question, "Is there evidence in the case study that suggests Ms. Jenkins incorporated understandings from this book?" Place one X anywhere on the line in each area to indicate whether there was little evidence, some evidence, or extensive evidence of that specified component. Be sure to complete this reflective activity before reading on.

It is your task to consider how well Ms. Jenkins incorporates the features of effective instruction and the critical components of reading instruction. Also, consider what additional information might be helpful to collect about the students to assist in planning and progress monitoring. What recommendations can you suggest to improve or adapt instruction for students with varying levels of achievement?

Once you have completed the chart, proceed to the last section of the chapter, Application Assignments, and follow the instructions to review and make recommendations for how Ms. Jenkins could improve the instruction. Also, consider what you might do differently when teaching older students.

Additional Considerations

When planning, keep in mind that context is key. Effective instruction integrates all of the critical components of reading. The amount of time allotted for each critical component varies at the different grade levels and for individual students. Vaughn and Linan-Thompson[7] created a continuum of critical components of reading and when each should be taught. It is adapted in Table 16.6 to provide you an overview of the critical components of reading instruction typically taught in specific grade levels.

Table 16.6. Continuum of critical components

	Phonological awareness	Phonics	Fluency	Vocabulary	Comprehension
Kindergarten	Syllables Onset/rime Phoneme level	Print awareness Alphabetic principle Decoding Irregular word reading		Oral vocabulary	Listening comprehension Sense of story
First grade	Phonemic awareness	Alphabetic principle Decoding Irregular word reading Decodable text reading	Connected text (second semester)	Oral and reading vocabulary	Listening comprehension Reading comprehension
Second grade			Connected text	Reading vocabulary	Reading comprehension in a narrative and expository text
Third grade			Connected text	Reading vocabulary	Reading comprehension in a narrative and expository text
Fourth grade			Connected text	Reading vocabulary	Reading comprehension in a narrative and expository text
Fifth grade			Connected text	Reading vocabulary	Reading comprehension in a narrative and expository text
Sixth grade			Connected text	Reading vocabulary	Reading comprehension in a narrative and expository text

Source: Research-Based Methods of Reading Instruction Grades K–3 (p. 127), by Sharon Vaughn & Sylvia Linan-Thompson. Alexandria, VA: ASCD. © 2004 by ASCD. Adapted with permission. Learn more about ASCD at www.ascd.org

CONCLUSION

Becoming an efficient and effective reader is the goal for all students and is the result of instruction and practice in the critical components of reading. Effective educators use data to plan and provide instruction for students. They focus on high-quality instruction and the use of effective instructional strategies to teach the critical components of literacy. This type of high-quality, evidence-based instruction benefits all students, including students learning English as a second language, those receiving accelerated instruction, those needing scaffolded supports, and students identified as requiring special education services. By studying this text and completing the application assignments, you will become an effective literacy teacher.

APPLICATION ASSIGNMENTS

In-Class Assignments

1. With a partner, review the case study. You will need four pieces of paper, one for each topic. The topics are: (1) the five features of effective instruction, (2) oral language development, (3) the essential components of reading instruction, and (4) evidence-based writing instruction. For each topic, answer the three questions below, a, b, and c.

   a. What is the evidence that Ms. Jenkins incorporated the feature or component into her instruction? Use Figure 16.3 to guide your analysis.

   b. What other things could she do to address the feature or component more thoroughly?

   c. What are three ways she could adapt the instruction to meet the needs of students who are English language learners? Who have reading difficulties? Who are accelerated?

   For example, the first page will consider the five features of effective instruction: systematic instruction with scaffolding, explicit instruction with modeling, multiple opportunities for response, progress monitoring, and corrective feedback. With these features in mind, address the questions.

   Continue to address the same questions, focusing on oral language development, then the essential components of reading instruction (phonemic awareness, phonics, vocabulary, fluency, and comprehension), and lastly Ms. Jenkins' writing instruction. Refer to previous chapters to review the essential, evidence-based practices that should be emphasized in the classroom.

2. Using Table 16.1, determine which students Ms. Jenkins should target with more instruction in specific skills. List the initials of the students in the column under each category.

Homework Assignments

1. Read *Teaching Reading Is Rocket Science: What Expert Reading Teachers Should Know and Be able to Do* by Louisa Moats, 1999. It is available to download from http://www.readingrockets.org/guides/teaching-reading-rocket-science

2. Write a one-page essay discussing the major points of the article and what you have learned about those points. List the areas in which you feel you need to learn more and make a plan to do so!

Tutoring Assignments

Most likely, this is the last session you will have with your student(s). You should spend your last hour with your student completing the following:

1. Complete a post-test, using a different form of the assessment you used the first time you assessed your student. A final oral reading fluency assessment would be appropriate.

Circle the level at which each item was addressed in the case study. The levels are (1) little evidence, (2) some evidence, (3) extensive evidence.

Reflection Activity 1

Planning for literacy
    1   2   3

Feature of effective instruction: Explicit instruction
    1   2   3

Feature of effective instruction: Systematic instruction with scaffolding
    1   2   3

Feature of effective instruction: Frequent opportunities to practice
    1   2   3

Feature of effective instruction: Immediate corrective feedback
    1   2   3

Feature of effective instruction: Ongoing progress monitoring
    1   2   3

Oral language and listening skills development
    1   2   3

Phonemic awareness and alphabetic principle
    1   2   3

Phonics, structural analysis, and spelling
    1   2   3

Fluency
    1   2   3

Vocabulary
    1   2   3

Comprehension
    1   2   3

Written expression
    1   2   3

Reflects current laws, policies, standards, initiatives, and response to intervention
    1   2   3

Planning for literacy instruction
    1   2   3

Figure 16.3. Reflection activity. (*Source:* Heacox, 2009.)

2. Allow your student to count the number of words read and to complete the graph (see Chapter 8, page 133).
3. Re-read a favorite book with your student doing most of the reading.
4. Point out all the things your student has learned while working with you. Be specific. For example, specify which letter sounds were mastered, which comprehension strategies were used, and the new spelling patterns your student learned.
5. Play a favorite education game and again reinforce what your student has learned.

6. Thank your student for letting you work with him or her. Your students will always be your best teachers so appreciate them!

7. Give your student a written thank you note and provide one for the student's parents/caregiver, teacher, and principal. Be sure they know how much you appreciate the opportunity to work with them.

ENDNOTES

1. Moats (1999).
2. Scarborough (2001).
3. For more information on Positive Behavior Intervention & Support, go to the Department of Education, Office of Special Education Programs, Technical Assistance Center on Positive Behavioral Interventions & Supports: http://www.pbis.org/

4. Sugai & Horner (2008).
5. Children's Learning Institute at The University of Texas Health Science Center at Houston (2008).
6. Children's Learning Institute at The University of Texas Health Science Center at Houston (2009).
7. Vaughn & Linan-Thompson (2004).

REFERENCES

Children's Learning Institute at The University of Texas Health Science Center at Houston. (2008). *Ready, set, teach: A back to school module*. Austin, TX: University of Texas System and Texas Education Agency.

Children's Learning Institute at The University of Texas Health Science Center at Houston. (2009). *GK: Routines and teaching tools*. Austin, TX: University of Texas System and Texas Education Agency.

Hasbrouck, J. (2012). Fluency instruction. In M. Hougen & S.M. Smartt (Eds.), *Fundamentals of literacy assessment and instruction*. Baltimore: Paul H. Brookes Publishing Co.

Heacox, D. (2009). *Making differentiation a habit: How to ensure success in academically diverse classrooms*. Minneapolis, MN: Free Spirit Publishing Inc.

Henkes, K. (1991). Chrysanthemum. NY: Harper Collins Publisher.

Meadows Center for Preventing Education Risk. (2007). Foundations of reading instruction, Module 13, Handout 2. Austin, TX: Texas Education Agency/University of Texas System.

Moats, L. (1999). *Reading is rocket science: What expert teachers of reading should know and be able to do*. Washington, DC: American Federation of Teachers. Available to download at http://www.aft.org/pdfs/teachers/rocketscience0304.pdf

National Reading Panel. (2000). *Teaching children to read: An evidence-based assessment of the scientific research literature on reading and its implications for reading instruction*. Rockville, MD: National Institute of Child Health and Human Development.

Scarborough, H.S. (2001). Connecting early language and literacy to later reading (dis)abilities: Evidence, theory, and practice. In S. Neuman & D. Dickinson (Eds.), *Handbook for research in early literacy* (pp. 97—110). New York: Guilford Press.

Sugai, G., & Horner, R. (2008). What we need to know about preventing problem behavior in schools. *Exceptionality, 16*, 67—77.

Vaughn, S., & Linan-Thompson, S. (2004). *Reading: Effective instructional activities for elementary students*. Alexandria, VA: Association for Supervision and Curriculum Development.

17

Ten Tips to Becoming an Effective Teacher

by Martha C. Hougen
and Susan M. Smartt

The conclusion to this text provides 10 tips for becoming an effective teacher. The authors hope that these tips will accelerate your becoming an effective, efficacious teacher who enjoys a fulfilling and long career in education.

A veteran teacher defined the true test of an effective teacher: when you run into one of your former students and you ask, "What do you remember learning while in my class?" and the student quickly remembers two or three critical concepts. It is even better if the student adds this comment, "You were the hardest teacher I ever had, and you were my favorite."

We are hopeful that you learned many critical concepts while studying this text and tutoring your student. We realize that you have much more to learn about teaching literacy, and we trust you will endeavor to continue to improve your knowledge and expertise. There are, however, a few crucial concepts we hope you will remember for the duration of your teaching career and that will accelerate your becoming an effective teacher.

TEN TIPS TO BECOMING AN EFFECTIVE TEACHER

1. **Continually examine your instructional practices.** If your students are not achieving as you had hoped, consider the features of effective instruction. Do you need to be more explicit? Teach more systematically and directly? Provide more time for practice? Be more thorough in your assessments so that you are building upon what students know and need to know? Provide more specific feedback?

2. **Communicate a sense of urgency.** Now more than ever before, all citizens need to be able to read and write at high levels. All students, except for the few with severe disabilities, can be prepared for college and a career: the critical, required skills are the same for both higher education and a lifelong career. Your excellent instruction, ongoing support, and high expectations enable and motivate students to succeed. You owe it to your students to be prepared, supportive, knowledgeable, and sensitive to their needs so that they are given the tools to be productive. Do not waste a moment of their time with unproductive, purposeless activities.

3. **Communicate high expectations** while recognizing in each of your students his or her strengths and areas in need of support. When you respect each student, differentiate instruction for them as needed, and communicate your high expectations, students will feel worthy. Your actions, even more than your words, communicate how students are to treat each other.

    High expectations must be attainable. When students have a perceived probability of success they are motivated to sustain their efforts. It is up to you to teach in a way that allows them to feel that they can learn the material, to perceive the probability of being successful so that they remain engaged and motivated.

4. **Continue to read research,** communicate with experts, and increase your knowledge in order to improve your instruction. The more you know, the more you practice, the more you critique your own teaching and improve, the more your students will benefit. Read, respect, and implement current research and join professional organizations that will assist you in increasing your expertise.

5. **Recognize the positive intent** of your students, their parents, and your colleagues. Most of the time, people act with a positive intent. That means that parents, students, and colleagues generally want to do good things, though sometimes it may not appear so to you. If you discover the positive intent of another person, your understanding of that person will increase. For example, when a student refuses to read aloud when you ask him or her to, what could possibly be the student's positive intent? It could be he or she cannot read and wants to avoid embarrassment. Here is another example. A student copies from someone's work. What could be his or her positive intent? He or she may be motivated to perform well, which is a positive trait. In both of these cases, you can address their positive intent by understanding their motivation and supporting them so they can achieve their intent in appropriate, rather than unacceptable, ways.

6. **Become a caring, creative, and courageous teacher.** Effective teachers have the "3 Cs" traits and are not afraid to show it!

   You have heard the phrase: "Students don't care how much you know until they know how much you care." Students learn more from teachers when teachers show they care and when students care about their teachers. Just a moment of focused time or a quick personal comment directed at a student communicates that you care about your students as individuals. Every day, create a few moments to show your students how much you care about them.

   Teaching requires creativity. Every year, you will have a student who perplexes you. Nothing you have tried in the past works. It is time to think outside the box and determine what will unlock learning for this student. Be creative, and you will find that key to unlock their learning.

   Effective teachers are courageous. They have the courage to advocate for their students, to do what is best even if it is not the norm of the school. Effective teachers have the courage to share with parents and students information about the students' progress or lack thereof. They have the courage to try new things and, even more importantly, the courage to cease ineffective practices.

7. **Be explicit** with your students about why they must learn what you are teaching. You may have heard that listening to Mozart makes you smarter. That is not supported by research, though it is a good story. There is, however, a radio station that, if you play it in your classroom, your students will be motivated to learn. The station is WII-FM. Have you heard of it?

   Actually, WII-FM is an acronym for a popular saying: What's In It For Me. This is what your students are thinking. What's in it for them to learn to read, especially when it is so difficult for some? What's in it for students to learn to write when they would rather play video games? If you cannot convince students that what you want them to learn will help them have better lives, you should not be teaching it.

8. **Consider doing the opposite** of what you feel like doing. Remember this when you are presented with a noisy disrespectful class and you feel like screaming. Rather, whisper, and the class will soon become quiet as they strain to hear what you are saying. When a student misbehaves and you feel like wringing his neck, try giving him a hug instead. When a student will not stop talking and you are so tired of her ramblings that you want to put a muzzle on her, tell her you will arrange a special time for her to tell you her tales, later, and be sure to give her that promised time. When a parent continually criticizes your actions, rather than get defensive, ask him or her to advise you on how to support their child. You are human, you get tired and frustrated and impatient. That is okay, but you have to control those reactions and maintain your professional demeanor, no matter what.

9. **Engage your students.** Student behavior improves and learning increases when students feel they are contributing and are connected. This is one reason elementary teachers have tasks or roles for each student. Being selected to clean the blackboard chalk erasers used to be a huge honor. These days, it may be an honor to turn the computers on and off, to be the webmaster, or to be the buddy of the new student. Students who contribute to the well-being of their class feel connected and empowered.

   Of course, engaging your students in their learning is most important. When they are active, thinking, and responding, they are engaged. Provide multiple opportunities for your students to practice the new learning, to talk with others, and to be fully engaged in the process. Students learn best when they are fully engaged.

10. **Model** what you want your students to learn, how they should act, and how they should treat others. For example, share your enthusiasm for reading and learning, and your students will be enthusiastic about reading, too. Treat all students respectfully, and your students will treat each other with respect. Whether you are cognizant of it or not, your students are always watching you, and you are always providing a model for them. Therefore, be thoughtful about what you do and say, as your students will do what you do!

    You are about to enter a wonderful, challenging career, one that will fulfill you in a way no other career can do. Each time you receive a letter from a student from long ago thanking you for teaching him or her to read, each time a student tracks you down to introduce you to his or her spouse and child, telling you it is because of you that he or she got to this happy point in life, your joy in your profession will increase. You will make a significant difference in the lives of many. You are now on the road to becoming an effective teacher.

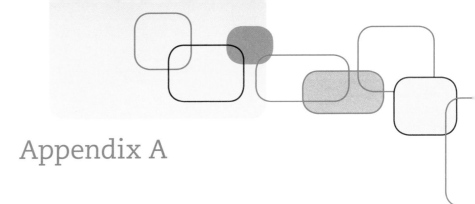

Appendix A

"Recipe" for a Sticky Board

Ingredients:

- 1 plastic rectangular tablecloth (use the inexpensive type ~ $3)
- 1/3 can temporary adhesive spray (e.g., Spray Mount by 3M)
- 1 roll blue painter's tape

Directions:

- Cut tablecloth in half to form two squares.
- Lay the square tablecloth on flat surface, or tape to a wall.
- Spray once and allow to dry for 1 minute.
- Spray two more times allowing to dry between applications.
- Adhere to wall with painter's tape when in use.
- Fold to store, sticky sides together (can be used repeatedly).

Recipe makes two reusable boards. You can make smaller sticky boards for individual students or larger ones for things such as word walls.

Suggested uses include the following:

1. Word sorts
2. Brainstorming
3. Graphic word organizers
4. Tier 1, Tier 2, and Tier 3 words
5. Vocabulary words for units being taught
6. Display of student work
7. Webbing diagrams
8. K-W-L charts (easily modified as more is learned)
9. Modeling of activities
10. Assigning small group membership

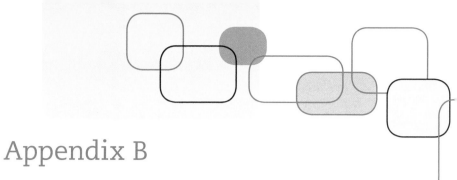

Say It and Move It Card

——————————

⬤————————————➤

From Blachman, B.A., Ball, E.W., Black, R., & Tangel, D.M. (2000). *Road to the code: A phonological aware-ness program for young children*. Baltimore: Paul H. Brookes Publishing Co.; reprinted by permission.

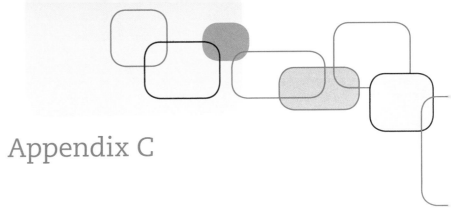

Appendix C

Helpful Web Sites

ASSESSMENT RESOURCES (UNIVERSAL SCREENING AND PROGRESS MONITORING)

AIMSweb: http://www.aimsweb.com   Formative assessment of early reading, intermediate reading, writing, and spelling skills. (Math probes are also available.)

Curriculum-Based Measurement in Reading—(CBM-R): http://www.rti4success.org/screeningTools   A chart of curriculum-based reading measures with descriptions and documentation of adequacy (e.g., reliability, validity, efficiency of use, and more).

DIBELS: http://www.dibels.org   A formative assessment of early literacy skills.

TPRI: http://www.tpri.org   A screening and diagnostic tool designed for students in kindergarten through third grade.

Reading Assessment Database: http://www.sedl.org/reading/rad/database.html   Searchable database that describes in detail early literacy assessment tools; Pre-K–3.

OSEP National Center on Student Progress Monitoring: http://www.studentprogress.org   Chart of progress monitoring tools, web resource library with PowerPoint presentations, links to additional resources.

OSEP National Center on Response to Intervention: http://www.rti4success.org   Resources for Essential Components of RTI: Screening, Progress Monitoring, Multi-level Prevention System, Data-Based Decision Making.

ADDITIONAL ASSESSMENTS

San Diego Quick Assessment: http://www.homeschooling.gomilpitas.com/articles/060899.htm   Quick word list reading assessment providing insight into independent, instructional, and frustration levels of student.

Irregular Word Test: http://www.scoe.org/depts./ell/5thacademicsuccess/irregularwords 10_06.pdf

Word Reading Test: nifl.gov/readingprofiles/QARI_combined.pdf   Word Reading test for grades 4 and above.

WIST: Word Identification and Spelling Test: http://www.proedinc.com/customer/ProductView.aspx?ID=2031&sSearchWord=Barbara+A.+Wilson   Measures word identification, spelling, and sound-symbol knowledge; ages 7–0 through 18–11 years.

Test of Word Reading Efficiency: http://lincs.ed.gov/readingprofiles/TOWRE.htm   Standardized test composed of subtests for sight word reading efficiency (reading real words) and phonemic decoding efficiency (reading pseudo words).

TOSWRF: Test of Silent Word Reading Fluency: http://www.proedinc.com/customer/ProductView.aspx?ID=3088&sSearchWord=   Measures student's ability to recognize printed words accurately and efficiently; ages 6–6 through 17–11 years.

Test of Reading Comprehension–Fourth Edition (TORC-4): http://www.proedinc.com/customer/ProductView.aspx?ID=4412&sSearchWord=   Tests silent reading comprehension; ages 7–0 through 17–11 years.

Alliteration or Rhyming Tasks from the Individual Growth and Development Indicators IGDIs (2001) suitable for children ages 3–5: http://ggg.umn.edu/get/procedures_and_materials/Alliteration/index.html

Comprehensive Test of Phonological Processing (CTOPP): http://www.pearsonassessments.com/HAIWEB/Cultures/en-us/Productdetail.htm?Pid=015-8735-03X&Mode=summary Helps identify students who need help in developing phonological awareness; ages 5–24.

Test of Preschool Early Literacy (TOPEL): http://www.proedinc.com/customer/productView.aspx?ID=4020 Helps identify preschool students who are at risk for literacy problems; ages 3 through 5–11 years.

Phonological Awareness Literacy Screening (PALS): http://pals.virginia.edu/tools-prek.html PALS-PreK A scientifically based phonological awareness and literacy screening that measures preschoolers' developing knowledge of important literacy fundamentals; offers guidance to teachers for tailoring instruction to children's specific needs. Screening, diagnostic, and progress monitoring tool (see similar tests for K through third grade).

Reading Fluency Benchmark Assessor (RFBA): http://www.readnaturally.com Includes benchmark passages, software guide, and software to assist with record keeping; grades 1 through 8.

INTERVENTION PROGRAMS

Useful in finding evidence-based educational interventions:

The What Works Clearinghouse: http://ies.ed.gov/ncee/wwc/reports/topicarea.aspx?tid=01 Reports that evaluate research on beginning reading curricula and instructional strategies, grades K–3. For a similar report for grades 4–12, go to http://ies.ed.gov/ncee/wwc/reports/topic.aspx?tid=15

Doing What Works: http://dww.ed.gov/ Videos, slideshows, and tools for using proven teaching practices. Based on findings from the What Works Clearinghouse.

The Promising Practice Network: http://www.promisingpractices.net/programs.asp Summaries of programs that are proven to improve outcomes for children.

Center on Instruction: http://www.centeroninstruction.org Offers materials and resources on literacy and language arts that help educators improve academic outcomes.

Pacific Resources for Education & Learning: http://www.prel.org Provides a range of products and services in the areas of reading and literacy development across the grades for multi-language and multicultural communities.

FOCUS ON FLUENCY PROGRAMS & ASSESSMENTS

Great Leaps: http://www.greatleaps.com/

Quick Reads: http://www.pearsonschool.com

Read Naturally: http://www.readnaturally.com

FLUENCY ASSESSMENTS

AIMSweb: http://www.aimsweb.com Pearson Education, Inc.

Curriculum-Based Measurement in Reading—(CBM-R): http://www.rti4success.org/screening Tools

FAIR: Florida Assessments for Instruction Reading: http://www.justreadflorida.com/instrreading.asp Florida Department of Education, (2009). Tallahassee, FL: Author

DIBELS Next (seventh edition):   Dynamic Indictors of Basic Early Literacy Skills   http://www.dibels.org. (2010). Dynamic Measurement Group, Eugene, OR: Author

Reading Fluency Progress Monitor (RFPM):   http://www.readnaturally.com/products/rfpm.htm   Read Naturally Inc., n.d., 19 Oct. 2011 http://

Reading Fluency Benchmark Assessor (RFBA):   Read Naturally Inc., n.d., 19 Oct. 2011 http://www.readnaturally.com/products/rfba.htm

TPRI: Texas Primary Reading Inventory http://www.tpri.org Austin, TX: Author

Tejas LEE: "El Inventario de Lectura en Español de Tejas" http://www.tejaslee.org/ Austin, TX: Author

FOCUS ON VOCABULARY

Florida Center for Reading Research: http://www.fcrr.org/FCRRReports/contents.htm   Analysis of commercial programs and teacher centers used by skilled teachers to provide effective instruction.

VOCABULARY OR MORPHOLOGY INSTRUCTION

Colorín Colorado: http://www.colorincolorado.org   Ideas for teaching ELL.

Free Rice: http://www.freerice.com   Players earn virtual rice to feed the hungry for every vocabulary question answered correctly, available in dozens of levels to suit every grade.

More Words: http://www.morewords.com/examples   Provides a list of words that share the same spelling pattern, to find morphologically related words.

Online Etymology Dictionary: http://etymonline.com   Provides the roots and affixes that make up a word and gives word origins.

Memidex: http://www.memidex.com   Multipurpose reference tool: dictionary, thesaurus, pronunciation by dialect, etymology, etc.

PrefixSuffix.com: http://www.prefixsuffix.com   Lists common prefixes and suffixes, with meanings and origin.

Spanish Cognates Dictionary: http://www.latinamericalinks.com/spanish_cognates.htm   Many words in Spanish resemble words in English (Spanish cognates) and if studied will provide the Spanish student a quick source of building a strong Spanish/English vocabulary.

Visual Thesaurus: http://www.visualthesaurus.com   Graphic word webs, plus many other tools and teaching tips.

VocabAhead: http://www.vocabahead.com/Default.aspx   Brief videos teaching academic words.

Vocabulogic: http://vocablog-plc.blogspot.com   Created for teachers, published by Susan Ebbers with numerous expert guest authors.

CORE PROGRAMS (REVIEWS)

Florida Center for Reading Research: http://www.fcrr.org/FCRRReports/contents.htm   Analysis of commercial programs and teacher centers used by skilled teachers to provide effective instruction.

What Works Clearing house: http://ies.ed.gov/ncee/wwc/reports/topic.aspx?tid=15 Source for review of adolescent literacy programs; grades 4–12.   http://ies.ed.gov/ncee/wwc/reports/advancedss.aspx   Source for review of elementary literacy programs.

Center on Instruction: http://www.centeroninstruction.org/   Offers materials and resources on literacy and language arts that help educators improve academic outcomes.

Identifying and Implementing Educational Practices Supported by Rigorous Evidence: A User Friendly Guide http://www2.ed.gov/rschstat/research/pubs/rigorousevid/rigorousevid. pdf Helps identify whether an intervention has strong or possible evidence to support it.

ENGLISH LANGUAGE LEARNERS (ELLs)

Colorín Colorado: http://www.colorincolorado.org Ideas for teaching ELL students; site filled with useful information, strategies, activities, and resources for all teachers of ELLs, whether an English as second language (ESL) teacher or a content area teacher with one or two English learners in your class.

Teaching Diverse Learners: http://www.lab.brown.edu/tdl/elemlit/index.shtml Information on ELL challenges and teaching practices; grades K through 6.

POLICY AND STANDARDS

Reading First/SBRR: http://en.wikipedia.org/wiki/Reading_First Provides summary of Reading First and valuable links to connected content such as NCLB and scientifically based reading instruction.

Put Reading First: http://lincs.ed.gov/publications/pdf/PRFbrochure.pdf Small brochure for educators, parents, and caregivers explaining the results of the National Reading Panel and SBRR specifically.

Put Reading First, kindergarten through grade 3: http://lincs.ed.gov/publications/pdf/ PRFbooklet.pdf Small booklet for educators, parents, and caregivers explaining the results of the National Reading Panel in plain talk and SBRR specifically.

Literacy Information and Communication System: http://lincs.ed.gov/

No Child Left Behind (NCLB): http://www2.ed.gov/nclb/landing.jhtml Provides not only the 2001 NCLB Act but current updated material as well. http://en.wikipedia.org/wiki/ No_Child_Left_Behind_Act

The Elementary and Secondary Education Act (ESEA, 2001): http://www2.ed.gov/policy/ elsec/leg/esea02/index.html Provides law in its entirety.

The Individuals with Disabilities Education Improvement Act: http://idea.ed.gov/ Provides complete law. Law is also known as IDEA, [34 CFR 300.8(c)(10)] http://nichcy.org/ disability/categories A web site that includes definitions and other information about IDEA and students with disabilities.

International Reading Association Standards for Reading Professionals: http:www.reading. org/Libraries/Reports_and_Standards/bk889.sflb.ashx IRA document designed to ensure that all students are knowledgeable and proficient users of language so they may achieve school and life success.

The Common Core State Standards: http://www.corestandards.org/ The Common Core State Standards provide a consistent, clear understanding of what students are expected to learn, so teachers and parents know what they need to do to help them.

The International Dyslexia Association, Knowledge and Practice Standards for Teachers of Reading: http://www.interdys.org/Standards.htm Serves as a guide to endorsing programs that prepare teachers in reading and/or programs that specialize in preparing teachers to work with students who have difficulties or disabilities.

The Texas College & Career Readiness Standards: http://www.thecb.state.tx.us/college readiness/crs.pdf These standards specify what students must know and be able to do to succeed in entry-level courses at postsecondary institutions in Texas.

READING/LITERACY GENERAL

Anita Archer video series: http://www.scoe.org/pub/htdocs/rla-media.html Literacy expert provides videos of vocabulary, retelling, engagement, modeling.

Children of the Code: http://www.childrenofthecode.org/   Public television documentary and social education project; videos; answering questions such as who is at risk, what is at stake, and what is involved in learning to read.

National Reading Panel: http://www.nichd.nih.gov/publications/pubs_details.cfm? from=& pubs_id=89   Report of the National Reading Panel: Teaching Children to Read, executive summary.

National Reading Panel: http://www.nichd.nih.gov/publications/pubs_details.cfm?from=& pubs_id=88   Report of the National Reading Panel: Teaching Children to Read: full report.

Put Reading First: Kindergarten through Third Grade: http://lincs.ed.gov/publications/ pdf/PRFbooklet.pdf   The Research Building Blocks for Teaching Children to Read; simple, easy-to-read format.

Reading A-Z: http://www.readinga-z.com/   Web site provides teachers instructional reading materials; K–5; leveled texts, decodable readers, poetry, letter flashcards, handwriting pages and more.

ReadingRockets: http://www.readingrockets.org/teaching/reading101-course/toolbox/teacher-toolbox   Teachers' toolbox for struggling readers.

Doing What Works: http://www2.ed.gov/nclb/methods/whatworks/   Site that translates research-based practices into practical tools used to improve classroom instruction.

Ivy's Dictionaries for Kids: http://www.aboutus.org/IvyJoy.com   Provides links to reference web sites and fun word tools such as FactMonster, Bartleby.com   WordNet, Encarta and Merriam-Webster, Anagram Server, Tongue Twisters, Visual Thesaurus.

Kids Read: http://www.kidsreads.com/ Designed to be used during literature circles or guided reading; newest books for children, trivia games/word puzzles; useful for planning before/during/after reading to build vocabulary and comprehension.

Neuhaus Education Center: http://www.neuhaus.org/ Provides teacher continuing education online classes, onsite classes and effective teaching strategies and materials to prevent reading failure.

Lexile Levels at   http://www.lexile.com   If you want to check out titles of books that you are reading, you can find their lexile levels here.

The Meadows Center for Preventing Educational Risk: http://www.meadowscenter.org/vgc/.

Resources, research, and instructional materials to teach reading to students, Pre-K–12, English language learners, and students with reading difficulties, including:

Essential Reading Strategies for the Struggling Reader

Reading Strategies & Activities Resource Book for Students at Risk for Reading Difficulties, Including Dyslexia

Supplemental Instruction for Struggling Readers Grades 3–5: A Guide for Tutors

A New Light on Literacy: Early Reading Interventions for English Language Learners

Text Project: http://textproject.org/   Aims to bring beginning and struggling readers to high levels of literacy through a variety of strategies and tools, particularly the texts used for reading instruction.

RTI

National Research Center on Learning Disabilities: http://www.nrcld.org   Site provides integrated research with improved policies and classroom practices See the article: "Understanding Responsiveness to Intervention in Learning Disabilities."

National Center on Response to Intervention: http://www.rti4success.org   Site provides "all you need to know about Response to Intervention"; learn about the essential components of RTI.

Florida Center for Reading Research: http://www.fcrr.org/interventions/RTI.shtm   Provides information about using ongoing progress monitoring to improve reading outcomes.

Center on Instruction: http://www.centeroninstruction.org/topic.cfm?k=R Site offers materials and resources on effective instruction within the RTI framework and implementation guidelines.

Intervention Central: http://www.interventioncentral.org   Site provides tools and resources needed for all aspects of RTI implementation.

Research Institute on Progress Monitoring: http://www.progressmonitoring.org   Progress monitoring tools and other resources helpful for RTI implementation.

RTI Wire: http://www.jmwrightonline.com/php/rti/rti_wire.php Site provides tools and resources needed for all aspects of RTI implementation.

Building RTI: http://buildingrti.utexas.org/   Dessimination of information, resources, and tools designed to enhance instructional decision-making model in reading, mathematics, and behavior. Includes presentations slides and videos.

What Works Clearinghouse: http://ies.ed.gov/ncee/wwc/   Various articles and practice guides for use in RTI model.

READING PROGRAM SELECTION

What Works Clearinghouse: http://ies.ed.gov/ncee/wwc/   Find what works in reading programs by using this site.

Florida Center for Reading Research: http://www.fcrr.org/fcrrreports/LReports.aspx   List reading programs and their evaluation; suspended in 2008.

The Institute for Development of Educational Achievement, The University of Oregon: http://idea.uoregon.edu/

PROFESSIONAL ORGANIZATIONS

Council for Exceptional Children: http://www.cec.sped.org

International Literacy Association   https://www.literacyworldwide.org/

National Center for Learning Disabilities: http://www.ld.org

The International Dyslexia Association: https://dyslexiaaida.org

TECHNICAL ASSISTANCE AND RESEARCH CENTERS

University of Kansas Center for Research on Learning: http://www.ku-crl.org

Center for Applied Linguistics (National Literacy Panel on Language Minority Children and Youth):   http://www.cal.org/

The IRIS Center: http://iris.peabody.vanderbilt.edu/

Texas Center for Learning Disabilities: http://www.texasldcenter.org

Center on Instruction: http://www.centeroninstruction.org

Consortium on Reading Excellence: http://www.corelearn.com

National Center on Intensive Intervention   http://www.intensiveintervention.org/

National Center for Systemic Improvement   https://www.wested.org/project/national-center-for-systemic-improvement/

CEEDAR Center   www.ceedar.org

Meadows Center for the Prevention of Learning Difficulties   www.meadowscenter.org

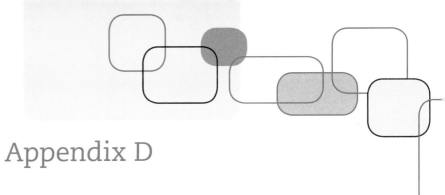

Appendix D

Lesson Plan Template

Date: Teacher:

Target students *(Whole class or small group. Identify specific students who need differentiated instruction.)*

Objective of the lesson:

Required resources

Review of previous learning

I do

Teacher:
- Explicit instruction with modeling
- Systematic instruction with scaffolding

(continued)

We do

Teacher guides instruction focusing on:
- Providing immediate corrective feedback
- Providing multiple opportunities for students to respond and practice

You do

Students practice skill independently, in pairs, or in small groups

Differentiation

Accelerated students:

English language learners:

Students needing additional scaffolding:

Progress monitoring

Teacher conducts an assessment of student progress

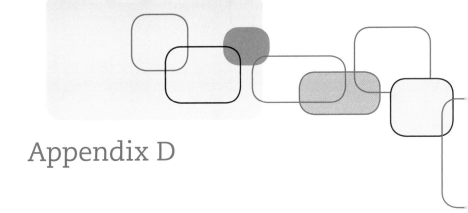

Appendix D

Lesson Plan Template: Example

Kindergarten or First-Grade Small-Group Intervention

Note: The text in handwriting font is what you could say verbatim. When you first begin teaching, you may want to write down every word you are going to say. Later, once you have learned the patterns and routines, you don't need to write down each word.

Date: 1/10/12   Teacher: Ms. Wilson

Target students *(Whole class or small group. Identify specific students who need differentiated instruction.)*

Five students—Jimmy, Kaitlin, Meagan, Beth, Wilber

Objective of the lesson:

The students will be able to blend and segment three phoneme words using Say-It-Move-It charts. Targeted words: dog, cat, bird, top, sun.

Required resources

Chips and Say-It-Move-It charts for each student; list of words to teach.

Review of previous learning

Review of segmentation of two-phoneme words: at, it, in, so.
"Let's review words that we segmented yesterday. Remember, to segment means to pull apart. Everyone, say at. Yes, at. Now let's say the sounds of at. Fingers up. Say /a/. Raise one finger. Now say /t/. Yes, /t/. Second finger up. Let's say both sounds in at. /a/ /t/. Yes! Now blend the two sounds together to form a word. What word? Yes! At."
(Continue reviewing the next four words it, in, so at a faster pace.)

I do

Teacher: Blending and segmenting three-phoneme words

Teacher models skill to be taught using:

- Explicit instruction with modeling
- Systematic instruction with scaffolding

"Today we are going to learn how to blend and segment words with three sounds. Listen: cat. Now I am going to say the sounds in cat slowly and for each sound I slide one chip down onto this line. Watch me. /c/ (slide a chip). /a/ (slide a chip). /t/ (slide a chip). Now I'll say the word fast: cat."

We do

Teacher and students: Students blend and segment words with teacher guidance

Teacher guides instruction focusing on

- Immediate corrective feedback
- Providing multiple opportunities for students to respond and practice

(Present each child with an Elkonin or "Say-It-Move-It" chart and three chips.)

"Try one with me. Everyone, say this word: cat. Yes, cat. What is the first sound you hear in cat, Jimmy? Yes, /c/. Slide one chip down to the line. Let's say the word again: cat. What is the next sound, the middle sound, of cat? Meagan? Yes, /a/. Everyone, say /a/ and slide a chip down. Say the word one more time, listening for the very last sound: cat. What is the last sound in cat, everyone? Yes! /t/ is the last sound in cat. Slide a chip down to the line. What word? Cat."

Corrective Feedback: (Wilber said kit). "Let's try that word again. Listen. The word is cat [emphasize the /a/]. What word? Yes, cat. Wilber, what word? Yes! Cat. Wilber, try this word: /d/ /o/ /g/. What word? Yes! Dog. Great job everyone! Let's try some more words."

(Follow the model for two more words, bird and top.)

You do

Students: Practice blending and segmenting

Students practice skill independently, in pairs, or in small groups.

Practice words: sun, leaf, road

"Try the next one by yourself. The word is sun. What word? Yes, sun. Say the word quietly and move a chip down for each sound."

If the children are doing well, add additional words such as: leaf, road.

(continued)

Differentiation

Challenge words for accelerated students (provide them an additional chip): tree (3), slip (4).

English language learners: Avoid confusing sounds.

(When first teaching the concept of blending and segmenting phonemes, avoid letters and sounds that may be pronounced differently in the child's first language. For example, most Spanish speakers pronounce ll as /y/ and /v/ as /b/, so avoid words that contain the letters v, l, and y and the sounds /v/ and /y/. Also, be cognizant that many vowels are pronounced differently than in English. You can say to the child, "In your first language, (or home language or whatever term you are to use in your district), you pronounce the letter a differently than it is pronounced in English. In English the letter a is pronounced /a/, as in apple.)

However, if your objective is ensuring the child knows how to segment words into phonemes, do not be too concerned if the phonemes are mispronounced as long as he is aware of how many phonemes there are and can segment them. That is your instructional objective. Later you can focus on the correct pronunciation of the sounds.

Additional scaffolding:

Provide a "Say-It-Move-It" chart with circles for the chips and dotted lines from the circle to the bottom line so that students know exactly how to move the chips.

Try hand over hand: place your hand on the child's and guide the movement of the chips as the child says the sounds.

If the child has difficulty with identifying the sounds, go back to the first sound and ask the child to identify the first sound only. When the child has mastered identifying the first sound, ensure the child can identify the last sound, and finally, the medial sound before asking the child to identify all the sounds in a three-phoneme word.

Provide additional guided practice

Progress monitoring: Students segment and blend two out of three words;

Teacher conducts a quick assessment of student progress

(One by one, give students a word and ask them to say the individual phonemes, then to blend it into a word. Note which children are still struggling and attend to them in a 1:1 format later in the day.)

Objectives for the next lesson

The students will match the sounds to letters in three phoneme words and blend the letters to form a word.

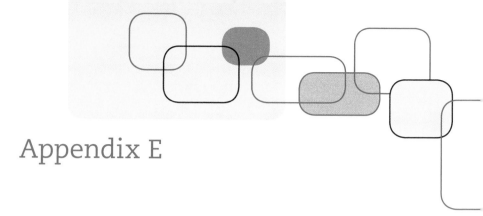

Appendix E

Glossary

academic English   The English language ability required for academic achievement in context-reduced situations, such as classroom lectures and textbook reading assignments, sometimes referred to as cognitive/academic language proficiency (CALP).

accelerated students   Those who learn quickly and may need to be challenged with more advanced material. These students are referred to as gifted and talented, advanced, or exceptional.

accuracy   The ability to recognize words correctly.

adequate yearly progress (AYP)   An individual state's measure of yearly progress toward achieving state academic standards. "Adequate Yearly Progress" is the minimum level of improvement that states, school districts, and schools must achieve each year.

affixes   Word parts that are "fixed to" either the beginnings of words (prefixes) or the endings of words (suffixes). The word *disrespectful* has two affixes, a prefix (dis-) and a suffix (-ful).

alphabetic principle   The basic idea that written language is a code in which letters represent the sounds in spoken words.

analogy or analogy phonics   Finding words or patterns within words that the student may already know in order to decode an unfamiliar word.

attention deficit disorder (ADD)   Attention deficit disorder is an older name for attention deficit hyperactivity disorder.

attention-deficit/hyperactivity disorder (ADHD)   Refers to the inability to use skills of attention effectively. Studies suggest that 5% to 10% of children, adolescents, and adults may have ADHD.

automaticity   A general term that refers to any skilled and complex behavior that can be performed rather easily with little attention, effort, or conscious awareness. Skills become automatic after extended periods of training. With practice and good instruction, students become automatic at word recognition, that is, retrieving words from memory, and are able to focus attention on constructing meaning from the text, rather than decoding.

base words   Words from which many other words are formed. Base words can stand alone, unlike root words. Examples of a base word and various forms is migrate: migration, migrant, immigration, immigrant, migrating, migratory.

benchmark assessments   Periodic assessments to measure student achievement, usually given during three different points in the year (beginning, middle, and end) to assess student progress and provide data for teachers to adjust their instruction to target student weaknesses.

bilingual education   An educational program in which two languages are used to provide content matter instruction. Bilingual education programs vary in their length of time and in the amount each language is used. The goal is that students become fluent in both languages.

blend   Two or three consonants together, before or after a vowel within a syllable, such as /cl/ close, /str/ strap, or /nt/ front; a blend is the same as a consonant cluster.

breve   is a diacritical mark ˘, shaped like the bottom half of a circle. The breve sign indicates a short vowel, as opposed to the macron ¯ which indicates long vowels, in academic transcription.

cognates Words in different languages related to the same root, e.g., *family* (English) and *familia* (Spanish); often share similar spelling, pronunciation, and meaning.

collaborative strategic reading (CSR) A framework for reading narrative or expository text that is based on extensive research demonstrating success for students with a wide range of ability levels, including English language learners and students with learning disabilities. CSR combines specific reading comprehension strategies with structured cooperative learning for students in upper-elementary and middle school.[1] CSR has a highly specific lesson format that must be followed with integrity to achieve positive results.[2]

Common Core State Standards Initiative The National Governors Association Center for Best Practices and the Council of Chief State School Officers developed a set of state-led education standards, called the Common Core State Standards. The English-language arts and mathematics standards for grades K–12 were developed in collaboration with a variety of stakeholders including content experts, states, teachers, school administrators, and parents. The standards define the knowledge and skills students should have within their K–12 education careers so that they will graduate from high school fully prepared for college and careers. The standards are aligned with college and work expectations; are clear, understandable, and consistent; include rigorous content and application of knowledge through higher order skills; build upon strengths and lessons of current state standards; are informed by other top-performing countries, so that all students are prepared to succeed in our global economy and society; and are evidence- and research-based.

comprehension strategies Techniques to teach students tools to comprehend text, including summarization, prediction, and inferring word meanings from context.

comprehension strategy instruction The explicit teaching of techniques that are particularly effective for comprehending text. Steps include direct explanation, teacher modeling ("think-aloud"), guided practice, and application. Direct explanation (the teacher explains to students why the strategy helps comprehension and when to apply the strategy), modeling (the teacher models, or demonstrates, how to apply the strategy, usually by

"thinking aloud" while reading the text that the students are using), guided practice (the teacher guides and assists students as they learn how and when to apply the strategy), and application (the teacher helps students practice the strategy until they can apply it independently).

context clues Sources of information outside of words that readers may use to predict words and meanings of unknown words; may be drawn from the immediate sentence containing the word, from text already read, from pictures accompanying the text, or from definitions, restatements, examples, or descriptions in the text.

continuous sound A speech sound that may be held or hummed until the speaker runs out of breath (/m/ /s/ /v/).

criterion-referenced measures (tests) Intended to measure how well a person has learned a specific body of knowledge and skills.

curriculum-based assessment (CBA) A method of monitoring students' educational progress through direct assessment of academic skills. CBAs usually consist of short tests, called probes, to ascertain student achievement on basic reading, math, writing, and/or spelling.

curriculum-based measure (CBM) Assessment of what students' have been learning. Usually has standardized instructions, a stop-watch or timer, a set of passages, scoring procedures, and record forms or charts. CBMs are often used for progress monitoring because they are well-suited for repeated use.

decoding The ability to translate a word from print to speech (written words into vocal speech), usually by employing knowledge of sound–symbol correspondences. Also considered the act of deciphering a new word by sounding it out.

diagnostic assessment Assessments used to pinpoint specific areas of weakness; provide more in–depth information to clarify students' skills and instructional needs.

discrepancy model Is used to determine whether a child qualifies for special education services, that is, whether an IEP is required. It is a measure of how far a child has fallen behind his peers.

dyslexia   A language-based disability that affects both oral and written language. It may also be referred to as reading disability, reading difference, or reading disorder; neurological in origin. Typically results from an unexpected (when compared with other cognitive abilities) deficit in the phonological component of language, resulting in poor or inaccurate word recognition and poor spelling and decoding abilities. Secondary problems may occur in reading comprehension and vocabulary development.

English language learner (English learners)   Students whose first language is not English and who are in the process of learning English.

ESL   The common acronym for English as a Second Language, an educational approach in which English language learners are instructed in the use of the English language.

fast mapping   Forming phoneme–grapheme (i.e., letter–sound) representations for words in memory.

fluency   The ability to read a text accurately, quickly, and with proper expression (prosody) and comprehension. Because fluent readers do not have to concentrate on decoding words, they can focus their attention on what the text means.

formal assessment   Refers to tests that have been standardized, i.e., given to a comparable group of students (the normative group) for the purpose of comparing one group's performance to another. See *normative assessment.*

grapheme   A letter or letter combination that spells a single phoneme (sound). In English, a grapheme may be one, two, three, or four letters, such as *e, ei, igh,* or *eigh.*

graphic organizers   Diagrams used to support comprehension when reading narrative (fiction) text or informational and expository texts. Graphic organizers (GOs) are linked to improving reading outcomes for students in general education, English language learners, and for those with disabilities. Graphic organizers include the following terms: cognitive maps, semantic maps, story maps, Venn diagrams, framed outlines, or advanced organizers.[3] GOs offer a "visual-spatial display of information extracted from text passages."[4]

guided practice   Typically, the teacher guides and assists students as they learn how and when to apply strategies.

high-frequency word   Words that are encountered frequently in the text and are important to know.

inference   To infer or arrive at a conclusion by reasoning from evidence. Use inferential questions in teaching comprehension— i.e., questions for which the answer is implied, not directly stated in the text.

informal assessment   Typically, commercial or teacher-made assessments that are curriculum based, no normative sample for comparison.

informational texts   Same as expository texts, which provide facts about the natural or social world. Students read two types of texts: factual texts and story or narrative text.

irregular words   Words that do not follow typical letter–sound correspondences, usually found in the vowel sound(s), such as *cough* and *there.*

lexile system   A recent type of readability formula that uses digital technology to measure the complexity of text. To obtain lexiles, words in samples of a text are compared to a database that began with a group of approximately 135,000 unique words and now has expanded to include many more unique words. A log of the mean frequency of the words in the text is used in a formula with the mean sentence length. The computation produces a lexile that can be placed on a scale, which spans 0 (easiest texts) to 2000 (most complex texts).[5]

long vowel sounds   Vowel sounds that are also letter names such as the /<a>/ as in *cake,* /<e>/ as in *eat,* /<i>/ as in *bite,* /<o>/ as in *coat,* and /<oo>/ as in *cube.* Long vowel sounds have a slightly longer duration than short vowel sounds.

macron   diacritical marking symbol (¯) that appears over a vowel grapheme that indicates a long or tense pronunciation of the vowel.

manipulatives   In education, hands-on objects used for instruction (e.g., blocks, plastic chips, felt squares).

manuscript writing   Form of handwriting, letters are separate from one another, unlike cursive. Also called printing.

metacognition   Act of reflecting on and monitoring cognitive (thinking) activity.

metalinguistic awareness   Ability to think about and reflect on the nature and function of language.

modeling   Refers to the practice of teacher modeling, or demonstrating how to apply a strategy. One strategy often modeled is "thinking aloud," i.e., sharing the comprehension thought process verbally while reading the text that the students are using.

morpheme   Smallest meaningful unit in a word.

morphology   Study of meaningful units of language and how they are combined in forming words.

multisensory instruction   Instruction that simultaneously links visual, auditory, and tactile–kinesthetic modalities (senses) to enhance memory and learning.

multisyllabic   Having more than one syllable.

narrative text   Typically tells a story. May include fables, poems, science fiction, short stories, novels, folk tales, and other text considered literary nonfiction. Usually has a predictable story structure: setting, characters, plot, theme, often contrasted with expository text.

No Child Left Behind Act of 2001 (NCLB)   The most recent reauthorization of the Elementary and Secondary Education Act of 1965. The act contains four basic education reform principles: stronger accountability for results, increased flexibility and local control, expanded options for parents, and an emphasis on teaching methods based on scientifically based research.

norm-referenced assessments (tests)   Intended to compare a person's score against the scores of a group of people who have already taken the same exam, called the "norming group."

onset   The part of a syllable before a vowel, such as /b/ in the word *bat*.

open syllable   A syllable ending in a vowel sound, making the vowel sound long, such as *so*, and *de* part, *va ca* tion.

orthography   A writing system; spelling system of language.

outcome assessment   Used to provide a bottom-line measure of students' progress; overall effectiveness of reading program. Annual state tests are outcome assessments.

percentile score   Scores showing how a student's performance compares with others tested during test development. A student who scores at the 50th percentile performed at least as well as 50% of students his age in the development of the test. A score at the 50th percentile is within the average range.

phoneme   The smallest unit of sound that changes the meanings of spoken words. Example: change the first phoneme in *bat* from /b/ to /p/, the word *bat* is changed to *pat*; English has about 41–44 phonemes; a few words, such as *a* or *oh*, have only one phoneme; most words have more than one phoneme; Example: The word *if* has two phonemes /i/ and /f/.

phonemic awareness   Awareness of the individual sounds that make up words and the ability to manipulate those sounds in words.

Stages of phonemic awareness development:
- Phoneme addition. In this activity, children make a new word by adding a phoneme to an existing word. (Teacher: What word do you have if you add /s/ to the beginning of *park*? Children: *Spark*.)
- Phoneme blending. In this activity, children learn to listen to a sequence of separately spoken phonemes, and then combine the phonemes to form a word. (Teacher: What word is /b/ /i/ /g/? Children: /b/ /i/ /g/ is *big*.)
- Phoneme categorization. In this activity, children recognize the word in a set of three or four words that has the "odd" sound. (Teacher: Which word doesn't belong? *bun, bus, rug*. Children: *Rug* does not belong. It doesn't begin with a /b/.)
- Phoneme deletion. In this activity, children learn to recognize the word that remains when a phoneme is removed from another word. (Teacher: What is *smile* without the /s/? Children: *Smile* without the /s/ is *mile*.)
- Phoneme identity. In this activity, children learn to recognize the same sounds in different words. (Teacher: What sound is the same in *fix, fall*, and *fun*? Children: The first sound, /f/, is the same.)

- Phoneme isolation. In this activity, children learn to recognize and identify individual sounds in a word. (Teacher: What is the first sound in *van*? Children: The first sound in *van* is /v/.)
- Phoneme segmentation. In this activity, children break a word into its separate sounds, saying each sound as they tap out or count it. (Teacher: How many sounds are in *grab*? Children: /g/ /r/ /a/ /b/. Four sounds.)
- Phoneme substitution. In this activity, children substitute one phoneme for another to make a new word. (Teacher: The word is *bug*. Change /g/ to /n/. What is the new word? Children: *bun*.)

phoneme awareness   See *phonemic awareness*.

phonics   A teaching method that uses letter–sound correspondences in reading and spelling; study of relationships between letters and sounds they represent.

phonological awareness   A global awareness of large chunks of speech, such as syllables, onset and rime, and the phoneme level. Typically includes ability to manipulate (blend or segment) at different levels of speech–sound system. Example: syllables within words (e.g., *cupcake* is made up of *cup* and *cake*), and onset and rime (i.e., that *dog* begins with /d/ and ends with /og/).

phonology   The study (science) of speech sounds; the rule system within a language; the speech–sound system of language.

pragmatics   System of rules and conventions for using language and related gestures in social situations; the study of that rule system.

prefix   A morpheme that comes at the beginning of a word *and* changes the meaning of the word, such as *happy, unhappy*.

prereading stage   Related to the stage of reading development that comes before children understand the alphabetic principle.

printing   See *manuscript writing*.

progress monitoring assessment   Used to determine whether students are making adequate progress. May be curriculum embedded (measuring to what extent students have mastered curriculum) or general/ external (measuring critical reading skills such as phonemic awareness, phonics fluency, vocabulary, or comprehension). They serve to predict success in meeting grade-level expectations.

prosody   One of three necessary components or characteristics of a fluent reader. Prosody is the ability to read with good expression; includes the pitch, tone, volume, emphasis, and rhythm in speech or oral reading.

rapid automatized naming (RAN)   Refers to the rapid, automatic naming of colors, numbers, letters, and objects that has been shown to be related to reading success.

r-controlled vowel   Refers to a vowel immediately followed by the consonant /r/ and whose sound is altered or modified by the /r/, such as *bar, for, her, sir,* and *fur*.

reading comprehension   A multicomponent, highly complex process that involves many interactions between readers and what they bring to the text (previous knowledge, strategy use) as well as variables related to the text itself (interest in text, understanding text types).[6]

reading fluency   The ability to read a text accurately, quickly, and with proper expression (prosody) and comprehension. Because fluent readers do not have to concentrate on decoding words, they can focus their attention on what the text means.

reciprocal teaching strategy   An evidence-based framework for improving reading comprehension. Effective for students in general education and for students who speak English as a second language.[7] In reciprocal teaching, the adult and students take turns serving as the teacher. This model teaches students to apply four reading strategies: prediction, summarization, question generation, and clarification.

repeated and monitored oral reading   An instructional activity, in which students read and reread a text a certain number of times or until a certain level of fluency is reached; has been shown to improve reading fluency and overall reading achievement; four re-readings are usually sufficient for most students; students can also practice reading orally through the use of audiotapes, tutors, peer guidance, or other means.

rime Linguistic (language) term, the part of a syllable that begins with the vowel and includes what follows; different from rhyming, which is a language activity. Example: onset /b/, rime /at/. What word? *Bat.*

root Main part of a word; affixes are added to make new word. Example: sect, intersect, intersection.

scaffolded instruction Temporary support to help a student until the student can complete the task independently; Examples of instructional scaffolds that you will note in this text are additional modeling, providing more examples, breaking the task down into smaller parts, providing part of the answer, reinforcing an easier skill, using physical movements to reinforce a skill, providing additional practice, and providing instruction in a small group or one-to-one.

schwa Neutral vowel in unaccented syllable in English; example: asleep, the /a/ pronunciation is the schwa sound; is the symbol for schwa.

scientifically based reading strategies Reading strategies are said to be scientifically based when they meet criteria based on scientifically based reading research (SBRR). Scientifically based reading research is determined when application of rigorous, systematic, and objective procedures are applied to obtain valid knowledge. SBRR studies are studies 1) that have been published in a peer-reviewed journal or approved by a panel of independent experts, 2) results of the study have been replicated by other scientists, and 3) there is agreement in the research community that the study's findings are supported by a critical mass of additional studies that point to a particular conclusion.[8]

screening assessment Used to identify students who may be at risk for reading difficulty. In some cases, may be referred to as benchmark assessment.

semantic features Concrete method for classifying abstract ideas or features, used to enhance comprehension.

semantics Study of word and phrase meanings.

short vowel sounds Sounds of /ă/ as in *pat*, /ĕ/ as in *Ed*, /ŏ/ as in *octopus*, /ĭ/ as in *igloo*, and /ŭ/ as in *up*; have relatively short duration (compared with long vowel sounds); (See *long vowel sounds.*) Also know as lax vowel sounds.

sight words Words that can be identified as a whole and do not require sounding-out or decoding. Students have learned to recognize the word automatically. Words that do not have to be sounded out; also known as whole words, nonphonetic words, irregular words, outlaw, or heart words. Example: said, know, their.

significant discrepancy A statistical term that is commonly used as a component to guide states/districts in determining eligibility for special education services for a learning disability. A significant discrepancy between a student's ability (intelligence score) and academic achievement is used to represent the degree a student's achievement is affected by the student's disability. For example, if a student had an IQ score of 100 (Mean 100; Standard deviation 15), and an achievement score in basic reading of 80, then a statistically significant difference or discrepancy is said to exist (more than one standard deviation). Recently, flaws in the discrepancy model have resulted in different approaches to identifying students with learning disabilities. One approach includes data determining a student's response to intervention instruction. Lack of response to specialized instruction may indicate the student has a learning disability.

standard score Standard scores help teachers determine how a child performs compared with other students. They also allow teachers to compare a student's performance on different tests. Test developers calculate the statistical average based on the performance of students tested in the norming process of test development. That score is assigned a value. Different performance levels are calculated based on the differences among student scores from the statistical average and are expressed as standard deviations. These standard deviations are used to determine at what scores fall within the above average, average, and below average ranges. Standard scores and standard deviations are different for different tests. Many of the commonly used tests, such as the Wechsler Intelligence Scales, have an average score of 100 and a standard deviation of 15.

stop sound A consonant speech sound that is spoken with a break in the airstream; the sound may not be held or hummed (/p/ /t/ /b/).

strategic instruction   Instruction that aims to promote student engagement in strategic processes. The goal is to teach students how to be metacognitive learners, to approach learning thoughtfully, with a plan in mind, and to evaluate the effectiveness of their approach to learning.

suffix   Morpheme added to the end of a base (root) word; creates new word with a different meaning or grammatical function. Example: add *or* to *act*. Result = *actor*. Changes grammatical form from verb to noun.

syllabication   Process of dividing words into syllables.

syllable   A unit of speech (pronunciation) that contains a vowel; may or may not have consonants before or after the vowel.

syntax   The way words are put together to form phrases, clauses, or sentences.

synthetic phonics (inductive phonics)   Method of teaching in which students are taught letter–sound correspondences and then how to blend sounds into whole word.

systematic   Definite method for a procedure, carried out by a step-by-step process.

tense vowel sound   See *long vowel sounds*.

think-alouds   The "think-aloud" strategy means encouraging students to verbalize their thoughts during reading in order to make text connections and encourage active thinking and questioning.[9] Teachers model the think-aloud strategy all year whenever they read to students. Teachers stop and make connections to their lives, to other books, and to the world (like a news story).

universal screening assessments   Type of criterion-referenced assessments, designed to be teacher friendly so that they can be quickly administered to all children in your class several times per year. The screening assessments help you determine which students are achieving as expected and which are at risk in specific components of reading.

VCE syllable   See *vowel-consonant-e* syllable.

voiced consonant   Consonant sound produced in which vibration of vocal chords is present (/b/, /d/).

vowel   Speech sound produced by the free flow of air through the vocal tract; most common vowels, a, e, i, o, u, sometimes y.

vowel-consonant-e (VCE) syllable   Syllable ending in a vowel, consonant and an *e*; example, *rate*.

vowel digraph syllable (vowel team syllable)   Syllable containing a vowel digraph such as *read, train*.

vowel team   A vowel grapheme or spelling made up of two or more letters forming a single speech sound; *ea* in *read*, *ou* in *route*.

word identification   Pronunciation of unfamiliar words using such methods as phonics, structural analysis, context clues.

word recognition   Quick identification (recognition) of a previously learned word and its meaning.

World Wide Web (WWW or W3 and commonly known as the Web)   A system of interlinked hypertext documents accessed via the Internet. With a web browser, you can view web pages that may contain text, images, videos, and other multimedia and navigate among them via hyperlinks.

ENDNOTES

1. Vaughn, Dimino, Schumm, & Bryant (2001).
2. Klingner, Vaughn, & Schumm (1998).
3. Kim, Vaughn, Wanzek, & Wei (2004).
4. Griffin, Simmons, & Kame'enui (1991).
5. http://www.lexile.com/about-lexile/lexile-overview/ retrieved 10-17-2011.
6. Klingner, Vaughn, & Boardman (2007).
7. Klingner & Vaughn (1996); Palinscar & Brown (1986).
8. The following web sites can be useful in finding evidence-based educational interventions: The What Works Clearinghouse (http://www.w-w-c.org/) and The Promising Practice Network (http://www.promisingpractices.net).
9. Oster (2001).

REFERENCES

Griffin, C.C., Simmons, D.C., & Kame'enui, E.J. (1991). Investigating the effectiveness of graphic organizer instruction on the comprehension and recall of science content by students with learning disabilities. *Reading, Writing, and Learning Disabilities, 7,* 355–376.

Henry, M.K. (2010). *Unlocking literacy: effective decoding and spelling instruction,* 2nd edition. Baltimore: Paul H. Brookes Publishing Co.

Kim, A., Vaughn, S. Wanzek, J., & Wei, S. (2004). Graphic organizers and their effects on the reading comprehension of students with LD: A synthesis of research. *Journal of Learning Disabilities,* 37, 105–118.

Klingner, J.K., & Vaughn, S. (1996). Reciprocal teaching of reading comprehension strategies for students with learning disabilities who use English as a second language. *The Elementary School Journal,* 96(3), 275–293.

Klingner, J.K., Vaughn, S., & Schumm, J.S. (1998). Collaborative strategic reading during social studies in heterogeneous fourth-grade classrooms. *The Elementary School Journal,* 99(1), 3–22.

The Merriam-Webster Dictionary, 11th edition (2008). Springfield, MA: Merriam-Webster, Inc.

Moats, L.C. (2000). *Speech to print: Language essentials for teachers.* Baltimore: Paul H. Brookes Publishing Co.

Palinscar, A.S., & Brown, A.L. (1986). Interactive teaching to promote independent learning from text. *The Reading Teacher,* 39(8), 771–777.

Vaughn, S., Dimino, J., Schumm, J.S., & Bryant, D.P. (2001). *Collaborative strategic reading: From click to clunk.* Longmont, CO: Sopris West.

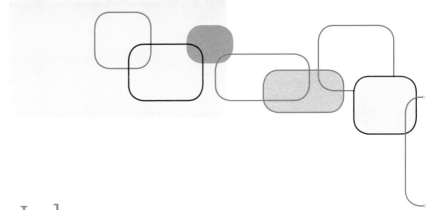

Index

Tables, figures, and notes are indicated by *t*, *f*, and *n*, respectively.